# An Introduction to International Relations and Religion

## Second edition

## JEFFREY HAYNES

**PEARSON**

Harlow, England • London • New York • Boston • San Francisco • Toronto • Sydney
Auckland • Singapore • Hong Kong • Tokyo • Seoul • Taipei • New Delhi
Cape Town • São Paulo • Mexico City • Madrid • Amsterdam • Munich • Paris • Milan

**Pearson Education Limited**
Edinburgh Gate
Harlow CM20 2JE
United Kingdom
Tel: +44 (0)1279 623623
Fax: +44 (0)1279 431059
Web: www.pearson.com/uk

---

First published 2007 (print)
**Second edition published** 2013 (print and electronic)

© Pearson Education Limited 2007 (print)
© Pearson Education Limited 2013 (print and electronic)

ISBN: 978-1-4082-7736-2 (print)
      978-0-273-78285-8 (PDF)
      978-0-273-78183-7 (eText)

**British Library Cataloguing-in-Publication Data**
A catalogue record for the print edition is available from the British Library

**Library of Congress Cataloging-in-Publication Data**
A catalog record for the print edition is available from the Library of Congress

10 9 8 7 6 5 4 3 2 1
16 15 14 13 12

Print edition typeset in 10.5/14.5pt Sabon LT Std by 35
Print edition printed and bound in Malaysia (CTP-VVP)

NOTE THAT ANY PAGE CROSS REFERENCES REFER TO THE PRINT EDITION

# An Introduction to International Relations and Religion

# Contents

## Contents

# Acknowledgements

*We are grateful to the following for permission to reproduce copyright material:*

## Tables

Table 10.1 from Pew Global Attitudes Survey 2005: 3, Pew Research Center's Global Attitudes Project; Table 12.1 from Islamic NGOs in Africa. The promise and peril of Islamic Voluntarism, Centre for African Studies, University of Copenhagen

## Text

Article 6 from The Arab Spring: Prospects and Pitfalls by Jeffrey Haynes, www.gpilondon.com

In some instances we have been unable to trace the owners of copyright material, and we would appreciate any information that would enable us to do so.

# 1 | Religion and international relations: what are the issues?

Mounting concern over the threat posed by pirates and Islamic insurgents in Somalia has led Britain and other EU nations to consider the feasibility of air strikes against their logistical hubs and training camps.

(Hopkins and Norton-Taylor, 2012)

US and Nato forces rushed yesterday to apologise for discarding and possibly burning copies of the Qur'an, as thousands of Afghans gathered to protest outside Bagram military airbase.

(Graham-Harrison, 2012)

Tibetans in north-west China have marked a tense traditional new year with prayer, the sounding of a gong and subdued defiance, in the wake of a string of self-immolations and protests against Chinese control . . . At least 16 Tibetans are believed to have died after setting themselves on fire in protest since March, most of them Buddhist monks in Tibetan parts of Sichuan and Gansu provinces.

(http://www.guardian.co.uk/world/2012/feb/22/tibetans-china-new-year-losar?INTCMP=SRCH)

Britain and other EU nations target militarily 'Islamic insurgents' in Somalia. American and North Atlantic Treaty Organization (NATO) troops burn the Muslim holy book – the Qur'an – in Afghanistan, setting off a fire storm of anger in the country. Growing numbers of Buddhist monks – over 30 at the time of writing (May 2012) – kill themselves through self-immolation in Tibet. All these stories were in just one British newspaper, *The Guardian*, over just two days, 22 and 23 February 2012. What do they have in common? What differentiates them from each other? What do they have to do with 'religion in international relations', the subject of this text?

The first story on Somalia covers a core international relations concern: foreign policy and a perceived security threat to a nation's wellbeing. The second story focuses on the problems of continuing US involvement in Afghanistan, more than ten years after it began, shortly

1

after 11 September 2001. The third story highlights a controversial and disputed area of China – Tibet – which sees itself as an independent country with a particular Buddhist history, religion and culture. Each of the stories involves a government – the British, the American and the Chinese – and a 'non-state actor': 'Islamic insurgents' in Somalia, Afghan protesters and Tibetan monks.

These news items provide evidence that religion has an impact on international relations in two main ways. First, governments may make issues linked to religion a focal point of their foreign policies. Second, non-state actors inspired by religious concerns may engage politically with governments, whether within countries or across state borders. The first thing to note, however, is that there are very few governments with foreign policies *consistently and centrally* focused on religious issues. The governments of Iran and Saudi Arabia are two prominent examples of such governments. The reason in both cases is that both countries underwent major political upheavals that led to religion becoming a focal point of government policy, both at home and abroad. Iran underwent an 'Islamic revolution' in 1978–79, which turned the country from a secular, West-focused, country into an Islamist theocracy, that is, a state where Islamic principles take strong precedence over secular – that is, non-religious – ones. The Kingdom of Saudi Arabia is a special place for Muslims. Founded in 1932, Saudi Arabia is the place where the Muslim religion was founded by the prophet Mohammed in the first decades of the seventh century. Saudi Arabia contains two of the holiest places in Islam: Mecca and Madinah. Saudi Arabia did not undergo an 'Islamic' revolution like Iran, yet its government adopted the Muslim holy book – the Qur'an – as the country's constitution. The overall point is that while both governments organise their states very differently, with very different political principles – one is revolutionary, the other very conservative – both claim to be explicitly and consistently guided by Islamic ideas and principles. These beliefs and values centrally inform state policy at home and abroad. Iran and Saudi Arabia are, however, very unusual in today's international relations.

Today, there are nearly 200 countries. Apart from Iran and Saudi Arabia, no other governments consistently use religion as a guiding principle in domestic policies and international relations. Put another way, *no* countries explicitly have Christian, Buddhist, Hindu, or Jewish values and beliefs guiding state behaviour and policies. For example, while Israel is a 'Jewish country', in the sense that its population mainly comprises Jewish people, the country has been officially *secular* since its founding in 1948. To say that Israel is secular is to highlight that over the last six decades successive governments of the country have *not* adhered to religious values, norms or principles in *either* domestic *or* foreign policy. Yet, governments in Israel *do* have one 'religious' concern in particular. This is a consistent state goal, for both religious and security reasons: not to cede control of the Jewish holy city of Jerusalem to the mainly Muslim Palestinians. To complicate matters, Muslims everywhere regard Jerusalem as the third most holy city in Islam after Mecca and Madinah.[1] And what are we to make of the United States which, between 2001 and 2009, had a president – George W. Bush – whose approach to foreign policy, especially in relation to the Middle East, was heavily affected by his personal Christian beliefs? This was apparent to the extent that Bush believed that it was God's will that the USA helped to spread religious freedom and democracy in the region (Marsden, 2008, 2011). In other words, US foreign policy during the administration of George W. Bush had goals explicitly linked to the president's Christian beliefs, which informed the USA's foreign policy in the Middle East.

The overall point is that nearly all countries officially organise both domestic and foreign policies according to 'secular' principles – that is, where religious beliefs do not significantly inform decision making. The widespread absence of religious ideas or principles in governments' foreign policies is the result of a basic principle of international relations, established in Europe over 350 years ago, following the Peace of Westphalia (in today's southern Germany) in 1648. Over time, this principle was spread throughout the rest of the world by the expansion of European influence – via imperialism, colonialism and trade expansion. The result is that secularity became the dominant principle of international relations, with the result that formerly powerful religious leaders were over time excluded from the public realm. The perceived superiority and desirability of secular power and authority over religion was made explicit, the key ideological and organisational principle, of both the American (1776) and the French Revolutions (1789). Over the next decades, all European states adopted the principle of the superiority of secular political power over that of religious authority. Spread to the rest of the world via European colonialism and imperialism in the eighteenth, nineteenth and early twentieth centuries, the outcome for international relations was that by the twentieth century, governments the world over pursued secular international relations.

Now, however, the situation has changed and religion has returned to international relations. This does not imply that most governments have suddenly decided that they now wish to run their countries according to religious principles and ideas. Instead, the most significant category of religious actor[2] in international relations today is not the state; it is numerous *non-state religious actors*. Examples include the Roman Catholic Church, with its headquarters, the Vatican, in Rome; the Anglican (in America, Episcopal) Church, with its centre of operations in Canterbury, England; the World Council of Churches, a group of around 350 Protestant churches with its head office in Geneva, Switzerland; the Organisation of the Islamic Conference, a 57-member intergovernmental organisation of Muslim countries, whose HQ is in Jeddah, Saudi Arabia; and a variety of transnational Islamist insurgents – for example, in Somalia, which affiliated to al Qaeda, are a concern for British and EU security.

Two or three decades ago, religion was rarely mentioned in international relations analysis. Today's concern with religion is both unexpected and surprising. To some extent, as we shall see, current international relations interest in religion is linked to the al Qaeda attacks on the USA on 11 September 2001. Yet, this is not the whole story. Instead, we are witnessing a development which has built over the last three decades, at least since the end of the Cold War in the late 1980s. Thus, to explain why we are today concerned about religion in international relations when a few years ago we were not, we need to refer both to a specific event and to longer-term developments. The specific event is the 11 September 2001 al Qaeda attacks on the USA, commonly known as '9/11', after the American habit of putting the month (9) before the day (11) in shorthand designations of day and date. On 9/11, three aeroplanes on domestic flights in the USA were hijacked by Muslim extremists. While most were nationals of either Saudi Arabia or Egypt, their main allegiance was not to a country or a government; instead, it was to Osama bin Laden and his transnational Islamist

4

terrorist organisation, al Qaeda. The al Qaeda operatives compelled the aeroplanes' pilots to divert their flight paths and to turn the aeroplanes into weapons of mass destruction. Two of the planes hit their intended targets – the Twin Towers of the World Trade Center in New York and the Pentagon in Virginia – with the collective loss of around 3,000 lives. For the al Qaeda personnel, the selected targets were highly symbolic of American capitalist (Twin Towers) and military (the Pentagon) power. The outcome of the attacks was that for international relations 12 September 2001 was a very different day compared to 10 September that year. Suddenly, religion was back on the international relations agenda and the world had changed in a flash.

What was the impact of 9/11 on international relations? Was 9/11 the first shot in an inevitably escalating conflict between Americans and extremist Islamists focused in al Qaeda? Or was it the last gasp in a clash which had actually begun many years earlier in 1978 when the Soviet Union (also known as the Union of Soviet Socialist Republics [USSR]) invaded mainly Muslim Afghanistan? The USSR's aim was to keep Afghanistan's communist president in power following an insurgency by local Islamists (Burke, 2010). This failed and the Soviet Union's defeat in Afghanistan was one of the factors that led to its sudden collapse a dozen years later.

The USSR's disintegration also heralded the end of the Cold War, a conflict between the United States and the Soviet Union, which had started soon after the Second World War ended in 1945. The Cold War centred on a battle for supremacy between competing secular ideologies: liberal democracy/capitalism (USA) and communism (Soviet Union). Religion was not a factor in the Cold War. The importance of the Cold War was so great for international relations that most analysts were not that concerned with anything else for 40 years after the Second World War until the Cold War ended. Suddenly, the pre-existing international system had changed dramatically. The 'bipolar' – that is, two poles, the USA and the USSR – system was abruptly replaced by a more fragmented power structure, a multipolar – that is, a 'many poles' – system, with several significant countries, including: China, Brazil, India, the USA, Germany, France and the United Kingdom.

The key point is that the quarter century between the USSR's invasion of Afghanistan in 1978 and the events of 11 September 2001 was a period of fundamental change for international relations. We can add to these two events a third factor of major – and continuing – importance for understanding religion's return to international relations: the impact of globalisation. A key component of globalisation is an accompanying technological revolution – involving in particular the internet and instant electronic communications methods. The implication of this for our purposes is that numerous non-state religious actors can now organise activities across state borders, that is, they form transnational networks. Apart from solely religious goals, many transnational religious actors also pursue a range of secular objectives, including: cooperation, conflict, development, democracy, security and human rights.

## Religion as distinctive subject matter in international relations

Having noted the return of religion to international relations, the next step is to understand what it means for analysis. American academic Jack Snyder (2011: 1) poses two useful questions:

- What is distinctive about religious subject matter in international relations?
- What are the 'implications for the kinds of [international relations] theories and methods that are needed to study' religion?

Snyder (2011: 1) asserts that, 'Religion is one of the basic forces of the social universe, not just an "omitted variable".' For a pair of American international relations (IR) analysts, Timothy Samuel Shah and Daniel Philpott (2011: 24), 'religion is older than the state, and its aims encompass not just politics but all of life'. Chris Seiple (2011: 292), also a US international relations analysis, claims that as religion 'pre-dates the field of international relations' it 'has been and will always be integral to human identity'. These comments underline that for these four American IR analysts, religion is of such great importance in today's world that it is inevitable that it will be of importance to IR analysis. For them, as religion is a universal phenomenon, it has both social and political importance for billions of people around the world. These include key political decision makers, including, presidents, prime ministers, foreign ministers, and so on. But the preferences of individual decision makers are not the only factor we need to take into account when thinking of religion in IR. The importance of religion in current international relations is manifested in three further ways. First, religions go beyond state borders – that is, they are very often cross-border or, in IR terminology, they are 'transnational actors'. Second, because of its wide-ranging concerns, religion affects many of society's institutions, norms and values – that is, religion may affect how actors in international relations behave. Third, religions may strongly inspire believers to act in certain ways and not others – that is, religion can be a stimulus to action both for individuals and for groups.

But to understand today's return of religion to international relations we need to locate current events in a historical context. During the development of secular international relations from the sixteenth and early seventeenth centuries, Europe's political map was fundamentally affected by the Christian Protestant Reformation. This led to the end of the previous dominance of the Roman Catholic Church. Beyond religion, the Reformation was a tumultuous upheaval which greatly affected Western Europe, politically, economically and socially. Formerly dominant religious ideas were replaced by new secular ideologies over the next century, manifested in the revolutions in America (1776) and France (1789) which stressed the importance of representation, legitimacy and popular authority. One reason why this historical precedent may be very important in thinking about religion in current international relations is that, as Snyder remarks, it 'raises the possibility that comparable new [religious] upheavals could once again produce far-reaching changes in the international system' (Snyder, 2011: 3). Snyder is thinking in particular of the impact of 9/11 on international relations. A few years before 9/11, an American academic, Samuel Huntington (1993, 1996), had controversially argued that in the post-Cold War world international relations was becoming characterised by what he called a 'clash of civilisations'. This referred to what Huntington saw as an emerging conflict between 'Islam' – that is, the large bloc of 'Muslim' countries – and the 'West', that is, western European and North American states. Actually, Huntington turned out to be wrong, as no such clash has ensued. Yet the impact of his thesis has had an important effect upon how many people, including some policy makers, understand and view international relations. We can understand the increased involvement of the USA and other Western countries, including the United Kingdom, in the Middle East in the decade since 9/11 as being directly linked to a Huntingtonian view of the world, reflected in continuing Western involvement in Afghanistan, Iraq and Libya. In each case, the main concern is to deter extremist Islamists and encourage 'moderate' Muslims. So, to answer Snyder's first question – What is distinctive about religious subject matter in international relations? – we can respond that it is distinctive in the sense that it brings into IR issues of norms, values and beliefs that go beyond the traditional secular concerns of international relations – war, peace, security – while opening up the terrain of IR analysis to involvement of numerous non-state actors motivated by religious concerns.

## Methods and theory in IR

Snyder's second question is: What are the implications of the return of religion to international relations for the theories and methods that we use to study it? What methods of analysis are most appropriate to explain religion's increased involvement in today's international relations? When we talk about 'methods' in international relations, we are referring to what ways are best systematically to test theories. The best methods to find out things in international relations are reflected in the research programmes we devise in order to investigate a hypothesis. (A hypothesis is a supposed or proposed explanation put forward with only limited evidence, which is a starting point for further exploration in a research programme.) 'Raising' a hypothesis is useful in helping to ascertain if at the beginning of investigations something *appears* to be true or not. The research programme helps us to confirm or deny the starting assumptions we have.

To assess the plausibility of a hypothesis in international relations, we need to start by assuming various things about actors and what they do. The purpose of a hypothesis is to help focus our thoughts and aid us in seeking to confirm – or reject – it. We can use either quantitative or qualitative methods. Quantitative methods, which, most analysts agree, do not lend themselves particularly well to the study of religion in international relations, and qualitative research often involving examining of empirical case studies. The primary method of this text is to rely on an examination of specific cases in several countries and regions. The aim is to illuminate the extent to which, and the ways in which, 'that dynamic results in effective political action' by selected religious actors (Byrnes, 2011: 10).

Having arrived at an appropriate method, we can then use this to test what we know theoretically. What is a theory? The *American Heritage Dictionary* (1985) defines a theory as 'systematically organized knowledge applicable in a relatively wide variety of circumstances, *especially a system of assumptions, accepted principles, and rules of procedure devised to analyze, predict, or otherwise explain the nature or behavior of a specified set of phenomena*'. The 'specified set of phenomena' in which we are interested in this text are 'selected religious actors' in international relations. In this text, a 'religious actor' is defined as an entity – it might be a state or a national or international non-governmental organisation – which we can plausibly characterise as being motivated significantly by religious belief, norms and values. We need an appropriate theoretical approach in order to try to understand such actors and to attempt to provide clear and precise explanations as to what they do and why they do it. This is because theories focus scholarly attention on puzzles that set the research agenda for those interested in studying that particular area. Ideally, theory should also offer a set of testable and falsifiable hypotheses, thus encouraging systematic re-evaluation of main arguments through different research methods.

Thinking about how to theorise religion in international relations, we have already noted the changed international context of the last two decades, that is, since the post-Cold War ended and the speed of globalisation increased. During this period, in response to growing economic interdependence and other profound changes in international relations, issues are often collected together under the rubric of 'globalisation', meaning that IR analysis has expanded in new directions. Many IR scholars now tackle 'new' – or at least newly noted issues – including: religion, human-centred security, international environmental politics, human-centred development and democracy promotion (Haynes et al., 2011).

Note, however, that while IR certainly has new issues upon which to focus, it is widely accepted that religion has distinct characteristics that fit awkwardly within the secular concepts conventionally employed to study the field. This is partly because most conventional theoretical approaches to study IR – especially the most influential, realism and liberalism – analytically privilege states, especially secular states, that is, the vast majority. Nevertheless, nearly all IR analysts would accept the importance of the small number of states with religion as a key focal point of domestic and foreign policies, such as, Iran and Saudi Arabia. There are also large numbers of significant non-state religious entities, including the Vatican and al Qaeda. Yet, what non-state religious actors do is itself controversial and under-examined in IR. For example, they may support the state and work with it to achieve shared goals. Or they may pursue their own autonomous goals, using the state as a means to try to achieve them. Some seek to employ the state as a way of increasing their own leverage in pursuit of goals which they may or not share with the state. Finally, they may wish radically to challenge international order, including by using violent methods, such as employed by al Qaeda on 9/11. As Snyder (2011: 5) puts it: 'Religion may shore up the state-centered international order as it is conventionally understood and help to explain it, but it may also work at cross-purposes to that order.'

Non-state religious actors in international relations are nearly always transnational, and their scope is often broader than that of single-issue, secular transnational activist networks, such as Greenpeace International (the natural environment), Amnesty International (human rights) or Transparency International (government and business corruption). Like a 'nation', a religious community is an 'imagined community' (Anderson, 1983), which 'rationalizes self-sacrifice across space and time, but unlike nationalism, religion holds out the prospect of individual salvation and is less tied to territory' (Toft, 2011: 116). The religious 'imagined community' holds to norms of behaviour that also set 'standards of appropriate behavior, as do norms that originate from non-religious sources, but as Toft's chapter on war shows, norms with divine authority may produce different kinds of commitment' (Snyder, 2011: 3–4). For these reasons, a conventional theoretical tool kit that is limited to the mundane secular politics of states and nations may struggle to comprehend the role of religion in international relations. These initial thoughts about how to theorise religion in international relations will be pursued in Chapter 3.

To conclude this section, it is useful to restate that religion is broader than politics. This implies that what religious actors do in IR often has implications for various aspects of politics as well as for societal relations and, in some contexts, economics – for example when religious conflict affects a country's economic position. Overall, religion affects:

- who the actors in world politics are;
- what they want;
- what resources they bring to the tasks of mobilising support and making allies;
- what rules they follow.

While some of these varied and encompassing effects of religion might be grasped within conventional frameworks for studying international politics, it is important to note that conventional theories of IR are mainly concerned with secular actors, especially states, and their analysis of religion is often piecemeal and unsatisfactory. This is because religion can play a role in informing actors and what they do in international relations, while also inhibiting or encouraging that behaviour. In addition, religious actors can be tactical and scheming, yet simultaneously politically influenced by their understandings of the divine and the sacred. In other words, both conventional (secular) power calculations and goals linked to religious concerns may at the same time play a role in state calculations about agreement and antagonism in foreign policy and international relations more widely.

## 'Religious resurgence' and 'post-secular IR'

It is now time to set out the approach I adopt in this text. Many studies of international relations aim to be comprehensive, seeking to explain a broad range of political interactions involving states and non-state actors. This text is no exception. My aim is to explain how, why and for what goals religious actors involve themselves in international relations. To do this I examine a range of religious actors, both state and non-state entities. We shall learn how religious actors can affect national foreign policies as they seek to persuade governments to adopt a certain foreign policy. We also find out about a range of non-state religious actors and how they can significantly affect international relations, either by linking up with governments or by independently pursuing their own agendas. In the course of the text, various issues and topics emerge as significant, including: international conflict, cooperation, human rights, democratisation and development. We shall explore these issues in later chapters.

We approach the topic of religion in international relations in the following way. Following this introductory chapter, Chapter 2 examines global religious resurgence and its impact upon international relations, leading to the emergence of what some call post-secular international relations. Chapter 3 discusses theoretical and analytical concepts related to the issue of religion and international relations. We examine how various theories of International Relations[3] seek to explain what religion does. In recent years, several scholars have sought to present their view on how best religion can be theorised in relation to international relations. Most agree that there is no need for a new theoretical paradigm centring on religion, contending that existing theories can accommodate religion. Chapter 4 looks at the issue of state foreign policies and the extent to which religion is a factor. Chapter 5 examines transnational religious transnational actors, explaining what they do and how they do it. Chapters 6, 7, and 8 focus consecutively on three important issues upon which religion has had a significant impact in recent years: democratisation and democracy; development; and conflict and cooperation. Chapters 2–8 comprise the first part of the text. The second part of the text, Chapters 9–14, is devoted to regional and country case studies, focusing on: the United States of America, Europe, the Middle East and North Africa, sub-Saharan Africa, South Asia and Pacific Asia. Chapter 15 is the concluding chapter, summarising the key points of the text and drawing relevant overall conclusions.

## Changes to the second edition

This is the second edition of a text that was originally published in 2007. It gives me an opportunity to rectify mistakes, shortfalls and omissions found in the first edition. In a fast-moving field, the first edition is now outdated, lacking coverage of several important topics which have recently emerged. Several recent developments stand out. These include, in no particular order, a change of president in the USA in 2009 and subsequent reappraisal of the country's relationship with Muslim countries, especially in the Middle East and North Africa (MENA). Second,

Osama bin Laden, leader of the most egregious religious terrorist organisation, al Qaeda, was assassinated in May 2011 by US action, which stimulated further debate about both the role of al Qaeda and that of the USA in international relations, albeit without leading to any significant popular complaints at bin Laden's death, even from those who might be expected to mourn his death: extremist Islamists. Third, Pope Benedict XVI delivered a contentious lecture in 2006 in which he argued that Christianity is 'rational' while Islam is 'irrational', which led subsequently to increased friction between the Catholic Church and some Muslim countries, including Muslim-majority Turkey, a candidate for European Union membership. The pope's speech highlighted how Turkey's candidature is highly controversial in some European countries, as many people fear the entry into the Union of Muslim-majority Turkey (Lindquist and Handelman, 2011: 15). Fourth, the position of Europe's Muslims came under renewed scrutiny in the wake of 9/11, Madrid's 21 April 2004 bombings and those in London on 7 July 2005. These events had the effect of encouraging European governments to pay attention not only to the issue of multiculturalism but also to reconsider the secular nature of their societies during a time of general 'religious resurgence'. These concerns encouraged European governments to adopt new and innovative approaches to public religion. Fifth, since late 2010 events in the Middle East and North Africa – collectively known as 'the Arab Spring' – have focused attention on the relationship between religion and politics in the more than 20 countries, nearly all Muslim-majority states, which comprise the MENA. A general aim of the second edition is to incorporate these and other recent events and developments into the case study chapters in the second half of the text, as well as informing the theoretical and historical chapters in the text's first part.

A second general issue focused upon in the second edition is more attention to international relations theory. The first edition was quite weak in this respect and for the second edition to be of maximum utility as a student textbook, especially those taking degrees in International Relations, I place more emphasis on how best to factor religion into key International Relations theories and approaches, examining, in Chapter 3: realism, liberalism, neo-Marxism/critical theory, constructivism and the 'English School'.

A third innovation in the new edition is that it expands coverage of key thinkers in the context of religion and international relations. These include the US political theorist Reinhold Niebuhr, and an idea with which he is often associated: Christian Realism, which is examined in Chapter 3 in the context of IR theories. In Chapter 8, we examine another important issue, omitted from the first edition: the 'dialogue of civilisations', the mirror image of Huntington's 'clash of civilisations'. The 'dialogue of civilisations' was the brainchild of a former president of Iran, Mohammed Khatami, which developed from 2005 into the 'Alliance of Civilizations' under United Nations (UN) auspices. The dialogue/alliance sought to counter the destructive ideas captured in the 'clash of civilisations' thesis and to suggest practical ways in which 'civilisations' could work together and not be pulled apart.

Fourth, in addition to recent empirical developments in country and regional contexts, enhanced focus on theory and theoretical issues, and the impact of important developments such as the 'Alliance of Civilizations', the second edition has dedicated chapters on issues of great importance to many non-state, transnational religious actors in international relations. These are: democratisation and democracy (Chapter 6); development (Chapter 7); and conflict and cooperation (Chapter 8). Chapter 6 focuses on the relationship between religion, democratisation and democracy, highlighting Western countries' attempts to promoted democracy in non-democratic states in the developing world. Chapter 7 examines the relationship between religion and development by examining two issues: the UN-supported Millennium Development Goals (MDGs) and the role of the World Bank in liaising with selected religious actors to help achieve the MDGs. Chapter 8 focuses on the role of religion in international conflict and cooperation, including the activities of the UN-sponsored Alliance of Civilizations, a riposte to Samuel Huntington's (1993, 1996) 'clash of civilisations'.

## Defining and explaining key terms: 'international relations' and 'religion'

The aim of the text is to assess the influence of state and non-state 'religious actors' in international relations and to explain how, why and when they are important. The issue is worth looking at because, while today many international relations specialists would accept that religion can be an important issue in world affairs, until quite recently it was ignored (Petito and Hatzopoulos, 2003; Fox and Sandler, 2004; Haynes, 2007a; Snyder, 2011). But, first things first. What, you might ask, do I mean by the key terms, 'international relations' and 'religion'?

## International relations

'Narrow' definitions of international relations primarily focus upon relations between the world's governments, represented by senior politicians – such as, Britain's foreign secretary, William Hague, or Hillary Clinton, the US secretary of state – whose jobs are to try to put into effect their government's foreign policies and external programmes. A more inclusive definition, one that is adopted in this text, understands international relations as both more comprehensive and interdisciplinary. This 'broad' understanding of international relations not only engages with subject matter drawn from various fields of study but also includes a focus on both state and non-state actors. The following subject areas inform the broad version:

- *Economics* is given a key focus in a specific area of international relations, known as international political economy (IPE). IPE involves the politics of international economic relationships. These include: trade and financial relations between states (for example, in the European Union); North–South development issues, including international debt and economic dependency; and the impact of World Bank and the International Monetary Fund policies on states.
- *Politics* within the subject matter of international relations includes, on the one hand, political relations between states and, on the other, various international organisations, such as, the United Nations, the European Union and the Organisation of the Islamic Conference.
- *Security studies* is a traditional issue in international relations, originally focusing on war, peace and diplomacy, but now covering 'new' areas, including economic, environmental and anti-terrorism security.
- *History* informs international relations by making clear the main events in the past that inform and influence the present.

15

## *Religion*

For Snyder (2011: 3), 'Religion is one of the basic forces of the social universe, not just an "omitted variable".' Huntington (1996: 27) believes that, 'In the modern world, religion is central, perhaps *the* central, force that motivates and mobilizes people.' These comments suggest that, for many people, religion is a central component of what it means to be human. Yet, *defining* religion satisfactorily seems to be impossible (Fitzgerald, 2011). Marty (2000) begins his discussion of religion by listing 17 different definitions, before commenting that: 'Scholars will never agree on the definition of religion.' Marty identifies several 'phenomena that help describe what we're talking about' when discussing religion. He lists five features of religion that 'help point to and put boundaries around the term'. For Marty, religion:

- focuses our 'ultimate concern';
- builds community;
- appeals to myth and symbol;
- is enforced through rites and ceremonies;
- demands certain behaviour from its adherents (2000: 11–14).

From this we can see that religion can be thought of as (1) a system of beliefs and practices – often but not necessarily related to an ultimate being, beings, or to the supernatural – and/or (2) that which is sacred in a society – that is, ultimate beliefs and practices which are inviolate (Aquaviva, 1979). For purposes of social investigation, religion may be approached: (1) from the perspective of a body of ideas and outlooks – that is, as theology and ethical code; (2) as a type of formal organisation – that is, the ecclesiastical 'church'; or (3) as a social group – that is, religious groups and movements. There are two basic ways that religion can affect the world: by what it *says* and by what it *does*. The former relates to religion's doctrine or theology, the latter to its importance as a social phenomenon and mark of identity. This can work through a variety of modes of institutionalisation, including church–state relations, civil society and political society.

It is important to distinguish between religion at the individual and group levels – because only the latter is normally of importance in international relations, although individual religious figures, such as Pope John

Paul II, the Dalai Lama and Osama bin Laden, have significantly influenced international relations in recent years. From an individualist perspective, it is useful to think of religion as 'a set of symbolic forms and acts that relates man [sic] to the ultimate conditions of his existence' (Bellah, 1964: 359). This is religion's *private*, spiritual side. We are, however, primarily concerned in this text with *group* religiosity, whose claims and pretensions are very often to some degree political. For Ramet (1995: 64), there is no such thing as a religion without consequences for value systems. Group religiosity is a matter of collective solidarities and of inter-group interactions. Sometimes this focuses on cooperation with other groups; sometimes on tension and conflict, concerned either with shared or contested images of the sacred, or on cultural and class concerns. To complicate matters, however, such influences may well operate differently and with 'different temporalities for the same theologically defined religion in different parts of the world' (Moyser, 1991: 11). Buddhism, Christianity, Confucianism, Hinduism, Islam and Judaism: basic beliefs.

To understand how and why many religious traditions and movements are involved in international relations, it is useful to become aware of some of the basics of their belief systems – as they will inform what religious actors actually do. We examine the basic beliefs of several religious traditions upon which we focus in this text: Buddhism, Christianity, Confucianism, Hinduism, Islam and Judaism. Our focus is on these 'world religions' because most of the significant actors in contemporary international relations come from these faiths.

There is potential for religions to act in international relations in ways that increase chances of cooperation, conflict resolution and peacebuilding. For example, with regard to Islam, 'Islam has a direct impact on the way that peace is conceptualised and the way that conflicts are resolved in Islamic societies, as it embodies and elaborates upon its highest morals, ethical principles and ideals of social harmony' (Bouta et al., 2005: 11). The Dalai Lama, leader of Tibetan Buddhism living in exile in India as a result of China's takeover of the country, has remarked that: 'Every religion emphasizes human improvement, love, respect for others, sharing other people's suffering. On these lines every religion had more or less the same viewpoint and the same goal' (quoted in Hirohita, 2002). Gopin suggests that it is very likely that all religions

**17**

have developed laws and ideas that provide civilisation with cultural commitments to critical peace-related values. These include: empathy, an openness to and even love for strangers, the suppression of unbridled ego and acquisitiveness, human rights, unilateral gestures of forgiveness and humility, interpersonal repentance and the acceptance of responsibility of past error as a means of reconciliation, and the drive for social justice (Gopin, 2000: 13). However, religious involvement in international relations is also sometimes characterised by competition and conflict.

## Buddhism

Buddhism is both a philosophy and a moral practice. Its purpose is to work towards the relief of suffering in existence by ridding oneself of desire. In the early 2000s, there were an estimated 350 million Buddhists, divided into three main schools: Mahayana (56 per cent), Theravada (38 per cent) and Vajrayana (6 per cent). Rather than a religion as such, Buddhism is often regarded as a philosophy based on the teachings of the Buddha, Siddhartha Gautama (in the Sanskrit form, Siddhattha Gotama in the Pāli form). He lived between c.563 and 483 BCE. Buddhism began in India, and gradually spread throughout Asia to Central Asia, Tibet, Sri Lanka and South East Asia, as well as to China, Mongolia, Korea and Japan in East Asia. At the current time, several Asian countries have majority Buddhist populations: Thailand (95 per cent Buddhist), Cambodia (90 per cent), Myanmar (88 per cent), Bhutan (75 per cent), Sri Lanka (70 per cent), Tibet (a region of China; 65 per cent), Laos (60 per cent) and Vietnam (55 per cent). Other Asian countries with significant Buddhist populations include: Japan (50 per cent) and Taiwan (43 per cent). Overall, there were more than 380 million Buddhists in the world in 2005 (http://www.buddhanet.net/e-learning/history/bstatt10.htm).

While there are very large differences between different Buddhist schools of thought, they all share an overall purpose and aim: to liberate the individual from suffering (*dukkha*). While some interpretations stress stirring the practitioner to the awareness of *anatta* (egolessness, the absence of a permanent or substantial self) and the achievement of enlightenment and Nirvana, others (such as the 'Tathagatagarbha' sutras) promote the idea that the practitioner should seek to purify him/

herself of both mental and moral defilements that are key aspects of the 'worldly self' and as a result break through to an understanding of the indwelling 'Buddha-Principle' ('Buddha-nature'), also termed the 'True Self', and thus become transformed into a Buddha. Other Buddhist interpretations beseech bodhisattvas (that is, enlightened beings who, out of compassion, forgo nirvana (or heaven) in order to save others) for a favourable rebirth. Others, however, do none of these things. Most, if not all, Buddhist schools also encourage followers to undertake both good and wholesome actions, and consequently not to do bad and harmful actions.

## Christianity

Christianity is a faith with foundations in the teachings of Jesus, regarded by Christians as the Son of God. Jesus is the second component of a Trinity, comprising God the Father, Jesus the Son, and the Holy Spirit. Christians believe that Jesus' life on earth, his crucifixion, resurrection, and subsequent ascension to heaven are signs not only of God's love for humankind but also his forgiveness of human sins. Christianity also includes a belief that through faith in Jesus individuals may attain salvation and eternal life. These teachings are contained within the Bible, especially the New Testament, although Christians accept also the Old Testament as sacred and authoritative Scripture.

The ethics of Christianity draw to a large extent from the Jewish tradition as presented in the Old Testament, notably the Ten Commandments. There is, however, some difference of interpretation between them as a result of the practice and teachings of Jesus. Christianity can be further defined generally through its concern with the practice of corporate worship and certain rites. These include the use of sacraments – including the traditional seven rites that were instituted by Jesus and recorded in the New Testament and that confer sanctifying grace (the Eastern Orthodox, Roman Catholic, and some other Western Christian churches) and in most other Western Christian churches, by two rites: Baptism and the Eucharist, instituted by Jesus to confer sanctifying grace.

There were an estimated 2.1 billion Christians in 2005 (http://www.adherents.com/Religions_By_Adherents.html) found in probably every country but with major populations found in Europe, the Americas, Africa and parts of Asia.

## Confucianism

Confucianism is a religious and philosophical system that developed from the writings attributed to the Chinese philosopher Confucius (the latinised version of Kung Fu-tzu (that is, Master Kung), who was a teacher in China (*c.*551–479 BCE). Confucianism focuses mostly upon the relationships between individuals, between individuals and their families, and finally between individuals and general society. Confucianism profoundly influenced the traditional culture of China and countries that came under Chinese influence, including Korea. Confucianism places a high value on learning and stresses family relationships, and is the name given by Westerners to a large body of Chinese scholarly works, which the Chinese refer to as 'the scholarly tradition'. Historically, Confucianism has been culturally and politically influential in several East and South East Asian countries, including China, Hong Kong, Japan, Singapore, Taiwan and Vietnam. It has long been an important influence in Chinese and Chinese-influenced attitudes towards life, suggesting patterns of living and standards of social value, while providing a backdrop to Chinese political theories and institutions. Key teachings are concerned with principles of good conduct, practical wisdom, and 'proper' social relationships. Recently, Confucianism has aroused interest among Western scholars because the ideas it represents are widely regarded as an important component of the concept of 'Asian values'. Various Asian countries including China, Korea, Japan and Singapore have cultures strongly influenced by Confucianism.

## Hinduism

Hinduism is the Western term for the religious beliefs and practices of the vast majority of the 1.2 billion people who live in India. One of the oldest living religions in the world, Hinduism is unique among the world religions in that it had no single founder but grew over a period of 4,000 years in syncretism with the religious and cultural movements of the Indian subcontinent. Hinduism is composed of innumerable sects and has no well-defined ecclesiastical organisation. Its two most general features are the caste system and acceptance of the Veda – that is, the oldest and most authoritative Hindu sacred texts, composed in Sanskrit and gathered into four collections – as the most sacred scriptures.

Hinduism's salient characteristics include an ancient mythology, an absence of recorded history (or 'founder'), a cyclical notion of time, a pantheism that infuses divinity into the world around an immanentist[4] relationship between people and divinity, a priestly class, and a tolerance of diverse paths to the ultimate ('god'). Its sacral language is Sanskrit, which came to India about 5,000 years ago along with the Aryans, who came from Central Asia. It is a varied corpus, comprising religion, philosophy and cultural practice that are both indigenous to and prevalent in India. The faith is characterised by a belief in rebirth and a supreme being that can take many forms and types, by the perception that contrasting theories are all aspects of an eternal truth, and by its followers' pursuit of liberation from earthly evils.

Of the total global Hindu population of more than 870 million (http://www.adherents.com/Religions_By_Adherents.html), about 94 per cent (818 million) live in India. Other countries with a significant Hindu population include: Nepal (22.5m.), Bangladesh (14.4m.), Indonesia (4.3m.), Pakistan (3.3m.), Sri Lanka (3m.), Malaysia (1.5m.), Mauritius (600,000), Bhutan (560,000), Fiji (300,000), and Guyana (270,000). In addition, the Indonesian islands of Bali, Java, Sulawesi, Sumatra and Borneo all have significant native Hindu populations.

## Islam

There were an estimated 1.3 billion Muslims in the word in 2005 (http://www.adherents.com/Religions_By_Adherents.html). Like Christians, Muslims are found in probably every country in the world with major populations throughout the Middle East, Africa and parts of Asia.

The origins of Islam are found in an allegiance to God, articulated by his prophet Mohammed (c.570–632 CE). Mohammed was born in Mecca (in present-day Saudi Arabia) and over a period of 23 years received revelations from an angel (Jibreel, or Gabriel), who Mohammed believed was relaying the word of God. For Muslims, Mohammed was the last in a series of prophets, including Abraham, Moses and Jesus, who refined and restated the message of God. After Mohammed's death in 632, Muslims divided into two strands: Shia and Sunni. The Shiites are followers of the caliph (that is, leader of an Islamic polity, regarded as a successor of Mohammad and by tradition always male) Abu Bakr and those who supported Mohammed's closest relative, his son-in-law, Ali ibn Abi Talib. Overall, Shiites place more emphasis on the guiding role of the caliph. The Sunni, however, are the majority sect within Islam, followers of the *custom* of the caliphate rather than an individual caliph, such as Ali. The Shia–Sunni division still persists, although both share most of the customs of the religion. About 90 per cent of the world's Muslims are Sunni and about 10 per cent Shia.

Shias and Sunnis share five fundamental beliefs:

- *Shahada* (profession of faith in the uniqueness of Allah and the centrality of Mohammed as his prophet);
- *Salat* (formal worship or prayer);
- *Zakat* (giving of alms for the poor, assessed on all adult Muslims as 2.5 per cent of capital assets once a year);
- *Hajj* (pilgrimage to Mecca, which every Muslim should undertake at least once in their lifetime; the annual hajj takes place during the last ten days of the twelfth lunar month every year);
- *Sawm* (fasting during Ramadan, the holy ninth month of the lunar year).

## Judaism

Judaism is a term with several distinct meanings: (1) the Jews' monotheistic religion, with origins back to Abraham and with spiritual and ethical principles mainly contained in the Hebrew Scriptures and the Talmud; (2) compliance with the Jewish religion's traditional ceremonies and rites; (3) the Jews' religious, cultural and social practices and beliefs; and (4) the people or community identified as Jews. There were over 15 million Jews worldwide in 2005 (http://www.adherents.com/Religions_By_Adherents.html), many but by no means all living in Israel among its population of more than six million people.

All these aspects of Judaism have an essential shared characteristic: belief in one God who created the universe and continues to rule it. The

God who created the world revealed himself to the Israelites at Mount Sinai. The content of that revelation makes up the Jewish holy book, the Torah, with God's will for humankind stated in his commandments. In Judaism, a second major concept is that of the covenant, or agreement, between God and the Jewish people. The covenant worked like this: Jews would acknowledge God, agreeing to obey his laws and in turn God would acknowledge the Jews as his 'chosen people'.

Jews believe that goodness and obedience will be rewarded and sin punished by God's judgement after death. Then at the end of times, God will send his Messiah to redeem the Jews and deliver them to their Promised Land. Although all forms of Judaism come from the Torah, Judaism is mainly derived from the rabbinic movement during the first centuries of the Christian era. At the turn of the third century, the rabbis (Jewish sages), produced the *Mishnah*, the earliest document of rabbinic literature.

## Conclusion

The aim of the text is to examine how religion affects international relations today. It starts from the following premises:

- *Religion's impact on international relations is not clear or straight-forward.* On the one hand, religion is associated with conflict – for example, 9/11, 7/7, Spain 2004 – while, on the other, it is associated with cooperation – for example, working to help deliver the Millennium Development Goals. It is now widely agreed that the multiple and complex ways that religion impacts upon international relations requires a nuanced treatment.
- *Religion has an important function in engendering and influencing values,* which in turn affects formulation of foreign policies by (a few) states, as well as what religious transnational actors do (Haynes, 2012b).
- *To understand how religion impacts upon international relations, we need to examine interactions between domestic and international spheres.* In other words, it is no longer fruitful – as a result of deepening globalisation – to see the domestic and the international as separate areas of analysis.

We conclude this section by noting that all six religious traditions we examine bring together an array of beliefs and understandings. Partly as a result, to try to bring together the spheres of religion and international relations and to discern and interpret significant patterns and trends is not a simple task. But, in attempting it, three points should be emphasised. First, there is something of a distinction to be drawn between looking at the relationship in terms of the impact of religion on international relations, and that of international relations on religion. At the same time, they are interactive: effects of one stimulate and are stimulated by the other. As we are broadly concerned with how *power* is exercised in international relations and the way(s) in which religion is involved, then the relationship between religion and international relations is both dialectical and interactive: each shapes and influences the other. Both causal directions need to be held in view.

Second, *all* religions are both creative and constantly changing; consequently, their relationships with other religious – as well as secular – actors may vary over time. The nature of the relationship between religion and secular power may suddenly – and unexpectedly – change. For example, in Iran in the late 1970s, and in Eastern Europe, Latin America and Africa in the 1980s and 1990s, leading religious institutions and figures shifted – apparently abruptly – from support to opposition of incumbent authoritarian regimes. This led in Muslim Iran to a theocracy, while in Eastern Europe, Latin America and Africa religious actors, notably Roman Catholic figures, were in the forefront of moves towards popular, democratically elected governments. Later, during the 1990s and early 2000s, religious actors from numerous faiths became involved in both domestic and international attempts to resolve conflicts and build peace (Bouta et al., 2005).

In sum, religions may not have a fixed, immovable position on various issues. This is because what is judged to be religiously appropriate for some believers may not be seen like that for others. In addition, religious understandings and meanings are affected by the broader context within which believers live. In this text we are concerned with two interactive issues: (1) how religious belief or affiliation can affect outcomes in international relations, and (2) how specific international contexts and factors affect what religious actors do. This points to the analytical importance of a range of state and non-state actors and of interactions between domestic and international spheres, in order to explain and account for outcomes in international relations that involve religious actors. I take the view that heuristically it is useful to dichotomise such actors' international involvement. On the one hand, especially since the end of the Cold War in the late 1980s, there have been a number of national and international conflicts with roots in religious, cultural and ethnic divisions. On the other hand, religion is also an increasingly important source of cooperation, often focusing upon conflict resolution and peacebuilding, as well as human and social development.

## Notes

1. According to a *New York Times* website (About.com: Islam), 'Jerusalem was the first *Qiblah* for Muslims — the place towards which Muslims turn in prayer. It was many years into the Islamic mission (16 months after the *Hijrah*), that Mohammed (peace be upon him) was instructed to change the *Qiblah* from Jerusalem to Mecca (Qur'an 2: 142–144). It is reported that the Prophet Mohammed said, 'There are only three mosques to which you should embark on a journey: the sacred mosque (Mecca, Saudi Arabia), this mosque of mine (Madinah, Saudi Arabia), and the mosque of Al-Aqsa (Jerusalem)' (http://islam.about.com/od/jerusalem/a/quds.htm).
2. Toft et al. (2011: 23) define a religious actor as 'any individual, group, or organization that espouses religious beliefs and that articulates a reasonably consistent and coherent message about the relationship of religion to politics'. A religious actor is encouraged to undertake action by religious faith. Such actors include: churches and comparable religious organisations in non-Christian religions; religious social movements, whose main motivating factor is their members' religious beliefs; and political parties, whose ideology has roots in identifiable religious beliefs and traditions.
3. According to International Relations theorist Chris Brown, the academic discipline of 'International Relations' (upper case) studies 'international relations' (lower case), that is, interactions between numerous state and non-state 'actors' (Brown, 2001: 1).
4. Immanentism refers to something existing in the realm of the material universe and/or human consciousness.

## Questions

- What is 'secularisation' and how does it affect the relationship between religion and politics both within and between countries?
- Why are religious actors nearly always overlooked in international relations theory?
- How does globalisation facilitate development of networks of religious transnational actors?
- Does 9/11 and its aftermath provide evidence for Samuel Huntington's claim that 'Islam' and 'the West' are incompatible and bound to come into conflict?

## Further reading

T. Bouta, S. Ayse Kadayifci-Orellana and M. Abu-Nimer, *Faith-Based Peacebuilding: Mapping and Analysis of Christian, Muslim, and Multi-faith Actors*, The Hague: Netherlands Institute of International Relations, 2005. This is a useful introduction to interfaith dialogue involving three world faiths: Christianity, Judaism and Islam.

T. Byrnes, *Reverse Mission. Transnational Religious Communities and the Making of US Foreign Policy*, Washington, DC: Georgetown University Press, 2011. Byrne's book examines three US-based, transnational Christian networks that exert an important influence on US foreign policy involving communal not national loyalties.

J. Haynes, P. Hough, S. Malik and L. Pettiford, *World Politics*, London: Pearson, 2011. The authors provide a wide-ranging introduction to the field of international relations, useful as background and complementary reading to the present text.

S. Huntington, *The Clash of Civilizations*, New York: Simon and Schuster, 1996. Now more than 15 years old, Huntington's seminal – and still highly controversial – articulation of his (in)famous thesis – that the world is entering an era of 'civilisational clashes', especially between Islam and Christianity – is still much debated, especially since 11 September 2001.

J. Snyder (ed.), *Religion and International Relations Theory*, New York: Columbia University Press, 2011. Snyder and his co-authors provide an interesting account of the current 'state of play' in international relations scholarship concerning how to theorise religion's involvement in world politics.

# Part One

# Theory and practice

# 2 | Religious resurgence and post-secular international relations

Until recently, few social scientists anticipated that today religion would still play a significant social or political role. Anybody who had predicted that the first decades of the twenty-first century would see 'a resurgence of religion, with great new cathedrals, mosques, and temples rising up, with the symbols and songs of faith everywhere apparent, would, in most circles, have been derided' (Woollacott, 1995). This is because most social scientists, including virtually all international relations experts, accepted the ideas of 'secularisation theory'. That is, social scientists tended to believe that, as a result of technological advancements and undermining of traditional cultures due to modernisation, religion would inexorably decline. Everywhere, it was assumed, people would lead increasingly secular lives, with religion playing a diminishing role.

'Secularisation' implies a significant diminishing of religious concerns in everyday life. It was once thought to be a unidirectional process, characterising progress from tradition to modernity. As societies moved in this direction, it was thought inevitable that they would progress from a sacred condition to one where religion had decreasingly less ability to influence public outcomes. The point would eventually be reached whereby the sacred would become both socially and politically marginal. According to what was known as 'secularisation theory', religion was destined *universally* to become 'only' a private matter, losing its public significance. As Shupe (1990: 19) notes, 'the demystification of religion inherent in the classic secularisation paradigm posits a gradual, persistent, unbroken erosion of religious influence in urban industrial societies'. Such was secularisation theory's hold on the understanding of successive generations of social scientists, that the Spanish sociologist José Casanova (1994: 17) was correct when he wrote that secularisation theory 'may be the only theory which was able to attain a truly paradigmatic status within the modern social sciences'. Casanova's comment

followed the understanding of most of the leading figures of nineteenth-
and twentieth-century social science – such as, Auguste Comte, Emile
Durkheim, Sigmund Freud, Karl Marx, Talcott Parsons, Herbert Spencer
and Max Weber. All agreed that secularisation is an integral facet of
'modernisation', a global trend of major developmental relevance everywhere as societies modernised. They 'all believed that religion would
gradually fade in importance and cease to be significant with the advent
of industrial [that is, modernised] society. The belief that religion was
dying became the conventional wisdom in the social sciences during
most of the twentieth century' (Norris and Inglehart, 2004: 3). As modernisation extended its grip, so the argument went, religion would everywhere be 'privatised', losing its grip on culture, becoming a purely personal
matter. Thus religion would no longer be a *collective* force with significant
mobilising potential for social and/or political changes. In short, secularisation, the US sociologist, Donald Eugene Smith proclaimed, was
'the most fundamental structural and ideological change in the process
of political development' (Smith, 1970: 6). It was thought a one-way
street: societies gradually – but inexorably – move away from being
focused around the sacred and a concern with the divine to a situation
characterised by significant diminution of religious power and authority.

Secularisation theory turned out to be wrong. Instead of fading away
as prophesised, religion made a return to prominence in many countries, especially in the developing world. Most international relations
scholars would now accept that the opposite to religious marginalisation has recently occurred: religious *resurgence*, with ramifications for
how we understand international relations (Moghadam, 2002; Petito
and Hatzopoulos, 2003; Fox and Sandler, 2004; Thomas, 2005; James,
2011; Toft et al., 2011). Religion's social and political influence is said
to be growing in many parts of the world, not 'only' in much of the
developing world, but also in a key Western, 'developed' country: the
USA. Whereas in the 1960s and 1970s secularisation theorists predicted
the 'death' of religion, now many accept they were wrong. For example,
a senior American sociology professor, Peter Berger (1999: 3), once a
leading proponent of the secularisation thesis, today accepts that, 'far
from being in decline in the modern world, religion is actually experiencing a resurgence . . . the assumption we live in a secularized world is
false. . . . The world today is as furiously religious as it ever was'.

Contrary to conventional wisdom, 'modernisation' did not actually weaken religion – but instead strengthened it, leading to a widespread religious resurgence. We are now as a result experiencing a religious revival, which consequently brings religion into renewed activity and prominence including in international relations. While, as Norris and Ingelhart (2004: 215–216) note, 'some of these reported phenomena [of religious resurgence] may have been overstated' it is the case that 'the simplistic assumption that religion was everywhere in decline, common in earlier decades, ha[s] become implausible to even the casual observer'.

---

### BOX 2.1 Religious resurgence in the early twenty-first century: the regional picture

Many religious organisations and communities have not adapted to secular culture merely in order to survive – but instead have successfully developed their own identities and retained a focus on the supernatural in their beliefs and practices. Today, numerous religious actors are interested in and have an impact upon key areas of concern for politics and international relations, including: human rights (including, social justice, gender issues and democracy), human and economic development, and conflict and cooperation. Numerous countries and regions provide evidence of continuing or growing interaction of religion and politics. These include the *United States*, with continuing vitality of what is variously called the 'Religious', 'Christian' or 'Protestant' Right; *Latin America*'s Protestant evangelical surge which is undermining the historical hegemony of the Roman Catholic Church and which has social and in some cases political ramifications; a post-communist emphasis on religion in *Central and Eastern Europe* which has widely brought religion back into the public realm; widespread Islamic renaissance in the *Middle East and North Africa* affecting political outcomes from Morocco to Egypt; continuing high profile of public religion in many countries in *sub-Saharan Africa*, which sometimes, as in Nigeria, leads to serious political conflict; continuing political significance of the 'Hindu nationalist' political party, the Bharitiya Janata Party in India; and, finally, in *Pacific Asia*, where countries, including China and South Korea, are experiencing a strong growth of Christianity.

---

Among the world regions, only Western Europe continues to experience a waning of the public importance of religion. Religion's decline is often measured by falling income levels for institutionalised religions – in Western Europe, this means long-established Protestant and Catholic churches – as well as declining ordinations of religious professionals, diminishing church attendances, and declining popular observance of traditional church-dictated codes of personal behaviour in relation to conventions regarding sexuality, reproduction and marriage. Overall, in Western Europe, these trends point to 'a process of decline in the social significance of religion' (Wilson, 1992: 198; Davie, 2007; Bruce, 2012). Overall, institutionalised Christianity in Western Europe has now lost many of the functions it once fulfilled for other social institutions. For example, the Christian religion once provided legitimacy for secular authority in a number of ways. It not only endorsed public policy while sustaining with 'a battery of threats and blandishments the agencies of social control', but also claimed to be the only fount of 'true' learning (Wilson, 1992: 200). The Church was also largely responsible for social-ising the young and sponsoring a range of recreational activities. Signs of religious decline have long been observable in north-western Europe. In addition, over the last 30–40 years the same process has been occur-ring in the predominantly Catholic south of the region. For example, both Italy and Spain have seen rapid decline in the authority and pres-tige of the Catholic Church (Moore, 1989; Davie, 2007). Yet even in Western Europe we observe primarily a shift in the institutional location of religion, not unabashed secularisation (Davie, 2002). Many Western European *societies* are undoubtedly becoming even more secular while many *individuals* who live in the region continue to seek religious or spiritual objectives (Lindquist and Handelman, 2011).

But while such facts are not seriously in dispute, recent works on the sociology of religion concerned with several highly secular societies in Europe – including, those of France, the United Kingdom, and Sweden – point out that 'secularisation' may not be the right term to apply to what has happened. This is because there is much evidence that reli-gious belief survives, most of it Christian, despite widespread alienation from the established Protestant and Roman Catholic Churches. British sociologist Grace Davie (2002) suggests that an important distinction can be drawn between 'belonging' and 'believing' in Western Europe. She contends that in Western Europe traditional mainline Christian religious institutions have undoubtedly lost public influence. At the same time, religious beliefs and practices continue to be important in the lives of millions of Europeans. Sometimes this takes the form of new or renewed religious expressions, with associated increments of religious fervour, often focused in what Berger (1999) refers to as religious grass-roots movements.

---

### BOX 2.2 Grace Davie on religious belief in the United Kingdom

Grace Davie (2000, 2002, 2007) argues that in Britain the shrinking number of people attending church services has not been accompanied by a widespread decline in religious beliefs. She also claims that similar patterns can be observed overall in Western Europe. Davie concludes that overall Western Europeans are 'unchurched' populations, not simply secular. She makes this claim because, as she observes, while there has been a marked falling-off in religious attendance (especially in the Protestant north) this has not resulted, yet, in the renunciation of religious belief.

---

Yet while a strong argument can be made for a continued decline in support for many of the established churches in Western Europe, this does not imply that leaders of the mainline churches are necessarily silent on issues of social concern, including: economic development, war and peace, human rights and social justice. For example, Britain is a remarkably secular country. In Britain, religion is privatised, with institutionalised religious organisations, including the state church, the Church of England, no longer having the *right* to be actively or regularly engaged in public life. This does not, however, necessarily imply that people in Britain are necessarily becoming less interested in spiritual matters. Rather, secularisation refers to: (1) dwindling social and moral influence of most religious leaders and institutions, including the Church of England, and (2) government policies pursued without clear heed to specifically religious injunctions or interdictions.

In the light of these developments, how is it possible to explain the continued social and political importance in Britain of some religious leaders and thinkers, including the Archbishop of Canterbury, Dr Rowan Williams, the Chief Rabbi, Jonathan Sacks, as well as the Muslim public intellectual, Professor Tariq Ramadan? One answer is to assert that the paradox of a growing, public role for such 'religious thinkers' in the UK not only reflects a popular turning away from the state to seek solutions to existential problems but also suggests the impact of globalisation, revealing that in recent years there has been a near-global resurgence of religion which even in highly secular Britain has led to a situation where in some circumstances the opinions of some religious leaders and thinkers are taken seriously by government.

The notion of religious resurgence has two connotations. First, it implies a growing public voice for religion, in the sense that issues are increasingly viewed or framed through a religious lens. In addition, it is not only religious leaders and intellectuals, such as Dr Rowan Williams, Dr Jonathan Sacks and Professor Tariq Ramadan, who are publicly concerned with economic and social justice issues. Around the world, numerous religious leaders and intellectuals now make public their desire to make societies more just, more equal, and more focused on spiritual issues. In pursuit of such objectives, they use a variety of tactics and methods some, such as the Anglican Church in Britain, lobby, protest and publish reports at the level of civil society. What encourages religious leaders to voice their social and economic concerns? Berger maintains that what they have in common is a critique of secularity, because human 'existence bereft of transcendence is an impoverished and finally untenable condition'. He argues that a human desire for transcendence – that is, a state of being or existence above and beyond the limits of material experience – is an integral part of the human psyche, and secularity – that is, the condition or quality of being secular – does not allow for this necessary sense of transcendence. Without a sense of transcendence, Berger asserts, life for many people is unsatisfactorily empty (Berger, 1999: 4). However, many people now appear to reject established institutional forms of religion, and the search for transcendence is often expressed in membership of grass-roots religious movements (Bruce, 2012; Haynes and Hennig, 2011; Rosenberger and Sauer, 2012).

For many people, the sense of the apparent emptiness of modern life – of which the search for transcendence is a characteristic – is captured in the concept of the 'postmodern condition'. The term 'postmodernism' is said to have been invented by a French philosopher, J.-F. Lyotard (1979). Postmodernism decisively reflects the end of belief in the Enlightenment project in two key ways: (1) assumptions of universal progress based on reason, and (2) in the 'modern Promethean myth of humanity's mastery of its destiny and capacity for resolution of all its problems' (Watson, 1994: 25).[1] Post-modernism is centrally concerned with 'incredulity toward meta-narratives' – that is, rejection of absolute, unquestionable ways of speaking truth. It reflects an undermining of the certainties by which many people, especially in the West, have hitherto lived for decades – which may help to explain popular support for various grass-roots religious movements (Lyotard, 1979: xxiv–xxv).

For many people, this disaffection with the scientific rationalism of Western thought is a consequence of secularity (Berger, 1999). Overall, the 'postmodern condition' offers opportunities for various religious actors to pursue a public role in a variety of areas, including social justice, encouraged by widespread feelings of economic, social, and political instability. This reflects the exigencies of an epoch that De Gruchy (1995: 5) identifies as 'turbulent, traumatic and dislocating, yet also . . . potentially creative'. One of the most important aspects of postmodernism is the cultural/interpretative dimension, with various religious 'fundamentalisms' a key manifestation, as well as the philosophy of the Religious Right in the United States, the evangelical revival in Latin America, and various expressions of 'militant' and 'moderate' Islamism (Cox, 1984; Ahmed, 1992; Simpson, 1992; Berger, 1999; Kamrava, 2011b). In addition, as a result of the communications revolution that characterises globalisation, more and often better sources of information are widely available, encouraging many people – for example, in Eastern Europe during the declining years of the communist era – to demand their rights, including religious freedoms (Ahmed, 1992: 129).

Clearly, the Enlightenment belief that all societies would inevitably secularise along a linear path as they 'modernise' was wrong. Instead, the combined impact of modernisation (involving urbanisation, industrialisation and swift technological developments) – coupled with a growing lack of faith in secular ideologies and belief in the inevitability of 'secular progress' – has left people around the world with growing feelings of loss rather than achievement and satisfaction. The result in many cases is a (re)turn to seeking after transcendence, often focused in various religious vehicles, not necessarily associated with the traditionally dominant religious faiths, which in Western Europe would be the Catholic and various long-established Protestant (Anglican, Lutheran, etc.) churches. Undermining 'traditional' value systems and allocating opportunities in highly unequal ways within and among nations, secularisation helped produce in many people a deep sense of alienation, helping to stimulate for some a search for identity to give life meaning and purpose; many people found what they wanted in various religious expressions, including grass-roots religious movements. In addition, the rise of global consumerist culture has led to expressions of aversion, sometimes focused in the concerns of religious groups. The overall result is a wave of resurgent religious expressions – with far-reaching implications for social integration, political stability and, in some cases, regional and international peace and security. Religious resurgence is occurring in a variety of countries with differing political and ideological systems, at various levels of economic development, and with diverse religious traditions. But all have been subject to the destabilising pressures of state-directed pursuit of modernisation and secularisation; in other words, all are experiencing to some degree the postmodern condition – characterised by a lack of clarity and certainty about the future direction of society.

But resurgent religion does not only relate to personal beliefs but can also lead to a desire in both individuals and groups to seek to grapple with what are perceived as interlinked social, economic and political issues. 'Because it is so reliable a source of emotion', Tarrow (1998: 112) remarks, 'religion is a recurring source of social movement framing. Religion provides ready-made symbols, rituals, and solidarities that can be accessed and appropriated by movement leaders.' Such religious actors are found in most different faiths and sects, and share a key characteristic: a desire to change domestic, and in many cases international, arrangements, in order to 'do good' or 'do better' by projecting the influence of their religious faith into this-world action. Religious actors will adopt various tactics to try to achieve their goals. Some protest, lobby, or otherwise engage with decision makers at home and abroad. Others focus reform intentions through the ballot box or via civil society. Still others – a tiny minority – may even resort to political violence or terrorism in order to try to pursue their objectives. Overall, numerous religious actors of various kinds seek to engage in current political, economic and social debates, in both domestic and international contexts.

## Post-secular international relations

*Secularism* is defined as the state or quality of being *secular*, the end result of a process of secularisation. Secularism is a term that was for decades associated in Western social science, including International Relations, with terms such as 'worldly' and 'temporal'. 'Secular' implied a lack of reference to a transcendent order, that is, one involving a divine being or beings, such as God or gods. The notion of secularism became normatively associated both with universalist pretensions – that is, it would become a global phenomenon – and a claim to superiority over each and every set of religious ideas, irrespective of their origin, content, philosophy, or approach. Over time, especially after the Second World War, secularism became an ideology of domination, implying the marginalisation, downgrading and, in some cases, belittling of religious ideas, in the pursuit of 'progress' and modernisation'. The domain of the secular became characterised by normatively desirable attributes, such as, tolerance, common sense, justice, rational argument, public interest and public authority. Religion was pejoratively regarded as the antithesis of secularism (Hurd, 2008).

The secularisation thesis was a core assumption of Western social sciences for 40 years following the Second World War. It animated two highly significant sets of social scientific ideas: modernisation theory in the 1950s and 1960s, and dependency theory in the 1960s and 1970s. Both schools of thought maintained – or rather implicitly accepted the then conventional wisdom, then at its most unchallenged – that the course of both international relations and of integrated nation-states necessarily lay squarely in secular participatory politics. In an example of theory guiding 'real world' politics, many political leaders – especially in the developing world, vast areas of which were emerging from colonial rule in the decades after the Second World War – worked implicitly or explicitly from a shared premise. It was that – sometimes irrespective of their own religious beliefs and cultural affiliations – they must for ideological reasons *necessarily* remain neutral in respect of entanglements stemming from particularist religious and cultural claims *if* they wanted to build successful nation-states and conduct flourishing international relations. Not to do so would serve both to encourage dogmatism and reduce tolerance ('isn't this what "history" tells us?', they queried) and as a result be antipathetic to the development of viable nation-states, democracy and the smooth running of the secularised international system. As Juergensmeyer (1993: 27) notes, 'secular nationalism was thought to be not only natural but also universally applicable and morally right'. This is an example of a normatively desirable set of ideas that would replace religion's perceived normatively undesirable characteristics: atavism, tradition, backwardness, rivalry and conflict. It is important to note that a core development in international relations – a universal system of secular, politically centralised states – occurred from the seventeenth century via European colonialism, first in East Asia, Latin America and the Caribbean and, later, in South Asia, sub-Saharan Africa and the Middle East and North Africa. During the nineteenth century, the rise of secular nationalism, first in Europe and then via the French and American Revolutions and European colonisation of the rest of the world, led to the apparent triumph of the secular over the religious. The effect for international relations – and a little later, for International Relations – was that religion was a 'Bad Influence' which needed to be removed if international relations had any chance of being cooperative rather than filled with conflict as Europe was before the Peace of Westphalia (1648). Religion's demonstrable 'Bad Influence' was reflected in numerous religious wars between Christians, on the one hand, and Muslims and Christians, on the other. The consequence was that in international relations religion was relegated to the category of a dangerous but eventually minor issue that must nevertheless be prevented from intruding into the search for domestic national unity and international political stability and progress.

But rather like what occurred within countries where secularisation theory turned out to be wrong, so too did the idea of an unchangingly secular international relations. During the twentieth century, the rise and fall of two extremist secular ideologies – fascism and communism, which led in both cases to extreme tyranny and to the deaths of millions of people by the state in Nazi Germany and the Soviet Union – fatally shook the perceived moral superiority of secular thinking and ideas over religious ones. Clearly, religion did not have a monopoly on conflict and repression and by the end of the Cold War the certainties of a 'superior' secular world order were severely shaken. The demise of optimism about the superior secular values of international relations gave way to a growing willingness to accept that maybe, after all, religion did have something to tell us about how to run international relations better. After the Cold War, religion began its public rehabilitation in international relations, although 9/11 rather set things back in this regard.

Religion values and norms began to reassert themselves, regaining influence in world affairs after centuries of global marginalisation, albeit in fragmented, partial and issue-specific ways. Two of the world faiths – Christianity and Islam – have more of a persistent impact on international affairs, compared to the others: Buddhism, Hinduism and Judaism. For example, in nominally Christian Western Europe, many Muslim immigrant communities now seek to assert themselves, in many cases becoming increasingly confident that they are pushing with the tide, in an environment where religion is making something of a public comeback after years of marginalisation (Rosenberger and Sauer, 2012; Haynes and Hennig, 2011). Contrasting with the idea of *inevitable* secularisation, these events and developments are conceptualised as characterising a new *post-secular* situation, in terms of culture and to some extent organisation. The American philosopher Charles Taylor (2007: 534) argues that it is likely that 'the hegemony of the mainstream master narrative of secularisation will be more and more challenged'. The 'master narrative' to which Taylor refers is the notion that secularisation is a linear regression in belief and practice caused by an 'incompatibility between some features of "modernity" and religious belief' (2007: 530), which has not in fact disappeared from 'modern' settings and, according to some, is making a comeback (Lindquist and Handelman, 2011: Chapter 1).

What, if anything, does the idea of the post-secular connote for understanding and analysing international relations? Many International Relations scholars would agree that since the Iranian revolution of 1978–79 and the end of the Cold War a decade later, there is 'more' religion noticeable in international relations. As a result, it is no longer appropriate to interpret international relations as singularly or even perhaps mainly a secular terrain. This is because there are many religious actors involved in international relations; some are states, most are not. Their influence tends not to be ephemeral; and some are persistently significant, such as the Vatican, successive popes, Osama bin Laden and al Qaeda, and conservative Protestant Evangelicals in the USA, comprising the core of the Religious Right in that country. This allows us to underline that we have now moved away from understanding that international relations is emphatically secular to a situation where the relevance of religion to outcomes in international relations is widely noted and accepted.

## BOX 2.3 What is the post-secular and what has it to do with international relations?

The term 'post-secular' is now widely used in various academic disciplines, including sociology, political science, political philosophy, theology, history and, increasingly, IR. Sociologists understand the 'post-secular' in the context of a (generally) unexpected return of religion into previously secularised societies. In this view, the post-secular is characterised by new visibility of religious practices and religious attitudes in previously secular public spaces, including those in Western Europe, previously believed to be inexorably secularising. For political scientists, evidence of post-secularity is to be found in the necessity of re-evaluating how governments engage with religion and adapting their policies to requirements of increasingly religiously pluralist societies in, for example, Western Europe, long regarded as moving inexorably along the path of secularisation. In addition, there is the issue of religious freedom and the role of religious actors in the public sphere in Western Europe's increasingly multicultural national environments. Political philosophers view 'post-secularity' as a normative challenge that, on the one hand, defines the place of religious viewpoints in the democratic public sphere and, on the other, serves to formulate a political ethic with general validity among citizens, irrespective of which faith – if any – they belong to. Philosophers address questions about the relevance of religiously informed arguments in morality and ethics debates, including those to do with gender equality, women's right and access to abortion services, and the scourge of HIV/AIDS and how to deal with the pandemic. Theologians tend to examine 'post-secularity' as a condition within which Christian churches and other institutionalised religious identities strive to find both place and role in relation to the state and civil society, which are no longer solely determined – at least in Western Europe – by exclusively secularist criteria. Finally, historians place 'post-secularity' in the broader historical context of modernisation and cultural history, aiming to identify specific historical processes and conditions that led to secularisation and now, perhaps, lead out of it.

The varied and various ideas expressed by sociologists, political scientists, political philosophers, philosophers, theologians and historians to include the 'post-secular' suggests that the term is not static or its meaning agreed; it means different things to different people in different contexts. That is, 'post-secular' does not have clear and consistent meaning in any of these disciplinary contexts. Yet, there are also discernible commonalities. There is a shared understanding that the relationship between religion and politics, society, philosophy, and so on, is in need of re-conceptualisation in the light of a continued – or renewed or increasing – religious presence, even in societies, such as those in Western Europe, which were once almost unanimously believed to be inexorably secular-ising, as a crucial aspect of the perceived linear trajectory from tradition to modernity. One way of thinking of this idea of religious resurgence and factoring it into analysis of international relations – along with political science, perhaps the most secular of all of the social sciences – is to go for the lowest common denominator which runs through the various definitions provided in the paragraph above. There, 'post-secular' refers in essence to a 'renewed openness to questions of the spirit' (King, 2000), with a post-secular society identified by Dalferth (2010) as one with new or 'renewed interest in the spiritual life'.

What does this mean for our understanding of international relations? First, we need to remind ourselves that international relations was for hundreds of years conventionally 'secular' – increasingly since the Peace of Westphalia (1648) which ended Europe's decades-long inter-Christian (Protestants and Catholics) conflicts. What does it mean for our under-standing of international relations to make the claim that we now inhabit a 'post-secular' global environment? According to Geoghegan (2000: 205–206):

> [S]ecularism is a complex and multifaceted process which emerged out of the European wars of religion in the sixteenth century, post-secularism is a heu-ristic and political device to address aspects of that process. *Post-secularism is a contested concept that lends itself to ambiguity.* It could suggest a deeply antagonistic stance toward secularism, involving the call for a resurgent religiosity, where 'post' really implies 'pre' – a *dismantling of the secular culture of the past few centuries.* (My emphasis)

To focus on these issues, it is useful to start by identifying what 'post-secular' might mean in international relations, so we can seek to opera-tionalise it analytically.

- Does the small yet arguably growing influence of religious entities in some states' foreign policies indicate that IR more generally is now characterised by 'post-secularity'?
- Is there persuasive evidence of a shift in IR from the dominance of secular concerns to a situation where religious actors of various kinds are now consistently able to influence outcomes?

Increasing numbers of monographs, book chapters, journal articles and conference papers testify to renewed interest in the role of religion in international relations. As noted in Chapter 1, many scholars characterise this as 'resurgent', 'returning', or 'rejuvenated' religion and, by implication, this could amount to a no-longer-secular, actually post-secular global environment (Fox and Sandler, 2004; Norris and Inglehart, 2004; Thomas, 2005; Micklethwait and Wooldridge, 2009; Toft et al., 2011). The analytical and conceptual problem, however, is that the expression 'post-secular' – rather like the earlier term, 'post-modern' – is both vague and hotly debated. Or, as Geoghegan puts it in the quotation above, post-secular is a 'contested concept that lends itself to ambiguity'. Given this lack of clarity, is it possible to identify what post-secular international relations would look like? It seems hard to argue that we are seeing a 'dismantling of the secular culture of the past few centuries'. One way of assessing whether international relations is becoming 'less secular' is to examine state foreign policies, and the impact of religion on their formation and execution. Yet, perhaps the biggest problem for clarity regarding the post-secular in IR is that the still state-centric environment of IR has so few demonstrably religion-influenced state foreign policies. Very few countries – identified in Chapter 1 as Iran and Saudi Arabia – officially have a leading role for religion in their foreign policies. Others, including the USA, especially during the presidency of George W. Bush (2001–09), Israel, especially over the contested issue of who controls Jerusalem, and maybe India during the rule of the Hindu nationalist Bharitiya Janata Party (1996–2004), intermittently take religion seriously in their foreign policies (Warner and Walker, 2007; Haynes, 2008a). To date, however, to my knowledge there is no plausible, universally relevant, theoretical framework to explain how, why, when and under what circumstances does religion manage to acquire centrality in foreign policy formation and execution (Warner and Walker, 2007; Haynes, 2008a; Toft et al., 2011; Snyder, 2011; Fitzgerald, 2011). When, however, scholars do perceive foreign policies to be closely and persistently linked to religious goals, it is usually domestic, religious lobby groups that encourage such policies. Religious lobby groups seek to persuade, encourage, cajole and/or threaten governments into pursuing religious concerns in foreign policy (Marsden, 2008). Generally, however, it appears that today few governments are ditching their embedded secular national interest concerns – such as, national security, protection of trade and territory, or seeking to dissuade potential enemies from embarking on conflict with them – in order to overtly imbue their foreign policies with religious concerns. As a result, it is not necessarily in the context of state foreign policies that we can identify a turn to the religious which would characterise post-secular international relations.

International relations has been dominated by Western countries – first, various European countries, including the United Kingdom, France and Russia, and latterly the USA – for at least 300 years. International relations became emphatically secular over this period with questions of spirituality and religion given short shrift by the powerful players in the pursuit of 'national interest', including even those which, like the USA, are relatively religious countries when compared to other Western states. When President George W. Bush claimed to be guided by God in his policy towards Iraq in 2003, it was unusual, and there is no evidence that Bush's view necessarily held sway over other – more secular – interpretations of the USA's goals in Iraq held, for example, by those identified as the 'neoconservatives', with decidedly secular views about what was good for the USA's national interest (Marsden, 2011). It may be useful to emphasise again that recent international relations was primarily a secular environment and it was very uncommon for religious actors to make an impact which was not merely transitory. From the time of the Peace of Westphalia in 1648, international relations developed impeccably secular credentials which led, first, to the secularisation of Western Europe and then, via various colonialist and imperialist mechanisms, to the rest of the world. During this process, religion was everywhere privatised, becoming secondary to secular, state-led domination of both domestic and international spheres (Halahoff and Wright-Neville, 2009: 923). 'Religious resurgence' and the related idea of 'post-secularity' would necessarily entail a reverse process: a definitive process of religious 'deprivatisation' (Casanova, 1994). This implies widespread, consistent and clear assertion of religion's socio-political relevance for understanding outcomes in international relations. Thus a post-secular IR could be characterised by, first, a greatly increased, consistent, importance for spiritual issues – including but not restricted to those linked to specific religious faiths' particularistic concerns – and, second, to a re-conceptualisation of core international relations concerns, away from secular, material and 'rational' (guided by 'national self-interest') objectives, towards spiritually and religiously relevant goals and objectives.

With this in mind, what might post-secular international relations look like? Is there persuasive evidence that IR is now characterised to a significant extent by a 'renewed openness to questions of the spirit' leading to a 'renewed interest in the spiritual life'? Among other factors, declining membership of organised religions and growth of secularism, especially in the West, have led to a broader view of spirituality. 'Spiritual' today is often used in contexts where 'religion' would once have been the preferred term. While the term 'post-secular' is used in a variety of ways, most meanings point to 'complex and diverse changes that in different ways involve a resacralisation[2] or revitalisation of religion'. However, this new situation provides researchers with not only a theoretical challenge but also a methodological one for understanding impact on international relations. For example, as a result of the changes that may be occurring, it becomes difficult to focus only on religious groups, organisations or movements as many and varied forms of post-secular religious phenomena now exist – for example, spiritual practices that are not associated with any religious faith or tradition (Sutcliffe, 2003). Traditionally, as we shall see in Chapter 3, theorists of IR have mostly sought to reduce the study of religion in IR to a small number of discrete actors: religious organisations of various kinds, including interest groups with moral and/or ethical concerns at one end of the spectrum to extremist and terrorist entities at the other end. There is also awareness that at least one important school of thought in IR, the 'English School', also examined in Chapter 3, allows the perusal of what are seen as generic principles that are synonymous with international norms.

## BOX 2.4 Jürgen Habermas on 'post-secular' Europe

There have been various attempts to conceptualise the post-secular in international relations, including in the works of the American political philosopher Charles Taylor (2007) and that of the German sociologist and philosopher Jürgen Habermas (2006). Habermas states that he is trying to answer the question of why we can now term some 'secularised' societies in Europe as 'post-secular'. In such societies, including for example, the UK, Germany and the Netherlands, various religious actors seek greater public influence, relevance and significance. This comes in the context of earlier secularistic certainty losing explanatory power for what is happening in Europe, with the continuing general impact of globalisation and that of the post-2008 economic crisis.

Habermas notes that at some stage what is now a 'post-secular' society must at some point have been located in a 'secular' country. Logically, then, the controversial term 'post-secular' can only be applied to the apparently secular societies of Europe, as well as countries such as Canada, Australia and New Zealand. In each, popular religious ties have steadily lapsed, often dramatically in recent decades. These countries and regions show pretty conclusively that citizens live in a secularised society. Habermas notes that in terms of sociological indicators in such places, there is no widespread return to religious behaviour and associated convictions among local populations. Trends towards de-institutionalised and new spiritual forms of religiosity have not offset the tangible losses by the major religious communities. According to Habermas, three overlapping phenomena converge to create the impression of a worldwide 'resurgence of religion', including Europe: an expansion in missionary activities; a 'fundamentalist' radicalisation; and a political instrumentalisation of the potential for violence innate in many of the world's religions.

Post-secular international relations and what it may mean for our understanding raises a number of important questions:

- Does post-secular means *after* the secular? If so, how might this be expressed and understood?
- What is the relationship between post-secularity and modernity?
- What are the implications of these debates on the post-secular for thinking about international relations and global politics?
- Will a post-Westphalian international system necessarily be a post-secular one? If so, what are the implications for post-secular domestic and international order?
- How can a focus on post-secularity inform debates and understandings about important current issues in international relations, including: conflict, cooperation, political violence, democracy and development?

Such questions are of major importance, although not necessarily easy to answer. They are crucial, however, if we want to engage meaningfully with current international relations and the extent to which it is informed more by issues of religious and spiritual concerns than formerly. The questions are also of relevance when thinking about what I have suggested is the most important body of actors in today's international relations consistently informed by religious and spiritual issues: non-state, religious transnational actors (RTAs). A focus on RTAs fits well with a separate argument often seen in the context of the post-Cold War impact of globalisation: states are said to be losing their pre-eminent position in international relations, challenged by an array of important non-state actors, with financial or diplomatic clout. They include: transnational business corporations; international financial institutions, especially the World Bank, International Monetary Fund and World Trade Organisation; and powerful regional inter-governmental organisations, including the European Union; and multi-regional cultural entities, such as the Organisation of the Islamic Conference. In widely cited contributions, Susanne Hoeber Rudolph (1997a, 2005) claims that we are witnessing the *de facto* 'fading of the state', which provides opportunity for spiritually and religiously informed, cross-border, 'transnational civil society' to build a universal, poly-religious 'ecumene' to fill the existing transnational space. This is to say that, assuming that forms of polity and forms of religiosity have an effect on each other, we can hypothesise that the claimed 'thinning' and increased 'porousness' of state boundaries as a result of globalisation and consequential expansion of transnational political, social and economic institutions and epistemes[3] will affect both forms of religiosity and capacity to achieve religious goals in international relations. In this vein, Toft, Philpott and Shah argue that

> [m]odern communication and transportation . . . [have] propelled one of the most striking dimensions of the [religious] resurgence – *the evolution of religious communities into transnational political actors*. The Muslim Brotherhood spans multiple countries and communicates its ideas globally. Hindu nationalists in India are supported by equally ardent Hindus in the United States. National Catholic churches around the world were supported by the Vatican – though to different degrees – in their confrontations against dictatorships. *Religious communities have spilled over the confines not only of the private and the local but also over the borders of the sovereign state.*
>
> (2011: 14–15; my emphases)

## Conclusion

This chapter has indicated that the post-Cold War era, that is, since the late 1980s, is characterised both by a widespread although not universal religious resurgence and, more tentatively, by a gradual, patchy post-secularisation of international relations. The latter development is characterised mainly by the growth and increase in influence of an array of diverse religious transnational actors. What they have in common is not only increased ability, as a result of the technological revolution at the heart of developing globalisation, to spread their ideas, norms and values nationally, regionally and, in many cases, globally, but also to begin to inform international relations with increased concern with moral and ethical ideas, including the role of justice and fairness in a world which seems ever more characterised by a lack of both. This is not to assert by implication that involvement of RTAs in international relations is necessarily normatively benign or 'progressive'. A quick perusal of the ideology of, say, al Qaeda would disabuse us of that notion. Yet we at least have a starting point for our examination in later chapters: a widespread assumption that religion now takes on more importance in international relations compared to the past. Some even contend that we are moving into an era of post-secularity, which would influence how and for what purposes international relations takes place. However, as we saw in the chapter, there is no agreed definition of post-secular, which makes it difficult for analysis. Subsequent chapters will enable us to see if there is anything substantive in the notion that we have moved into a post-secular era of international relations. We will do this by looking at a number of issues – democracy, development, and conflict and cooperation – and by assessing the influence of religion on both state and state actors. We start in the next chapter by looking at how religion is theorised in International Relations theory in order to put into perspective what a difficult job it is to factor into a decidedly secular social science discipline a consistent and informed concern with the influence of religion and spirituality.

## Notes

1. For a discussion of postmodernism and Christianity, see Simpson (1992) and in relation to Islam see Ahmed (1992).

2. Resacralisation refers to the return of religious meanings to the public realm, including in relation to politics, the arts and resistance to secularisation, especially from religious believers.
3. An episteme is a set of linked ideas that, taken together, serve to provide the basis of the knowledge that is widely believed to be intellectually certain at a particular era or epoch.

## Questions

- How do we know that religion is 'returning' to public life in both domestic and international contexts?
- What do you understand by the term 'post-secular'?
- Have we entered a new era of post-secular international relations? If so, what is the evidence that this shift has occurred?
- To what extent does globalisation encourage the growth and spread of religious transnational actors?

## Further reading

P. Berger (ed.), *The Desecularization of the World. Resurgent Religion and World Politics*, Washington, DC: Ethics and Pubic Policy Center, 1999. This volume challenges the belief that the world is increasingly secular, showing that while modernisation does have secularising effects, it also provokes a reaction that more often strengthens religion.

J. Habermas, 'Religion in the public sphere', *European Journal of Philosophy*, 14, 1, 2006, pp. 1–25. This article is widely cited in relation to the notion of the post-secular in international relations. It focuses upon the most secular of regions – Europe – and seeks to assess the extent to which it can now be understood as post-secular.

J. Haynes, *Religious Transnational Relations and Soft Power*, Aldershot, UK: Ashgate, 2012. The aim of this book is to examine selected religious transnational actors (RTAs) in international relations, with a focus on both security and order.

P. Norris and R. Ingelhart, *Sacred and Secular. Religion and Politics Worldwide*, Cambridge: Cambridge University Press, 2004. This book develops a theory of secularisation and existential security and compares it against survey evidence from almost 80 societies worldwide.

# 3 | Religion and International Relations theory

Religious concerns stand at the center of international politics, yet key paradigms in international relations, namely realism, liberalism, and constructivism, barely consider religion in their analysis of political subjects.

(Snyder, 2011: back cover)

The assumption that the religious revival in today's world heralds a new era is
not supported by the evidence. Data and analysis both suggest a continuing,
complex, hierarchical and multipolar, but also interdependent and multilateral,
global system. Those acting under the inspiration of a creed will, in the long
run, have to adapt to the secular concepts that underpin the foundations of
the world order rather than the other way around.

(Merlini, 2011: 127)

Until recently International Relations (IR) theory had little to say
about religion. Today it is difficult to avoid religion when talking
about IR theory, as the recent publication of a number of books and
articles makes very clear (Snyder, 2011; James, 2011; Toft et al., 2011;
Fitzgerald, 2011). Why is this and why have things changed? The quota-
tions above suggest that this is a controversial issue in IR theory,
characterised by a diversity of views about how to interpret and understand religion's current involvement in international relations. What
does Snyder mean when he asserts that 'Religious concerns stand at
the center of international politics'? What is Merlini actually claiming
when he says that, 'Those acting under the inspiration of a creed will,
in the long run, have to adapt to the secular concepts that underpin the
foundations of the world order rather than the other way around'? If
religion stands at the 'centre of international politics', then it cannot be
of such unimportance that 'secular concepts [still] underpin the foundations of the world order'. They cannot both be right! Merlini is saying
that although there may be 'more' religion in international relations
compared to the past, this does not imply that we need to change how

we understand how the world works. Snyder seems to be implying the opposite. We have already seen in earlier chapters that there is little evidence that the fundamentals of international relations have suddenly changed as a result of the current religious resurgence, no compelling evidence that post-secular international relations is clearly different from secular international relations, as it evolved over the centuries since the Peace of Westphalia in 1648. To what extent do we need to change our perception of religion's minor role in international relations in order to inform IR theory? In this chapter, I shall argue that we still live in a 'hierarchical and multipolar, but also interdependent and multilateral, global system', just as we did a quarter of a century ago. For IR theory, religion is not a 'game changer', although its various manifestations – expressed in how it affects both states and transnational non-state actors – can at times and in relation to certain issues be significant. However, religion's 'return' to international relations does not mean that we must fundamentally adjust our understanding of how international relations 'works'. The long-running focus on the activities of states – which, do not forget, still in the main adhere to secular principles and objectives in their international relations dealings – is still to be captured within the existing IR theories which collectively see little consistent significance for religion.

Despite religious resurgence and claims of post-secular international relations, the important actors in IR have not fundamentally changed in recent years: powerful states still dominate most of the time, although in certain contexts and in relation to some issues we cannot overlook the importance of a range of secular and religious non-state actors. On the one hand, states (or governments, the two terms are used synonymously in the IR literature) in various ways, in various contexts and with various outcomes may connect their policies to religious concerns. They typically do this in order to justify or legitimate their foreign policies. It is not necessarily the case that they believe that religion is telling them to act more morally or ethically and, as a result, this implies that they must adjust policies. On the other hand, there are non-state actors in international relations employing religion either domestically, to try to encourage governments to act in one way rather than another, or in relation to foreign policy, seeking to adjust, amend or change a country's international relations in order to be more in line with their religious principles. Sometimes they may act as religious transnational actors (RTAs), working alone to try to effect policy change in relation to various issues.

The main reason that IR theory has little to say about religion is because of the background, history and development of the discipline of IR. As we noted in earlier chapters, for hundreds of years, international relations, especially in the West, has been both state-focused and secular in outlook. In recent centuries, very few states – especially in the secular West – have had an organising ideology that regards religion as more significant than secular – that is, non-religious – principles, such as liberal democracy, capitalism, or communism.

> Since September 11, 2001, religion has become a central topic in discussions about international politics. Once Islamic terrorism put religion in the international spotlight, this realm suddenly seemed to teem with lively issues: the foreign policy predilections of the [US] Christian Right towards Israel and Southern Sudan, the complications of faith-based Western activism abroad, the Dalai Lama and the Falun Gong as potential destabilizers of officially atheist but increasingly neo-Confucian China, and the Myanmar military regime's fear of a potential alliance of Burmese monks and international refugee organizations. Perhaps religious international politics had been there all along, but it suddenly became harder to ignore.
>
> (Snyder, 2011: 1)

Snyder mentions four of the world faiths in this quotation – Buddhism, Christianity, Confucianism, and Islam. We could add both the influence of Hinduism in India's foreign policy, especially in relation to (Muslim) Pakistan during the rule of the Hindu nationalist Bharatiya Janata Party in the late 1990s and early 2000s, and that of Jewish political parties in Israel particularly regarding the Palestinians and the status of Jerusalem, a holy city for both Jews and Muslims. We saw in Chapter 2 that overall some claim that there has been a significant shift in world politics, necessitating more consistent attention paid to religion as a result of a perceived shift to 'post-secular' international relations (Habermas, 2006; Barbato and Kratochwil, 2009). While such a shift is open to question, it is clear that the recent resurgence of religion noted on many levels of social activity – including international relations/International Relations[1] – significantly undermines the deep-rooted, secular stubbornness of Western social sciences to take religion seriously. As Snyder notes in the quotation at the beginning of this chapter, three of the most significant theoretical approaches applied to the study of international relations – realism, liberalism and constructivism – have all struggled to factor religion into their paradigms. In this chapter, we shall review each of these approaches and find out why they have a problem with religion in their theorising.

This neglect by these theoretical approaches does not do justice to the current importance of religion in international relations analysis. Although studies are accumulating, how (or whether) religion as a variable can be integrated into mainstream IR thinking still remains in question. First, we examine approaches to understanding religion in international relations, which seek to make religion central to theory. Next, we look at three important paradigms in IR theory – realism, liberalism and constructivism – to see how within those frameworks a concern with religion – an identity-related variable – might contribute to our understanding of international affairs.

The starting point, however, is to underline that to date, as Snyder (2011: 1) puts it, 'the main canonical works of international relations theory, which continue to shape much empirical academic work, hardly mention religion'. Over the last decade, however, a number of works have appeared which have collectively begun to show how international relations scholarship can usefully turn its attention to the fact of religion. Nonetheless, even in 2012, most scholarly and policy discussion of religion in international relations is located in current affairs, area studies, or comparative domestic politics.

> One reason for this neglect is that mainstream international relations scholars find it difficult to integrate religious subject matter into their normal conceptual frameworks. The foundational statements of the three leading paradigms – by Kenneth Waltz for realism, Michael Doyle and Robert Keohane for liberalism, and Alexander Wendt for constructivism – offer no explicit guidance on how to do this, and in some cases imply that a role for religion may not be allowable within the logics of their paradigms. Realists ask 'how many divisions has the Pope?' Liberals tend to accept the secular modernist presumption that religion is an atavism to be superseded. Constructivism, with its central role for identity, norms, and culture, has provided more natural intellectual terrain on which to integrate religion into international relations theory, and yet the index of Wendt's field-defining book does not have a single entry for religion.
>
> (Snyder, 2011: 1)

As Snyder notes, religion does not feature in the 'foundational state-ments of the three leading paradigms'. How, then, can we conceptualise its involvement in today's international relations? Four approaches are worthy of consideration. First, we might work within mainstream theoretical paradigms, looking into how religion has occasionally been influential in shaping the international system, helping to define its key actors – states – and significantly informing key concerns and views.

A second approach, most nearly represented by Samuel Huntington's 'clash of civilisations' thesis, holds that religion has become so central that it should supplant existing paradigms and become the main prism for thinking about international politics. None of the ten contributors to Snyder's (2011) recent edited book on religion in international theory – all of them are US IR experts – believe that this view is accurate. However, they do agree that the role of religion: (1) in international relations has never been small and (2) has been rising in recent decades. For example, in many countries, especially in the developing world, religion is increasing its importance and profile, often as a form of populist politics which followed a general discrediting of secular political ideologies, such as 'African socialism', 'Arab socialism' and communism.

Third, Elizabeth Shakman Hurd (2008, 2011) has argued persuasively that the long-term core value of international relations concept and practice – secularism – is usefully thought of not as an opposite, a mirror image, of religion but rather as an analogous kind of worldview that draws on and competes with religious views. This can be seen in both domestic and international contexts. In the latter, many countries' foreign policies are overtly and explicitly secular. 'Seen in this light, the subject of religion is sufficiently pervasive and distinctive that it requires adjust-ing our basic conceptual lenses to view international relations properly, while not abandoning insights from the traditional paradigms' (Snyder, 2011: 2). Utilising the third approach that Snyder refers to, Nexon (2011) calls for what he refers to as a 'relational-institutional' theoretical approach. This involves drawing on both realism and constructivism, with the aim of analysing 'competitive interplay of discursive frames and transnational networks in an anarchical setting' (Snyder, 2011: 2).

The fourth approach eschews the value or desirability of trying to understand the 'big picture' in favour of examining 'more focused hypotheses in which religion is a causal variable. For example, Monica Toft's (2011) chapter in Snyder's book argues that differing characteristics of the world faiths affects the likelihood of war.

The current chapter will restrict itself to looking at the first two categories noted above: mainstream IR theories and dedicated religion-focused approaches. Chapter 4, which looks at the role of religion in state foreign policies, will focus upon secularism in international relations. Chapter 8 looks at the issue of conflict in international relations, seeking to understand if some religions are more prone to conflict and violence than others.

## Religion and International Relations theory

Since the foundation of Western social sciences in the nineteenth century, religion has been dismissed as of diminishing importance in modern(ising) societies. As discussed in Chapter 1, the theory of secularisation was for decades highly influential. The core of the theory was that religion would everywhere eventually disappear from the public realm, becoming a private, spiritual issue without profound consequence for political developments, whether within countries or internationally. Secular societies, which would base their approach to life on the application of science and rationality, would eventually exclude religion from public concern. Secularisation theory deeply influenced social scientific thinking, including the discipline of International Relations. As a result, according to Sandal and James (2011: 3)

> Until the end of the Cold War, it is not an exaggeration to say that only a few theorists of International Relations (IR) or policy-makers engaged in either substantial investigation or articulation of the links between cultural variables like religion and ethnicity on one hand and international affairs on the other.

Many sociologists of religion and political scientists now fundamentally question the assumptions of secularisation theory, which seem to them both erroneous and wrong, as it does not any longer have empirical validity. This is captured in the idea of a resurgence of religion, with clear international implications, including but not restricted to the events of 9/11 and the murderous attack on the USA which killed around

3,000 people. Yet despite this apparent re-entry of religion in international relations, most IR scholars have been loath to accord religion a central or even important role in IR theories. Is this because most scholars of international relations really do not think that religion matters? Or is it because the most widely accepted theories of IR are actually incapable of factoring in religion to their paradigms? Or is the explanation a combination of both factors?

I adopt the following approach in this text in relation to this issue. I think it is important to incorporate various manifestations of religion into IR analysis, as overall it is too important to be ignored. However, I do not believe that religion is always or even very often the most important factor when it comes to explaining international events and outcomes. I will argue that religion deserves an explanatory place among other, non-religious, factors when seeking to explain international relations outcome, although its validity and explanatory power depends upon the issue and the context.

## BOX 3.1 The impact of the Iranian revolution and 9/11 on International Relations analysis

The Iranian revolution of 1978–79 is an important point for seeing a re-insertion of religion into international relations. Before the revolution, international relations experts took little or no account of religion in their understanding of world affairs; after the revolution, some did, not least because it appeared to affect US foreign policy and national interests. Later, other events, most obviously 9/11, also nudged IR scholars to examine the role of religion, once again mainly because of how it affected the USA. The perceived unimportance of religion in IR before Iran's revolution was closely linked to the prominence of secular international security issues during the Cold War, between the late 1940s and late 1980s. Underpinning this view were two widely accepted assumptions in American–European – that is, 'Western' – social science: (1) rationality and secularity go hand in hand, and (2) 'modern', political, economic and social systems are *only* found in societies that are 'modern', becoming so via a process of secularisation, which seeks publicly to marginalise or 'privatise' religion (Casanova, 1994). We discussed these issues in Chapter 1. I am mentioning them again now both to remind us of their importance and to serve as a useful entry point into the theoretical study of religion in the academic discipline of International Relations.

Earlier, in Chapter 1, we examined the phenomenon of widespread religious resurgence (see, for example, Norris and Inglehart, 2004). We saw that Western Europe appeared for a while to be an exception to the trend of religious resurgence, with most regional countries still characterised by continuing secularisation. However, the importance of the Italian-based pope, John Paul II, in Catholic Poland's post-communist democratisation, the rise of 'Muslim cultural politics' in Britain, France, the Netherlands and elsewhere in the 1990s, and the unavoidable religious factor in Turkey's long-running bid to join the European Union, have all underlined that, 'even' in secular Western Europe, religion is now a component of many domestic political and social issues, while also influencing regional international relations.

One of the perceived strands of religious resurgence was that after the Cold War ended in the late 1980s, there were increased instances of conflicts both within and between countries, which some analysts characterised as mainly about cultural/civilisational issues, which also often involved religion (Huntington, 1993, 1996). Since the Iranian revolution of 1978–79, many observers have pointed to increased political involvement of Muslim political actors – usually referred to as 'Islamists' – in the Middle East and North Africa (MENA), the Horn of Africa, West Asia and elsewhere. At the time of writing (mid-2012), the role of Islam and Islamists in the Arab Spring involving various countries in the MENA is widely debated.

When seeking to interpret these events, it may be useful to try to apply an International Relations theory. But why can we not take each event as it comes and understand each one as an autonomous event? Let us remind ourselves of the points made in Chapter 1 as to the importance of theory for understanding International Relations. We noted that we need theory[2] to provide clear and precise explanations of a 'specified set of phenomena'. This refers to various entities which we can plausibly identify as 'religious actors', including both states and non-state actors. More generally, theory focuses scholarly attention on puzzles that set a research agenda for interested students and researchers. At its most useful, theory offers a set of testable and falsifiable hypotheses, thus encouraging systematic re-evaluation of its main arguments through different research methods.

Linked to issues about theory is the question of which research method is most appropriate to find out about various phenomena. We saw in

Chapter 1 that research methods are systematically structured or codified ways to test theories. Research methodology is particularly relevant in the context of a research programme where we raise a hypothesis, examine evidence and seek to determine whether it is accurate or not. Given a range of assumptions about the properties of actors and their interactions, various hypotheses can be arrived at, ideally supported – or not supported – by empirical case studies or via quantitative research. In this text, we adopt the qualitative, case study approach as a way of finding out whether, for example, selected religious actors are pro- or anti-democracy, pro- or anti-development, pro- or anti-human rights, pro- or anti-conflict, or pro- or anti-cooperation. The task then is to examine the evidence to see if initial hypotheses are correct.

To answer the question, what is theory *for* – we can now state that the purpose of any theory and methodological approach is to understand the world better than we would do without them. We can see this in the context of understanding religion in international relations, where two key developments – the end of the Cold War in the late 1980s and the continuing impact of globalisation – together form an important backdrop to assessment of today's role of religion in international relations. These developments were symptomatic of a new era of international relations, one that compelled novel ways of explaining increasingly integrated domestic and international political developments and outcomes.

## Religion in International Relations theory

In this section, we examine the position of religion in the following IR paradigms:

- Realism;
- Christian Realism;
- English School;
- Liberalism;
- Neo-Marxism and Critical Theory;
- Constructivism.

The overall aim of this section is to examine how these approaches regard religion in international relations, how they factor it into their analytical frameworks and how they understand more generally how religion influences international relations outcomes.

We have already noted that most IR scholars – like their counterparts in the social sciences more generally – have long been subject to what might be called a powerful secularist consensus. This has led to a number of widely held assumptions about religion. One is that there are two kinds of religion: 'good' religion and 'bad' religion. 'Good' religion is linked to a 'modern' individual who regards religion as primarily a confidential, personal matter, implying a set of privately held beliefs that are largely irrelevant to politics and, by extension, international relations. 'Bad' religion, however, is associated with the violent history of Europe's past, particularly the sectarian violence of the Wars of Religion in the seventeen century, during the European Reformation of the same period, and today with mainly Islamist religious terrorism. Most liberal, realist, constructivist and English School approaches have picked up on these working definitions of 'good' and 'bad' religion and adapted them to their theoretical paradigms. Consequently, most work on the assumption that 'good' religion is that which has been confined to the private sphere or has disappeared altogether, while 'bad' religion is that which stubbornly refuses to be privatised and instead acts in various ways to destabilise or challenge international order. Many recent contributions to the study of religion in international relations highlight the importance of marginalising 'bad' religion, associating it with division, violent behaviour and narrow-mindedness (James, 2011). 'Good' religion, however, is seen as potentially able to contribute to public life by helping pursue global justice, improved peacebuilding and facilitating post-conflict reconciliation, while offering in its 'moderate' guise an alternative approach to religious terrorists (Johnson, 2011).

## Realism

Emerging as an academic discipline after the First World War, International Relations initially reflected the view that, with the apparent emphatic development and embedding of secularisation, religion would henceforward be of very limited importance in explaining how the world worked. Consequently, religion was afforded little attention or emphasis, especially in the United States, where most international relations scholars live. In the USA, the approach known as Realism achieved dominance from the 1940s and 1950s, not least because the paradigm's core beliefs appeared to reflect what was actually happening in the world at the time: prominence of first fascism and then communism and their collective, strong challenge to the West's preferred organisational framework, liberal democracy. Realism is based on three fundamental premises:

- States' foreign policies have two main goals – accumulate both material goods and resources and as much power as possible.
- All states share similar international motivations and goals. Because of perceived unity of purpose, what goes on within state policy making processes and structures can be safely placed in a 'black box' – and ignored.
- The international system is a chaotic, self-help system characterised by competition, conflict and cooperation.

Religious movements and actors could well play a role in the competition for resources but, like Realism itself, the levels of analysis problem likely leaves out less well-defined and armed actors. Realism in its various incarnations has not done well in anticipating or predicting significant shifts in world politics (Stack, 2011: 26). As the American politician and sociologist Daniel Moynihan, noted at the time of the collapse of communism in 1989–91: '[Realism] made no provision for the passions – the appeal of ethnic loyalty and nationalism, the demands for freedom of religious practice and cultural expression, and the feeling that the regime had simply lost its moral legitimacy' (Moynihan quoted in Stack, 2011: 27).

Realism contends that the state is *always* the most important factor in international relations because there is no higher authority; international organisations, such as the United Nations or the European Union, are regarded as always subservient to the dominant states. For Realists, the global system is emphatically a global *states* system grounded in competition, conflict and cooperation. Consequently, all states must rely upon their own resources to achieve the power they need to thrive, even if they are prepared, as most are, to collaborate from time to time with others to achieve shared goals. Serious conflict is not the usual status of international relations because peace is usually maintained through local and global balances of power. Realism also emphasises how hegemonic powers, such as the United States, have an important role in establishing and maintaining order in the international system and stresses that the structure of power in the international system shapes the character of the political order (Bull, 1977). In short, Realist analyses places great stress on the significance of military power, because states must ultimately rely on their own efforts to achieve their goals. It ignores or seriously downplays the role of religion, not least because very few – if any – states proclaim that their foreign policies are driven by religious factors (Stack, 2011: 25–27).

## Christian Realism

There is one approach broadly within the Realist paradigm which pays attention to the role of religion in international relations, or, to be precise, Christianity. The approach is known as Christian Realism, whose focus is both normative and historical. Christian Realism can be thought of as a 'moral' version of Realism, usually regarded as amoral and strictly utilitarian, that is, that actions are believed to be appropriate if they are demonstrably useful or for the benefit of a majority. Christian Realism, however, seeks to offer a competitive explanation of right and wrong in international politics. It is often applied to the study of US foreign policy, as we shall see in Chapter 9.

### BOX 3.2 Reinhold Niebuhr and Christian Realism

The key ideas of Christian Realism are strongly associated with the American theologian and IR scholar Reinhold Niebuhr (1892–1971). Niebuhr contends that Realism leaves a contradiction, which the logic of its value systems cannot resolve. That is, for Christian Realists such as Niebuhr, Realism cannot resolve a deep-seated tension between *motive* and *action*. That is, Realists use empirical observation and deductive reasoning in order to identify what is most useful in terms of actions, yet, Christian Realists point out, this leaves something lacking: when such a method is used to infer utility in international relations, it cannot cover all dimensions of an issue, as utility is more than a hard empirical object. For example, how can this perception of utility on its own adequately explain the continuous contradictions and tensions we observe in international relations?

What Christian Realists see as an obvious gap in the Realist assessment of international relations is its unresolved contradiction deriving from an arguably incomplete assumption of what human nature does comprise and entail. Christian Realists contend that Christianity and attendant beliefs offers a plausible understanding of both human nature and the human condition. In this conception, 'faith' is also 'reason'. This is carried in the Christian belief that humans were created by God in God's image. As a result, reflecting God's own concerns, people desire justice, want to develop virtue not vice and seek diligently peace. Moreover, so the argument goes, around the world, wherever we look, both natural law and moral justice are found, regardless of culture or religious belief. Thus, it was not the Enlightenment of the seventeenth and eighteenth centuries, or the consequential advance of civilisation or learning that accounts for a global set of moral laws. It was the inherent God-given qualities of people, which Christian Realism uses to explain the perceived existence of good in international relations, in clear contrast to the pessimistic Realist view of human nature. Instead, Christian Realism offers some guiding principles for states and other actors in international relations to encourage behaviour to improve not make worse international outcomes.

## English School

Realism developed primarily in the USA in the context of that country's conflict in the Cold War. According to Niebuhr, the kingdom of heaven cannot be achieved on earth because of people's inherent corruption. Due to earthly injustices, a person is therefore forced to compromise the ideal of the kingdom of heaven on Earth. Niebuhr also contended that human perfectibility was an illusion. He highlighted the sinfulness of humanity at a time, the 1940s and 1950s in particular, when international relations was confronted by the experience of Hitler and the Holocaust, and Stalin.

The nature of the anti-totalitarian conflicts of the 1940s and 1950s encouraged a rather stark view of the world, with first Nazi Germany and then the Soviet Union engaged in a battle for supremacy with the USA. In the United Kingdom, like the USA a key centre of international relations enquiry, analysis took a different turn to Realism and Christian

Realism from the 1950s. It may be that Britain, after the Second World War, was no longer a global power, severely wounded in the Second World War, and thus UK-based IR scholars did not necessarily see the world in the same stark terms as many of their counterparts in the USA. Unlike US-based Realism, the 'English School' approach focused on something quite different: perceived evolution and development of a new 'international society', characterised by the creation and development of the various United Nations organisations. The English School acquired its name because many of its key figures, while not necessarily English by birth, worked in English universities, including the London School of Economics and Political Science, and Oxford and Cambridge universities. Key names associated with the English school include: Martin Wight, Hedley Bull, R. J. Vincent, James Mayall, Robert Jackson, Barry Buzan, Tim Dunne and Nicholas J. Wheeler. According to Buzan, 'The English School can be thought of as an established body of both theoretical and empirical work' (2004: 6). What primarily distinguishes the English School from the Realist approach is, like Christian Realism, a concern with morality. This leads to a distinctive 'English' approach to the study of international relations, emphasising problems of coexistence, cooperation, and conflict, especially in the relations between sovereign states (Jackson and Owens, 2005: 46; Brown, 2005: 51).

The idea of international society involves 'relations between politically organised human groupings, which occupy distinctive territories and enjoy and exercise a measure of independence from each other' (Jackson and Owens, 2005: 46). Conceptually the idea of 'international society' stresses a network of 'autonomous political communities' – typically, states – that are independent of any higher juridical authority, such as, regional or global governments. For Hedley Bull, a founder of the English School, the 'starting point of international relations is the existence of states, or independent political communities, each of which possesses a government and asserts sovereignty in relation to a particular portion of the earth's surface and a particular segment of the human population' (Bull, 1977: 8). Thus for Bull, the main focus of study of IR is the 'world of states' not sub-state entities – such as ethnic or religious communities – or universal categories, such as 'humanity'.

## BOX 3.3 English School, international society, international system

It is a key premise of the English School approach that when states interact regularly and systematically they do not merely form an international *system* – that is, a purely functional arrangement for mutual benefit – but comprise an international *society*. An international society differs from an international system by virtue of the fact that the former is a 'norm-governed relationship whose members accept that they have at least limited responsibilities towards one another and to the society as a whole. These responsibilities are summarised in the traditional practices of international law and diplomacy' (Brown, 2005: 51).

Interest in the role of religion in international relations raises an important theoretical question in relation to the English School approach: is an international society possible in today's world – above all, a multicultural and multi-religious international environment? For Brown, it makes sense to think of the idea of international society as 'an occasionally idealized conceptualisation of the norms of the old, pre-1914 European states system' (Brown, 2005: 51). If this is right, can such a conception of 'international society' be a satisfactory starting point when we bear in mind that most existing states are not European? It might be that the pre-First World War international order functioned relatively well because of a quite high level of cultural homogeneity among the members of international society. This may have been in part because Europeans have a mutual history informed by common Graeco-Roman cultural and Christian religious origins. This relationship was not, however, always peaceful: many historical relationships between European states were intermittently or regularly based on competition and sometimes conflict between, for example, followers of the (Greek) Orthodox and (Roman) Catholic Churches or between Protestant and Catholic interpretations of Christianity. How much more likely now is the potential for competition and perhaps conflict – given that the normative basis for international society (based on shared religious and cultural underpinnings of Europe) – has given way to international relations comprising not only Christian-rooted conceptions but also others deriving from, for example, Islam, Hinduism, Confucianism, Buddhism, Judaism and so on?

## Liberalism

The liberal paradigm begins from the premise that the state is no longer automatically the primary actor in world politics. The growth of transnational relations points to the significance of non-state actors, especially transnational corporations and international organisations of various kinds – including cross-border religious groups, such as al Qaeda – which can be independent of any individual state's or group of states' control (Haynes, 2001b, 2005b). Indeed, the state itself is not regarded as a unitary actor. Rather, it consists of a body of bureaucratic organisations and institutions. The global system is perceived as an aggregate of different issue areas, such as trade, finance, energy, human rights, democracy and ecology, in which domestic and international policy processes merge. The management of global interdependencies is carried out through processes of bargaining, negotiation and consensus seeking. Order is maintained not by a balance of power, as Realists contend, but by the consensual acceptance of common values, norms and international law. In other words, global order is maintained because states have a vested interest in so doing, while the global political process does not involve states alone but also includes a variety of non-state actors. Despite the fact that the liberal internationalist perspective recognises that religious actors can be important transnationally, their importance is seen in terms of particular issues – for example, in relation to democracy or development – rather than generally. We shall examine the Liberal view further in the context of our focus of specific issue areas involving religion in Chapters 6–8, when we focus on, respectively, democratisation, development and cooperation/conflict.

## Neo-Marxism and Critical Theory

The neo-Marxist view sees political processes at the global level primarily as expressions of underlying class conflicts, which develop from their starting points in domestic political competition and conflict. Religion is not seen as an important facet of class issues. Overall, 'materialist' approaches, including neo-Marxism and Critical Theory tend to understand religion (whether in its 'good' or 'bad' guise) as largely epiphenomenal. This means that religion is understood to be an effect of or a cover for more fundamental material considerations, especially economic interests and power politics. Talal Asad (1993: 46) has observed that materialist approaches, such as neo-Marxism and Critical Theory, usually dismiss religion 'as a mode of consciousness which is other than consciousness of reality, external to the relations of production, producing no knowledge, but expressing at once the anguish of the oppressed and a spurious consolation'. Materialist IR approaches differ from Realists in not conceiving of global order as based upon an interlinked structure built of military and economic power, or as sustained by networks of interdependence as Liberals do. One of the dominant characteristics of the global order for neo-Marxists and Critical Theorists is the structural differentiation of the world into core, peripheral and semi-peripheral centres of economic power. While originally this was regarded as the division between the 'North', 'South' and the communist Eastern bloc, the emergence of the East Asian Newly Industrialising Countries in the late 1970s and the demise of the Eastern communist bloc a decade later comprehensively undermined this simple (and increasingly simplistic) three-way international economic division. Today, both Critical Theorists and neo-Marxists tend to look to the allegedly baleful conditions of globalisation and neo-imperialism to explain inequities and injustices in international relations. Global order is today preserved through the interactive power of the leading capitalist states, international organisations, such as the United Nations and the European Union, transnational corporations, and international regimes based on the hierarchical dominance of these actors, which together serve to legitimise a global diffusion of a dominant ideology of liberalism and Western-style modernisation.

## Constructivism

Constructivism is not, strictly speaking, a theory or a paradigm. Instead, it is an approach to understanding international relations that is not restricted to one single form, view or concept. What constructivist approaches have in common is the aim of understanding the behaviour of agents, states and non-state actors alike, in social and cultural contexts. For Constructivists, political decision making is understood in both ideational and material terms. Theoretically, then, Constructivists

**65**

might be expected to consider to a greater degree than positivist approaches, including Realism, Liberalism, neo-Marxism and Critical Theory, various factors, including: culture, history and religion. This is because they appear to be influential in helping shape significant outcomes in international relations, including, but not restricted to, those achieved by states. Constructivism, with its central role for identity, norms and culture, provides a potentially favourable theoretical environment in which to bring religion into international relations theory. Consequently, constructivist approaches would seem most likely to provide an analytical environment to encourage understanding of religion in international relations. This is because constructivism is generally concerned with the impact and power of ideas, norms, identity and culture on behaviour. Constructivism is intrigued by the ways that as people interact they construct a *social* world from the *material* world around them, and as a result shape themselves. The implication is that constructivism confronts and challenges a positivist approach to understanding, which insists that science objectively observes the outside world. Constructivism, conversely, constructs.

## BOX 3.4 Peter Katzenstein and Europe: a constructivist view

We can see the potential value of constructivism for understanding outcomes in international relations when we turn to a specific issue: religion in Europe's contemporary international relations. American IR scholar Peter Katzenstein (2006) notes that scholars usually examine *secular* Europeanisation, including the impact of the European Union (EU) on key areas, including: national administrative practice, monetary affairs, human rights, democracy and environmental policy. In such examples, the influence of the EU on individual member states is clear – although outcomes can vary from country to country. Over time, during the process of expansion from six to the current 27-member EU, the main IR scholarly concern has been exploration of the effects of multiple secular issues on the EU's growth and development. Now, however, according to Katzenstein (2006: 1), 'European enlargement is infusing renewed religious vitality into Europe's political and social life, thus chipping away at its exceptional secularism.' Katzenstein (2006: 1) contends that there are three reasons why this development is worthy of attention for IR scholars: 'First, religious vitality has the potential to revive political recognition of the Christian and specifically Catholic foundations of European integration. Second, renewed attention to religious differences could ignite political reactions that in the foreseeable future may well impede Europeanisation. Third, the growing salience of religion is likely to demand new terms of coexistence with secularism.' Legal and cultural Europeanisation has left problematic and undefined the core of the European project. In the future religion may help fill that core by offering a focal point for political debate, engagement, and conflict.

# Dedicated religion-focused approaches in IR

In this section, we examine two theories that claim that religion is so central that it should supplant existing paradigms and become the main prism for thinking about international politics. The first is Samuel Huntington's 'clash of civilisations'. The second is Vendulka Kubálková's international political theology approach. We shall see that while both are interesting and thought-provoking, neither has the capacity to act as an overall or comprehensive theoretical approach to understanding the various ways in which religion affects outcomes in international relations.

## Samuel Huntington's 'Clash of Civilisations'

We have referred briefly to this approach in Chapter 1. We will have occasion to examine it in more detail in Chapter 8, when we look at conflict and cooperation in international relations. As a result, we shall only engage with it briefly here.

The changing post-Cold War international environment encouraged some IR theorists to take religion seriously. One of the first to do so was the US academic Samuel Huntington. In an article (1993) and a subsequent book (1996), Huntington presented an interesting attempt to make religion central to IR theory. Huntington controversially argued that in the post-Cold War world, international relations was characterised by what he called a 'clash of civilisations'. This referred to what Huntington saw as an emerging conflict between 'Islam' – that is, the large bloc of 'Muslim' countries – and the 'West', that is, western European and North American states. Actually, Huntington turned out to be wrong, as no such clash has ensued. Yet the impact of his thesis had an important effect upon how many people, including some policy makers, understand and view international relations. We can understand increased involvement of the USA and other Western countries, including the United Kingdom, in the Middle East in the decade since 9/11 as being directly linked to a Huntingtonian view of the world, reflected in continuing Western involvement in Afghanistan, Iraq and Libya.

Huntington's 'clash of civilisations' approach holds that religion has become so central that it should supplant existing paradigms and become the main prism for thinking about international politics. Very few scholars who have looked at this issue share his view. For example, none of the ten contributors to Snyder's (2011) *Religion and International Relations Theory* takes this view. They do, however, concur that the role of religion in international politics has never been small, is now increasing and has been for some time, and informs a widespread rise in the last 20–30 years of generically similar forms of populist politics in many developing countries and regions, consequential to extensive discrediting of once popular secular political ideologies, such as nationalism and socialism.

## Kubálková's 'International Political Theology'

A few years after Huntington's thesis appeared, another US academic, Vendulka Kubálková, also sought to outline a new theoretical approach to theorise about religion in international relations. Kubálková called her approach international political theology (IPT). In the same vein as international political economy (IPE), which is the application of political concerns to the study of international economics, Kubálková explained that the purpose of IPT was to look at the growing need for meaning in a world deeply affected by globalisation, be that 'transcendental' or 'secular', and wanted to try to incorporate this very human reaction into IR studies.

Kubálková poses a key question: how can IR as an academic discipline usefully contribute to the study of the widespread resurgence of religion and its effects upon outcomes in global politics? This question is important, since the new visibility of religions occurs in a global context which is the primary domain of IR expertise. It is also one that has been overlooked or under-examined by most IR scholars. So far, the contribution of IR to the study of the resurgence of religion has been limited by the social-scientific and materialistic cast of the discipline: religion stands in sharp contrast to reason and is not to be taken seriously. The interests of states are understood in the IR mainstream, particularly in the US, as exogenously given, that is, all conform to a set of universal 'national interest' aspirations, inherent within the Realist approach. Religions, however, are understood in mainstream IR theory as different kinds of actors, which do not conform to the territorial boundaries so essential to state-centric IR studies. To rectify this omission, Kubálková proposed creating IPT to take on a systematic omission in IR, which she saw as neglect of the role of religions, culture, ideas, ideologies and rules in social-science accounts of global politics. IPT would, she argued, focus on those discourses in global politics which search for, or claim to have found, a response – transcendental or secular – to the human need for meaning. For Kubálková, the multifaceted phenomenon of globalisation has encouraged 'an intensified human search for meaning that reaches beyond the restricted empirical existence of the here and now. Globalisation may be one of the possible causes of the increased visibility of religions worldwide, and IPT is a response to this development' (2003: 87).

Kubálková points to a fundamental difference between religious and secular discourses, that is, their 'ontological' presumptions. According to Gruber (1993: 199), 'ontology is a description (like a formal specification of a program) of the concepts and relationships that can exist for an agent or a community of agents'. Kubálková contends that 'most religions' share 'basic ontological characteristics', a contention with which Fitzgerald (2011) strongly disagrees, not least because there are many religions, especially so-called 'Eastern religions' – such as Buddhism, Confucianism and Shinto – which lack a key characteristic of the Abrahamic faiths – Christianity, Islam and Judaism – that is, a single God.

Kubálková proposes what she calls 'a rule-oriented constructivist framework' which enables a serious treatment of 'religion' on a par with other ideas, ideologies and IR theories. Kubálková's approach is novel, not least because she argues explicitly for an ontological distinction between religious and secular thought (Kubálková, 2003: 87). However, according to Fitzgerald (2011: 23), she makes 'wild generalizations about what "all religions, western and eastern" share', which undermines dramatically the explanatory power of her IPT paradigm.

## Conclusion

Until recently, International Relations (IR) theory had little to say about religion. Today, however, many scholars seek to theorise about religion when talking about IR theory. This chapter sought to examine how International Relations theory seeks to engage with religion. We saw that the issue is controversial and there is no consensus about what is the best approach. We have already seen in earlier chapters that there is little evidence that the fundamentals of international relations have suddenly changed as a result of the current religious resurgence. In addition, there appears to be no compelling evidence that post-secular international relations is clearly different from earlier secular international relations, which evolved over the centuries following the Peace of Westphalia in 1648. To what extent do we need to change our perception of religion's minor role in international relations in order to inform IR theory? In this chapter, I argued that we still live in a 'hierarchical and multipolar, but also interdependent and multilateral, global system' (Merlini, 2011: 127), just as we did a quarter of a century ago. For IR theory, religion is not a 'game changer', although its various manifestations – expressed in how it affects both states and transnational non-state actors – can at times and in relation to certain issues be significant. However, religion's 'return' to international relations does not mean that we must fundamentally adjust our understanding of how international relations 'works'. The long-running focus on the activities of states – which, do not forget, still in the main adhere to secular principles and objectives in their international relations dealings – is still to be captured within the existing mainstream IR theories which collectively see little consistent significance for religion. Two theories focusing upon religion as a central component of their explanations for outcomes in international relations, those associated with Samuel Huntington and Vendulka Kubálková, were both rejected in terms of their explanatory potential.

## Notes

1. Remember that the academic discipline of international relations is denoted as 'International Relations', while a more general focus, without theorising, is denoted as 'international relations' (lower case).

2. I understand theory as 'systematically organized knowledge applicable in a relatively wide variety of circumstances, especially a system of assumptions, accepted principles, and rules of procedure devised to analyze, predict, or otherwise explain the nature or behavior of a specified set of phenomena' (*American Heritage Dictionary*, 1985).

## Questions

- To what extent have mainstream theories of International Relations successfully factored in religion into their explanatory frameworks?
- Is religion in international relations too diverse to be easily and simply theorised about?
- Do you find either Samuel Huntington's or Vendulka Kubálková's theories convincing?
- What IR theory would you use to explain the impact of Iran's revolution in 1979 on international relations?

## Further reading

T. Fitzgerald, *Religion and Politics in International Relations. The Modern Myth*, New York: Continuum, 2011. Fitzgerald discusses how, in his modern myth, 'religion' appears as a force of nature which either assists or threatens the sacred secular order of things.

P. James (ed.), *Religion, Identity and Global Governance*, Toronto: University of Toronto Press, 2011. James contends that to understand international relations today, we must take into account the issue of religion.

J. Snyder (ed.), *Religion and International Relations Theory*, New York: Columbia University Press, 2011. Snyder and his co-authors provide a definitive account of the current 'state of play' of how usefully to examine religion in international relations.

M. Duffy Toft, D. Philpott, and T. Samuel Shah, *God's Century*, New York: W.W. Norton and Co., 2011. This book is an important contribution to the contemporary debate about the role of religion in international affairs. They seek to explain why the political consequences of religion differ from time to time and place to place, both historically and in the current era.

# 4 | States, religion and international relations

Numerous recent books, book chapters, journal articles and conference papers testify to renewed interest in the role of religion in international relations. Many scholars characterise this as 'returning', 'resurgent' or 'rejuvenated' religion, leading to the 'desecularization of the world' (Berger, 1999; Fox and Sandler, 2004; Norris and Inglehart, 2004; Thomas, 2005; Micklethwait and Wooldridge, 2009; Toft et al., 2011). However, we have already noted in earlier chapters that this assertion is only the first step in a more complex process: examining systematically and purposively what new religious resurgence means for our understanding of international relations. Put another way, while many argue that there is now something emerging which can be conceptualised as 'post-secular' international relations (Barbato and Kratochwil, 2009; Habermas, 2006), the term 'post-secular' remains vague and under-analysed, as we saw in Chapter 2. Perhaps the biggest problem for clarity regarding the post-secular in IR is that the still state-centric environment of IR has few states with demonstrably and consistently religion-focused foreign policies. Observers characterise a small number of countries – no more than four or five – as having foreign policies consistently or intermittently informed by religious concerns. These include, as noted in Chapter 1, Iran and Saudi Arabia. Others with at least intermittent centrality of religion in their international relations include: the USA, especially during George W. Bush's presidency (2001–09) (Marsden, 2011), India under Bharitiya Janata Party rule (1996–2004), and Israel (Judis, 2005; Haynes, 2008a). Yet, to my knowledge, there is no well-advanced theoretical framework to explain how, why, when and under what circumstances religion informs foreign policy as a central component of focus and objectives (Warner and Walker, 2007; Haynes, 2008a; Toft et al., 2011, Snyder, 2011; Fitzgerald, 2011). When scholars do perceive foreign policies to be closely and persistently linked to religious goals, they often note that domestic religious lobby groups are significant, seeking to persuade, encourage, cajole and/or threaten governments into pursuing religious concerns in foreign policy (Warner and Walker, 2007; Haynes, 2008).

Does the so far limited yet maybe growing influence of religion in some states' foreign policies indicate that international relations more generally is now characterised by 'post-secularity'? In other words, is there persuasive evidence of a shift in international relations from the dominance of secular concerns to a situation where religion is now consistently able to influence outcomes? When we looked at this issue in Chapter 2, we saw that to try to ascertain whether this is true we need to be clear what 'post-secular' *means* so as to be able to operationalise it in analysis. The starting point, however, is to assess what the reinsertion of religion into international relations analysis means for our understanding. As Hurd (2008: 1) notes,

> Religion is a problem in the field of international relations at two distinct levels. First, in recent years religious fundamentalism and religious difference have emerged as crucial factors in international conflict, national security, and foreign policy. This development has come as a surprise to many scholars and practitioners. Much contemporary foreign policy, especially in the United States, is being quickly rewritten to account for this change. Second, the power of this religious resurgence in world politics does not fit into existing categories of thought in academic international relations. Conventional understandings of international relations, focused on material capabilities and strategic interaction, exclude from the start the possibility that religion could be a fundamental organizing force in the international system.

Religion has 'returned' to international relations and, according to Hurd (2008), it poses two 'problems'. On the one hand, many governments, 'especially' that of the United States, must now deal with 'religious fundamentalism and religious difference', as Hurd puts it in the quotation above in an obvious allusion to 9/11, which necessitates refocusing foreign policy in order to confront consequential 'international conflict [and] national security' issues. On the other hand, this 'return' of religion to international relations poses a more general difficulty for international relations analysis, as we saw in the preceding chapter. Following the Peace of Westphalia in 1648, religion was supposed to be permanently excluded from international relations and now we find that it is not. How then do we factor it into our theoretical approaches and empirical analyses? Hurd refers to 'conventional understandings of international relations', which focus on 'material capabilities and strategic interactions'. This is a reference to two theories of IR that we examined in Chapter 3: Realism and Liberalism. We saw that Realism especially is concerned with analysis of international relations, focusing upon what states do and why they do it, largely contoured by their pursuit of power. We have seen that only a handful of states in contemporary international relations have religion as an acknowledged focal point or guiding principle of their international relations. The second issue that Hurd raises – that religion is only of importance in international relations because of the problem it poses for the United States in terms of international conflict and national security – fits in with these analytical perspectives. The problem, however, is that it ignores other crucial issue areas that religion significantly affects, including: democratisation, development and cooperation – concerns driven to a considerable degree by the activities of religious transnational actors (RTAs), the focus of the next chapter (Haynes, 2012b).

In this chapter we are concerned, first, with the role of religion in building states in the context of the expansion of nationalism in the nineteenth and twentieth centuries. We then turn to the issue of contemporary state foreign policies and explain the relative lack of religion among most. We seek to explain religion's relative absence in relation to how international relations has developed over time, which emphasises the importance of secular principles and ideologies.

## Religion and foreign policy in historical perspective

In order to understand the long-term 'exclusion' of religion from international relations and subsequent surprise from observers and analysts at its 'return', we need to understand why religion was excluded in the first place and what it has meant over time for the development of international relations. The Peace of Westphalia (1648) is a useful and specific starting point. It was the year that, following a decades-long religious war, European governments agreed to follow specific rules of conduct governing their diplomatic and commercial interactions which would seek to exclude religion from the international public realm.

It is commonly agreed among IR scholars that the Peace of Westphalia is one of the most important points marking off the mediaeval from the modern period in European and international relations. This is because it marks the starting point, and is a key source of, a new international system based on secular, normative aspirations, not divisive, particularistic religious principles which, it was believed, led to decades of inter- and intra-state conflict in Europe. Secular norms embedded in the Peace were highly influential in creating the foundations of a new secular European and international system, which followed the collapse of its predecessor: a Christianity-based concept and structure called 'Christendom', under the control and authority of the pope. As an organising principle, Christendom had existed in Europe for a thousand years prior to the Peace. From that time, secular international law – that is, the body of international rules and regulations that today covers how states and non-states should behave in international relations – became the key organising principle of Europe's international relations.

## BOX 4.1 The Peace of Westphalia (1648) and its importance for international relations

The main importance of the Peace of Westphalia for international relations was primarily because it instituted increasingly definitive secular principles covering increasingly comprehensive inter-state interactions. Note, however, that while the Peace had fundamentally important secular aspects, it was signed into authority by leaders of two warring Christian sects: Catholics and Protestants. The agreement followed decades of inter-Christian conflict, great wars of religion (including the Thirty Years' War), which had raged across much of Western Europe for a hundred years or more. While the causes and trajectory of the initial conflict were complex, its results were clear enough: millions of dead, wounded and displaced people, with between one-third and half of the populations of many areas in Europe affected. There was massive destruction of property, as well as famines and widespread disease. In fact, the wars of religion in Europe were comparable to the twentieth century's two world wars, in terms of both their comparative destructiveness and the way that they spurred a quest for new, post-war international relations. The end of Europe's religious wars resulted in the eclipse of the concept of Christendom which had dominated ideologically the region's mediaeval principles, structures and institutions. For centuries, Christendom had ostensibly sought to promote the common good but had instead led to an increasingly unrestrained contest for power among political and religious heavyweights, leading to the breakdown of relations typifying the wars of religion which ended with the Peace of Westphalia.

By the time of the Peace of Westphalia, Europe's political leaders were accepting that the previous system based on an inspirational but actually unachievable Christian unity under the aegis of the pope was both outmoded and unworkable. This was primarily because of the immutable division in Christianity between Catholics and Protestants; in addition, references to 'the shared values of Christendom' were no longer adequate or effective as a legitimising ideal which could effectively control the actions of leaders of European countries. The post-Westphalia fragmentation of power in Europe, which focused on individual nation-states rather than the collective authority of the pope, was over time legitimised, while religious authority and power declined. The new set of organising values centred on sovereign equality of states, with individual rulers having absolute authority within their own domains. As a consequence of the steady advance of secular, centralised states, the international system developed from the seventeenth century via exclusion of the public centrality of religion. It was relegated to the category of a potentially dangerous but actually rather minor issue that must not be allowed to obstruct the successful search for both domestic national unity and international political stability and progress. From the chaos of Europe's religious wars came a revolutionary change in the region's political leaders as they sought to order their international relations. The Peace of Westphalia – comprising two separate treaties – created the basis for the first time of a European-wide decentralised system of sovereign and legally equal nation-states. Following the Peace, a key principle – that is, decentralised, scattered power – underpinned first Europe and later via colonialism and imperialism the European system developed into a global system of international relations.

## Nationalism, religion and international relations

Religion was excluded from political power in Europe as a key mechanism for trying to keep international relations peaceful, harmonious and cooperative. Over the course of three and a half centuries – roughly from the time of the Peace of Westphalia (1648) until the end of the Cold War (1988) – international relations developed as a highly secular environment, with no public place for religion. Now, however, there is de facto consensus among IR scholars that religion has 'returned', both within countries and in international relations. Consequential to religion's 'return', international relations scholars now interrogate the previously anodyne and uncontroversial concept of 'secularism', defined here as state promotion of secular policies at home and abroad.

---

## BOX 4.2 The Politics of Secularism in International Relations

Elizabeth Shakman Hurd's book *The Politics of Secularism in International Relations* (2008) provides a comprehensive overview of the issue of secularism in international relations. She explains that the field of international relations has seen controversy about the so-called Westphalian Settlement (or System), the interplay between modernity and the nation-state, and the ideology of secularism. Other international relations scholars, including Fox and Sandler (2004) and Thomas (2005), have also engaged with the theme of secularism in international relations. They conclude that while conflicts involving religion have returned to the forefront of international relations, many analysts and policy makers still assume that ordinarily religion is privatised, and that it is anomalous for it to seek to re-enter the public realm, especially in Western Europe, long regarded as the most secular region. However, as Hurd (2008) notes, this secularist assumption tends to overlook or at least underplay two key questions in current international relations: (1) What does 'secularity' mean and imply for international conflict and cooperation? (2) How far is it defensible to argue that religion still plays a minor role in such issues?

---

Hurd (2008: 1) argues that the two problems identified in these questions are actually two sides of the same coin: the unquestioned acceptance of the secularist division between religion and politics. The consequence of the return of religion to international relations, however, is to make re-examination necessary of both religious privatisation and absolute differentiation between religion and politics. The point is that secularism needs to be analysed as a form of political authority or ideology in its own right, entailing that its consequences need to be evaluated for their impact on international relations. This is Hurd's objective in her book and subsequent work (see Hurd, 2008, 2011). Her central motivating question is: 'how, why, and in what ways does secular political authority form part of the foundation of contemporary international relations theory and practice, and what are the political consequences of this authority in international relations?' (Hurd, 2008:

1). She argues that the secularist separation of religion and politics is not fixed or inevitable. Instead, it was both socially and historically constructed by political leaders for their own ends. Second, the failure to recognise constructed reality involving religion and politics helps explain why many IR scholars fail to recognise the real power of religion in global affairs. Third, overcoming this problem should lead to a better 'handle' on critical observed problems in international relations, including: conflict between the USA and Iran and between Israel and the Palestinians, controversy over Turkey's bid to join the European Union, the rise of political Islam throughout the Middle East and elsewhere in the Muslim world, and the broader religious resurgence noted in many countries around the world.

After the Westphalian Settlement, secular nationalism replaced religion as the key organising ideology of nation-states in Europe. The term 'nationalism' is usually understood in two overlapping ways: as both dogma and political movement. It emphasises that a nation – defined here as a group of people of indeterminate but normally considerable size often in the context of a particular territory, who believe themselves linked by sometimes intense feelings of community – believes it has the right to constitute itself into an independent, sovereign political community. This is for two reasons: shared history and perceived common destiny. For nationalists, it is only right and proper that state borders should dovetail, as precisely as possible, with the boundaries of the nation. In extreme cases, the state regards its nationalism as *the* supreme facet of a person's identity, such as that demonstrated in the ideology of Nazi Germany.

The nature of the relationship between religion and nationalism is, however, both indistinct and contentious. Some authors writing on the topic of nationalism – such as Ernest Gellner (1983) and Eric Hobsbawm (1990) – do not believe a focus on religion is necessary when discussing the origin and practice of nationalism, preferring instead to highlight the importance of various secular – especially historical and economic – factors. Increasingly, however, experts on nationalism recognise that to present a complete and well-rounded understanding of the development of nationalism, covering both developed and developing countries, it is necessary to take into account religion's indirect and direct influence on the development and practice of nationalism (Reiffer, 2003).

The British political scientist Anthony D. Smith is a key authority in this regard. Discussing the relationship between religion and nationalism, Smith (2003: ix) claims that 'perhaps more detrimental than anything to our understanding of these phenomena has been the general trend to dismiss the role of religion and tradition in a globalising world, and to downplay the persistence of nationalism in a "post-national" global order'. Smith's book *Chosen Peoples* (2003), which builds on earlier articles published in 1999 and 2000, is an effective reply to this trend, providing a persuasive account of the long-term relationship of religion and nationhood.

There are important connections between the secularist tradition and contemporary forms of nationalism. As Anthony Marx argues, 'despite denials and formal commitments to liberal secularism, the glue of religious exclusion as a basis for domestic national unity has still not been fully abandoned'. Taking Marx's argument about religious exclusion and national unity as a starting point, it is useful to shift the focus from religion and towards the ways in which modern forms of secularism have been consolidated both through and against religion as bases of unity and identity in ways that are often exclusionary for religion. The US-based anthropologist Talal Asad examines 'how certain practices, concepts, and sensibilities have helped to organize, in different places and different times, political arrangements called secularism' (2006: 217).

When there is a demonstrable relationship between religion and nationalism, scholars use the term 'religious nationalism'. Religious nationalism is an important component of present-day international life, defining a nation in terms of shared religion, although not necessarily exclusively; it may also be connected to other components of identity, including culture, ethnicity and language. Religious nationalism is identified in various contexts, leading to different outcomes. When the state, as in present-day Iran or Saudi Arabia, or in Afghanistan under the Taliban (1996–2001), derives its political legitimacy primarily from public adherence to religious, not secular, doctrines, then what we have is a theocracy: the state is dominated by officials who believe themselves or are widely thought to be divinely guided. Overall, we can note several ways in which religion and nationalism interact, identifying a number of degrees of influence which religion has on nationalism. In the first category, *religious nationalism*, religion and nationalism are inseparable.

In other national movements, however, religion plays a less dominant role, 'merely assisting the more prominent nationalist movement as a cohesive element' (Reiffer, 2003: 215). Many examples of primarily ethnic and cultural nationalism, especially in the developing world, also include important religious aspects. However, they are a variable marker of group identity, not necessarily a *fundamental* impetus for nationalist claims. In other words, religion does not *necessarily* occupy an influential or central position in a nationalist movement. It may be that the secular goal of a nation-state is the primary concern, but this does not imply that religion is utterly irrelevant to such a movement, rather that it may become significant as a supporting element that can help bring together a community in pursuit of a nation-state. Reiffer calls this 'instrumental pious nationalism', and notes the following examples among Muslim liberation movements: the Palestinians, Chechens, Filipino Moros, and Kashmiris, as well as India's Sikhs (2003: 225–226, 229).

## BOX 4.3 Religious nationalism

The term 'religious nationalism' is also used in the literature concerned with the national and international relations of many Middle Eastern and Asian countries in the context of anti-colonialist, indigenous nationalism in the early and mid-twentieth century (Haynes, 1993; Engels and Marks, 1994; Furedi, 1994). During colonial rule in these regions, Western powers, including Britain, France, Belgium and Portugal, sought to administer secular regimes. These proved, however, to be consistently unpopular and unworkable with indigenous populations who were nearly always inspired by religious, not secular, principles. Often, anti-secular agitation inspired anti-colonialist, religion-inspired, indigenous opposition campaigns. Hinduism, Buddhism and Islam all underwent periods of intense political activity in various countries during the period from the end of the First World War (1918) until the 1960s, when most countries in Africa, Asia and the Middle East had won their independence. For example, after the First World War, the rise of Arab nationalism was often intimately associated with Islam, as part of the opposition ideology (Khan, 2006). In addition, following the abrupt withdrawal of British colonial rule, Pakistan was explicitly founded as a *Muslim* state in 1947, religiously and culturally distinct from Hindu-dominated India. Turning to South East Asia, we can note the importance of Buddhism as an anti-colonialist ideology, stimulating nationalists in Burma and Vietnam, in the context of their struggle for liberation from, respectively, British and French colonial rule.

Links between religion and nationalism are not only of historic interest and importance in the context of anti-colonial struggles. Little notes that many contemporary nation-building projects are 'deeply infused with religion'. Consider the following quotation:

> Whether the issue is building, restructuring or maintaining a nation, the process is, all over the world, deeply infused with religion. How else are we to understand Northern Ireland, Israel, Lebanon, the Sudan, Sri Lanka, or Iran? Or, more immediately, how else are we to understand former Eastern European satellites like Poland or Bulgaria, or the so-called 'Soviet Nationalities,' such as the Ukraine, Lithuania, or Azerbaijan and Armenia? Nor, for that matter, are the developed countries altogether exempt from the effects of religious nationalism. The influence of the Moral Majority and related movements on American public life during the 1980s left no doubt about that.
>
> (Little, 1994: 84)

Efforts to build a nation-state utilising either secular methods or, as in Israel, combining both secular and religion-inspired doctrines, are made more problematic when, as with the mainly Muslim Palestinians and the mostly Jewish Israelis, there are fundamental disputes about which group has the definitive right to control territory and build a nation-state. Thus, it is not only the case that religious nationalism occurs when the population of a territory is relatively religiously homogeneous, but it also emerges when territory is contested: a threat to a religious group's identity and wellbeing from a rival can spur contesting religious nationalisms. For example, in early 2008, the declaration of independence by 90 per cent Muslim Kosovo from mainly Christian Serbia (78 per cent of Serbs profess allegiance to the Serbian Orthodox Church) led to an increase in religious nationalist sentiments on both sides – and this after nearly a century of aggressively secularising nationalist ideology following Yugoslavia's establishment in 1918.

A further kind of religious nationalism can be manifested when a religious or cultural group is situated in a territory that it believes is surrounded by a different – and hostile – religious denomination. The result is that the perceived or actual threat from the latter can foster religious nationalism and can aid in mobilising a movement or political party informed by religious fundamentalist ideas. In India, a contemporary form of Hindu nationalism is focused in both a political party, the

Bharatiya Janata Party (BJP), and a national movement, the Rashtriya Swayamsevak. The BJP dominated India's politics for a decade until the May 2004 elections, when it lost power at the national level to the resurgent – and officially secular – Congress (I) Party. However, the BJP retained its hold both on India's commercial capital – Mumbai – and on the Maharashtra state, where it rules today in coalition with a staunch ally, the Shiv Sena. By 2012, when the next Maharashtran local elections are due, the Shiv Sena would have ruled over Mumbai for an uninterrupted spell of 20 years.

It is not, however, the case that religious nationalists necessarily wish to see a nation *within* a defined state. For Juergensmeyer (1993), the term 'religious nationalism' – which he equates with 'religious fundamentalism' – can imply either national or transnational goals. He particularly emphasises 'Islamic fundamentalism' of the many religious nationalisms, contending that it stands out by virtue of its extent and the depth of its hold on followers. In addition, Juergensmeyer notes similarities between the now defunct international, theoretically stateless, revolutionary Marxist–Leninist challenge to the Western order and the post–Cold War threat posed by religious fundamentalism. This is because in both cases the confrontation was 'global in its scope, binary in its opposition, occasionally violent, and essentially a difference of ideologies' (Juergensmeyer, 1993: 5).

This account of the rise of 'secular' nationalism during the nineteenth and twentieth centuries, first, in Europe, and subsequently via European colonialism and imperialism to much of the rest of the world, highlights the increasing significance of secular organising principles for states. It also emphasises that despite a process of secularisation of international relations over time, even the decidedly secular notion of nationalism is also often informed by religious principles. To what extent, if at all, is a similar process to be observed in the creation and development of states' foreign policies, especially during the current era of religious resurgence and post-secular international relations?

## Religion and foreign policy

All states have foreign policies that officially focus on securing a set of 'national interest' goals. A state's foreign policy should be flexible enough to follow the changing contours and dynamics of international politics while simultaneously seeking to preserve and promote what the government of the day decrees are the country's national interests. Most IR scholars would agree that a country's domestic environment has a role in shaping its foreign policy. For Frankel (1963), foreign policy is to a large extent a reflection of a country's domestic milieu, its needs, priorities, strengths and weaknesses. This suggests that a state's foreign policy is thought to be influenced by certain 'objective' conditions – such as history, geography, socio-economic conditions, and culture – that interact with the changing dynamics of international politics to produce identifiable foreign policies. For a country to enjoy a successful foreign policy – that is, one that manages most of the time to achieve the national interest goals that the government identifies – it is necessary to achieve a balance between domestic and external dimensions. In sum, national foreign policies reflect (1) a country's overall power indices (including, geo-strategic location; economic wealth and health; military strength; and domestic political stability) and interactions with (2) the prevailing international environment.

Only a few governments have foreign policies and more generally international relations ostensibly or significantly motivated by religion. Below we shall look briefly at the USA, India, Saudi Arabia and Iran, before focusing upon them more fully in the relevant chapters in the second half of the text concerned with regions and individual countries. How and under what circumstances might religion influence a state's foreign policy, including in relation to national interest goals? The question can be approached in two separate ways. First, it can refer to policies a state adopts in order to deal with religious actors it encounters in trying to put into effect its foreign policy beyond the country's borders. Second, it can refer to actions and policies of domestic religious actors seeking to influence state foreign policies.

## USA

In relation to both aspects of the question, a useful starting point is to note that as 'religion plays an important role in politics in certain parts of the world' then it is likely that there will be 'greater prominence of religious organisations in society and politics' in some countries compared to others (Telhami, 2004: 71). Second, ability of domestic religious actors to translate *potential* ability into *actual* influence on a state's foreign policies will depend to some degree on whether the former can consistently access and influence what relevant decision makers decide. Third, religious actors' ability to influence foreign policy is also linked to ability to influence policy in other ways. For example, the USA has a democratic system with relatively accessible decision-making structures and processes, potentially offering actors – both religious and secular – opportunities to influence domestic and foreign policy decisions (Hudson, 2005: 295–297). However, the idea that religious actors must 'get the ear of government' directly is a very limited and traditional understanding of influence. As Mearsheimer and Walt (2006: 6) note, 'interest groups can lobby elected representatives and members of the executive branch, make campaign contributions, vote in elections, try to mould public opinion etc'.

It is important to note, however, that religions are not just run-of-the-mill lobby groups. There are in addition key aspects of influence that are indirect but nevertheless help construct the mindset that engages with such issues: What questions are raised? What issues are of concern? What terms are used? How are they thought about? And even if a religious actor gets access to formal decision-making structures and processes, it does not guarantee the ability significantly to influence either policy formation or execution. To have a profound policy impact, it is necessary to build relations with key players in both society and politics, as well as to foster good relations with influential print and electronic media. Overall, religious actors' ability to influence state foreign policies is likely to be greatest when, as in the USA after 9/11, there was pronounced ideological empathy between key religious groups and secular power holders. In this context, we can note, first, the post-9/11 influence of the Religious Right in relation to US foreign policy in the Middle East, including the thinking of the then president, George W. Bush (Marsden, 2008, 2011). Leading figures, both secular and religious, whose interests and goals dovetailed – including, Gary Bauer, the late Jerry Falwell, Ralph Reed, Pat Robertson, Dick Armey and Tom DeLay – all enjoyed close personal relationships not only with President George W. Bush but also with several of his close confidantes, such as John Bolton, Robert Bartley, William Bennett, Jeane Kirkpatrick and

George Will (Walt and Mearsheimer, 2006: 6; Marsden, 2011). Second, there is a wider coalition – involving Christian conservatives, mainline Protestants, Catholics, Jews and others – successfully using its soft power to encourage successive US governments under both Bill Clinton and George W. Bush to pass various laws – the International Religious Freedom Act (1998), the Trafficking Victims Protection Act (2000), the Sudan Peace Act (2002) and the North Korea Human Rights Act (2004) – that collectively focus upon social welfare and human rights issues as a focal point of US foreign policy (Haynes, 2008a, 2008b). We shall examine this issue in more detail in Chapter 8, dealing with the issue of religion and international relations involving the USA.

## India

India provides a second example of how religious actors, in this case not the Christian Right as in the USA, but Hindu nationalists, have sought to influence foreign policy regarding Pakistan. Hindu nationalists have focused on this issue since at least the mid-1990s, in relation to the Indian state of Kashmir, the only one in the country with a Muslim majority population. According to Hindu nationalists, Kashmir is a key focus of Pakistan's foreign policy, whose main goal is to destabilise India, Pakistan's arch rival. Like the USA, India is another established democracy with governmental decision makers open to a variety of non-state actors seeking to influence both domestic and foreign policies. In relation to (Hindu) India's long-running conflict with (Muslim) Pakistan over Kashmir, we can note the influence of Hindu nationalists over the years. Their influence was especially important in relation to ideologically compatible governing coalitions from the mid-1990s to the mid-2000s, a time during which India's national government was dominated by the Hindu nationalist Bharatiya Janata Party (BJP).

Like the Religious Right in the USA, which has sought to build influence since the 1970s, Hindu nationalists have been a factor in India's politics for decades. Achieving independence in 1947 from British colonial rule, India was ruled for the next 30 years by the secular Congress Party. During this time, India's foreign policy was characterised by moderation and pragmatism, and its foreign policy centred on the following objectives:

- continuous dialogue with Pakistan;
- strengthening of trade and investment relations with China;
- developing stronger ties with Russia, Japan, the European Union, and the United States;
- efforts to work towards construction of a South Asian regional organisation, the South Asian Association for Regional Cooperation (Katyal, 2004).

The end of the Cold War in the late 1980s and simultaneous deepening of globalisation coincided with the rise to power of the BJP in India. What impact did this have on India's foreign policy? MacFarquhar (2003) argues that the coming to power of the BJP shifted India's foreign policy from moderation, pragmatism and non-alignment to an obsession with the role of Pakistan in sponsoring 'Islamist terrorism' in Kashmir. Thirumalai claims that, following the BJP's ascent to power, 'the role of religion in India's foreign policy cannot be exaggerated. Hindus claim to be the most tolerant of all religious groups. But this claim has been continuously shattered, resulting in certain adverse reactions among various nations'. For Thirumalai this was because

> India has to come to grapple with the fact that Hinduism is more or less a single nation religion, whereas Islam, Christianity and Buddhism are religions practiced and encouraged in many and diverse nations. The view the practitioners of other religions hold regarding Hinduism and Hindus certainly influences the foreign policy of these nations towards India. India's insistence on its secular credentials may be appreciated in the academic circles all over the world, but India continues to be a Hindu-majority nation, a Hindu nation, in the minds of lay Christians, Muslims, and Buddhists all over the world. The foreign policy formulations of other nations do not fail to recognize that India is a Hindu nation, despite India's claims to the contrary.
>
> (Thirumalai, 2001)

For Marshall, perceptions of India as a Hindu nation were reinforced as a result of increasing Hindu extremism and terrorism from the 1990s. Globally, however, especially since 9/11, there was much attention paid to Islamic extremism and terrorism but relatively little overt concern with what some commentators saw as violent trends in Hindu extremism, supported by 'allies in the Indian government, which until mid-2004 was led by the BJP' (P. Marshall, 2004). Instead, a political focus of Hindu nationalism was given attention. Bidwai suggests that 'if the ideologues of India's Hindu-supremacist Bharatiya Janata Party and key policy-makers in the coalition government it leads in New Delhi had their way, they would bring into being just such an alliance or "Axis of Virtue" against "global terrorism"', involving the governments of India, USA and Israel (Bidwai, 2003), with Pakistan as a key target.

## BOX 4.4 India, foreign policy and the 'Axis of Virtue'

In May 2003, India's then national security adviser, Brajesh Mishra, advanced the 'Axis of Virtue' proposal in Washington DC. Mishra was addressing the American Jewish Committee (AJC) at an event where there were also many US Congressmen and women present. Mishra emphasised his desire to help fashion an 'alliance of free societies involved in combating' the scourge of terrorism. Apart from the fact that the US, Israel and India were all 'advanced democracies', each 'had been a significant target of terrorism', in India's case at the hands of Pakistan in Kashmir. As a result, Mishra declared, the four 'advanced democracies must jointly face the same ugly face of modern-day terrorism'. The 'Axis of Virtue' aimed to 'take on international terrorism in a holistic and focused manner . . . to ensure that the global campaign . . . is pursued to its logical conclusion, and does not run out of steam because of other preoccupations. We owe this commitment to our future generations' (Mishra quoted in Embassy of India, 2003). A month later, also in Washington, DC, the then deputy prime minister, Lal Krishna Advani, spoke in glowing terms about the proposal. He stressed 'similarities' between India and the US, calling them 'natural democracies'. He praised the relationship 'developing between our two countries [that is, India and the USA], which is powerfully reflected' in President George W. Bush's then recently announced National Security Strategy document. Obliquely referring to Pakistan, he added, 'it is not an alliance of convenience. It is a principled relationship' (Advani quoted in Bidwai, 2003). According to Bidwai, 'The BJP's ideology admires people like [the then Israeli prime minister, Ariel] Sharon for their machismo and ferocious jingoism. It sees Hindus and Jews (plus Christians) as "strategic allies" against Islam and Confucianism. Absurd and unethical as it is, this "clash-of-civilisations" idea has many takers on India's Hindu Right' (Biswai, 2003).

Overall, according to Biswai, there were three main reasons why the BJP wished to move India closer to Israel and its ideology of Zionism:

- a wish to build closer relations with Israel's main ally, the USA, and thus try to isolate Pakistan;

- shared 'Islamophobia' and anti-Arabism;
- shared commitment to an aggressive and dynamic nationalism (Bidwai, 2003).

In conclusion, the influence of Hindu nationalists in India's foreign policy vis-à-vis Pakistan was reflected in a shift in India's foreign policy from moderation, pragmatism and non-alignment to a fundamental concern with Pakistan, perceived sponsor of 'Islamic terrorism' in Kashmir, and the wish to build an 'alliance of civilisations' with the United States and Israel.

## Saudi Arabia

A third example of the influence of religious actors in relation to foreign policy is to be found in the case of Saudi Arabia. For decades Saudi foreign policy has been based on ostensibly religious considerations. For decades after the Second World War, the government was fervently and consistently opposed both to Jewish Israel and the atheist Soviet Union, while also promoting Islam in various ways around the world. We can see the influence of financial clout in operation here: following the onset of oil prosperity in the 1970s, the Saudi government began to donate millions of US dollars annually to support Islam in various ways, including the building of mosques and printing and distribution of numerous copies of the Qur'an. In addition, Saudi Arabia serves as the chief patron of the Muslim duty to make a pilgrimage to Mecca, expanding arrangements to house and transport the millions of pilgrims who visit the holiest site in Islam: Mecca, located in Saudi Arabia. In addition, Saudi Arabia has made major financial contributions to the creation and development of the World Muslim League, a religious-propagation agency founded in 1962, with headquarters in Mecca. Finally, Saudi Arabia is a leading member of the Organisation of the Islamic Conference (OIC), a multinational grouping of 57 Muslim countries whose role is to defend and advance the interests of Islam around the world.

The influence of Islam in Saudi Arabia's foreign policy is not only because two of the holiest places in Islam, Madinah and Mecca, are located within the country. It is also because the ideology underpinning the rule of the government is an expansionist strand of Islam, called

Wahhabiya. The influence of Wahhabiya is reflected in the fact that the country is run as a theocracy, under the aegis of the king, who claims religious credentials for his power, authority and legitimacy. *Shariah* (Muslim) law is the law of the land and Islamists have access to all the levers of power in the country. Note, however, that Saudi Arabia's foreign policy does not only reflect religious goals. Like every other state, Saudi Arabia has important security goals unconnected to religious objectives. As evidenced by the fear of invasion by Iraq at the time of the first Persian Gulf War in 1990–91 when Iraq invaded Kuwait and seemingly threatened Saudi Arabia, the kingdom's leaders recognise that the country's security is best protected by its alliance with the non-Muslim, United States of America. Saudi Arabia seeks to balance both religious and secular security goals in its foreign policy. To avoid what might have been unacceptable levels of conflict with the USA, the ruler of Saudi Arabia, King Abdullah, sought to block the support for al Qaeda and other radical Islamist organisations from his then main rival for power, Prince Nayef. Fear of offending Washington has also prevented a Saudi/OIC stand against US sanctions on Iran for its alleged attempt to develop nuclear weapons. We can conclude that Saudi Arabia has a mixture of religious and secular foreign policy goals and that when the government feels that the country's security is being threatened, then it is willing to work with states which are not Muslim in order to achieve them.

## *Iran*

The Islamic Republic of Iran is another example of a country whose government has foreign policies influenced by religion. Like Saudi Arabia, Iran is a theocracy strongly influenced by Islam (in Iran's case, Shia Islam, contrasted with the rival Sunni faith, religiously dominant in Saudi Arabia). No other nations today have so clearly articulated as post-revolution Iran an official religion-based ideology and view of the state as an instrument of that ideology. But Iran's foreign policies and activities are not always characterised by a clearly religious dimension, but, like Saudi Aarbia, also by an observable discrepancy between the country's theocratic ideology and secular security imperatives. Overall, seeking to defend Shia Islam and advancing the cause more generally of

Islam are core aspects of Tehran's foreign policy, although at times non-religious goals take priority (Afrasiabi and Maleki, 2003).

According to Sarioghalam (2001: 1), 'Iran's foreign policy is shaped, not mainly by international forces, but by a series of intense post-revolutionary debates inside Iran regarding religion, ideology, and the necessity of engagement with the West and specifically the United States.' When Iran's secular security interests conflict with commitments to 'Islamic solidarity', Tehran gives preference to the former. Indeed, Iran often uses religion to pursue material state interests – as a way of contending with neighbouring regimes or trying to force changes in their policies. For example, it promotes Islamist radicalism and anti-regime movements in, for example, Palestine (Hamas) and Lebanon (Hezbollah), yet does not work to undermine secular Muslim regimes such as Turkmenistan if that regime's relations with Tehran are good (Takeyh, 2009).

Kemp (2005) notes a particular context where Iran's religious and security concerns dovetail: in relation to Iran's neighbour, Iraq. Iran is 90 per cent Shiite and Iraq is between 60 and 65 per cent Shiite, while about one-third of Iraqis are Sunnis. These factors have facilitated the ability of Iran to achieve considerable power and influence in Iraq since the fall of Saddam Hussein in March 2003. Initially, Iran actively supported the position of the United States in wanting to see national elections in Iraq. The main reason was that by the use of its religious influence Iran had a practical way to try to facilitate the political dominance of Iraq's Shiite majority, and, as a result, the government hoped to consolidate its political and religious position in Iraq. Iran's post-Saddam position contrasts with the approach it adopted in the immediate aftermath of the 1979 revolution when the government focused efforts on hard power strategies, for example, seeking to export the revolution 'through the funding of Shiite resistance groups'. Now, however, 'current circumstances encourage Iran to use soft power to help create some sort of Islamic government in Iraq' (Kemp, 2005: 6).

In the medium term, Iran is likely to continue to promote democratic structures and processes in Iraq – as a strategy to try to consolidate a dominant Shiite voice in Iraq's government. On the one hand, Iran is likely to seek to continue to use its religious influence as a key short- and medium-term means to try to facilitate its main objectives in Iraq:

political stability and an accretion of influence. On the other hand, Iran's continuing involvement in Iraq is also part of a long-term security strategy that may not have much to do with religious goals but primarily reflects the importance of secular security goals.

## Conclusion

We have seen that while nationalism is a primarily secular ideology, it also often has important religious foundations or influences. It suggests that when thinking about today's mainly secular countries in international relations, we can still trace how religion has in many cases impacted upon existing forms of nationalism. We also saw that nationalism is both a key factor in the construction and development of modern states and an important component of many foreign policies seeking to achieve national interest goals.

In terms of state-related religious power, our examples – the USA, India, Saudi Arabia and Iran – collectively underline 'that religion's greatest influence on the international system is through its significant influence on domestic politics. It is a motivating force that guides many policy makers' (Fox and Sandler, 2004: 168). To understand and account for the influence of religious actors on foreign policy in relation to the USA, India, Saudi Arabia and Iran, we saw that their wielding of soft power is the best – actually, the *only* way – to influence foreign policy. We also learnt that while it is obviously important for religious actors directly to get the ear of government through various available mechanisms – both formal and informal – in order to have a chance of their preferred policies being put into effect, there are also additional means, including: trying to mould public opinion through the media, demonstrations, or via think tanks, that might be used. In sum, religious actors may try to influence outcomes in international relations by encouraging states to adopt foreign policies that they believe are most in tune with their religious values and goals. We shall examine this issue further in later chapters.

We also saw that there is another category of religious actors – non-state religious actors – who attempt to influence international relations through a focus on transnational civil society. Transnational religious networks have received growing attention since the end of the Cold War in 1989, but the ability of such actors to influence outcomes in international relations is variable. The influence on international relations of transnational religious actors forms the focus of Chapter 4.

In sum, we saw in this chapter that both state-related and non-state religious actors can be of significance for outcomes in international relations. Overall, four main points were made in this chapter:

- State foreign policies can be motivated or significantly influenced by religious actors.
- Domestic religious actors can cross state borders and become internationally significant.
- These transnational religious phenomena use various strategies to try to achieve their goals.
- Religious norms and values can affect international relations in various ways.

## Questions

- Why do so few states have religion as a focal point of their foreign policies?
- What is religious nationalism and how does it affect international relations?
- To what extent, if at all, is the foreign policy of the United States affected by religious concerns?
- To what extent, if at all, is the foreign policy of Iran affected by religious concerns?

## Further reading

M. Barbato and F. Kratochwil, 'Towards a post-secular political order?', *European Political Science Review*, 1, 3, 2009, pp. 317–340. The 'return of religion' as a social phenomenon has stimulated at least three different debates, with the first being the 'clash of civilisations', the second criticising 'modernity', and the third focusing on the public/private distinction. This article uses Habermas' idea of a post-secular society as a prism through which the authors examine the return of religion and impact on secularisation.

J. Fox, 'Clash of civilizations or clash of religions. Which is a more important determinant of ethnic conflict?, *Ethnicities*, 1, 3, September 2001, pp. 295–320. Fox examines the extent to which ethnicity and nationalism are important components of contemporary international relations.

M. Juergensmeyer, *The New Cold War? Religious Nationalism Confronts the Secular State*, Berkeley: University of California Press, 1993. Will the religious confrontations with secular authorities around the world lead to a new Cold War? Mark Juergensmeyer paints a provocative picture of the new religious revolutionaries altering the political landscape in the Middle East, South Asia, Central Asia and Eastern Europe.

E. Shakman Hurd, *The Politics of Secularism in International Relations*, Princeton, NJ: Princeton University Press, 2008. While conflicts involving religion have returned to the forefront of international relations, many political scientists and policy makers still assume that religion has long been privatised in the West. Hurd argues that this secularist assumption ignores the contestation surrounding the category of the 'secular' in international politics.

# 5 | Religious non-state actors and international relations

Secular certainties of international relations developed from the Peace of Westphalia in 1648. They were informed by the understanding that religion was permanently excluded from international relations. Today, however, it is impossible to understand international relations (IR) as completely secular. Instead, we have entered a new, post-secular, era. Now, however, there are a number of important religious actors active in international relations. Some are states. But most are non-state actors. We saw in Chapter 4 that in relation to states this encourages re-examination both of motivations for undertaking specific foreign policies and of how religious belief can be linked to countries' national priorities and outlook. In the current chapter, we switch focus to religious transnational actors (RTAs). RTAs are non-state religious actors that are not formally or consistently connected to states.

In recent decades, various RTAs – including the Roman Catholic Church, networks of mainly USA-based Protestant evangelical Christians, Islamist jihadi entities, including al Qaeda and Lashkar-e-Taiba, and 'moderate' Islamist groups, such as *Tablighi Jamaat* – have sought to develop their transnational links and have had, as a result, significant impacts on international relations (Haynes, 2001b, 2009, 2012b; Rudolph and Piscatori, 1997; Shani, 2008). We can understand the increasing profile of RTA activities as consequential to wider changes in IR, which we characterised in Chapter 2 as a recent shift from secular to 'post-secular' international relations. This is a context where, more than in earlier periods, we see a variety of religious actors in IR, active in relation to various issue areas, including: democratisation, development, cooperation and conflict, issues we examine in Chapters 6–8. Many IR scholars would agree that the post-secular nature of today's international relations is the consequence of two separate but linked events: (1) changes to international relations following the end of the Cold War in the late 1980s and (2) the simultaneous deepening and widening of globalisation over time since then. Together, these two developments are representative of a dramatically changed environment of IR which leads in turn to increased awareness of new actors, issues and concerns.

---

### BOX 5.1 Susanne Hoeber Rudolph and the fading of the state

The US academic Susanne Hoeber Rudolph (1997a, 2005) argues that the post-Cold War period is marked by states losing their pre-eminent role in IR. She claims that we are witnessing a 'fading' of the state, providing opportunity for spiritually- and religiously-informed cross-border religious actors – in our terminology, RTAs – to increase their influence compared to an earlier era where states collectively appeared to many IR scholars to have unchallenged dominance. Rudolph contends that the 'thinning' and increased 'porousness' of state boundaries as a result of globalisation and consequential expansion of transnational political, social, and economic institutions and epistemes[1] affects forms of religiosity and capacity to achieve religious goals in international relations.

---

In a recent contribution, Toft et al. also highlight how globalisation leads to increased opportunities for at least some RTAs to influence international relations outcomes. They note that

> [m]odern communication and transportation . . . [have] propelled one of the most striking dimensions of the [religious] resurgence – *the evolution of religious communities into transnational political actors.* The Muslim Brotherhood spans multiple countries and communicates its ideas globally. Hindu nationalists in India are supported by equally ardent Hindus in the United States. National Catholic Churches around the world were supported by the Vatican – though to different degrees – in their confrontations against dictatorships. *Religious communities have spilled over the confines not only of the private and the local but also over the borders of the sovereign state.*
> (Toft et al., 2011: 14–15; my emphases)

The comments of Rudolph, and Toft et al. point to the fact that, over the last quarter century, cross-border networks involving growing numbers of RTAs have expanded and deepened. Rudolph and Piscatori's edited book from 1997 contains a number of case studies of RTAs, indicating that concerns go beyond the narrowly religious to incorporate: human rights (including democratisation, and democracy and religious freedom), human development, and an attempt at strengthening inter-religious cooperation in order to try to avoid communitarian and sectarian conflicts.

This chapter focuses on RTAs in order to explain what they do and why they do it. We start with a brief survey of what I have referred to as the post-Cold War 'changed landscape' of IR. After that, we explore the activities and goals of selected RTAs in the context of post-secular international relations. We look at the largest Christian church, the Roman Catholic Church; the largest Muslim transnational network, *Tablighi Jamaat*; and a large and important cross-border network of mainly American, conservative, Protestant, evangelical Christians. Each is an example of a particular kind of RTA, which we identify as: the *extended*, the *negotiated* and the *state-linked*.

## Religious transnational actors and the changed landscape of IR

One of the main reasons that we now pay increased attention to religion in international relations is the rise – in both numbers and influence – of religious transnational actors (RTAs) (Thomas, 2005; Shani, 2009; James, 2011; Toft et al., 2011; Haynes, 2012b). This is not, however, to suggest that the involvement and influence in international relations of *any* transnational actors – whether secular or religious – is altogether new. Following the end of the Second World War in 1945, various transnational actors took advantage of improving communications conditions to become purveyors of important ideas, both secular and religious. Secular ideas which developed and spread include: Zionism (the idea that the nation of Jews deserves their own state), anti-colonialism (the movement to free countries in the developing world from European control), anti-imperialism (the movement against European empires, also in the developing world), anti-racism (the idea that to discriminate against someone because of their race or skin colour is wrong), pan-Africanism (the notion that Africans must unite in order to be strong), pan-Arabism (the idea that Arabs were disunited by European colonialism and imperialism and needed to work against an 'artificial' state border to maximise international influence), and 'Afro-Asian solidarity' (the idea that peoples in the developing world in both Asia and Africa suffered similar disadvantages because of colonialism and now is time to work together to improve the position) (Florini, 2000).

There were fewer transnational religious ideas and movements appearing after the Second World War, although 'pan-Islam' was one such notion. Pan-Islam was the notion that Muslim countries should work together to improve their collective position in international relations. The 57-member Organisation of the Islamic Cooperation, founded in 1969, was the material manifestation of this aspiration (Haynes, 2001b). In June 2011, the organisation changed its name to the Organisation of Islamic Cooperation.

Transnational ideas, both secular and religious, can be influential in international relations when they encourage groups of people in different countries to work together in pursuit of their goals. Nye (1990, 2004a) refers to this ability to encourage others to act in certain ways, without force, the threat of force or material inducements, as 'soft power'. When ideas, arguments and campaigns – whether secular or religious – appeal to sufficiently large numbers of people, then there is a possibility that they can influence outcomes, particularly by the capacity to encourage decision makers to make one decision rather than another. Thus the power of soft power is unlike hard power. Soft power reflects the power and force of *ideas* while hard power draws its strength from *material* capabilities, including force or the threat of force and/or economic threats and rewards. Soft power *persuades* or *encourages* decision makers to act in one way rather than another. It does not *force* or *compel* them to do so by the threat or use of hard power.

## BOX 5.2 Religious soft power

The idea of 'religious soft power' involves encouraging both followers and decision makers to change behaviour because they are convinced of the appropriateness of a religious organisation's goals. If international relations is now characterised by a shift to 'post-secular' concerns, then religious soft power ideas are an important component in that change (Barbato and Kratochwil, 2009; Haynes, 2012b). It is clear that at least some religious transnational actors – for example, the Roman Catholic Church (in relation to democratisation during the third wave of democracy) and al Qaeda (in relation to terrorism and extremism before and after 9/11) – significantly affect both domestic and international agendas because of their capacity to affect outcomes. However, using conventional measures (such as economic resources, diplomatic leverage, threat or actual use of force; in short, hard power) overall states, especially the most powerful countries, such as the USA and China, still clearly dominate international relations. Precious few governments – we can count them on the fingers of one hand – are unequivocally or consistently ideological purveyors of religious ideas in international relations. That is, *secular* ideas dominate *most* states' foreign policies – even, arguably, the few that claim to be motivated primarily or significantly by religious goals (such as Iran and Saudi Arabia). Does this mean that, lacking material 'divisions' – to refer to the dismissive comment made by the former leader of the Soviet Union, Josef Stalin, when referring to the lack of hard power of the Roman Catholic Church after the Second World War, implying to him that the Church would have no say in Europe's post-war direction – religious actors, including RTAs, are without ability to influence outcomes in international relations? It may well be that if religious actors, including RTAs, are to achieve their goals then they may find it expedient to ally themselves with (secular) state actors and, when necessary, to benefit from states' hard power, adding to their own capability to wield religious soft power.

Thomas (1999: 30) argues that, as a result of increased capacity to wield soft power, religious transnational actors 'represent – or are seen to represent by individuals and groups in the international community – ideas whose "time has come", increasingly shaping values and norms of the international system'. Sometimes, as Jefferis (2011) notes, RTAs focus on 'contentious politics' and are the focal point of 'social movements'. However, we have an analytical problem to contend with: 'transnationalism' and 'transnational actors' are imprecise, contested research areas (Levitt, 2009). Their study spills over the borders of several academic disciplines in the social sciences, including sociology, political science, international relations and economics.

What we can say is that in recent years the number of RTAs appears to have increased,[2] and so has their analytical significance. The context, already noted, is that of deepening and widening globalisation, which enables ideas to spread with greater ease than in earlier periods, as a result of the multifaceted communications revolution. Globalisation has encouraged RTAs – like their secular counterparts – to look beyond the borders of a state, to pursue transnational and international goals by

linking up with like-minded individuals and groups in different countries
(Thomas, 2005; Haynes, 2009). The general issue of transnational relations opens a wide research agenda. It involves numerous cross-border,
non-state actors participating in myriad regional and global exchanges.
Various kinds of transnational actors not only RTAs but also others –
including multinational corporations, international non-governmental
organisations, terrorists, criminal actors, and diasporas and ethnic
actors – exert variable, yet overall considerable, influence on politics
across borders.

Globalisation generally facilitates such links between many kinds
of state and non-state actors, religious and secular, making shared
concerns widespread, of cross-border importance. In other words,
geographical distance and international borders are no longer major
barriers to consistent communication and persistent collective action.
For transnational actors generally, globalisation theoretically increases
ability to spread messages, information, ideas and funds and, as a result,
link up across international borders with like-minded groups. In addition, over the past two decades or so, global migration patterns have
also helped spawn myriad active transnational religious communities
(Levitt, 2004; Cesari, 2010). Overall, for a variety of reasons, cross-
border links involving religious actors have recently multiplied, and so
have their international and transnational concerns (Rudolph and
Piscatori, 1997; Haynes, 2001b, 2008b, 2012b; Fox and Sandler, 2004;
Thomas, 2005). The outcome is that globalisation strongly encourages
more active religious transnational communities, creating a powerful
potential force in international relations (Banchoff, 2008).

Reflecting these developments, the period since the early 1990s has
seen growing scholarly and policy interest in the study of RTAs and
their impact on international relations. Yet there is little agreement as
to what observers see. On the one hand, some see many – but by no
means all – RTAs as central to the emergence of a generally benign,
politically and socially progressive, transnational civil society. Certain
RTAs, for example, the World Council of Churches, the Roman Catholic
and Anglican Churches, and individual religious actors, such as Archbishop
Desmond Tutu, Pope John Paul II, Dr Rowan Williams, and the Dalai
Lama, all of whom claim to speak for specific religious communities,
have high profiles (Florini, 2000; Held and McGrew, 2002; Lerchner

and Boli, 2008). On the other hand, other RTAs, such as al Qaeda, have a quite different impact on international relations: neither benign nor progressive, but radically destabilising and order-challenging. The overall point is that it is impossible to do purposeful theorising about the nature of current international relations without taking into account both normatively 'benign' and 'malign' RTAs (James, 2011; Byrnes, 2011; Snyder, 2011; Toft et al., 2011).

The goals of normatively 'benign' and 'malign' RTAs differ, but they also have commonalities. First, they pursue goals with a mix of religious, spiritual, social and political concerns. For example, the Roman Catholic Church, the Anglican Church, and al Qaeda each have multifaceted – albeit different – interests and objectives. Second, RTAs typically pursue increased justice for their members and followers, understood as striving to achieve better – religious, social and/or political – outcomes for the disadvantaged or unfulfilled. For example, in the 1980s and early 1990s, the then pope, John Paul II, spearheaded the defence of Polish Catholics against the influence of the atheistic Soviet Union and in the process was instrumental in ending the Cold War and bringing down the system of communist rule in Central and Eastern Europe. More widely, during this time the Roman Catholic Church collectively had great significance during the 'third wave of democracy' in the 1980s and 1990s, encouraging many authoritarian governments in Africa, Central and Eastern Europe, and Latin America to democratise (Huntington, 1991; Toft et al., 2011). We shall look at this issue in greater detail in a later chapter.

Human rights were another concern. For example, during 2011, the alleged persecution of Anglicans in Zimbabwe was a major concern of the leader of the global Anglican Church, Dr Rowan Williams. Dr Williams expressed his concerns during an October 2011 official visit to Zimbabwe, during which he had an audience with Prime Minister Robert Mugabe (Butt and Smith, 2011). However, Dr Williams was met with a decidedly dusty response by Mr Mugabe, who proceeded to lecture the Archbishop on the problematic issue of allowing gay men to have a leading role in the Anglican Church. These variable outcomes underline that the democratising and pro-human rights influence of various Christian leaders and organisations do not necessarily lead to success.

## BOX 5.3 Jihadi transnational actors

Jihadi transnational actors are collectively important actors in international relations, because of their effects on security, order and stability.[3] Examples include the perpetrator of 9/11, al Qaeda ('The Base'), al Shabaab ('The Youth') in Somalia which is trying to take over the government, and Pakistan-based Lashkar-e-Taiba ('Army of the Righteous'). The latter is not only well known for its terroristic activities in the Indian state of Kashmir but was also responsible for the November 2008 siege of the Taj hotel in Mumbai which led to over 170 deaths (Burke, 2010). Jihadi transnational actors have a conflictual understanding of the world. For example, al Qaeda's rage at governments in the Middle East and North Africa being the stooges of US interests is a key component of its continuing campaign to change regional power configurations and international relations.

Unlike Islamist-nationalist groups, such as Hamas in Palestine and Hezbollah in Lebanon, which seek to use Islamist jihad as an ideology to rid their territories of Israel and Israeli influence, both al Qaeda and Lashkar-e-Taiba regard local conflicts, such as ongoing insurgencies in Afghanistan, Pakistan, Somalia and Yemen, as particular aspects of a wider regional and global battle: to establish a borderless Islamic state (*khalifah*).[4] Thus al Qaeda, Lashkar-e-Taibar, al Shabaab, and other jihadi organisations explicitly reject and seek to destroy the international system's foundational norms, values, institutions and rules. These have long been dominated by a small group of Western states, especially the United States, and Western-led international organisations, including the United Nations, the World Bank, the International Monetary Fund and the World Trade Organisation (Haynes, 2005c; Haynes et al., 2011). Jihadi transnational organisations pursue a competing logic to the Western- and sovereignty-dominated international system, working to replace (Sunni) Muslims' allegiances to their nation state and national government by adherence to a border-less, (Sunni) nation, the *ummah* (Rudolph and Piscatori, 1997: 12; Haynes et al., 2011).[5] The key way they seek to fulfil their goals is via violence and conflict with the goal of destabilising the current international order. This was made explicit in recent *Human Security Reports* which noted that international terrorism – including, importantly, that perpetuated by transnational jihadi

**101**

organisations – was at the time 'the only form of political violence that appears to be getting worse. Some datasets have shown an overall decline in international terrorist incidents of all types since the early 1980s, but in the mid-2000s there was a dramatic increase in the number of high-casualty attacks since the September 11 attacks on the US' (*Human Security Report*, 2005). The 2010 *Human Security Report* highlighted the continued destabilising effect of transnational jihadi organisations. They had a major role in destabilising four of the world's most fragile states – Iraq, Afghanistan, Pakistan and Somalia – and were centrally involved in more than 25 per cent of serious conflicts which began during 2004–2008 (*Human Security Report Project*, 2010).

However, even the most high-profile jihadi transnational organisation – undoubtedly, al Qaeda – has not been able to control territory for long. Territory is a very important resource in international relations because every state bases its significance ultimately on the territory it controls. One of the characteristics of RTAs is that their importance does not come from territory but from ability to encourage followers to act in certain ways. For example, the headquarters of the global Roman Catholic Church – the Vatican, located in Rome, Italy – is territorially tiny comprising only one square kilometre, although the influence of the Church on its hundreds of millions of followers is huge. Al Qaeda was able to control territory in Afghanistan between 1996 and 2001 – due to the complicity of the theocratic Taliban government, although lack of territory has not been a barrier to al Qaeda managing to win hearts and minds, because of the attractiveness to some of its militant ideas.

'Failed' states, such as Somalia, and 'failing' states, such as Pakistan, are often a safe haven for jihadi transnational groups, such as al Qaeda, Lashkar-e-Taibar and al Shabaab. This is because the state is just too weak to prevent their activities, allowing by default much freedom of action. The overall point is that jihadi transnational actors exploit the circumstances of failed and failing states in order to try to achieve their objective: overthrow the existing international order and replace the current configuration of nation-states with a Islamic border-less religious community, known as the *ummah* ('community' or 'nation'). The success or failure of jihadi transnational groups is not linked to their ability to command significant military resources or territory. Instead, progress towards achieving their goals is dependent on the capacity to convince Muslims of the appropriateness and desirability of their goals. In other words, jihadi transnational groups need to have sufficient soft power – the ability to persuade, cajole or encourage – to achieve success. What the activities of jihadi transnational actors have in common with the Roman Catholic Church's championing of democracy or the Anglican Church's defence of co-religionists in Zimbabwe is that to achieve their objectives they must convince key decision makers to act in certain ways and not others. Put another way, the Roman Catholic and Anglican Churches, jihadi transnational actors and other RTAs all have one thing in common: the objective of shaping 'the norms and values of the international system' (Thomas, 1999), by the only means they have at their disposal: soft power.

## Religious transnational actors: influence in international relations

Domestic religious concerns may spill over to become transnational political issues, in relation to, inter alia, Muslim communities or Christian churches. In general, religious transnational actors can affect international relations in three ways which, while heuristically separable, in practice often overlap. First, there are notable religious transnational actors, which although diverse in orientation, capacity and goals, influence *political* outcomes. They include various cross-border Islamic movements – including, extremist Sunni organisations such as al Qaeda or Lashkar-e-Taiba and Shia movements in the Middle East, such as Hezbollah in Lebanon, which are often believed to be working to help (Shia) Iran achieve its foreign policy goals (Louer, 2008; Salamey and Othman, 2011). Second, religious transnational actors can affect international outcomes through ability to 'influence . . . domestic politics. It is a motivating force that guides many policy makers' (Fox and Sandler, 2004: 168). For example, we noted above Pope John Paul II's involvement in Poland's democratisation and associated decline of communism and Russian hegemony in the late 1980s and early 1990s. Third, there are conservative protestant evangelicals in the USA who, as we note briefly below – and explain in Chapter 7 in more detail – work closely with the US government to try to deliver developmental goals, especially increased religious freedoms in countries that deny them. These examples collectively highlight the coming together of religious and secular issues in the pursuit of various political goals in international relations, involving both state and non-state actors motivated to some degree by religious concerns.

---

### BOX 5.4 Religious non-governmental organisations

Some scholars refer to 'religious', 'spiritual', or 'faith-based' non-governmental organisations as 'religious non-governmental organisations' (RNGOs). According to Dicklitch and Rice (2004: 662), RNGOs are 'non-state actors that have a central religious or faith core to their philosophy, membership, or programmatic approach, although they are not simply missionaries'. For Berger (2003: 16), RNGOs are '[f]ormal organisations whose identity and mission are self-consciously derived from the teachings of one or more religious or spiritual traditions and which operate on a non-profit, independent, voluntary basis to promote and realise collectively articulated ideas about the public good at the national or international level'. This is a way of saying that such organisations have concerns that are not limited narrowly to the task of religious conversion alone. Such organisations may both explicitly represent certain religious traditions and, in addition, seek goals in accordance with faith-based values that go beyond narrow faith issues to 'spill over' into various 'humanitarian' tasks both at home and abroad.

---

I employ the term 'religious transnational actor' (RTA) rather than 'religious non-governmental organisation' mainly because the latter can refer to entities that work in solely domestic environments, without 'spilling over' into transnational activities. Nonetheless, as we have already noted, the term 'religious transnational actor' can cover a variety of entities with an assortment of concerns and objectives, both religious/spiritual and secular. However, what RTAs have in common, minimally, is desire – and sometimes capacity – to act purposively and consistently across state borders and be legitimately characterised to some extent by the pursuit of religion-influenced objectives which, nevertheless, may spill over to include social and/or political goals. This is not to try to gloss over the fact that so far we have developed little in the way of robust knowledge about RTAs. This is due to (1) conceptual ambiguities, (2) uncertainty as to some RTAs' claims to be representative of a specific religious identity, such as Hindus or Muslims, (3) myriad activities, structures, sizes, intents, forms and practices, defying easy or precise categorisation, and (4) doubt as to how 'religious' RTAs actually are, in terms of piousness.[6] That is, the 'degree' or 'amount' of religiousness that characterises RTAs is difficult or impossible to measure in the absence of a reliable database on such organisations, although it is reasonably certain that they vary considerably (Berger, 2003: 25).

What is clear is that RTAs typically have various and variable goals: some of which can be conventionally defined as 'religious' or 'faith-based'. More widely, however, and to put this issue into conventional social scientific terminology, some RTAs pursue conflict, while others pursue cooperation. Jihadi transnational actors such as al Qaeda seek to revolutionise international relations by seeking to do away with individual Muslim nation-states and instead bring into being a transnational, nation-less *ummah*. But most RTAs do not pursue such violently system-changing goals. They may well seek to change outcomes more incrementally, informed by religious principles, in pursuit of a variety of human rights and/or development concerns (Haynes, 2007a, 2007b; ter Haar, 2011; Jefferis, 2011). Overall, transnational conflict (à la al Qaeda) and cooperation (à la World Council of Churches) are common factors characterising existing networks of religious transnational actors. They are generally reflective of a new religious pluralism that impacts upon transnational and international relations in two key ways. First, 'global religious identities' are emerging that can lead to increasing interreligious dialogues, involving greater religious engagement around various issues, including international development, conflict resolution, and transitional justice. However, this globalising environment can also lead to greater, perhaps often more intense, interreligious competition and/ or conflict, between members of various religious faiths and traditions (Haynes, 2007a, 2007b).

## Categorising religious transnational actors

Levitt (2004) identifies and discusses two categories of religious transnational actors: 'extended' and 'negotiated'. I will add a third: 'state-linked'. Note that these three types of RTAs are examined here as heuristic devices not static, fixed categories. This is because boundaries between them are blurred and actors may move over time between types. The context for them all, however, is increased interest in religious objectives in international relations.

## Extended religious transnational actors

In recent times, activities of RTAs have come under increased scholarly scrutiny. However, with much of the attention dedicated to the rise of political Islam in the Middle East and newly influential forms of Christianity in the Americas, including Pentecostalism in Latin America, the single biggest and arguably most influential transnational religious actor – the Roman Catholic Church – is relatively under-examined. Levitt (2004) identifies the Roman Catholic Church as an 'extended' actor because of its widespread – near global – focus and because of its array of political, developmental and social concerns. The expansiveness of the Church's international focus changed following the Second Vatican Council between 1962 and 1965, known as Vatican II. From that time the Church became much more vocal in international relations, especially in relation to the third wave of democracy in the 1970s, 1980s and 1990s, and increased involvement in conflict resolution, especially in Africa and Latin America, where large numbers of Catholics live (Appleby, 2000; Haynes, 2007a), and human development issues, especially in relation to attempts to achieve the Millennium Development Goals (2000–15) (Haynes, 2007a, 2007b). Finally, most recently, coinciding with the accession of Pope Benedict XVI in 2005, following the death of John Paul II, the Church is active in debates about regional integration processes in Europe, especially the position and role of Muslim Turkey (Haynes, 2012a).

For over 150 years, the Church has sought to build and develop its influence as a transnational, publicly focused religious institution. A hundred years after the First Vatican Council (1869–70), Vatican II sought to reverse 'a century-long trend toward centralization' in the Church, by 'acknowledging the plurality of national Catholicisms while instituting a set of liturgical changes that homogenized Catholicism throughout the world. The same general ethos of the Church as a global institution that tolerates religious pluralism also encourages transnational ties' (Levitt, 2004: 5). For these reasons, the Church can be categorised as an *extended religious transnational actor*. The Church is an 'extended' entity as it integrates followers into powerful, well-established, cross-border networks, within which Catholics 'can express interests, gain skills, and make claims with respect to their home and host countries' (Levitt, 2004: 3).

Overall, the Church went through several stages in transnational engagement and foci during the twentieth century. During the first half, the Church was noted as an 'uncompromising opponent of liberalism and democracy' (Reuschmeyer et al., 1994), providing support for various unsavoury – including fascist – governments. All this changed following the Second World War. From the late 1940s, the Church enjoyed a close relationship with conservative – albeit thoroughly democratic – Christian Democrat parties (West) Germany, Italy and elsewhere. After Vatican II, the then pope, Paul VI, began publicly to express concern with human rights. Later, in the 1980s and 1990s, the Church became a leading player in democratisation demands in many parts of the world, including Latin America and some sub-Saharan African countries. The Church was able to develop its transnational globe and extend its range of interests because of its widespread – virtually global – transnational networks which integrated its tens of millions of followers into an extended, and highly influential, network with multiple concerns and foci.

## Negotiated religious transnational actors

Unlike the Roman Catholic Church and similar institutionalised Christian entities, including the global Anglican Church, *negotiated religious transnational organisations* do not have well-established, organisationally solid, cross-border structures. Instead, this second category of RTA incorporates members from different countries into *developing* or *evolving* cross-border organisational arrangements which, unlike the established structures of the Roman Catholic and Anglican Churches, 'are still being worked out. While ties between Catholic churches develop within the context of a strong, federated institutional structure', negotiated RTAs 'must negotiate power sharing, leadership, and financial management' (Levitt, 2004: 7).

Many Muslim RTAs fall into this category, not least because unlike Christian churches, Muslim religious organisations are more loosely organised and less hierarchical; there is no Muslim equivalent to the Vatican for Catholics or Canterbury for Anglicans. Our example in this section, *Tablighi Jamaat* (TJ),[7] is typical. TJ is the world's largest Muslim transnational organisation, yet lacks developed institutional structures reminiscent of the Roman Catholic and Anglican churches. TJ is an Islamic revivalist organisation which was founded by an Indian, Mohammed Ilyas al-Kandhlawi, in 1926. Today, its headquarters are in India's capital, New Delhi. Over the last 90 years, TJ has expanded from a local to a national to a transnational movement, extending from India to an estimated 150 countries worldwide. While exact numbers are unknown, TJ undoubtedly has millions of members around the globe (Howenstein, 2006). Over time, TJ has developed a global profile, primarily but not exclusively among Muslims of South Asian origin, utilising informal networks of believers to pursue a number of socially conservative social goals, including in relation to the societal position and role of women. More generally, working at the community level, TJ pursues members' spiritual reformation, via involvement of both male and female Muslims of all social and economic classes. The over-arching goal is to bring members closer to what is perceived as the 'true' practices of the Prophet Mohammed. Teachings of TJ focus on 'Six Principles' – originally advanced by the TJ founder, Mohammed Ilyas al-Kandhlawi – that continues to influence most of the movement's teachings today.[8]

Despite its size, worldwide presence, and tremendous religious, spiritual and social importance, TJ remains largely unknown outside the Muslim community. This is by design rather than accident. Unlike the Roman Catholic and Anglican churches, TJ officials work to remain outside both media and governmental notice. TJ neither has a formal organisational structure nor does it publish details about the scope of its activities, its membership, or its finances. According to Alexiev (2005), 'By eschewing open discussion of politics and portraying itself only as a pietistic movement, *Tablighi Jamaat* works to project a non-threatening image. Because of the movement's secrecy, scholars often have no choice but to rely on explanations from *Tablighi Jamaat* acolytes'. Rashid (2009: 358) contends that the issues which have moulded and continue to influence TJ's development and growth have roots in and are furthered by the conditions of current globalisation, such as 'contradictions of modernisation and social change, including urbanisation, proselytisation, secularisation, and religious and social marginalisation'.

Howenstein (2006) explains that TJ is a 'revivalist organization that eschews politics in its quest to reform society'. But TJ is hardly unique in this regard. Encouraged by globalisation and attendant swift, multifaceted changes leading to rapidly changing socio-political and economic conditions, numerous Muslims in many countries seek in various ways – via individual or group efforts – to restore traditional values and norms, which they firmly believe are core to important traditional Islamic teachings. According to Moghadam (2002), TJ philosophy fits in well with this observation, as it is delimited by 'rigid attitudes on moral, cultural, and social issues'. Unusually in this era of globalisation, when most religious actors – whether domestic or cross-border – use various forms of electronic media to spread their messages, norms and values, TJ 'has largely avoided electronic media and has emphasised a personal communication for proselytising' (Sunnideobandi, 2011). Metcalf (2003: 3–5) describes TJ as 'a movement in encapsulation' which 'stands apart from explicit concerns about public life and competition to secure communal interests in the larger society'. Standing in direct contrast to politically activist Muslim groups, such as al Qaeda, Hezbollah or Hamas, which all seek fundamental political and social changes via a focus on reforming or taking over state institutions, TJ 'depends on invitation and persuasion directed towards individuals'. Consequently, TJ has a society-orientated outlook emphasising that the way to deliver desirable changes is from the bottom up, whereby 'social transformation is possible only by changing the individuals' (Amin, 2011: 281).

Despite its apparent wish to avoid conflict, TJ has nevertheless appeared on the fringes of numerous terrorism investigations in recent years. Policy analysts and Islamist scholars are divided in their assessments of the organisation, with some seeing TJ as a front for terrorist activities (Alexiev, 2005; Howenstein, 2006). TJ's role as a springboard to terrorist organisations has been questioned several times yet there is no clear evidence that it deliberately acts, unlike, for example, al Qaeda, as a recruiting arm for jihadi groups. However, it may well be that TJ plays a significant role in fragmenting and contesting religious authority not only locally (in Pakistan and Indian subcontinent) but also globally by actively engaging South Asian Muslim diaspora in Europe, North America and Australia (Moghadam, 2002; Rashid, 2009).

## State-linked religious transnational organisations

While the Roman Catholic Church has a widespread influence by directing its activities towards state institutions and *Tablighi Jamaat* takes a bottom-up approach focusing upon organising individual and communities, US-based Protestant evangelical religious transnational organisations pursue a human rights agenda via a focus on the state, groups and individuals. This network pursues religious freedom goals, linking with American state foreign policy actors to try to achieve their goals. Conservative Protestant evangelicals have long had an important political and social voice in the USA, widely noted as having significantly influenced the outcomes of the 2000 and 2004 presidential elections, contests that led to the election and re-election of a conservative Christian evangelical, George W. Bush (Green et al., 2003). In addition, as explored in Chapter 7, conservative Protestant evangelicals have since the mid-1990s had an important and continuing impact upon US foreign policy in relation to human rights issues (Hehir et al., 2004; Seiple, 2011).

A more general issue in this context, one that informs much recent scholarship on the impact of religion on IR, is: what is the relationship between religion and politics and how, if at all, does it change when the relationship spills over from the domestic to the transnational context? To seek to answer this question, it is useful to bear in mind that, as already noted in relation to various Christian churches and jihadi transnational actors, many religious transnational actors seek a variety of objectives. For example, as Levitt (2004) notes, while Pentecostals are usually thought of as 'apolitical', there is growing evidence that in various parts of the world, including the USA, Latin America and sub-Saharan Africa, Christian Pentecostal[9] communities have both political and social interests, often extending to the pursuit of transnational concerns (Peterson et al., 2001; Menjivar, 1999; Corten and Marshall-Fratani, 2001; Haynes, 2008b; Englund, 2011). Levitt (2004) also notes that members of Pentecostal Churches often aim to fulfil 'multiple roles and participate in multiple settings' and as a result they both influence the secular world and are in turn influenced by it (Levitt, 2004; Englund, 2011). Yet Pentecostalists are not unique in sharing concerns for multiple (spiritual, religious, social and political) concerns which are pursued in both domestic and transnational activities.

To account for the influence of conservative Protestant evangelicals on US foreign policy, it is necessary to start by taking into account the general importance of norms, values and ideology in the making of foreign policy. As Finnemore and Sikkink (1998: 888) note, 'the ways in which norms themselves change and the ways in which they change other features of the political landscape . . . [make] static approaches to International Relations . . . particularly unsatisfying during the current era of global transformation when questions about change motivate much of the empirical research we do'. This highlights the importance of taking into analytical account the relationship between *ideational* and *material* issues to account for changes in US foreign policy from the mid-1990s in relation to human rights, including religious freedom. It would also appear to reflect a growing concern with 'post-secular' issues in US foreign policy which extends to concerns of the current president, Barack Obama (Haynes, 2012b). That is, this is a period when the predominance of secular foreign policy goals during the Cold War shifted to an emphasis on concerns linked to religion. For example, during the Clinton presidency (1993–2001), 'left-leaning [religious] activists' had access 'to top administration officials. After [George W.] Bush took office, evangelical Christian leaders were the ones able to arrange sessions with senior White House aides' (Page, 2005).

The foreign policy influence of conservative Protestant evangelicals began in the early 1980s, during the presidency of Ronald Reagan, a man who shared many of their ideals and goals. From this time, socially conservative Protestant evangelicals began to consolidate as a significant and focused lobby group (Haynes, 1998: 28–33; Halper and Clarke, 2004: 182–200; Judis, 2005). A second key component in the subsequent shift in US foreign policy was the rising influence of (secular) neoconservatives, whose growth in prominence coincided with the rise in the influence of conservative Protestant evangelicals. Both groups shared common ground and beliefs and the alliance between them deepened during the 1990s (Oldfield, 2004). Lieven (2004) notes five key developments in the 1990s that led to their deepening association:

(1) narrowing of Christian beliefs; (2) sense of being under threat from globalisation; (3) growing desire to resist external influences; (4) harking back to a golden age; and (5) readiness to use all available means to achieve successful policy outcomes in crucially important areas.

The most influential organisation among conservative Protestant evangelicals in the USA at this time was, and continues to be, the National Association of Evangelicals (NAE).[10] Leadership by the NAE was important in the desire to increase religious freedoms in countries that lack it, including communist states, such as North Korea, and mainly Muslim countries, such as Sudan (Seipel and Hoover, 2004). The root of conservative Protestant evangelicals' persuasiveness is found in a commonplace but crucial fact: unlike all other Western countries, the USA is a highly religious nation (Norris and Inglehart, 2004). And, because in the USA religion plays an important role in political life, there exists 'greater prominence of religious organizations in society and politics' (Telhami, 2004: 71). Yet, religious organisations are not mere run-of-the-mill lobby groups, nor are they necessarily monolithic in views, beliefs and expectations. Moreover, while the tangible resources of religious interest groups pales in comparison to corporate lobbies, religion can often wield indirect influence that can be instrumental in helping construct the mindset of policy makers, including in relation to international human rights in US foreign policy since the 1990s (Marsden, 2008, 2011).

## Conclusion

In this chapter I sought to address the following question: what is the role of religious transnational actors (RTAs) as a consequence of entering a post-secular IR environment, which is also characterised by deepening and broadening globalisation?

We noted earlier the wide agreement that religion now has more importance in international relations compared to the recent past, an understanding that leads to an understanding that we have now entered an era of 'post-secularity'. In this context we looked at three kinds of RTAs: extended, negotiated and state-linked.

Unlike states, RTAs do not have hard power. Instead they have varying degrees of soft power. This is a highly useful attribute as it helps

RTAs to achieve their goals. For example, we saw that the Roman Catholic Church was active in international democratisation attempts from the 1970s as a direct result of the changing ideas of what the Church should pursue, emanating from Vatican II. We also noted that, lacking an institutional and hierarchical structure like the Roman Catholic Church, the world's largest Muslim RTA, *Tablighi Jamaat*, pursued its goals via the individual and collective agreement of members to act in certain ways and not others because they are persuaded of the appropriateness of those goals. Finally, we saw that it can be important for RTAs to work closely with government in pursuit of shared goals. US conservative Protestant evangelicals were successful in pursuing their human rights objectives when they linked up with state power to encourage a change in US foreign policy towards countries denying religious freedoms. However, the Roman Catholic Church had a patchy – although on the whole significant – impact on democratising outcomes, although outcomes were partly dependent on the relationship between the state and Church in various countries. Certainly, the Church did not have the capacity to force through democratising outcomes if sufficient forces were arrayed against this happening. Finally, *Tablighi Jamaat* is an anomaly: a highly significant RTA in terms of numbers of followers and geographical coverage but which chooses to focus on the individual and communities rather than the state to try to achieve its objectives.

# Notes

1. An episteme is a set of linked ideas that, taken together, serve to provide the basis of the knowledge that is widely believed to be intellectually certain at a particular era or epoch.
2. There may be about 25,000 'active' transnational actors with broadly political goals and another 22,000 which are 'dead, inactive, and unconfirmed' (Anheier and Themudo, 2002: 195). An unknown proportion, maybe 10 per cent, may plausibly be classified as religious transnational actors.
3. Jihadi transnational organisations, such as al Qaeda and Lashkar-e-Taiba, pose significant threats to national and international security and hence order. Historically, Islamist movements, despite pan-Islamic ideologies, typically began as national (not *trans*national) movements in conflict with

their respective governments and their policies. As the case of the Muslim Brotherhood in Egypt demonstrates, this often implies use of nationalist besides religious sentiments and a sphere of overlapping ideology with secular organisations (Jefferis, 2011). So far in the twenty-first century, jihadi extremist pathologies have presented themselves in order-challenging ways, including: the 11 September 2001 outrages in the USA, the attacks on Madrid on 21 April 2004, the 7 July 2005 bombings in London and the 27 November 2008 atrocity in Mumbai, India, that killed 170 people and wounded many more at the Taj Hotel. Of course, none of this is meant to imply that all or even most Islamist transnational actors are religious or political extremists.

4. For practical reasons, such a state would perhaps be sub-divided regionally. *Khalifah* is the term used for the series of Muslim states that were formed following the death of the Prophet Mohammed in 632 CE.

5. Most transnational jihadi organisations, such as al Qaeda and Lashkar-e-Taiba, are Sunni organisations which identify Shia Muslims as a key enemy.

6. I understand piousness to be characterised by having or exhibiting religious reverence, indicating strong compliance with religious norms and showing a high level of religious devotion.

7. *Tablighi Jamaat* can be translated into English in various ways, including 'society for spreading faith', 'group to deliver the message of Islam' and 'the preaching and inviting society'.

8. (1) *Kalimah* – an article of faith in which the *tabligh* accepts that there is no god but Allah and the Prophet Mohammed is His messenger; (2) *Salaat* – five daily prayers that are essential to spiritual elevation, piety, and a life free from the ills of the material world; (3) *Ilm and Dhikr* – the knowledge and remembrance of Allah conducted in sessions in which the congregation listens to preaching by the *emir*, performs prayers, recites the Qur'an and reads *Hadith*. The congregation will also use these sessions to eat meals together, thus fostering a sense of community and identity; (4) *Ikram-i-Muslim* – the treatment of fellow Muslims with honour and deference; (5) *Ikhlas-i-Niyat* – reforming one's life in supplication to Allah by performing every human action for the sake of Allah and towards the goal of self-transformation; (6) *Tafrigh-i-Waqt* – the sparing of time to live a life based on faith and learning its virtues, following in the footsteps of the Prophet, and taking His message door-to-door for the sake of faith (Ali, 2003: 176–177).

9. 'Pentecostalism is a form of Christianity that emphasises the work of the Holy Spirit and the direct experience of the presence of God by the believer. Pentecostals believe that faith must be powerfully experiential, and not something found merely through ritual or thinking. Pentecostalism is

energetic and dynamic. Its members believe they are driven by the power of God moving within them' (http://www.bbc.co.uk/religion/religions/christianity/subdivisions/pentecostal_1.shtml).

10. The NAE, led by Leith Anderson, 'represents more than 45,000 local churches from over 40 different denominations and serves a constituency of millions' (http://www.nae.net).

## Questions

- Is the state fading as a result of the impact of globalisation?
- What is religious soft power and how does it affect international relations?
- To what extent do religious transnational actors seek similar goals?
- Does the growth in numbers and influence of religious transnational actors encourage the view that international relations is now post-secular?

## Further reading

M. Duffy Toft, D. Philpott, and T. Samuel Shah, *God's Century*, New York: W. W. Norton and Co., 2011. This book is an important contribution to the contemporary debate about the role of religion in international affairs. It seeks to explain why the political consequences of religion differ from time to time and place to place, both historically and in the current era.

J. Haynes, *Religious Transnational Relations and Soft Power*, Aldershot, UK: Ashgate, 2012. The aim of this book is to examine selected religious transnational actors in international relations, with a focus on both security and order.

S. Hoeber Rudolph and J. Piscatori (eds), *Transnational Religion and Fading States*, Boulder, CO: Westview, 1997. Focusing on the alleged dilution of state sovereignty, this book examines how the crossing of state boundaries by religious movements leads to the formation of transnational civil society.

S. Thomas, *The Global Resurgence of Religion and the Transformation of International Relations*, New York: Palgrave Macmillan, 2005. Thomas examines the current widespread resurgence of religion in international relations, arguing that it is more than a clash of civilisations driven by religious extremism, terrorism or fundamentalism.

# Part Two

# Current issues

# 6 | Religion and democratisation

Until quite recently, there were few democratically elected governments outside Western Europe and North America. Most countries, especially in the developing world, had various kinds of non-democratic governments, including: military, one-party, no-party and dictatorships led by individually strong leaders. During the 1970s, 1980s, 1990s and early 2000s, however, there was a pronounced shift from unelected to elected governments in many formerly authoritarian parts of the world, including: Southern Europe, Latin America, sub-Saharan Africa, East Asia and, more tentatively, South Asia. I say 'more tentatively' because several South Asia countries – including, Bangladesh, Pakistan and Nepal – have recently wavered between democratically elected and non-democratic governments. However, both India and Sri Lanka have consistently maintained their democracies, although the status of the latter is problematic because of a still unresolved, two-decade civil war between the majority Sinhala and minority Tamils, a conflict which has drawn a periodic response from Sri Lanka's giant neighbour, India.

The US academic Samuel Huntington (1991) deemed the democratic changes to be so significant that he gave them a name: the 'third wave of democracy'. As a result, the British academic Georgina Waylen (2003: 157) notes, 'competitive electoral politics is now being conducted in a record number of countries', including dozens of countries in the developing world. How best can we explain this important political development? Many analysts point to the importance primarily of various domestic factors, although external considerations are also widely noted, including so-called 'democracy promotion' efforts, especially conducted by the USA and the European Union (EU) (Pinkney, 1994, 2005; Green and Luehrmann, 2003; Haynes, 2001a). To examine this important issue and to assess the role of religious actors in it, we will focus on: the overall impact of the third wave of democracy on the developing world, the comparative significance of external and internal factors for democratic outcomes, and any significant links between democracy and economic growth in developing countries.

## The third wave of democracy

The third wave of democracy followed two earlier democratic 'waves'. The first took place during the last decades of the nineteenth and the early years of the twentieth century, a period during which various European and North American countries democratised. The second wave of democracy began directly after the Second World War, when several countries, including Italy, Japan and West Germany, moved from authoritarian to democratic rule, strongly encouraged by the government of the USA (Haynes, 2001a).

### BOX 6.1 The third wave of democracy

The third wave commenced in 1974 with democratisation in three southern European countries – Greece, Portugal and Spain. Later, in the 1980s and 1990s, numerous authoritarian regimes in Latin America, Eastern Europe, Asia and Africa democratised. The extent of these changes is shown by the fact that in 1972 only a quarter of countries had democratically elected governments. Twenty years later, the proportion had grown to over 50 per cent, and by 2002, around 75 per cent of the world's nearly 200 countries had democratically elected governments, a similar proportion to 2011, when the most recent count of democracies was undertaken by the US non-governmental organisation, Freedom House.

The trend towards democracy over the last four decades – from 1972 to 2011 – is summarised in Table 6.1. The question of how religious actors might affect democratisation has been a controversial issue for decades. Scholars have stressed the importance of what they call 'political culture' in explaining success or failure of democratisation after the Second World War in West Germany, Italy and Japan (Linz and Stepan, 1996; Stepan, 2000; Huntington, 1991). In addition, religious traditions – for example, Roman Catholicism in Italy and Christian Democracy in West Germany – are said to be important in the (re)making of those

**Table 6.1** 'Free', 'partly free' and 'not free' countries, 1972–2011

|      | Numbers of 'free' countries | Numbers of 'partly free' countries | Numbers of 'not free' countries |
| ---- | --------------------------- | ---------------------------------- | ------------------------------- |
| 1972 | 43                          | 38                                 | 69                              |
| 1982 | 54                          | 47                                 | 64                              |
| 1992 | 75                          | 73                                 | 38                              |
| 2002 | 89                          | 56                                 | 47                              |
| 2011 | 87                          | 60                                 | 47                              |

Source: Freedom House, 2003; and for 2011, 'Combined Average Ratings – Independent Countries' at http://www.freedomhouse.org/sites/default/files/inline_images/CombinedAverageRatings%28Independe ntCountries%29FIW2011.pdf. Note that the terms 'free', 'partly free' and 'not free' broadly correspond to the following terms: established democracy, transitional democracy and non-democracy.

countries' political cultures after their lengthy experience of totalitarian, Nazi and fascist regimes, from the 1930s until the mid-1940s (Casanova, 1994). During the 'third wave of democracy' (mid-1970s to early 2000s), a lot of attention was paid to the role of religion in democratisation (Huntington, 1991). For example, in Poland, the Roman Catholic Church played a key role in undermining the communist regime and helping to establish a post-communist, democratically accountable regime (Weigel, 2005, 2007). This had a wider political effect beyond Poland, extending from Central and Eastern Europe to Latin America, Africa and parts of Asia. There was also the rise of the Religious Right in the United States of America from the 1980s, and its subsequent impact on the electoral fortunes of both the Republican Party and the Democratic Party. Add to this widespread growth of Islamist movements across the Muslim world, with significant ramifications for electoral outcomes in various countries, including Algeria, Egypt, Morocco and Tunisia, electoral successes for the Bharatiya Janata Party in India, and substantial political influence over time for various 'Jewish fundamentalist' political parties in Israel, and we can see clear and sustained evidence of religion's recent democratic importance in international relations.

Focusing upon the East European democratising experience more generally, US-based academics Juan Linz and Alfred Stepan have argued that religion is *not* generally a key explanatory factor explaining democratisation outcomes (Linz and Stepan, 1996). In relation to Muslim countries, the late Fred Halliday (2005) argued that apparent barriers to democracy in some such countries are primarily linked to certain shared social and political features. These include in many cases long histories of authoritarian rule and weak civil societies and, although some of those features tend to be legitimised in terms of 'Islamic doctrine', there is in fact nothing specifically 'Islamic' about them. However, for Huntington (1993, 1996), religions have a crucial impact on democratisation. He claims that Christianity has a strong propensity to be supportive of democracy while other religions, such as Islam, Buddhist and Confucianism, do not.

The focus of this chapter is on the role of religion in recent democratisation in various parts of the world. It seeks to examine key debates on religion and democratisation from three main perspectives:

- Religious traditions have core elements which are more or less conducive to democratisation and democracy.
- Religious traditions may be multi-vocal – but at any moment there may be dominant voices more or less receptive to and encouraging of democratisation.
- Religious actors rarely if ever *determine* democratisation outcomes. However, they may in various ways and with a range of outcomes be of significance for democratisation. This may especially be the case in countries that have a long tradition of secularisation.

Our starting point is that generally around the world, religions have left their assigned place in the private sphere, with many becoming politically active in various ways and with a mixture of outcomes. This re-emergence from political marginality dates back until at least the early 1980s. As the US-based sociologist José Casanova notes, 'what was new and became "news" . . . was the widespread and simultaneous refusal of religions to be restricted to the private sphere' (1994: 6). This development involved a remodelling and re-assumption of public roles by religion, which theories of secularisation had long condemned to social and political marginalisation.

As we saw in Chapter 1, it was once widely believed that modernisation inevitably leads to religious privatisation and secularisation. As a result, there would be a fundamental, global decline in religion's social and political importance. This was believed to be the case, regardless of religious tradition or form of political power dominant in the context where religions operated. The 1978–79 revolution in Iran posed fundamental questions in relation to this conventional wisdom. At the same time, the Roman Catholic Church was beginning to play an increasingly important role in relation to democratisation in Central and Eastern Europe, Africa, East Asia and Latin America. These two developments not only collectively emphasised that modernisation does not always lead to secularisation but also that religion can sometimes play a fundamental role in issues of political representation and legitimacy. Contrary to secularisation theory, there has been in recent years a widespread – some say, global – resurgence of religion, often manifested as a political actor. This has involved various religious traditions. Overall, it emphasises not only that there is more than one relevant interpretation of modernisation but also that religion can and does play a role in political changes, even in secularising regions of the world, including Western Europe.

## Religious deprivatisation and political change: a worldwide phenomenon

Globally, two phenomena are simultaneously taking place. First, there is said to be an *increase* in various forms of spirituality and religiosity, although this also implies in many cases both fragmentation and decline in societal clout of hitherto leading religious organisations in many countries (Davie, 2007). The increase in spirituality and religiosity is manifested in various ways including 'new' religious and spiritual phenomena, including manifestations of 'New Age' spirituality; 'foreign', 'exotic' Eastern religions, including Hare Krishna; 'televangelism'; renewed interest in astrology; and 'new' sects, such as the Scientologists. Note, however, that such religious entities, as Casanova points out, are 'not particularly relevant for the social sciences or for the self-understanding of modernity', because they do not present 'major problems of interpretation . . . They fit within expectations and can be interpreted within the framework of established theories of secularization' (1994: 5). The point is that they are *normal* phenomena. They are examples of *private* religion. They do not individually or collectively question or challenge the extant arrangements of society, including political and social structures. Indeed, such religious phenomena are *apolitical*; and 'all' they really show is that many people are interested in spiritual issues and sometimes they involve new expressions. In addition, in many European countries where Roman Catholicism is the main religious faith – such as, Italy, Poland and Spain – the Catholic Church has long been losing moral authority, especially for many young people (Ceccarini, 2009; Hennig, 2009). Globally, the multiplicity of existing and new religious phenomena belies the idea that religion will *inevitably* lose its popular appeal, even in officially secular countries, including France and Turkey (Hurd, 2008).

Second, not only Christian churches – especially the Roman Catholic Church in both transnational and national contexts – but also Islamic religious actors in many countries, as well as Jewish entities in Israel, now openly seek to articulate viewpoints on a variety of political and social issues, more readily and openly than in the past. Such religious entities typically resist state attempts to sideline them, actively involving themselves in political debates, including those focused on democratisation and democracy.

Three questions are central in seeking to account for religion's widespread involvement in democratisation (the process of becoming democratic) and democracy (the process of embedding or consolidating democracy). First, *why* should religious organisations seek to become actors with political goals related to democratisation and democracy? Evidence suggests that this can occur when religious entities feel that change is necessary and that the state is not well equipped to oversee and lead such changes, not least because the solutions it seeks are secular ones; and they do not chime well with religious interpretations. Second, how *widespread* is the phenomenon? Evidence suggests that it is extensive. Third, what are the *political consequences* of religion's intervention in politics, especially questions of democracy? The short answer is that they are variable. For example, sometimes religion appears to have a pivotal influence on political outcomes – for example, the role of the Roman Catholic Church in Poland in relation to democratisation in the 1980s. Elsewhere, for example, recently in relation to Islamists in Egypt, Tunisia and Turkey, or Jewish fundamentalists in Israel, political outcomes are both unexpected and variable.

While differing in terms of specific issues that encourage them to act politically, religious actors commonly reject the secular ideals that have long dominated theories of political development in both developed and developing countries, appearing instead as champions of alternative, confessional outlooks, programmes and policies. Seeking to keep faith with what they interpret as divine decree, they typically refuse to render to secular power holders automatic material or moral support. Instead, they are concerned with various social, moral and ethical issues, which are, however, nearly always political to some degree. Religious actors may challenge or undermine both the legitimacy and the autonomy of the state's main secular spheres, including government and more widely political society. In addition, many churches and other comparable religious entities no longer restrict themselves to the pastoral care of individual souls. Now, they raise questions about, inter alia, interconnections of private and public morality, claims of states and markets to be exempt from extrinsic normative considerations, and modes and concerns of government. What religious actors also have in common is a shared concern for retaining and increasing their social importance. To this end, many religious entities now seek to bypass or elude what they regard as the cumbersome constraints of temporal authority and, as a result, threaten to undermine the latter's constituted political functions. In short, refusing to be condemned to the realm of privatised belief, religion has widely reappeared in the public sphere, thrusting itself into issues of social, moral and ethical – and in many places, political – contestation.

The overall aim of the chapter is to highlight that today religious entities are often also political actors, wielding varying degrees of influence on political outcomes, including democratisation and democracy, while sharing a focus on a key issue: a desire to change their societies in directions where what they regard as religiously acceptable standards of behaviour are central to public life, including political life. Pursuing such objectives, they use a variety of tactics and methods, operating either at the level of civil society and/or political society.

## Defining democratisation

Democratisation is best thought of as a process and may occur over time in four – not necessarily separate – stages: (1) political liberalisation; (2) collapse of authoritarian regime; (3) democratic transition; and (4) democratisation consolidation. *Political liberalisation* is the process of reforming authoritarian rule. *Collapse of the authoritarian regime* stage refers to the stage when a dictatorship falls apart. *Democratic transition* is the material shift to democracy, commonly marked by the democratic election of a new government. *Democratic consolidation* is the process of embedding both democratic institutions and perceptions among both elites and citizens that democracy is the best way of 'doing' politics.

The four stages are complementary and can overlap. For example, political liberalisation and transition can happen simultaneously, while aspects of democratic consolidation can appear when certain elements of transition are barely in place or remain incomplete. Or they may even be showing signs of retreating. However, it is nearly always possible to observe a concluded transition to democracy. This is when a pattern of behaviour developed ad hoc during the stage of regime change becomes institutionalised, characterised by admittance of political actors into the system – as well as the process of political decision making – according to previously established and legitimately coded procedures.

Until then, absence of or uncertainty about these accepted 'rules of the democratic game' make it difficult to be sure about the eventual outcome of political transitions. This is because the transition dynamics revolve around strategic interactions and tentative arrangements between actors with uncertain power resources. Key issues include: (1) defining who is legitimately entitled to play the political 'game'; (2) the criteria determining who wins and who loses politically; and (3) the limits to be placed on the issues at stake. What chiefly differentiates the four stages of democratisation is the degree of uncertainty prevailing at each moment. For example, during regime transition *all* political calculations and interactions are highly uncertain. This is because political actors find it difficult to know: (1) what their precise interests are; and (2) which groups and individuals would most usefully be allies or opponents.

During democratic transition, powerful, often inherently undemocratic, political players, such as the armed forces and/or elite civilian supporters of the exiting authoritarian regime, characteristically divide into what the US academic Samuel Huntington (1991) calls 'hard-line' and 'soft-line' factions. 'Soft-liners' are relatively willing to achieve negotiated solutions to the political problems, while 'hard-liners' are unwilling to arrive at solutions reflecting compromise between polarised positions. Democratic consolidation is most likely when 'soft-liners' triumph because, unlike 'hard-liners', they are willing to find a compromise solution.

## BOX 6.2 Consolidated democracy

A consolidated democracy is said to exist when political leaders, political parties, and the mass of ordinary people accept – openly or tacitly – formal rules and informal understandings that determine political outcomes, that is, who gets 'what, when and how' (Lasswell, 1936). If achieved, it signifies that groups are settling into relatively predictable positions involving politically legitimate behaviour according to generally acceptable rules. More generally, a consolidated democracy is characterised by normative limits and established patterns of power distribution. Political parties emerge as privileged in this context because, despite their divisions over strategies and their uncertainties about partisan identities, the logic of electoral competition focuses public attention on them and compels them to appeal to the widest possible clientele. In addition, 'strong' civil societies are thought to be crucial for democratic consolidation, in part because they can help keep an eye on the state and what it does with its power. In sum, there is democratic consolidation when all major political actors take for granted the fact that democratic processes dictate governmental renewal.

Despite numerous relatively free and fair elections over the last two or three decades in many formerly authoritarian countries, in most cases ordinary people continue to lack ability to influence political outcomes. In many cases, this may be because small groups of elites – whether, civilians, military personnel, or a combination – not only control national political processes but also manage more widely to dictate political conditions. Under such conditions, because power is still focused in relatively few elite hands, political systems have narrow bases from which most ordinary people are, or feel, excluded. This can be problematic because, by definition, a democracy should not be run by and for the few, but should signify popularly elected government operating in the broad public interest. In sum, during the third wave of democracy, increased numbers of governments came to power via the ballot box – yet not all of them have strong democratic credentials.

To try to bring together the relationship between democratisation and religious actors in all their varied aspects and then to discern significant patterns and trends is not a simple task. But, in attempting it three points are worth emphasising. First, there is something of a distinction to be drawn between looking at the relationship in terms of the impact of religion on democratisation and that of democratisation on religion. At the same time, they are interactive: one stimulates and is stimulated by the other. In other words, because we are concerned with the ways in which power is exercised in society, and the ways in which religion is involved, the relationship between religion and democratisation is both dialectical and interactive. Both causal directions need to be held in view.

Second, religions are creative and constantly changing; consequently, their relationships with democratisation can also vary over time. In this chapter, we are concerned with involvement of religious entities in democratisation outcomes both currently and over the last few decades.

Finally, as political actors, religious entities can only usefully be discussed in terms of specific contexts; the relationship with government forms a common, although not the sole, focal point. Yet, the model of responses, while derived from and influenced by specific aspects of particular religions, is not necessarily inherent to them. Rather, this is a theoretical construct suggested by much of the literature on state-society relations, built on the understanding that religion's specific role is largely determined by a broader context. The common assumption is that there is an essential core element of religion shaping its behaviour in, for example, Christian, Islamic, or Jewish societies and communities.

## Religion, political society, civil society and the state

To understand the general political importance of religious actors, and by extension how they may involve themselves in democratisation, it is necessary first to comprehend what they say and do in their relationship with the state. I mean something more than 'mere' government when referring to the state. The state is the continuous administrative, legal, bureaucratic and coercive system that attempts not only to manage the various state apparatuses, but in addition to 'structure relations between civil and public power and to structure many crucial relationships within civil and political society' (Stepan, 1988: 3). As a result, almost everywhere in the world, apparently regardless of the nature of political systems and/or the level of economic development in a country, states having over time sought to reduce and control religion's political importance and involvement. That is, around the world states have sought to privatise religion, and thus to reduce considerably its political impact. Sometimes, for example in Poland and Italy (Catholicism) and Turkey (Sunni Islam), states have attempted to erect a 'civil religion' arrangement, whereby a certain designated religious format effectively 'functions as the cult of the political community' (Casanova, 1994: 58). The declared purpose is to try to create and develop forms of consensual, corporate religion, claiming to be guided by general, culturally appropriate, specific religious beliefs of intrinsic societal significance. In short, when states seek to develop 'civil religions', it is an attempted strategy to try to avoid social conflicts and promote national coordination and cohesion.

## BOX 6.3 Religious actors and the state

Religious actors' relationships with the state are not limited to attempts by governments to try to build civil religions within their countries. In fact, in many countries, relations between religious entities and the state are not only now more visible, but also often increasingly problematic. Why is this the case? First, it may be that recent increases in religious challenges to the authority of the state are merely transitory reactions in the context of the onward march of secularisation. Second, even if the modern state is particularly vulnerable to legitimation crises, it does not necessarily mean that religion is again becoming *automatically* relevant to state functioning. Third, religion-based challenges to state hegemony have roots in endeavours by the latter to assert a monitoring role vis-à-vis religion, in effect to control it. We can see such a development at three levels: political society, civil society and at the level of the state itself.

I want to underline that in many countries religion is liberating itself from providing routine legitimacy to secular authority, whether democratically or not. Consequently, many religious actors are now willing routinely to criticise and challenge the state in various ways in relation to a variety of issues and themes. Yet, even if heightened concern about the state's policies can be held up as evidence of the regeneration of the socio-political power of religion, we still need to ask further questions. The issues are themselves secular and in so far as religious agencies are active in these areas, this is a radical shift of concern from the super-natural, from devotional acts, to what are largely secular goals pursued by secular means. However, a note of caution is in order: we need to bear in mind that when religious interests act as 'pressure groups' – rather than as 'prayer bodies' – they are not necessarily going to be effective in what they seek to achieve. This is because the more secular-ised a society, the less likely it is that religious actors will be able to play a politically significant role (Wilson, 1992: 202–203).

## Religion and political society

At the level of political society – that is, the arena in which countries specifically make arrangements to conduct political competitions for a government to exercise legitimate control over public power and the state apparatus – there are various religious responses whose nature depends in part upon how secular a country is. These include: (1) resist-ance to the disestablishment and the differentiation of the religious from the secular sphere; the goals of many so-called religious 'fundamental-ist' groups; (2) religious groups and confessional political parties' mobil-isations and counter-mobilisations against other religions or secular movements and parties; and (3) religious organisations' mobilisation in defence of religious, social and political freedoms – that is, demanding the rule of law and the legal protection of human and civil rights, pro-tecting mobilisation of civil society and/or defending institutionalisation of democratically elected governments. In recent times in pursuit of such goals, we can note Roman Catholic transnational political mobil-isation in and between various countries (Troy, 2011), as well as activi-ties of Islamist groups in various countries, including Turkey (Barras, 2009; Grigoriadis, 2009; Gozaydin, 2009), Egypt (Jamal, 2009), Mali and Indonesia (Künkler and Leininger, 2009).

## Religion and civil society

Civil society is the arena where various social movements – including, not only religious entities but also various secular bodies, such as, neighbourhood associations, women's groups and intellectual currents – join with various civic organisations, including, lawyers', journalists', trade unions' and entrepreneurs' associations – to constitute themselves into a collective entity to advance their interests in relation to the state. Sometimes, the concept of *civil* society is used in contrast to *political* society. Unlike the latter, civil society refers to organisations and movements – *not* political parties – formally uninvolved in both the business of government and the overt political management. Note, however, that this does not necessarily prevent civil society organisations from sometimes seeking to or actually exerting political influence, on various matters, including democratic outcomes and the content of national constitutions.

Regarding religion at the level of civil society, we can distinguish between dominant civil religions – such as Evangelical Protestantism in nineteenth-century America – and the recent public intervention of religious entities, concerned either with single issues such as anti-abortion or with morally determined views of wider societal development, for example, in relation to homosexual rights or appropriate days for shops to open (on the latter issue, see Jamal, 2011, for the current situation in Israel). In trying to influence public policy – without themselves seeking to become political office-holders – religious entities may employ a variety of tactics, including, in no particular order: (1) lobbying the executive apparatus of the state; (2) going to court; (3) building links with political parties; (4) forming alliances with like-minded groups, both secular and/or from other religious traditions; (5) mobilising followers to lobby and/or protest; and (6) working to sensitise public opinion via mass media. The overall point is that religious actors may use a variety of methods to try to achieve their objectives (Baumgart-Ochse, 2009; Ganiel, 2009)

## Religion and the state

Interactions between the state and religious entities are often referred to as 'church–state' relations. It is useful to point out, however, that one of the difficulties in seeking to survey contemporary 'church–state relations' is that the very concept of *church* is only directly relevant to Christian traditions. It is derived primarily from the context of British establishmentarianism – that is, maintenance of the principle of 'establishment' whereby one church is legally recognised in a country as the *only* established church. In other words, when we think of church–state relations we need to assume a single relationship between two clearly distinct, unitary and solidly but separately institutionalised entities. In this implicit model built into the conceptualisation of the religion–political nexus, there is but *one* state and *one* church; both entities' jurisdictional boundaries need to be carefully delineated. Both separation and pluralism must be safeguarded, because it is assumed that the leading church – like the state – will seek institutionalised dominance over rival religious organisations. For its part, the state is expected to respect individual rights even though it is assumed to be inherently disposed towards aggrandisement at the expense of citizens' personal liberty. In sum, the conventional concept of church–state relations is rooted in prevailing Christian conceptions of the power of the state of necessity being constrained by forces in society – including those of religion. For example, Ganiel (20011) shows, through a focus upon a specific Charismatic church in Zimbabwe, that churches can seek to pursue their objectives, even when the state is powerful and its orientation is not conventionally pro-democracy.

## BOX 6.4 Church–state relations in non-Christian contexts

Expanding the problem of church–state relations to non-Christian contexts necessitates some preliminary conceptual clarifications – not least because the very idea of a prevailing church–state dichotomy derives from Christian culture. As already noted, *church* is a Christian institution, while the modern understanding of *state* is deeply rooted in the Post-Reformation European political experience. In their specific cultural setting and social significance, the tension and the debate over church–state relationships are uniquely Western phenomena, referred to in the well-known saying in the Bible: 'render therefore unto Caesar the things which be Caesar's and unto God the things which be God's (Luke 21: 25). With their roots in Western/Christian cultural history, the two concepts of state and church are not always easily translated into non-Christian terminologies, for example, those involving Islam and Islamic perceptions of the religious and political worlds.

The differences between Christian conceptions of state and church and those of other world religions are well illustrated by reference to Islam. In the Muslim tradition, mosque is not church. The closest

Islamic approximation to 'state' – *dawla* – means, as a concept, either a ruler's dynasty or his administration. Only if we understand the term *church* as a term encompassing the notion of a *moral community, priest* as a generic term for *custodians of the sacred law*, and *state* for *territorially based political community* can we comfortably use these concepts in Islamic, Hindu, Buddhist and other non-Christian contexts.

The overall point is that tensions widely exist between secular power holders and religious actors of various kinds in the modern world, in relation to both democratisation and politics more generally. It is often the case that in some European countries, for example, some religious actors, apparently regardless of their religious persuasion, may work individually or collectively towards reducing the ability of the state to sideline them. Barras (2009) shows this in relation to France where recent years have seen a campaign by some Muslim women to wear the Islamic headscarf, even though the secular French government is staunchly opposed to it. While some Muslim women in France regard wearing the Islamic headscarf as a fundamental human right – that is, the right to dress as they wish without the state telling them what to do – the French state sees things differently: Muslim women's efforts to dress as they wish is regarded by the secularists as a direct contravention of a core principle of post-revolutionary France – subjugation of religion by the state. In effect, such religious challenges reflect a wider development: a wish on the part of some religious actors to reverse religious privatisation, a course of action which impacts on a variety of political and social concerns, including democratisation.

## Religion, democratisation and the Arab Spring

The issue of the Islamic headscarf is widely debated within France. It is not, however, an international issue. This is largely because most governments agree that the French state has the right to decide its relationship with religious actors, without encouragement or advice from anyone else (Barras, 2011). An issue that is of great international importance is that of the political direction of the Arab/Muslim countries of the Middle East and North Africa (MENA), a region largely untouched by the third wave of democracy. Since the demands for fundamental political changes in the MENA surfaced in the autumn of 2010, international attention has focused on what has become known as the 'Arab Spring'. Revolutions followed in Egypt and Tunisia and the existing government was overthrown in Libya following international intervention. However, at the time of writing, the Arab Spring has not reached a clear conclusion. In particular, the question of whether there will eventually be widespread, important political changes in the region is not resolved, and the issue remains of profound international importance, not least because of the attempt by the Assad government in Syria to hang on to power in the face of increasingly clear domestic challenges to its rule. Given the fundamental changes that have already occurred in Egypt, Tunisia and Libya, all of which are staunchly Muslim countries, then our starting point in this section is to underline that there is nothing inherent in Islam which means that Muslim countries – whether in the MENA or elsewhere – will necessarily lack capacity to change political arrangements, perhaps in a pro-democracy direction.

The Arab world is undergoing a series of uprisings and rebellions which began in Tunisia in January 2011 and led to the fall of the country's government. Soon after, the government of Egypt also collapsed. During 2011 and early 2012, there were major political upheavals in Libya, Syria, Bahrain and Yemen, and smaller, although still notable, expressions of political dissent in Algeria and Morocco. These concerns took a new turn in May 2011 with the killing by US agents in Pakistan of the al Qaeda leader, Osama Bin Laden, ramifications of which for regional and Western security are not clear.

## Democracy promotion and regime change

We have already noted that there was much analytical attention paid to processes of democratisation at the level of the nation-state during the third wave of democracy. Yet, deepening of globalisation after the Cold War served to focus attention on democratisation as a process that cannot be assessed by looking at internal factors alone. As a result, most international relations experts might now accept that democratisation within a country may be affected, perhaps significantly, by foreign states. For example, at the very least, democratisation requires that no foreign power, hostile to this development, interferes in the political life of a country with the intention of subverting the political system. Whitehead

(1993) argues that examples of democratisation during the third wave of democracy indicate that the influence of external actors is always secondary to domestic factors, while Huntington (1991) suggests that such actors can hasten or retard but not *fundamentally* influence – at least not for long – domestic political outcomes.

Two sets of external factors can be noted in relation to regime change and democratisation during the Arab Spring: (1) background factors; and (2) state actors and non-state actors.

## Background factors

The influence of generally favourable or unfavourable geostrategic circumstances in relation to regime change and democratisation are sometimes referred to as 'background factors' in the democratisation literature (Haynes, 2002). This is not a new phenomenon, and the significance of background factors has been noted in relation to regime change throughout much of the twentieth century. For example, after the First World War, President Woodrow Wilson's references to the desirability of 'national self-determination' in relation to the founding of the League of Nations encouraged nationalists in the Middle East and elsewhere to demand self-rule. A decade later, during the 1930s, tentative moves towards democracy in several Latin American countries could not make headway against a background of regional – and global – economic depression. During the 1960s and 1970s, US fears of the spread of the Cuban revolution led to a regional crackdown on calls for democracy and support for military governments throughout Latin America. More recently, in the 1980s and 1990s, global circumstances (the 'new world order') became more advantageous for democracy, following the unforeseen collapse of Europe's communist regimes. The overall point is that external background factors were influential in relation to regime change in various parts of the world during the twentieth century. However, background factors are never sufficient on their own to lead to fundamental changes of regime unless they interact with what actors in both civil society and political society are doing. During the Arab Spring period, background factors were quite unclear as the earlier Western support for democratisation found in the 1980s and 1990s had given way to an ambivalent position whereby Western governments weighed up the benefits to their perceived security of a country in the MENA becoming democratic. If this meant, for example, that Islamists would assume power, then Western governments might prefer a situation of non-democracy – without Islamists in power – if they believed that this would lead to more security.

### States and democracy promotion

Pridham (2000: 313–314) notes that 'the scope for external influences to determine the course of regime change . . . has certainly increased over time'. As a result of the influence of globalisation, Hague and Harrop (2001: 47) suggest that 'weak states must accept both the external setting, and their vulnerability to it, as a given. The task of their leaders is to manage external influences as best they can'. Jackson (1990: 189, 195) points to the fact that many post-colonial countries are not only weak but also characterised by 'negative sovereignty' with 'adverse civil and socioeconomic conditions'. Consequently, they may well be objects of other, stronger, states' policies.

But not even weak states are necessarily powerless in relation to powerful external states. For example, in the 1990s and early 2000s, the only remaining superpower – the USA – was not able decisively to influence incumbent governments in several 'weak' states, including: Afghanistan, Haiti, Iraq, Liberia, Nigeria, Somalia and Sudan. All had important 'negative' power resources that lay principally in their potential for 'chaos power', that is, capacity to create or make worse regional problems that powerful countries such as the USA might be expected – perhaps through the UN – to deal with. That is, the ability of external actors in this regard is linked to the presence or absence of functioning states in the countries they enter; when functioning states are particularly 'fragile' – as in most of the countries noted above – then even powerful external actors struggle to implement their preferred policies.

Where functioning states do exist, external state actors may encourage their political preferences, including democratisation, through the media of 'political conditionality'. There are two main forms: (1) 'positive' political conditionality to encourage further democratisation, and (2) 'negative' political conditionality to promote desired political reforms in hitherto unreceptive countries.

From the 1980s, the largest aid donors in quantitative terms – Britain, France, Japan, and the USA, plus the Scandinavian countries – sought to encourage both democratisation and economic liberalisation among countries receiving their aid. These governments, along with the International Monetary Fund (IMF) and the World Bank, attached political conditionality to aid, loans and investments to recipient countries. If the latter denied their citizens basic human rights – including democratically elected governments – they would be denied assistance. The reasoning behind political conditionality was partly economic. Western governments, the IMF and World Bank all claimed that economic failures were directly linked to an absence of political accountability. Consequently, without democratisation, economic liberalisation would not achieve beneficial results.

Crawford (2001) discovered that aid sanctions in the early 1990s led by the governments of the USA, Sweden, Britain and the European Union, were effective in promoting political reform in only 11 of the 29 cases (38 per cent) where they were applied. He concluded that aid penalties: (1) were most effective where they added to pressure on governments from internal reform pressures, and (2) failed when they met strong resistance from recipient governments or when they threatened donors' strategic or commercial interests.[1] Holland (2002: 132) provides further evidence of the patchy effectiveness of political conditionality. During the 1990s, the EU applied sanctions against 13, mainly African, developing countries. Holland notes there were contrasting outcomes in two of them: Fiji and Zimbabwe. While the latter's government seemed impervious to external encouragement to reform, Fiji's was not.

The United States is a key player in relation to democracy promotion, with both the government and various state-linked bodies, such as the National Endowment for Democracy, actively supporting democratisation and economic liberalisation (Carothers, 2002). This is not a new policy, but developed from the 1950s. Sixty years ago, then newly democratic governments in Latin America, including Costa Rica, Venezuela and Colombia, received financial and diplomatic support from the US government. Later, in the 1970s, US foreign policy goals were reflected in President Jimmy Carter's human rights policy, while in the 1980s President Ronald Reagan's government promoted democracy as a counter to perceived communist expansionism. In the 1990s, President Bill Clinton developed policies linked to political conditionality, a strategy continued during the administrations of George W. Bush (2001–09). The scale of US support in this regard can be gauged from the fact that during the 1990s alone, US governments provided over $700 million to over 100 countries to further democratisation (Carothers, 1997).

US academic Carothers (2004) notes that US state assistance is typically focused in what he identifies as a standard democracy template. This involves offering financial support to help develop electoral processes and democratic structures, including constitutions and political institutions, including, the rule of law, legislatures, local government structures, political parties, improved civil–military relations, and civil society. However, as Leftwich (1993: 612) points out, it takes more than simply external sources of finance to develop democracy. This is because money alone cannot create and embed concrete manifestations of 'good governance', without which democracy cannot develop. This outcome is 'not simply available on order', but requires 'a particular kind of politics . . . to institute and sustain it'.

Superficially, democratisation may be seen to be encouraged if foreign states limit their perusal of the democratic process to elections alone; indeed, some critics argue, international observation of elections often seems the only consistent test used to judge a shift from authoritarian to democratic rule. But when elections are complete, and the attention of the corpus of international observers moves on, 'democracy' is often at best only partially achieved. Anti-democracy elites, often in the military, can remain powerful, and political systems frequently retain narrow bases, characterised by the survival of 'authoritarian clientelism and coercion' (Karl, 1995: 74). In sum, external democracy promotion and associated funding will not be effective if target regimes are able to 'acquire democratic legitimacy internationally without substantially changing their mode of operation' (Lawson, 1999: 23).

Critics of political conditionality contend that Western governments focus more on security than democracy. Western aid-donating governments may seek to control the pace of democratisation, as 'too much' democracy too quickly can be politically destabilising and affect the stability of individual countries and their regional neighbours. Aid donating and aid recipient governments may share common interest in limiting the extent of political changes, a theory known as Low Intensity Democracy (LID) (Gills et al., 1993). LID is said to satisfy Western

governments' allegedly insincere concerns for democratisation in relation to non-democracies by encouraging strictly limited political reform
processes. In short, the LID argument is that in some circumstances
Western aid-donating governments prefer stable – even if authoritarian
– regimes, to unstable – even if democratically elected – governments
receiving their aid.

An example said to support this contention is that of Uganda, a small
country in east Africa (Haynes, 2001a). During the 1990s, Uganda's
president, Yoweri Museveni, made a successful diplomatic offensive to
sell his 'no-party' – that is, not conventionally democratic – political
system to the Western aid-donating governments. While neighbouring
countries, such as Kenya and Tanzania, were strongly encouraged to
adopt multi-party democratic systems, Museveni was able to persuade
them that his 'all-inclusive', party-less, system was (1) stable, (2) capable of dealing with violent challenges to the status quo, including from
the dreaded Lord's Resistance Army, and (3) willing to make innovative
appointments, such as that of Vice-President Specioza Wandira Kazibwe,
at the time the highest-ranking female politician in Africa (Haynes,
2003b).

In conclusion, it is difficult to be sure about when and why democracy promotion 'works', in the sense of demonstrably leading to significant political reforms. It is clearer that aid-donating Western states
were often important sources of encouragement to reform at the transition stage of democratisation – but less important later. This is because
building democratic structure and processes is linked to long-term
efforts that are rooted in the development of internal structures and
processes.

These points about the problematic intervention of foreign governments into continuing political challenges in non-democratic countries
are given credence by the issue of foreign democracy promotion during
the Arab Spring.[2] Western governments have been torn between wish-
ing to see more democracy in the MENA and the potential dangers to
Western security of having hostile Islamist governments in power, as
occurred in Afghanistan throughout 1996–2001 during Taliban rule.
The UK prime minister, David Cameron, was however moved to announce
in May 2011 that the UK would make a major financial donation
in support of democratisation and improved social welfare. The UK

government announced that £110 million would be siphoned off from the existing Department for International Development budget, to be focused upon encouraging democratisation in the MENA. In addition, the UK's Foreign and Commonwealth Office stated that up to £40 million would be spent over the 2011–15 period to try to improve three democratic cornerstones in the Arab Spring countries: increased political participation, improved rule of law, and greater freedom of the press. Finally, the UK pledged to donate a further £70 million, focused generally on economic reform and specifically on aiming to boost youth employment, strengthen anti-corruption measures and promote private sector investment. In sum, the UK government was committing extensive funds to the democratisation and improved social policy of the Arab Spring countries in a bid not only to spread democratic values but also to undermine religious extremism in the MENA.

However, a word of caution is necessary: for three main reasons, it is unlikely that the MENA region is about to jump from authoritarianism to democracy as many Central and Eastern European countries did between 1989 and 1991. One general reason is that the MENA region has widespread sectarian divisions – leading to conflict between different religious sects, including intra-Muslim (Iraq, Syria) and Muslim–Christian (Tunisia, Egypt) tensions. Religious competition and conflict is one dimension of a more general threat to a process of democratisation in the MENA. There are also generalised, serious economic problems throughout the countries of the MENA. Add to this a deadly rivalry between the region's two biggest rivals – the governments of Saudi Arabia and Iran – and the scene is set for prolonged political contestation without clear generalised signs of democratic advance.

Despite the coming together of people from all faiths in the protests that brought down their governments, both Egypt and Tunisia have recently experienced sectarian tensions and conflict, while Syria may be embarking on the same path. Egypt was the scene of a bloody attack against a Coptic church in Alexandria in December 2010, followed by a clash in the Imbaba district of Cairo which killed at least 15, both Copts and Muslims. Tunisia saw the murder of a Polish-born Catholic priest, Father Marek Rybinski, killed on the premises of an inter-denominational school in Tunis, while Islamist protesters gathered together outside the Great Synagogue of Tunis and a chapel was burned near Gabes. In Bahrain, the political violence pitted Shias against Sunnis. In Syria the Assad-led Alawite minority government seeks to exploit the country's latent sectarian divisions in its bid to stay in power.

Second, the region is undergoing a frightful economic slide. Gross domestic product (GDP) is down and social welfare declining, and all this in the context of some of the fastest-growing populations in the world. Egypt is a good example of what is happening. Arguably, much of the cause of the uprising which led to the overthrow of the Mubarak government in early 2011 was the result of economic frustration, especially among the young, those in the forefront of the rebellion. Egypt's economy contracted by 7 per cent in the first three months of 2011. Tourism revenue, the mainstay of the economy and the biggest single element in GDP, fell by 80 per cent in 2011, the stock market plummeted, and the IMF revised its growth estimate to a mere 1 per cent in 2011, following 5.1 per cent growth in 2010.

Third, both Saudi Arabia and Iran are deadly rivals in the MENA. Saudi Arabia has had to deal with the loss of its closest ally, the Mubarak government. Iran contemplates the fall of its ally, the Assad regime. The government of Bahrain is bolstered – but for how long? – by the injection of Saudi troops, while Iran seeks to exploit the growing anarchy in Yemen in order to destabilise its Saudi arch enemy.

Overall, evidence suggests that the prospects for a clear and linear path to democracy in the MENA region are currently poor. The most likely outcome is a gradual slide into entrenched and long-term political instability culminating in some cases in state failure with serious ramifications for regional and international instability.

## Conclusion

This chapter engaged with the relationship between religion and democratisation. The focal points were the third wave of democracy, between the mid-1970s and early 2000s, and the Arab Spring, which began in late 2010. We have seen that on occasion religious actors can be pivotal in relation to democratisation outcomes, as in Poland in the late 1980s. Most of the time, however, religious actors tend to have a rather ambivalent relationship with democratisation. This is partly because they are not necessarily recognised as legitimate actors in this context, a terrain where secular political actors are normally much more influential than religious actors.

We also saw that Western governments were often key supporters of the third wave of democracy. Embarking on often ambitious programmes of democracy promotion in the 1980s and 1990s, backed up by large sums of money in order to improve the prospects of democratisation, over time this fulsome support gave way to growing Western ambivalence about encouraging democracy, especially in regions such as the Middle East and North Africa (MENA) where a shift to democracy was likely to mean an increase in the capacity of Islamists to play a role in government. Not all Islamists, some Western governments believed, would necessarily be friendly to Western interests in the MENA region. However, the course of the Arab Spring has not been clear cut or unidirectional. In some cases, Islamists have achieved power (Egypt, Tunisia), while in others secular actors appear to be in charge following overthrow of an existing regime (Libya). The longer-term role of religious actors in political events in the MENA is by no means clear and it appears that the relationship with democracy that Islamists and others have varies from place to place and context to context.

## Notes

1. However, it became clear that it was easier to state the desirability of political and economic reforms than it was to achieve them. In many cases, attempts at economic reforms, expressed via structural adjustment programmes, and of political reforms, were disappointing.
2. The paragraphs at the end of this section are derived from an article of mine, dated 21 June 2011, published at http://www.gpilondon.com/?id=295.

## Questions

- What is democracy and what has religion got to do with it?
- Are religious actors necessarily democratic?
- What is democracy promotion and is it effective?
- Will the Arab Spring result in regional democratisation in the Middle East and North Africa?
- Is Islam pro-democracy?

# Further reading

T. Carothers, *Critical Mission: Essays on Democracy Promotion*, Washington, DC: Carnegie Endowment for International Peace, 2004. This book brings together a wide-ranging set of Carothers' widely cited essays, organised around four vital themes: the role of democracy promotion in US foreign policy; the core elements of democracy aid; the state of democracy in the world; and the American push in the 2000s to promote democracy in the Middle East.

J. Haynes (ed.), *Religion and Democratizations*, London: Routledge, 2011. This book examines key debates on religion and democratisation from three main perspectives: (1) religious traditions have core elements which are more or less conducive to democratisation and democracy; (2) religious traditions may be multi-vocal – but at any moment there may be dominant voices more or less receptive to and encouraging of democratisation; and (3) religious actors rarely if ever determine democratisation outcomes. However, they may in various ways and with a range of outcomes be of significance for democratisation.

S. Huntington, *The Third Wave: Democratization in the Late Twentieth Century*, Norman, OK: University of Oklahoma Press, 1991. Between 1974 and 1990 more than 30 countries in Southern Europe, Latin America, East Asia, and Eastern Europe shifted from authoritarian to democratic systems of government. Huntington analyses the causes and nature of these democratic transitions, evaluates the prospects for stability of the new democracies, and explores the possibility of more countries becoming democratic.

# 7 | Religion and development

Religious actors of various kinds are now widely recognised as important actors in development in the developing world, especially in the context of the aim of achieving the Millennium Development Goals (MDGs). The MDGs were announced by the United Nations in 2000 for achievement by 2015 (www.un.org/millenniumgoals/).

While the MDGs have focused attention on religious actors in development, there has also been a more general growth in concern by many religious actors in the developing world that development goals are not being met and, as a result, many are anxious to do what they can to try to improve matters. As a result, over the last few decades, religious actors of various kinds have increasing focused on development issues, seeking to employ their organisational capacities in this respect. The increase in religion's involvement in development reflected the impact of three linked but conceptually distinct developments: widespread religious resurgence; deepening globalisation; and rising popular concern with development shortfalls in many developing countries. These issues came together in the announcement of the MDGs. The MDGs were designed to have bottom-up input and not solely to be a top-down strategy designed and put into effect by governments and powerful international non-governmental organisations (INGOs) concerned with development, especially the World Bank (Haynes, 2007b, 2012c). The impact of both a general increase in religious actors' concern with development and the announcement of the MDGs combined to make it very difficult to ignore religion's influence on development, which has become a key factor in development outcomes in much of the developing world.

To understand the current role of religion in development outcomes in the developing world, which is the overall focus of this chapter, we can start by noting two generic kinds of religious actors active in development processes and outcomes: (1) those that are active in one country, and (2) those that are active in more than one country. Each kind of religious actor, whether nationally or transnationally focused, can impact on development issues and outcomes in the same way: by seeking to influence development policy and programme formation and execution.

Because of its potentially vast subject matter, it is not possible in this brief chapter to examine each and every area where religion has an impact on development in the developing world. Nor do we examine the issue region by region in the developing world to try to come up with a general understanding of the relationship between religion and development. Instead, the focus of this chapter is limited to brief analyses of: (1) why, how and with what effects selected religious actors have interacted in recent years with secular development agencies, notably the World Bank, and (2) general problems, opportunities and prospects of religious engagement with development in developing countries. The overall context is the coming together of secular and religious concerns on the slow and fragmentary pace of improved development in much of the developing world, which stimulated announcement of the MDGs in 2000.

The first section of the chapter briefly examines changing approaches to development in the developing world in the six decades since the end of the Second World War in 1945. The second section examines explicit links between religion and development. The third section focuses on the World Bank's decade-long engagement with selected religious actors, including the Anglican Church and the World Council of Churches, from the mid-1990s to the mid-2000s, an engagement which flourished for a time during James Wolfensohn's presidency of the World Bank between 1995 and 2005. The final section of the chapter focuses on problems and prospects of religion helping to bring about improved development in developing countries.

## Changing strategies to achieve improved development

The ideological power of neo-liberalism was at its height in 1989–91 when the Cold War came to an end and the Eastern European communist bloc spectacularly and swiftly collapsed. The swift disintegration of Europe's communist governing systems not only appeared to offer clear evidence of the superior power of capitalism and liberal democracy over communism, but also provided pro-market forces with ideological momentum. The then dominant neo-liberal development strategy – the so called 'Washington consensus' – reflected the pre-eminence of such ideas among key Washington, DC-based, institutions and actors, including, INGOs, such as the International Monetary Fund (IMF), 'the World Bank, independent think-tanks, the US government policy community, investment bankers, and so on' (Thomas and Reader, 2001: 79). Critics of the Washington consensus argued that the studiously pro-market view it endorsed gave insufficient emphasis not only to the essential developmental role of government, the only institution consistently with power and authority to alter prevailing socio-economic realities through application of appropriate policies and programmes, but also to that of relevant non-state actors – both secular and religious organisations – that could also be influential in helping to deliver improved human development (Taylor, 2005).

Critics' focus on the importance of non-state actors in relation to development goals in the developing world reflected the abject failure of many post-Second World War development strategies. Today, the developmental picture in many developing countries is still very gloomy, with rising global poverty and polarising inequality. After half a century of applied development policies and programmes, and a quarter century of neo-liberal economic policies, over a billion people in the developing world still live on less than US$1 a day. More than two billion people – nearly a third of the total number of people in the world – do not have access to clean drinking water. In addition, hundreds of millions of individuals, especially women and the poor, lack even basic health care and/or educational opportunities (World Bank, 2001).

The last half century has seen three stages of thinking about development in the developing world. First, during the 1950s and 1960s, when dozens of culturally, politically, and economically disparate post-colonial countries emerged, mainly in Africa, Asia and the Caribbean, the West's chosen strategy to achieve development was primarily via the application of appropriate levels of state-directed development aid. Second, during the 1970s, substantial oil price increases both underlined and hastened developmental polarisation, with some richer developing countries – such as South Korea, Taiwan and Singapore – managing to cope better than their poorer counterparts in Africa and elsewhere. Many developing countries also found their international debts fast rising at this time. Then, the West's contemporary development vision was on a 'basic needs' strategy. It was envisaged that development goals would be achieved via a strategy to ensure that *all* people had access to necessary 'basics', including: clean water, basic health care and at least primary education. This strategy generally failed, however, for two main reasons: first, the developmental issue became subsumed into the wider Cold War ideological division, with government-disbursed development funds not necessarily going to the most 'developmentally deserving' countries – but often instead to allies of the key aid providing countries; and, second, because of the frequent unwillingness of ruling elites and their supporters in many developing countries to facilitate the necessary financial transfers upon which the successful delivery of basic needs strategy fundamentally hinged (Haynes, 2007b; Taylor, 2005; Shaw, 2005).

The third phase followed in the 1980s. Developmental polarisation in the developing world led to renewed Western attempts to encourage poorer developing countries to reform their economic policies in order to try to stimulate increased economic growth and development. Western governments, including those of the USA, Britain and (West) Germany, and development-focused INGOs, including the World Bank, appeared to believe that in the developing world 'unacceptable' levels of state meddling, incompetence, and poorly developed and executed policies were the main causes of underachievement in attaining development goals. The proposed solution was to try to 'roll back' the state, believing that states had often 'tried to do too much', expending much effort and money but actually achieving relatively little. Instead, it was envisaged that private entrepreneurs would provide necessary new injections of dynamism, energy and funding to arrive at solutions to development shortfalls, which would usefully augment the state's developmental role. In pursuit of this strategy, Western financial assistance was henceforward to be focused on 'structural adjustment programmes' (SAPs), combining IMF and World Bank efforts, applied to dozens of developing countries, especially from the 1980s. According to Barber Conable, World Bank president between 1986 and 1991, SAPs reflected the belief that 'market forces and economic efficiency were the best way to achieve the kind of growth which is the best antidote to poverty' (Barber Conable, quoted in Thomas and Reader, 2001: 79).

## BOX 7.1 The World Bank and development

Barber Conable's statement – referred to above – reflected the intellectual pre-dominance of neo-liberalism in relation to development thinking in the 1990s. Neo-liberalism was an economic and political philosophy that ideologically underpinned the pro-market and monetarist ideas of various governments, including those of Britain's Margaret Thatcher (1979–90), Germany's Helmut Kohl (1982–98) and, in the USA, the administrations of Ronald Reagan (1980–88) and George H. W. Bush (1988–92). A core belief of neo-liberalism was that to achieve desirable development outcomes, government's role must be diminished, with private capitalists and entrepreneurs 'freed' from state control to apply their energies to economic growth strategies. Under pressure from Western governments and key INGOs – especially, the World Bank and the IMF – govern-ments of developing countries were strongly encouraged to put in place and develop neo-liberal policies. Outcomes, however, were on the whole dis-appointing in terms of reducing developmental inequalities (Stiglitz, 2006).

# Religion and development: what are the links?

Towards the end of the twentieth century, decades of failed develop-ment strategies in the developing world helped to stimulate a new look at development and how better to achieve it. Led by the United Nations, there was renewed interest in and focus on addressing glaring develop-ment shortfalls in the developing world. The international community set itself the challenge of a third millennium 'onslaught' on poverty and human deprivation, with efforts focused on the developing world, espe-cially sub-Saharan Africa, where human deprivation and poverty were most pronounced and widespread.

## BOX 7.2  The Millennium Development Goals

The aim of the United Nations Millennium Declaration was to diminish signifi-cantly human deprivation and poverty. In September 2000, the Millennium Development Goals (MDGs) were announced, with a deadline of 2015 to achieve the desired outcomes. The MDGs featured eight key objectives: eradicate extreme poverty and hunger; achieve universal primary education; promote gender equality and empower women; reduce child mortality; improve maternal health; combat HIV/AIDS, malaria, and other diseases; ensure environmental sustain-ability; and develop a global partnership for development.

(http://www.un.org/millenniumgoals/)

What was novel about this strategy was not that there were clear goals and a timeframe to achieve them. What was new was that the MDGs were drawn up from the assumption that to attain desired development outcomes across the developing world it was necessary for state *and* non-state actors – both secular *and* religious (or, 'faith-based', the term usually used) – to work together (Haynes, 2007b, 2012c; Lunn, 2009; ter Haar, 2011). At this time, the world's most influential and money-rich INGO, the World Bank, publicly accepted the need for a refocusing of developmental emphasis if development goals were to be widely achieved in the developing world. The Bank noted in its *World Development Report 2000/2001* that adjustments were necessary at both global and national levels. While the Bank did not specifically mention religion or religious organisations in the *2000/2001 Report*, there was a clear inference to its recommendations: to achieve improved developmental outcomes it was necessary to employ all currently under-used human resources, including those potentially available from religious organisations, especially at the grass-roots level.

As Lunn (2009: 937) notes, 'religion, spirituality and faith have suffered from long-term and systematic neglect in development theory, policy making and practice, although there has been a noticeable turnover in the past 10 years'. This is a pointer to the fact that in recent years – in the context of the end of the Cold War, deepening globalisation, 9/11 and successive global financial crises since 2008 – there has been much speculation about how developmental outcomes in the countries of the developing world are affected by these multiple and multifaceted global changes. What do they mean for chances of improved peace, prosperity, and justice – in short, for prospects of enhanced development – in the developing world?

As we have already noted in earlier chapters, it was once widely assumed that nations would invariably secularise as they modernised. It was believed that associated loss of religious faith and increasing secularisation would dovetail with the idea that technological development and the application of science to overcome perennial social problems of poverty, environmental degradation, hunger, and disease would result in long-term human progress. However, it is plausible to surmise that lack of success in this regard was one of the factors behind the recent increased focus on the developmental role of religion in the developing world (Berger, 1999).

Religion has had an increasingly clear impact upon development outcomes in many parts of the developing world over the last two decades or so (Haynes, 2007b; Lunn, 2009; Mesbahuddin, 2010). As a result, we can see that earlier confidence was misplaced, that growth and spread of urbanisation, education, economic development, scientific rationality and social mobility – in short, secularisation – would combine to reduce dramatically the public role of religion. Two broad trends can be noted. First, religion is often used politically – as a vehicle of opposition or as an ideology of community self-interest. Threats emanating either from powerful, outsider groups or from unwelcome symptoms of modernisation (such as, breakdown of moral behaviour and perceived over-liberalisation in education and social habits) serve to galvanise such groups. Second, failure of governments to consolidate programmes of developmental improvements also encouraged religious entities, some of which develop specific faith-based agendas of solidarity and development. Examples include Roman Catholic Basic Christian Communities, followers of the radical doctrine of liberation theology found throughout much of Latin America and in some sub-Saharan African and East Asian countries, and various Islamic development entities throughout the Muslim world.

Today, many religious entities seek to achieve improved development in the developing world. There is a growing literature on them (Alkire, 2006; Holenstein, 2005; Marshall, 2005a, 2005b; Haynes, 2007b; Rees 2009; ter Haar, 2011). Evidence suggests that religion can work to help to deliver improved development, including improved social services for people in the developing world whom national or local governments cannot or will not assist. Some service-oriented religious entities in the Middle East and sub-Saharan Africa enjoy annual budgets that in some cases can exceed that of the government agencies officially tasked to deliver social welfare goals, while procedures for accessing their direct assistance and welfare services can be more efficient and straightforward than those provided by the state in the public sector (Ellis and ter Haar, 2004; ter Haar, 2011). Others are more concerned with other issues, especially human rights, including: gender issues, democratisation, democracy and governance (ter Haar, 2011).

Alkire (2006) emphasises that in relation to both development and the linked issue of human rights, ideas of desirable outcomes expressed by religious leaders and organisations can differ significantly from those advanced in secular development models, including those put forwad by INGOs, such as the World Bank and the IMF. This is because from a religious perspective secular development programmes and policies are often regarded as 'one-eyed giants'. That is, they seek to 'analyse, prescribe and act *as if* man could live by bread alone, *as if* human destiny could be stripped to its material dimensions alone' (Goulet, 1980, quoted in Alkire, 2006). Such concerns are reflected in the views of those whose ideas are informed by specific religious perspectives. For example, writing from an Islamic viewpoint, Seyyed Hussein Nasr focuses on the link between modernisation and development, and emphasises how important it is for religious issues and concerns to be a factor in their achievement. For Nasr, 'development' without this religious focus would fatally distract Muslims from what is their true – that is, religious – nature and, as a result, seriously undermine their chances of living appropriately (Nasr, 1967, 1975, 1996).

Another example comes from Roman Catholic social teachings, which have long articulated a faith-based view of development. As Alkire (2004: 10) highlights, the Roman Catholic view emphasises the key contributions of 'spiritual disciplines and of ethical action to a person's "vocation to human fulfilment", [which must be] addressed alongside contributions made by markets, public policy, and poverty reduction'. A further articulation of concern about the goals and purpose of human development from a Roman Catholic perspective is found in a radical approach, known as 'liberation theology'. Liberation theology focuses on important structural developmental and political injustices which, it is argued, fatally undermines the chances of poor Roman Catholics, especially in the developing world, of achieving their full spiritual potential. The way of dealing with this, articulated by liberation theologists, was for increased engagement of Roman Catholics with political and economic institutions in order to try to encourage improved outcomes. A Peruvian priest, Gustavo Gutierrez, famously articulated liberation theology in his 1973 book, *A Theology of Liberation. History, Politics and Salvation.*

Representatives of other religious faiths, including Judaism and Buddhism, have also advanced similar kinds of theological/development interpretations to that of Gutierrez, underlining that several among the world work from a similar position in relation to many development issues. Various popular books have put forward strategies of people-centred, faith-based development perspectives, including: Bernardo Klicksberg's *Social Justice: A Jewish Perspective* (2003a), and from a Buddhist perspective, Sulak Sivaraksa's *Seeds of Peace* (1992; also see Marshall, 2011).

## The World Bank, religion and development

The previous section draws attention to the fact that ideas about development and how to achieve it tend to differ from religious and secular development perspectives. But this is not surprising when we consider that traditionally (secular) development strategies have been designed and devised by (secular) Western donors to try to improve the lives of people in the developing world who are, nearly everywhere, highly likely to be religious with associated worldviews. Mesbahuddin (2010: 221) notes that 'attempts have been made in the recent past to restore some of that imbalance by incorporating cultural issues and religious values into the international development policy network, but hostilities remain' between the two generic approaches. Two problems in particular are clear: first, development policies and practices continue to be articulated within a predominantly neo-liberal and secular framework which necessarily curtails the input from other ideological viewpoints, including religious views; second, within developing countries there are often divisions between religious communities and as a result it may be difficult to institute and develop a religiously focused development model which is both inclusive and does not serve to reinforce divisions.

At the beginning of the twenty-first century, the world's most important development-focused INGO, the World Bank, appeared to accept the need for a significantly different developmental emphasis if the United Nations-sponsored Millennium Development Goals (MDGs) had any chance of success by their designated achievement date, 2015. The Bank's *World Development Report 2000/2001* noted that 'adjustments' would be necessary at both global and national levels to achieve major developmental improvements in the developing world. The report claimed that MDG goals, including the promotion of opportunity, were inherently linked to increases in overall economic growth, as were patterns and quality of growth. The Bank believed that: (1) market 'adjustments' were central to achieving expanded opportunities for poor people in the developing world, and (2) 'adjustments' were also urgently needed in relation to local institutional and structural conditions which combined to undermine chances of improved development (World Bank, 2001).

The 2000/2001 report also emphasised the necessity of improving governance within developing countries, which involved 'choice and implementation of public actions that are responsive to the needs of poor people [and which] *depend on the interaction of political, social, and other institutional processes*' (emphasis added). That is, the Bank argued that more is needed to be done to encourage involvement of non-state actors – including by implication religious groups – in order to boost chances of achieving improved development outcomes, especially in the world's poorest, most under-developed countries, which nearly always contain very high proportions of religious believers among the populations.

The report also contended that improved development outcomes would be linked to (1) 'active collaboration among poor people, the middle class, and other groups in society', and (2) wider changes in style and outcomes relating to governance. These changes were necessary, the report stated, in order to make public administration, legal institutions, and public service delivery more efficient and accountable to and for *all* citizens – rather than primarily serving the interests of a privileged few with best access to the 'levers of power' (World Bank, 2001: 7). Finally, the report also claimed that to deliver enhanced participation in development required the inclusion of ordinary people and their representative organisations in decision-making structures and processes at various levels, from local to national. The report did not specifically mention faith-based organisations. Yet, anyone reading the report would gain a clear inference from its recommendations: to achieve the MDGs in just 16 years (2000–2015) would necessarily require full utilisation of *all* currently under-used human resources, including, where appropriate, those linked to religious entities.

## Religion and the state: strategies for improved development outcomes

Strategies and objectives stated in the 2000/2001 *World Development Report* were, at the time, central to the World Bank's two-pronged strategy for improved development outcomes in the poorest developing countries: (1) investing in and empowering people, and (2) improving climate for domestic and external financial investments in developing countries. The clear focus in the 2000/2001 report on communities and their importance in achieving improved development outcomes was welcome, not least because it served to emphasise more generally that development outcomes, ultimately, can only be measured in the extent to which they affect poor people's quality of life and the ways in which such people can influence output via collective efforts.

In the increased emphasis on the importance of harnessing community involvement to achieve better development outcomes, it is obvious that faith could be a factor. Religion could potentially play an important role in two main ways in community engagement with development:

- *Bottom-up influence on policy makers and consequential policy formation.* This could occur by engendering and/or influencing policy-makers values and outlooks, in turn affecting formulation of specific development policies.
- *Bringing together* or *dividing communities along religious lines.* This could either improve or worsen political conflicts centring on access to development and associated goods.

This should not, however, be taken to imply that relations between governments, secular development agencies and religious leaders and organisations is necessarily unproblematic. There is, however, widespread recognition that:

- Religious groups of various kinds – including, churches, mosques, religious charities and religious movements – are often important parts of civil society, whose involvement in policies and programmes can potentially help achieve increased tolerance, social cohesion and understanding.

- Religious entities can play a key role in providing education and achieving local and global justice, gender equality, and action for non-violent resolutions to conflict.
- The highlighting of religions' common values can help promote and develop religious/cultural understanding in many societies in the developing world.

Conversely, not everyone agrees that religion is, even potentially, a productive force that can help improve people's lives. Some believe that religion is inherently divisive, leading inevitably to complications and strife. In such views, serving humanity is most likely to be delivered through a focus on explicitly and consistently secular vehicles of social and economic reform and development. This problem surfaced during World Bank-led initiatives in the early 2000s to build a bigger role for religion in development programmes and policies in the developing world. Assorted multilateral development banks and other official development institutions actively sought, through various means, to engage in dialogue with a broad range of civil society institutions, including religious entities. Yet results were decidedly patchy. Questions were – and continue to be – asked about what is the best way forward in relation to the role of religion in development (Marshall, 2005a, 2009; Haynes, 2007b, 2012; ter Haar, 2011).

Religious entities face particular challenges not only in integrating their perspectives into the general state–civil society dialogue but also into the strategies and operations of development policy and programmes. This point can be illustrated by identifying problems which surfaced when trying to institutionalise relations between, on the one hand, governments, the World Bank and the IMF in the early 2000s, and, on the other, assorted religious leaders in relation to a joint World Bank/IMF initiative known as Poverty Reduction Strategy Papers (PRSP), introduced formally in 1999 in the build up to the Millennium Declaration of 2000. PRSP is a World Bank/IMF/government-devised approach to guide growth and poverty reduction within explicit strategic frameworks tailored for each client country. The purpose of PRSP is to outline a comprehensive strategy to encourage growth and reduce poverty in a developing country in order to collect together different actors' priorities and analyses – collectively working under the general rubric of 'development' – with the intention of increasing chances of complementarity and coherence. In pursuit of this goal, various forms of consultation are held in each affected country with prominent figures and organisations. Overall PRSP consultations: (1) seek to adopt growth and development strategies that are deemed to be 'economically rational', while (2) aiming to ensure that the policies and programmes that result are compatible with what a country's people regard as developmentally appropriate and sustainable. Once consultation is concluded, a PRSP would be finalised. The World Bank and the IMF would assess its strengths as the basis for a country to receive loans and credits. Note that this means that the parameters of each PRSP are bound by what the World Bank and IMF believed is appropriate in relation to development policy and programmes (Levinsohn, 2003).

---

## BOX 7.3 Civil society participation in development strategies

Civil society's participation is seen as both essential and central in relation to PRSP design, and some religious entities are recognised in this context as potentially important components in the process of PRSP formulation. However, there is no coordinated strategy necessarily to engage relevant religious organisations in PRSP processes, nor wide-ranging discussions to ascertain their views or evaluate experiences. The reason for this omission is that PRSP processes are primarily designed and led by governments and the aforementioned INGOs, and in many cases they do not actively seek relevant religious organisations' views, despite the fact that in each country adopting a PRSP, selected religious entities are identified as potential partners in the consultation and participation process (World Faiths Development Dialogue, 2003). In short, there are often problems of interaction between religious leaders, governments and INGOs in relation to PRSP formulation, planning and execution. For example, an initiative to institutionalise religion's involvement in development strategies, including PRSP, was set in train by the then president of the World Bank, James Wolfensohn, in 1998. Almost straightaway, however, Wolfensohn's initiative faced serious collective opposition from the World Bank's Executive Committee, a group of 24 country representatives with a pivotal role in setting World Bank policy. The executive directors raised fundamental objections to the idea of developing and institutionalising the Bank's development dialogue with religion. The result was that decreasing effort was then applied by the Bank, including reductions in institutionalised engagement with religion (Marshall, 2005a).

Some senior World Bank employees had long recognised the potential for religion to assist in achieving better development outcomes. The issue was explicitly raised in the late 1990s by the then president of the World Bank, James D. Wolfensohn. For Wolfensohn,

[t]his is a powerful idea – to tap the strengths of religions as development actors. Consider economics, finance and administration as disciplines that are deeply ethical at the core . . . they are about poverty reduction and employment creation. A vision without a task is boring. A task without a vision is awfully frustrating. A vision with a task can change the world.
(http://web.worldbank.org/WBSITE/EXTERNAL/EXTABOUTUS/
ORGANIZATION/EXTPRESIDENT2007/EXTPASTPRESIDENTS/
PRESIDENTEXTERNAL/0,,contentMDK:20091872~pagePK:139877
~piPK:199692~theSitePK:227585,00.html)

Wolfensohn was president of the World Bank between 1995 and 2005. An Australian Jew, he is said to be a man of strong personal religious convictions, although this was not the main reason for seeking to involve religion with development. The main reason was that Wolfensohn saw it as an opportunity being missed, as religious entities were empirically so central in many developing countries to community development, including in many cases the explicit goal of improving development outcomes. As a result, during his presidency of the Bank, Wolfensohn was personally instrumental in establishing various initiatives with important religious organisations, notably the World Council of Churches.[1] In addition, he personally created the World Faiths Development Dialogue (WFDD)[2] and the now-disbanded Development Dialogue on Values and Ethics (DDVE).

## BOX 7.4 Development Dialogue on Values and Ethics

The DDVE was a small unit at the World Bank whose purpose was to contribute to analytical work, capacity development and dialogue on issues related to values and ethics. Founded in 2000, for the next decade the DDVE served as the World Bank's focal point on the intersection of religion and development. In addition, the unit led a number of projects related to prominent development issues, such as the current economic crisis in Africa, with a focus on the difficult distributional trade-offs faced by various development actors in dealing with these issues. The DDVE was disbanded in July 2011 without replacement.

(http://web.worldbank.org/WBSITE/EXTERNAL/EXTABOUTUS/PARTNERS/EXTDEVDIA
LOGUE/0,,contentMDK:21966758~menuPK:5554943~pagePK:64192523~piPK:641924
58~theSitePK:537298,00.html)

Initially units of the World Bank entities, the WFDD and DDVE, were both established in 1998. The formal dialogue with the WCC began soon after, in 2002 but also later lapsed for unclear reasons ('The WCC-IMF-WB high-level encounter', 2004).

The problem of consistent engagement between governments, and development INGOs – such as the World Bank – and selected religious entities was highlighted during a four-day meeting held in Canterbury, England, in July 2002. Led by James Wolfensohn and George Carey, then Archbishop of Canterbury, the meeting brought together individuals from 15 developing countries, including several participants from various religions. Michael Taylor, then director of the WFDD, led the consultation. World Bank representatives were among the observers; the IMF was invited to participate but no representative could be present. The meeting's main purpose was to gain an understanding of whether religious entities at the meeting believed that their views were taken sufficiently into account when the Bank sought to draw up poverty reduction strategies in its programmes in developing countries (World Faiths Development Dialogue, 2003).

The meeting focused on a range of human development issues, including the potential for religion to help improve development outcomes. The gathering brought together an impressive group of religious leaders, key development organisations, and individuals from the private sector, including the worlds of entertainment and philanthropy. Discussions and presentations at the meeting focused on key development issues identified in the Millennium Declaration, including: education, poverty, HIV/AIDS, gender, conflict and social justice. Participants discussed various dimensions of and developmental ramifications of globalisation, including its differential impact on rich and poor countries. It was noted that poverty, HIV/AIDS, conflict, gender concerns, international trade and global politics bind all the world's countries and peoples into a global community, emphasising the urgency of shared responsibility and partnership. This sense of 'oneness' highlighted the urgency of developing shared responsibility and partnership to deal with collective problems facing humanity. The overall conclusion was that more was needed to be done to move from expressions of solidarity in the face of shared problems to the realisation of practical plans involving collaboration between the worlds of faith and development in confronting major development issues (Marshall and March, 2003). This illustrates that shared development concerns – especially poverty alleviation and improved human development more generally in the developing world – encouraged expansion of links between religious leaders and organisations and the World Bank.

Several faith participants not only emphasised that poverty is a complex phenomenon but also stressed that many people regard the importance of freedom and a satisfying life as a higher priority than simple gains in income or improvements in social indicators (Marshall and Keough, 2004). For example, according to a Sri Lankan at the meeting, aspirations of Buddhist Sri Lankans differ from those of people living in countries tightly focused on economic growth, commenting that: 'The middle path, path to the human liberation in Buddhism, guides people for a simple, happy and content life' (Tyndale, 2004; also see Marshall, 2011). In addition, two African participants highlighted that in popular perceptions of relative importance, opportunities in life can rival wealth acquisition in terms of popular priorities. A Tanzanian underlined the significance of rights in alleviating poverty, especially social wellbeing, as well as those related to security, justice, freedom, peace, and law and order. In relation to Zambia, it was claimed that opposition parties were weak; consequently, 'only the [Catholic] church speaks out'. In addition, Catholic social teaching was said to serve as a source of inspiration for many Zambians, with its focus on human dignity particularly important in contrast to the government view that 'economic growth equals development' *tout court*. The Zambian participant also stressed that 'if growth does not benefit the human being, then it is not development at all' (Tyndale, 2004).

Katherine Marshall was Mr Wolfensohn's right-hand woman in these initiatives, a senior World Bank official who headed the DDVE.[3] According to Marshall (2005a), the Bank did not believe 'that religion and socio-economic development belong to different spheres and are best cast in separate roles – even separate dramas'. Her observation was based on recognition that around the world many religious organisations and secular development agencies have similar key concerns, including how to improve: (1) the lot of materially poor people; (2) the societal position of those suffering from social exclusion; and (3) unfulfilled human potential in the context of glaring developmental polarisation within and between countries. In other words, while faith has often in the past been understood as 'otherworldly' and 'world-denying', Marshall (2005b) noted much agreement both in the World Bank and within other secular development agencies that increased cooperation with faith-based organisations can usefully contribute to the achievement of developmental goals, not least because issues of right and wrong and social and economic justice are central to the teachings of the world religions. Under Wolfensohn, the Bank's commitment to bringing religion into the pursuit of development in the developing world led to a major initiative, 'Shaping the Agenda – Faith & Development', which centred on three main areas of dialogue: (1) building bridges – stronger, bolder partnerships; (2) exploring a more 'comprehensive', 'holistic' and 'integrated' vision of development; and (3) transforming dialogue into practice and action ('JDW – Faith and development', 2011).

In addition to these World Bank initiatives, several United Nations agencies were also active at this time, developing dialogue with religious leaders and organisations. The International Labour Organisation (ILO) and the IMF began dialogue with the World Council of Churches. The Inter-American Development Bank (IDB), an affiliate of the World Bank, began an initiative entitled, 'Social Capital, Ethics, and Development' and 'approached religious leaders to try to win the backing of their moral authority . . . for its campaign in Latin America against corruption' (Tyndale, 2004: 2). A UN agency, the United Nations Fund for Population Activities (UNFPA), built links with various faith leaders, including Muslim imams in Africa and Bangladesh ('Married adolescents ignored in global agenda, says UNFPA', 2004). The UNFPA also collaborated positively with religious leaders in Africa and, via a dialogue characterised by sensitivity and respect, educational programmes and programmes for women's empowerment were instituted. Overall, as Tyndale notes, such collaborations became possible when both sides – that is, secular development agencies and religious leaders and organisations – acknowledged that neither alone had the whole answer to all development questions (Tyndale, 2004: 6).

Over time, however, fundamental objections raised by the World Bank's executive directors regarding an enhanced role for religion in development dialogues significantly inhibited this development. One sign of this was that the WFDD was cast adrift by the World Bank in

2006. Headed by Marshall who retired from the Bank in 2006, the WFDD then started a new life as a cash-strapped, yet independent, pro-development non-governmental organisation (NGO), based at Georgetown University, in Washington DC. The changing position of the WFDD – from established World Bank unit to independent NGO without significant financial resources of its own to call on – should not, however, be taken to imply that all Bank initiatives involving religion were henceforward forbidden. For example, if a World Bank country representative takes a personal initiative for local operational reasons to engage with a religious leader and/or organisation – for example, as occurred in Indonesia in the late 1990s and early 2000s – in pursuit of clear and explicit development goals, then the Bank would not expressly forbid such activity. Moreover, where religious entities are already important elements in civil society forums, as in, for example, Zambia, Indonesia and Ghana, then their continued involvement is often judged by the Bank to be both appropriate and desirable. Nevertheless, issues remain within the Bank concerning, on the one hand, pragmatic dialogue with selected religious entities in the context of individual countries and their specific development needs and priorities and, on the other hand, the idea of an institutionalised partnership with a large number of religious organisations as a key factor in pursuing development more generally in the developing world. The Bank – and by extension powerful governments which, it should not be forgotten, provide the financial resources for the Bank to function – have the following concerns:

- Disquiet about the nature and direction of development when religion is centrally involved.
- Apprehension about differences between secular and religion-based visions of development.
- Lack of agreement both within the higher echelons of the World Bank and among powerful governments on whether systematic or institutionalised dialogue with religion is actually desirable.

## Conclusion

In the late 1990s and early 2000s, various secular development agencies – including the World Bank, IMF, ILO and the UNFPA – sought to engage with selected religious organisations to pursue improved development, especially for the poorest people in the developing world. This followed collective realisation that secular and religious entities often share similar development concerns, especially commitment to poverty alleviation as a crucial first stage in improved development outcomes and better human rights. Common ground linked them to a growing consensus that underpinned both the UN-sponsored Millennium Declaration and achievement of the associated Millennium Development Goals (2000–2015).

A key question we have examined in the chapter is why do many religious leaders and organisations have a higher profile today in relation to development issues compared to a few decades ago? I have suggested that one important reason is that, after half a century, secular development policies and programmes had led to disappointing outcomes in many parts of the developing world and there was widespread realisation that something new and different needed to be tried. One result is that not only many religious leaders and the organisations they represent but also many ordinary people in the developing world may well believe that it is entirely correct that religion should be an influential voice in helping resolve development problems and be part of the quest for improved strategies in this regard. Yet, many governments – the huge majority of which are explicitly secular in their orientation and outlook – tend to regard the prospect of religion's institutionalised involvement in development with apprehension or suspicion, a perception often linked to what they see as problematic involvement of religions more generally in secular – political, social and economic – issues.

Second, there are marked differences in perceptions of poverty and development between religious entities, on the one hand, and government and secular international development agencies, on the other. That is, while governments and secular international development agencies still overwhelmingly prioritise economic growth in development, religious leaders and entities see things differently: they prioritise a range of ways of understanding the notions of poverty-reduction and development, over and above achievement of higher incomes. The key practical question is *how* and *in what ways* might secular development agencies and governments constructively integrate religious perspectives into poverty reduction strategies? Or, to put it another way, *how* and *in what ways* can religion constructively influence governmental and secular development agencies' perspectives on poverty reduction strategies and by extension development? It is apparent, however, that this is going to be a difficult issue to resolve – not least because religions often do not view poverty reduction as *the* central question in the creation of more fulfilling, sustainable lifestyles. Instead, they afford most importance to achievement of wider spiritual and religious goals.

Finally, while often paying lip service to the involvement of religion in development, it may be that both governments and, to an extent, development INGOs such as the World Bank, either lack ability or are simply not interested in integrating alternative – including religious – perspectives into wider development programmes and policies, including poverty reduction strategies. Over the years, this issue has often strained relationships and undermined confidence between international development agencies, including the World Bank and religious actors, with secular development agencies' own biases adding a layer of complexity; and this continues not only to curtail vigorous and constructive debate about poverty and how to reduce it but also to stymie development of comprehensive development programmes that can consistently draw on both secular and religious insights.

## Notes

1. The WCC was founded in Amsterdam in 1948. It is an international, inter-denominational Christian organisation which brings together around 350 – Protestant, Anglican and Eastern Orthodox – churches. WCC headquarters are in Geneva, Switzerland.
2. According to the WFDD website, 'The World Faiths Development Dialogue was set up in 1998 as an initiative of James D. Wolfensohn, President of the World Bank and Lord Carey, then Archbishop of Canterbury. Its aim is to facilitate a dialogue on poverty and development among people from different religions and between them and the international development institutions.' The focus is on the relationship between faith and development and how this is expressed, both in considering decisions about development policy and in action with impoverished communities all over the world (http://www.wfdd. org.uk/).
3. Marshall served as senior advisor for the World Bank on issues of faith and development. Her long career with the World Bank (1971–2006) involved a

wide range of leadership assignments, many focused on Africa. From 2000 to 2006 her mandate covered ethics, values, and faith in development work, as counsellor to the World Bank's then president, James Wolfensohn.

## Questions

- Can religion help improve development outcomes? If so, how?
- To what extent do religions share a concern with material, as opposed to spiritual, development?
- Why did the World Bank lose interest in the idea of institutionalised engagement with selected religious actors?
- Does the significance of civil society for achieving improved development outcomes in the developing world depend on the involvement of religious actors?

## Further reading

ter Haar, G. (ed.), *Religion and Development: Ways of Transforming the World*, London: Hurst and Co., 2011. Ter Haar's book looks at the ways in which a religious worldview can influence processes of development. Its originality lies in the fact that it does not concentrate primarily on religious institutions and organisations but on religious ideas themselves.

J. Haynes, *Religion and Development: Conflict or Cooperation*, New York: Palgrave Macmillan, 2007. This book adopts a chronological and conceptual approach to introduce undergraduate and postgraduate students to the central themes and theoretical perspectives in the study of religion and development in the developing world. It examines the emergence and consolidation of theories of development and explains how and why development outcomes in the developing world are often influenced by religion. Focusing on key themes including environmental sustainability, health and education, as well as detailing the principles of key religious groups, this essential text explores how religion impacts upon development practice.

Lunn, J., 'The role of religion, spirituality and faith in development: a critical theory approach', *Third World Quarterly*, 30, 5, 2009, pp. 937–951. Religion, spirituality and faith have suffered from long-term and systematic neglect in development theory, policy making and practice, although there has been a noticeable turnover in the past ten years. This article explores the role of religion, spirituality and faith in development in the past, present and future by applying three core concepts from critical theory – grounding of knowledge in historical context, critique through dialectical process, and identification of future potentialities for emancipation and self-determination. It concludes that religion, spirituality and faith have a role to play in the future of development, particularly in ensuring that it is appropriate and sustainable. The article also serves to counter critics who claim that critical theory has no resonance to contemporary social research.

Mesbahuddin, T., 'Religion in development. An Islamic model emerging in Bangladesh', *Journal of South Asian Development*, 5, 2, 2010, pp. 221–241. This article contends that recent attempts have been made to incorporate cultural issues and religious values into the international development policy network, but hostilities remain. Mesbahuddin argues that development practices continue to embrace a neo-liberal framework which limits other ideological viewpoints. Setting an Islamic context where greater emphasis is laid on values, Mesbahuddin asserts that in Bangladesh, Islamic solutions to development also have a utilitarian function in welfare terms.

# 8 | Religion, conflict and cooperation

Each of us has the right to take pride in our particular faith or heritage. But the notion that what is ours is necessarily in conflict with what is theirs is both false and dangerous. It has resulted in endless enmity and conflict, leading men to commit the greatest of crimes in the name of a higher power.

It need not be so. People of different religions and cultures live side by side in almost every part of the world, and most of us have overlapping identities which unite us with very different groups. We *can* love what we are, without hating what – and who – we are *not*. We can thrive in our own tradition, even as we learn from others, and come to respect their teachings.

(Kofi Annan, United Nations Secretary General, Nobel Peace Prize Acceptance Speech, 2001; http://nobelprize.org/nobel_prizes/peace/laureates/2001/annan-lecture.html)

The United Nations (UN) proclaimed the years 2001–2010 as the 'International Decade for a Culture of Peace and Non-Violence for the Children of the World'. A 'culture of peace' is defined by the UN as 'a set of values, attitudes, modes of behaviour and ways of life that reject violence and prevent conflicts by tackling their root causes to solve problems through dialogue and negotiation among individuals, groups and nations'.[1] The UN's concerns – rejecting violence and thus aiming to prevent conflicts – are central to the teachings of the world religions: Buddhism, Christianity, Hinduism, Islam and Judaism. They all share a concern with how to build peace and minimise tensions and conflicts between different religious and cultural groups. This issue has become a key feature of international relations in recent years, one with which the UN is centrally concerned. It seems plausible to suggest that religious teachings focused on the desirability of peace and operation and not conflict might be a very useful medium from which to address conflicts and work towards their resolution. This is especially the case in the context of today's international relations (IR), a post-secular context with religion making a notable and sustained return to world affairs. One key way in which religion has 'returned' to IR is in the domain of ideas, values and norms, which can broadly encourage religions to seek *conflict* or engage in *conflict resolution, peacemaking and peacebuilding*. To be true to their moral and ethical imperatives, religious leaders and their organisations have a duty to play constructive roles in helping to resolve conflicts and to facilitate peacebuilding in various ways, including: early warnings of conflict, good offices once conflict has erupted, as well as advocacy, mediation and reconciliation. Yet, religious involvement is only too common in conflict in current international relations, most egregiously in so-called 'inter-civilisational' conflicts, involving Islamist extremists and the West (Huntington, 1993, 1996).

Apart from a role in 'civilisational' conflicts, an issue we shall examine in the second half of the chapter, religious difference is also said to be a significant component in some inter-national conflicts. This is especially the case when the key issue is which group controls territory that both sides covert. We can see the centrality of both religion and territorial control in the long-running dispute between Israel and the Palestinians. Nearly all Palestinians are Muslims, and most Israelis are Jews. Increasingly, religion has come to define their key differences, centring on the issue of who controls Jerusalem – a holy city to Jews, Muslims *and* Christians. This is a – perhaps *the* – basic element not only upon which Jewish attachment to the territory of Israel is based but also which provides a key source of the political involvement of Palestinian Islamists. Like religious Jews, Palestinian Islamists also draw on core religious sources to justify, explain and underline attachment to the same piece of land.

In this chapter we look at religion's involvement in international conflict and cooperation. First, we examine the ambivalence of religion in this respect, that is, it can be central to *both* conflicts *and* attempts at cooperation, including conflict resolution and peacemaking, and post-conflict peacebuilding. Second, we turn to the issue of religion's involvement in inter-civilisational conflict and cooperation, especially after 9/11.

# Religion as a potential bridge in conflicts

## BOX 8.1 Peace and conflict in Israel/Palestine

Does resolution of conflicts become more or less easy as a result of inter-religious dialogue? Israeli academic Ben Mollov is sure that it helps. He conducted a quantitative empirical survey data among Israelis and Palestinians at a dialogue held in Khan Yunis in Gaza in 1999. To Mollov (2006), his findings provide convincing evidence that perceptions among those who are most religious and initially negative in attitude may improve as a result of inter-religious dialogue. Yet, over the time since Mollov conducted his survey, five significant events have occurred, which collectively may make attempts at inter-religious dialogue between Israelis and Palestinians more not less problematic: the 11 September 2001 ('9/11') attacks on the Twin Towers and the Pentagon; US/UK-led invasion and occupation of Afghanistan from late 2001; US/UK involvement in the overthrow of Saddam Hussein and the government of Iraq from March 2003; the subsequent – still unfinished – attempts to reassert the shattered state, build democracy, and diminish tensions between Iraq's different religious groups; finally, continued – seemingly unconditional – support for Israel's government from both the USA and many European governments may suggest to many Palestinians that the 'international community' may have no real interest in being even-handed in the conflict. While none of these issues is solely religious, it would be difficult to deny that religion provides a context and focus within which the Israel/Palestinians conflict can be approached.

The Israel/Palestinians issue highlights that inter-group conflicts can be framed in religious terms even when the key issue is not religious but territorial. The German academic Hans Kurtz contends that polarised religious worldviews can encourage radically differing allegiances and standards in relation to various fundamental areas, including the state, land and politics, as noted above in relation to the Israel/Palestinians issue. According to Kurtz (1995: 170), such conflicts can 'take on "larger-than-life" proportions as the struggle of good against evil'. In addition, the eminent German Roman Catholic theologian, Hans Kung, claims that:

> the most fanatical, the cruelest political struggles are those that have been colored, inspired, and legitimized by religion. To say this is not to reduce all political conflicts to religious ones, but to take seriously the fact that religions share in the responsibility for bringing peace to our torn and warring world.
>
> (Kung, quoted in Smock, 2004)

However, religious leaders can be effective as 'angels of peace'. This duality – between the two views of religion as a potential stimulator *and* resolver of conflict – encouraged the US religious historian R. Scott Appleby (2000) to coin the phrase: the *ambivalence of the sacred*. Appleby is referring to the fact that, ultimately, the relationship of the world religions, including Judaism and Islam, to violence is unclear. This is because they have evolved from traditions that, in certain circumstances, may legitimise force, claim victims in the battle for their own beliefs, and demonise believers in other religions. Yet, simultaneously, they all proclaim the *incompatibility* of violence with their core religious tenets, while expecting sacrifices for peace and respect for people of other religions. Holenstein (2005: 10) expresses the ambivalence in the following way:

> If we are to assume that, for the foreseeable future, the religions of the world will continue to be a factor in political conflicts, then it is high time that we strengthened the 'civilising' side of the sacred and made it more difficult for it cynically to be taken over by political interests. What is said here about the relationship of world religions to violence can be considered generally valid for religions overall.

## BOX 8.2 Religious ambivalence, conflict and cooperation

Religious ambivalence is especially notable when focusing upon religions' involvement in many recent and current conflicts, both within countries and between them. For example, much contemporary political violence in sub-Saharan Africa, Asia and other parts of the developing world is associated with religious tensions, competition and/or conflict (Haynes, 2007a, 2007b, 2012). However, as Barringer (2006: 2) notes, apparent religious tensions are very often themselves linked to other, non-religious, issues, including 'ethnicity, culture, class, power and wealth, played out both within' countries, for example, Nigeria, Fiji, Cyprus, Sri Lanka, and between them, for example, India/Pakistan and Israel/Palestine. The Middle East in particular seems especially prone to conflicts with a religious component. The region has long-running religious (and cultural) tensions and conflicts – between Israel and, inter alia, the (mostly Sunni Muslim) Palestinians and Lebanon's mainly Shia Hezbollah guerrillas. In addition, there are continuing conflicts within Iraq between Shia and Sunni Muslims and internationally between Shia Iran and Sunni Saudi Arabia (Haynes, 2008).

Such conflicts draw our attention to the fact that the Middle East is the emblematic birthplace of the three monotheistic world religions (Islam, Judaism and Christianity). The unfortunate result is a legacy not only of shared religious wisdom but also of many inter- and intra-societal conflicts, providing a complex environment affecting not only all regional countries, but also on some far away from the region, including the Philippines (which has seen growing numbers of Islamic extremist groups in recent years, in some cases apparently inspired by al Qaeda), as well as various Western countries, including the United States, the United Kingdom and Spain, all of which experienced Islamist bombing outrages between 2001 and 2005.

A key to eventual peace in the Middle East may well be the success of focused collaborative efforts by respected religious leaders and the organisations that dovetail with related efforts by various secular actors, including governments within the region outside, including those of the USA and European Union member states. Working together, religious and secular actors may be able to develop and embed work-able models of peace and co-operation to address at least some of the region's continuing conflicts. The aim, of course, is to facilitate the region's escape from what sometimes seems to be apparently endless cycles of religion-linked conflict. This emphasises that in the Middle East religion is intimately connected *both* to promulgation and prolongation of conflicts *and* attempts to end them. Religion can play a significant or fundamental role in contributing to conflicts in various ways, including how they are intensified, channelled or reconciled. However, it can also play an important role in seeking to resolve conflicts and then build peace. Yet, the ambivalence of the sacred is not limited to the Middle East. It is also present in recent and current conflicts in Asia (for example, the recently concluded internecine struggle between mainly Hindu Tamils and Buddhist Sinhalese in Sri Lanka, conflict between mainly Hindu India and Muslim-majority Pakistan, the China–Tibet imbroglio, involving radical members of Tibet's Buddhist *sangha* (monks)), in sub-Saharan Africa, for example, in unresolved conflicts between Muslims and Christians in Sudan and Nigeria, and in Europe where the mainly Muslim Kosovans remain in dispute with mostly Orthodox Christian Serbs more than a decade after their conflict offici-ally ended. Overall, these examples indicate that religions can be linked to violence and conflict both between and within religious groups, despite the fact that most religious believers would no doubt regard their chosen faith as both benevolent and inspiring.

A growing scholarly literature has appeared which focuses on religion-linked political conflicts, in both domestic and international contexts (for a major, if now a little dated, bibliography, see National Commission on Terrorist Attacks, 2004). Around the world, many armed groups claim religious justification for their activities. How shocking is it that religion is often implicated in both domestic and international conflicts? The answer is: it is not that surprising because religious faiths often contain within them – at least potentially – sources of related danger:

- *Religions are often focused on the absolute and unconditional and as a result can adopt totalitarian characteristics.* Christianity, Islam and Judaism – that is, the Abrahamic, monotheistic religions – may all have difficulty in trying to distinguish between, on the one hand, claims of the absolutely divine and, on the other, the traditions and history of human existence. This is a way of saying that if you believe that God wants you to do x or y, then it may be difficult to allow others to behave in ways which you believe are contrary to God's will.

- *When claiming both absolute and exclusive validity, religious conviction can lead to intolerance, over-zealous proselytisation – that is, the act of attempting to convert people to another religion – and religious fragmentation.* Such circumstances can make it very difficult or impossible to cultivate the kind of consensual and tolerant political culture where democracy can thrive.

- *Religious belief can increase aggressiveness and the willingness to use violence.* Added symbolic value can be an aspect of religious conviction, deriving from profane – that is, non-religious – motivation and aims that eventually become 'holy' objectives. This is a way of saying that religious belief can link up with political objectives and affect what goals are pursued.

- *Religious leaders may seek to legitimise abuses of power and violation of human rights in the name of religious zeal.* Because such leaders are nearly always men, there can also in addition be specific gender issues and women's human rights.

In addition, Holenstein (2005: 11) notes that what she calls 'religious power interests' may try to make use of the following susceptibilities:

- Domination strategies of identity politics which seek to harness real or perceived 'ethnic-cultural' and 'cultural-religious' differences.
- Misused religious motivation which informs some recent and current terrorist activities.
- Leaders of religious 'fundamentalist' movements which 'lay claim to a single and absolutist religious interpretation at the cost of all others, and they link their interpretation to political power objectives'.

---

**BOX 8.3 Religion and 'exclusive accounts of the nature of reality'**

The last bullet point relates to what Kurtz (1995: 238) calls 'exclusive accounts of the nature of reality', that is, some religious followers only accept religious beliefs that they regard as *true* beliefs. Examples include monotheistic 'religions of the book' – Christianity, Islam and Judaism – because each of these faiths claims authority deriving from authoritative interpretations of specific sacred texts. These 'exclusivist' truth claims can be a serious challenge to religious toleration and diversity, essential to peaceful co-existence in our globalised world, while perhaps making serious inter-religious conflict more likely. Yet, as already noted, religious traditions often contain important sets of beliefs that at least theoretically can help develop a more peaceful, multicultural, world. For example, from within Christianity comes the idea of non-violence, a key attribute of Jesus, the religion's founder, who insisted that all people are children of God, and that the test of one's relationship with God is whether one loves one's enemies and brings good news to the poor. As St Paul said, 'There is no Jew or Greek, servant or free, male or female: because you are all one in Jesus Christ' (Galatians 3:28).

---

## Conflict resolution and peacebuilding

I want to stress again that I am not arguing that religions are *necessarily* associated with conflict and violence. Religious leaders may play a pivotal role in helping resolve inter- and intra-group clashes and conflicts and in helping build peace. They may draw on key teachings of their religious faith, serving to emphasise that 'all religious traditions contain references in the form of didactical stories, teaching or even direct recommendation as to how the faithful should act in order to achieve harmony and peace within him/herself in the first place' (Bartoli, 2005: 5–6). Yet, nearly 20 years after publication of a path-breaking volume, Douglas Johnston and Cynthia Sampson's edited book, *Religion, the Missing Dimension of Statecraft* (1994), there are many examples of religion's involvement in *both* conflict *and* cooperation. Summarising an initial set of findings regarding religious peacebuilding and faith-based diplomacy, R. Scott Appleby (2006: 1) notes that:

- Religious leaders are uniquely positioned to foster non-violent conflict transformation through the building of constructive, collaborative relationships within and across ethnic and religious groups for the common good of the entire population of a country or region.
- In many conflict settings around the world, the social location and cultural power of religious leaders make them potentially critical players in any effort to build a sustainable peace.
- The multi-generational local or regional communities they oversee are repositories of local knowledge and wisdom, custodians of culture, and privileged sites of moral, psychological and spiritual formation.
- Symbolically charged sources of personal as well as collective identity, these communities typically establish and maintain essential educational and welfare institutions, some of which also serve people who are not members of their religious community.

From a variety of religious traditions, many religious leaders are actively involved in attempts to end conflicts and to foster post-conflict reconciliation and build peace (Bouta et al., 2005; Abu-Nimer and Augsburger, 2009). While in recent years the role of religious leaders in these respects has been highlighted, it is not an entirely new phenomenon. Religious individuals and/or representatives of various faith-based organisations have for decades carried out such mediations, with variable success. Examples include: mediation undertaken by a Christian sect, the Quakers, and financed by the US Ford foundation in the Nigerian Civil War, 1967–70; the work of the World Council of Churches and the All Africa Conference of Churches in mediating a cessation to the Sudan conflict in 1972; efforts made by a professor of International Peacebuilding at the University of Notre Dame, John Paul Lederach, in Nicaragua in the 1980s; and, in the 1990s and early 2000s, work by the Muslim Imam of Timbuktu in helping to mediate various West African conflicts (Conflict and Resolution Forum, 2001). Thus to focus exclusively and single-mindedly on *conflicts* within and between religions not only oversimplifies causal interconnections between religion and the absence of peace, in particular by disregarding important alternate variables, but also leads to a potential underestimation of attempts emerging from various religious traditions to help resolve conflicts and build peace. When successful, religion's role in helping resolve conflicts and build peace is a crucial component in helping achieve both peace and human development.

Success depends on the activities of the 'religious peacemakers', religious leaders, often representatives of religious organisations, who attempt to help resolve inter-group conflicts and build peace (Appleby, 2000, 2006; Gopin, 2000, 2005; ter Haar and Busutill, 2005; Abu-Nimer and Augsburger, 2009). Appleby (2006: 1) suggests that religious peacemakers are most likely to be successful when they: (1) have an international or transnational reach; (2) consistently emphasise peace and avoidance of the use of force in resolving conflict; and (3) encourage good relations between different religions in a conflict situation. The three 'religions of the book' – Christianity, Islam and Judaism – share a broadly similar set of theological and spiritual values and this can potentially underpin ability to provide positive inter-faith contributions to conflict resolution, peacebuilding and, more generally, inter-faith cooperation. Such efforts are increasing, with growing numbers and types of religious peacemakers working to try to build peaceful coexistence in multi-faith societies, while advocating reconciliation and fairness in a world increasingly characterised by economic polarisation, a key cause of both social and political strife (Bartoli, 2005). These observations lead to the following summary points regarding religious individuals/organisations and their contributions to conflict resolution and peacebuilding:

- Religious leaders and their organisations are active in attempts at peacebuilding.
- Religious leaders have a special role to play in zones of religious conflict, yet related peacebuilding programmes do not need to be confined to addressing religious conflict only.

- Although in some cases religious peacebuilding projects resemble very closely peacebuilding by secular peacebuilders, the religious orientation of religious leaders and organisations helps shape their peacebuilding attempts.
- Religious peacebuilding agendas are diverse, ranging from high-level mediation to training and peacebuilding-through-development at the grass roots.
- Peace can often be promoted by building peace-initiatives into wider relief and development activities, which do not necessarily have a religious component at all.

Overall, religious-focused efforts can contribute positively to peacebuilding in four main ways. They can: (1) offer 'emotional and spiritual support to war-affected communities'; (2) provide effective mobilisation for 'their communities and others for peace'; (3) supply mediation 'between conflicting parties'; and (4) serve as a conduit in pursuit of 'reconciliation, dialogue, and disarmament, demobilization and reintegration' (Bouta et al., 2005: ix). However, religious ambivalence can surface in two main ways: (1) some religious leaders fail to 'understand and/or enact their potential peacebuilding roles within the local community', and/or (2) lack the ability to 'exploit their strategic capacity as transnational actors' (Appleby, 2006: 2).

## Intercivilisational conflict and cooperation after 9/11

How to prevent conflicts developing in the first case and, when they do, how to bring them to a peaceful conclusion as quickly as possible? Some inter-faith religious organisations – for example, Religions for Peace,[2] established in 1970 – devote a great deal of time, energy and commitment not only to try to 'stop war', but also to related developmental and environmental concerns (such as, 'ending poverty' and 'protecting the earth') (http://www.religionsforpeace.org/about/). Overall, it is clear that, in various parts of the world, a variety of religious actors are engaged in peacemaking activities in many contexts.

Inter-religious dialogue and cooperation can be made extremely difficult – although not necessarily impossible – in the context of sudden, unexpected and damaging developments. I want to illustrate this contention in relation to the 9/11 attacks, subsequent US-led invasions of Muslim-majority Afghanistan (2001) and Iraq (2003) and successive bomb attacks in Madrid (2004) and London (2005). Together, these events almost certainly made inter-religious dialogue between Christians and Muslims more problematic than they might otherwise have been, while also stimulating an international effort to stress what 'civilisations' have in common and what can be done to minimise conflict and increase cooperation.

### BOX 8.4 Jonathan Fox on civilisations and religious conflict

Samuel Huntington's 'clash of civilisations' argument – that conflicts will increasingly be between 'civilisations' – is a source of considerable debate within international relations. Among the criticisms of this argument is the fact that there is a considerable overlap between Huntington's concept of civilisations and religion. In fact, only one of Huntington's eight civilisations has no obvious religious component. This raises the question of whether the concept of civilisations is really a proxy for religion. The Israel-based, US academic Jonathan Fox (2001b) examines the influence of both religion and Huntington's concept of civilisations on what he identifies as 'ethnic conflict' using well-developed data plus data on collected independently religion and civilisations. His results show that while there is considerable overlap between religion and civilisation, the two are not the same. Also, while it is not clear whether religious or civilisational differences have a greater impact on ethnic conflict, it is clear that neither are its primary cause. These results cast serious doubt on the validity of Huntington's hypothesis, at least as far as it concerns ethnic conflict.

In recent years, a new focus has emerged in international relations, that of 'intercivilizational conflict'. The focus on this issue was heightened after the 11 September 2001 ('9/11') attacks, as well as those on Madrid and London in 2004 and 2005, all carried out by al Qaeda-inspired activists against Western targets. A few years earlier, US academic Samuel Huntington (1993, 1996) had written about and popularised the notion of 'inter-civilisational' conflicts. For Huntington this was a key issue after the Cold War ended in the late 1980s. He believed that it would henceforward be a key focus of international tension and conflict. Although Huntington's thesis stimulated a lot of criticism, some accepted his argument that 'inter-civilisational' conflict was a fact of life in the post-Cold

War world, especially between 'Islam' and the 'West'. Some commentators argued that both the 9/11 attacks and subsequent US responses in relation to the 'war on terror', including the invasions of Afghanistan (2001) and Iraq (2003), were evidence that Huntington was right.

Huntington first presented his 'clash of civilisations' thesis in an article published in 1993, followed by a book in 1996. After the end of the four decades-long conflict between liberal democracy/capitalism and communism, Huntington's main argument was that there was now a new, global clash: a fight between the (Christian) 'West' and Muslim-majority countries, especially in the Middle East. Christianity is said by Huntington to be conducive to the spread of liberal democracy. In evidence, he notes the collapse of dictatorships in overwhelmingly Christian countries in southern Europe and Latin America in the 1970s and 1980s – they were mainly Roman Catholic but Orthodox Christianity was also represented, notably in Greece – followed by subsequent development of a full range of liberal democratic political norms (including, the rule of law, free elections, and multiple political rights and civil liberties). For Huntington, these events were proof of a demonstrable synergy between Christianity and liberal democracy, key foundations of a normatively desirable global order built on liberal values. Huntington contrasted this situation with that found, he alleged, in Islam; as a result, the West now found itself in conflict with radical Islam, a key threat to international stability. Radical Islam (covering related terms, such as 'Islamism', 'Islamist extremism' and 'Islamic fundamentalism') was a *political* movement concerned with fundamental changes in the international order, with its various elements not only united by antipathy to the West but also inspired by anti-democratic religious and cultural dogma, Huntington claimed. Huntington was not a lone voice; other senior academics also alleged that Islam is inherently undemocratic or even anti-democratic. For example, venerated US university professor Francis Fukuyama (1992: 236) suggested that 'Islamic fundamentalism' has a 'more than superficial resemblance to European fascism'.

There were, however, critics of Huntington. Many noted that it is one thing to argue that various brands of political Islam have qualitatively different perspectives on liberal democracy compared to many forms of Christianity, but quite another to claim that Muslims en masse are poised to enter into a period of conflict with the West. Critics also pointed out that there are actually many 'Islams' and only the malevolent or misinformed would associate the terrorist attacks with an apparently representative quality of a single – necessarily, extremist – idea of Islam. Second, the 11 September atrocities – as well as subsequent bomb outrages in London, Madrid and elsewhere – were not carried out by a state or group of states or at their behest, but by al Qaeda, an international terrorist organisation, as vilified by Muslim governments – including those of Pakistan, Saudi Arabia and Libya – as it is by Western states.

Third, the idea of inter-civilisational conflict is also implausible for another reason: it is very difficult or impossible clearly to delineate territorial boundaries between 'civilisations'; and even more tricky to perceive them as acting as coherent units. This underlines that, problematically, Huntington's scenario of 'clashing civilisations' focuses attention on a one-dimensional, undifferentiated category – 'civilisation' – and as a result places insufficient emphasis on various trends, conflicts and disagreements occurring *within* all religious and cultural traditions, including, Islam, Christianity and Judaism. The wider point is that cultures are not usefully seen as closed systems of essentialist values, while it is not helpful to try to understand the world as comprising a strictly limited, discrete number of civilisations or cultures, each with its own unique core beliefs.

Finally, the image of 'clashing civilisations' ignores the very important sense in which radical Islamist revolt generally and al Qaeda terrorism in particular is primarily aimed at governments *within* the Islamic world, especially those consistently accused of both corruption and 'un-Islamic' practices. Yet the rise of Islamist groups across a swathe of Arab countries and elsewhere in the Muslim world is not *only* consequential to failings of *individual* regimes – it is also the result of the failure of modernisation promises to deliver generally beneficial outcomes. That is, the contemporary Islamist resurgence – of which al Qaeda is an aspect but not of course the whole story – carries within it popular disillusionment at developmental and societal failures as well as widespread disgust at the spectre of corrupt and unrepresentative governments which, to add insult to injury, consistently refuse meaningfully to democratise political systems. As a result, confronted by state power that seeks to destroy or control communitarian structures and replace them with an idea of a national citizenry based on the link between state and individual, Islamist groups are to many Muslims important vehicles of popular political aspirations (Strindberg and Wärn, 2011).

It is useful to think of 'political Islam' as a variable and varied political ideology, as it is not necessarily associated with radicalism or extremism. Various expressions of political Islam are undoubtedly radical – for example, post-revolutionary Iran or Afghanistan, when governed by the Taliban between 1996 and 2001 – or extremist, such as al Qaeda and assorted Islamist terrorists from Morocco to Indonesia. But what the latter examples have in common – a willingness to use extremist tactics in order to achieve their political goals – does not imply that they see the world in the same way from a shared religious perspective. For example, the government of Shia Iran has evolved a unique system of administration which has almost nothing in common – beyond the rather opaque idea of a pursuit of 'Islamic principles' – with the form of government expressed in neighbouring Afghanistan by the Sunni Taliban in 1996–2001. Much more common are the myriad groups in the Muslim world which can be described as 'moderate', implying they eschew extremist tactics. Over the last two decades, Islamically orientated candidates and political parties in Algeria, Tunisia, Morocco, Egypt, Lebanon, Turkey, Jordan, Kuwait, Bahrain, Pakistan, Malaysia and Indonesia have all sought to utilise pluralistic pathways to electoral success. They have contested and won seats at both local and national levels, been invited to serve in cabinets and, in some cases, achieved power, as in Turkey, Egypt and Tunisia. Over the last decade, elections in, inter alia, Bahrain, Egypt, Iraq, Kuwait, Morocco, Palestine, Pakistan, Saudi Arabia, Tunisia and Turkey, have served to highlight the political salience of 'Islam' in numerous countries. Some such groups, it should be noted, are highly controversial, espousing militancy which has not necessarily endeared them to democrats everywhere; examples include Hezbollah in Lebanon and Hamas in Palestine. In both cases, however, the organisations combine the attributes of successful guerrilla groups with those of viable, grass roots-orientated political parties, which have achieved massive electoral successes.

Seeking to come up with workable policies in order to respond adequately to both 'moderate' and 'extremist' political Islam, Western foreign policy makers must learn to acquire better understandings of how global Muslim majorities see the world, including the West. A 2011 opinion survey, involving nearly 14,000 people in 14 countries by both telephone and face-to-face interviews, was conducted by the US-based Pew Research Center. It found that majorities in several mainly Muslim countries – the Palestinian Territories, Turkey, Lebanon, Egypt and Jordan – believed that 'relations are poor' between Muslims and Westerners, as did majorities in France, Germany, Spain and Britain. The same poll revealed that large majorities in Russia, Germany, USA, Britain, France and Spain were concerned about 'Islamic extremism', as were over half the respondents in various Muslim majority countries: the Palestinian Territories, Egypt, Lebanon, Pakistan, and Turkey (http://www.pewglobal.org/2011/07/21/muslim-western-tensions-persist/).

Such concerns can be linked to the ideas expressed in Huntington's 1996 book, *The Clash of Civilizations and the Remaking of the World Order*. Huntington's central argument is still widely discussed. That is, that the primary axis of conflict in the post-Cold War world would be along cultural and religious lines, a source of much ideologically fuelled violence and conflict. The findings in the large Pew Research Center survey highlight that, over a decade after 9/11, the tensions and distrust which that event helped to stimulate or reflect have still not gone away. In the dozen years since 9/11, there have been several international efforts to undermine the idea that civilisational conflict is a key feature of inter-national relations and to seek to build trust. In 2005, under the auspices of the United Nations (UN), the governments of Spain and Turkey established the 'Alliance of Civilizations'. The main aim of the Alliance of Civilizations is to improve understanding and encourage coopera-tive relations among nations and peoples across cultures and religions. Linked to this is a second objective: to seek to 'counter the forces that fuel polarisation and extremism' (http://www.unaoc.org/about/).

Since Huntington's contributions in the mid-1990s to the debate about civilisations and their propensity for violence and conflict with each other, a growing literature has emerged on the topic. Petito (2007, 2009) notes that partly in response to Huntington's claims, a counter argument has developed – starting with calls for a *dialogue* of civilisations – which eventually became institutionalised as the Alliance of Civilizations under UN auspices. The more general context for this development was the post-1989 debate on the future of world order, as noted in Chapter 1. That is, how to develop what is increasingly seen as a political necessity: a more peaceful, multicultural and just world order. Since 9/11, the idea of a dialogue of civilisations – and its related components of inter-cultural and inter-religious dialogue – has been the subject of a proliferation of public initiatives and international meetings, a level of interest which has not so far been seen in nor duplicated in IR writings.

A former UN Secretary General, Kofi Annan, formed an 18-person expert group – known as the 'High-level Group' – to look into the issue of civilisational conflict.[3] The High-level Group sought to achieve two main tasks: first, to explore what currently causes 'polarisation' between different societies and cultures, and, second, to determine a practical programme of action to address this issue. At the end of their deliberations, the High-level Group compiled and circulated a report providing analysis and practical recommendations forming the basis for the implementation plan of the United Nations Alliance of Civilizations (UNAOC). Following the report of the High-level Group, a former president of Portugal, Jorge Sampaio, was appointed in April 2007 as the High Representative for the UNAOC by current UN Secretary-General Ban Ki-moon. Sampaio's main task was to lead the implementation phase of what is now known as the 'Alliance of Civilizations' (www.unaoc.org/). From 2007, the UNAOC Secretariat, based in New York, sought to work with a network of partners, including: governments, international and regional organisations, civil society groups, foundations, and the private sector. The overall objective was to improve cross-cultural relations between sometimes diverse nations and communities. At the grass-roots level, UNAOC promotes various projects focused in four areas: youth, media, education and migration – that collectively seek to build trust, reconciliation and mutual respect.

In addition to the Alliance of Civilizations, there are also other high-level international attempts aiming to help build inter-civilisational trust. They include: actions by the United Nations Educational, Scientific and Cultural Organisation in support of the dialogue of civilisations (www.unesco.org/dialogue2001); the Islamic Educational, Scientific and Cultural Organisation (ISESCO) programmes on dialogue of civilisations, under the auspices of the 57-member Organisation of Islamic Cooperation (www.isesco.org.ma); a Russian-led initiative, the World Public

Forum 'Dialogue of Civilizations' (http://www.wpfdc.org/index.php?lang=en) and an initiative organised by a lay Catholic organisation, the Sant'-Egidio community, entitled 'International Meetings: Peoples and Religions' (www.santegidio.org/).

The UNAOC in particular has been critiqued by those who are not convinced of its ability to make a beneficial difference. Riem Spielhaus, a research fellow at the Centre for European Islamic Thought, Copenhagen, contends that the UNAOC starts from a disadvantage 'when it comes to making concrete progress as it is shackled by its own terminology. The two sides are often portrayed in simplistic terms'. In a 2010 interview in the German newspaper, *Deutsche Welle*, Spielhaus argued the main problem with the UNAOC approach is that it stems from a 'binary' – that is, comprising two autonomous parts – approach emphasised in the terminology of 'the West' and 'Islam'. While 'dialogue and direct communications between individuals are to be preferred to violent conflicts', she added, 'it remains questionable whether they will lead to solutions or further partitions if the terminology remains binary' (Amies, 2010). Another negative appraisal of the UNAOC comes from, David Bosold, head of the German Council for Foreign Relations' Forum on International Strategic Thinking, who argues that the UNAOC lacks fundamental ability to achieve its desired results (Amies, 2010). For Bosold, the main problem is that the UNAOC is top-down and lacks consistent connection with civil society organisations.

> UN initiatives such as the AoC are only useful in terms of symbolic politics by creating a more open atmosphere for political discussions among political leaders . . . In order to achieve concrete results, AoC lacks at least three aspects: it is not able to connect with civil society in both the Islamic world and the West in order to bring significant parts from both sides into a permanent dialogue; it is elite-driven and not a grass roots-level endeavour, notwithstanding its pretension to achieve that very end.
>
> (Aes, 2010)

The problem is made worse, according to Bosold, because the UNAOC does not have a framework outside that of the UN. Many now argue that the UN is simply not central to international relations in the ways it was planned to be when founded after the Second World War in 1945. This is a problem because the UN is recently seen to have lost relevance in international affairs. As Bosold argues, 'Since the Secretary Generals of the UN have increasingly lost the ability to set the international agenda, I don't see how this problem might be remedied when it comes to the AoC' (Amies, 2010).

## Conclusion

In this chapter we looked at some fundamental issues concerning the roles of religion in the context of conflict, conflict resolution, and peacemaking and building in today's international relations. Regarding conflict, we saw that inter-religion tensions and competition are often implicated in the 'politics of identity' which can lead to often serious conflicts between groups which see themselves as the defenders of their own identity against others' attacks. We also examined the potential and actual role of religious leaders and their organisations in attempts at conflict resolution and peacemaking and peacebuilding. While the contexts, issues, and religious faiths and actors differ from country to country, the common factor is that while religious causes of conflict receive much public attention, religious peacemakers' efforts in conflict resolution and peacebuilding tends to get much less attention and publicity, even when they are successful (Smock, 2004; Appleby, 2006). Research indicates, and this chapter would underline, that religious faith can encourage both religious leaders and the organisations they represent meaningfully to work towards resolving conflicts and develop peace (Bouta et al., 2005; Abu-Nimer and Augsburger, 2009). This is reflected in the fact that growing numbers of religious organisations seem to be looking for opportunities to promote peace, including in circumstances where religion itself is seen to contribute to conflict (United States Institute for Peace, 2003; Abu-Nimer and Augsburger, 2009).

Overall, it may be that, as a result of increased public recognition and support and development of more effective peacemaking strategies, conflict resolution and peacemaking skills of religious leaders are now developing towards achievement of their undoubted potential. Peacemaking ability is likely to develop in this way when, acting under the auspices of a religious group, individuals and their groups are seen to contain high moral standing, credibility, and stature, to the extent that they can be regarded by all interested parties as neutral in conflict situations. However, peacemaking should not only be about short-term building of peace, but should in addition aim to develop restorative justice and/or the establishment of what are considered 'right relationships' between formerly conflicting groups through acknowledgement of each other's position and accountability of those acting on behalf of religious communities. In some cases, however, religious individuals and organisations may enter a conflict situation and focus primarily on trying to resolve its immediate manifestations while not looking as closely at the structural problems that underlie the conflict and trying to work towards addressing important background issues that make conflict more likely.

We also looked at the United Nations Alliance of Civilizations, whose formation a few years ago was a direct result of the challenge to international peace and cooperation posed what see saw as an emerging post-Cold War 'clash of civilisations' (Huntington, 1993, 1996; for a counter view, see Petito, 2007, 2009). We saw that despite its no doubt commendable objectives, critics claim that the UNAOC is not an especially worthwhile medium as it may not be capable of achieving its goals. The main problem is perceived to be that the UNAOC is no more than a high-profile debating club, lacking focus, clout and capacity actually to change the conditions and issues that it seeks to improve. For example, regarding relations between two perceived distinct entities – 'the West' and 'the Muslim world' – it is sometimes contended that the latter has different values compared to those of 'the West', and that this is a source of competition, friction, and sometimes conflict. However, is the real issue alleged incompatibility of two sets of religion and culture, or is it more to do with international politics? For example, contemporary jihadism à la al Qaeda is clearly stimulated to a considerable degree by generic anti-Western focus, especially a pronounced anti-Americanism, perhaps given impetus by the US and other Western governments' support of egregiously undemocratic governments in the Middle East and the Muslim world more generally.

We noted recent opinion poll results which indicate that there is undoubtedly mutual suspicion, fear and misunderstanding between some Muslims and some Westerners. This has developed since 9/11 in particular. Yet, it is important to stress that it is *not* a clash driven by deep, unbridgeable civilisational differences but by extremists, in both the West and the Muslim world, who concur on the desirability of exploiting post-9/11 instability and suspicion between the world's cultures. Neither side knows about or wants to know about each other, it appears. Instead, they appear to be content to function as mutually hostile mirror images of each other. A shared lack of information on both sides helps fuel hostility and suspicion and does not make it plain that what is most apparent about 'Islam' and the 'West' is not their mutual differences but rather the diversity within both 'worlds'. The point is that both the 'West' and the world of 'Islam' are presented by the extremists as undivided blocks – even though the reality is that both are highly diverse, not least when it comes to how religion is regarded at both political and societal levels.

Finally, what is the potential of inter-civilisational dialogue to reduce tensions in one of the world's conflict hot spots, the Middle East, as well as more generally? *If* there is *realistically* potential to identify common ground and manage subsequently to develop dialogue based on areas of commonality, then it may be possible to foresee potential – and of course meaningful – negotiations between the government of Israel and the Palestinian leaders. This issue is widely seen as pivotal, as foundational, in attempts to make the Middle East region more not less conflict-prone. In this context, inter-religious dialogue could be a significant factor in helping achieve progress towards a lasting peace between Israel and the Palestinians as well as more generally. However, it would be naive to claim that injecting increased or better focused inter-civilisational/inter-religious dialogue into the situation would on its own lead to sudden or remarkable peace breakthroughs. This observation is informed by the fact that recent escalation of tensions in the Middle East have occurred *despite* the widespread agreement that increased (inter-religious) dialogue will improve chances of success in resolution of deep seated conflicts. In addition, the role of US foreign policy – in unconditionally supporting Israel – is problematic. It serves not only to aggravate pre-existing inter- and intra-religious tensions but also makes the pursuit of common ground – an essential first step – more not less difficult.

# Notes

1. UN Resolutions A/RES/52/13 1998: Culture of Peace and A/RES/53/243, 1999: Declaration and Programme of Action on a Culture of Peace, available at: http://www.unesco.org/cpp/uk/projects/2000res.htm.

2. 'Religions for Peace is the largest international coalition of representatives from the world's great religions dedicated to promoting peace. Respecting religious differences while celebrating our common humanity, Religions for Peace is active on every continent and in some of the most troubled areas of the world, creating multi-religious partnerships to confront our most dire issues: stopping war, ending poverty, and protecting the earth. Religious communities are the largest and best-organized civil institutions in the world, claiming the allegiance of billions across race, class, and national divides. These communities have particular cultural understandings, infrastructures, and resources to get help where it is needed most.

   Founded in 1970, Religions for Peace enables these communities to unleash their enormous potential for common action. Some of Religions for Peace's recent successes include building a new climate of reconciliation in Iraq; mediating dialogue among warring factions in Sierra Leone; organizing an international network of religious women's organizations; and establishing an extraordinary program to assist the millions of children affected by Africa's AIDS pandemic, the Hope for African Children Initiative' (http://www.religionsforpeace.org/about/).

3. Membership of the group can be found at: http://www.un.org/News/Press/docs/2005/sgsm10073.doc.htm.

## Questions

- Does the involvement of religion in a conflict make it easier or more difficult to resolve?
- Why do the teachings of most religions refer to both peace and conflict?
- Does conflict resolution work?
- What is more important: the Alliance of Civilizations or the Clash of Civilizations?

## Further reading

R. Scott Appleby, *The Ambivalence of the Sacred: Religion, Violence and Reconciliation*, Lanham, MD: Rowman and Littlefield, 2000. Appleby describes how both terrorists and peacemakers can emerge from the same community, and be followers of the same religion. One kills while the other strives for reconciliation. Appleby explains what religious terrorists and religious peacemakers share in common, what causes them to take different paths in fighting injustice, and how a deeper understanding of religious extremism can and must be integrated more effectively into our thinking about tribal, regional and international conflict.

T. Bouta, S. Ayse Kadayifci-Orellana, and M. Abu-Nimer, *Faith-Based Peace-building: Mapping and Analysis of Christian, Muslim, and Multi-faith Actors*, The Hague: Netherlands Institute of International Relations, 2005. This is a useful introduction to interfaith dialogue three specific religions: Christianity, Judaism and Islam.

D. Johnston, *Religion, Terror, and Error: U.S. Foreign Policy and the Challenge of Spiritual Engagement*, New York: Praeger, 2011. How should the United States deal with the jihadist challenge and other religious imperatives that permeate today's geopolitical landscape? Johnston argues that what is required is a longer-term strategy of cultural engagement, backed by a deeper understanding of how others view the world and what is important to them. The means by which that can be accomplished are the subject of this book.

M. Juergensmeyer, *Terror in the Mind of God: The Global Rise of Religious Violence*, Berkeley: University of California Press, 2000. Juergensmeyer documents the global rise of religious terrorism while seeking to comprehend the 'odd attraction of religion and violence'. Basing his study on scholarly sources, media accounts and personal interviews with convicted terrorists, Juergensmeyer exercises caution with the term 'terrorist'. He prefers to emphasise the large religious community of supporters who make violent acts possible rather than the relatively small number who carry them out. Juergensmeyer identifies certain 'cultures of violence' in many religions (Christianity, Judaism, Islam, Hinduism, Sikhism and Buddhism).

# Part Three

# Country and regional focus

# 9 | The United States of America

The Constitution of the United States of America (USA) makes it clear that there should be no institutionalised links between religion and politics. This is explicitly stated in the first amendment of the Constitution – 'Congress shall make no law respecting an establishment of religion or prohibiting the free exercise thereof'. The current understanding is that this implies that politics and religion belong to separate realms. Although some contest this interpretation of the non-admissibility of mixing religion and politics in the USA (see, for example, Patterson, 2011), it is the case that unlike some European countries there has never been an institutionalised relationship between religion and politics. For example, in some European countries – including, Germany, Italy and Sweden, Christian Democratic parties have been influential for decades. However, as Reichley (1986: 23) notes, 'religion has always played an important part in American politics'. The relationship between the two goes back to the republic's founders who commonly drew on religious values and rhetoric when forming the new nation at the end of the eighteenth century following the defeat of British colonialism. Over the next decades, Christian churches became centrally involved in the controversy about slavery and the resulting US civil war (1861–65). During the twentieth century, Christian churches were also active in various campaigns, including: prohibition of the sale of alcohol, enactment of women's right to vote, New Deal measures to increase social welfare in the 1930s, and the passage of laws covering increased civil and political rights for African-Americans in the 1960s (Wald, 2003).

It is important to bear in mind, however, that separation of Church and State, as specified in the US Constitution, guarantees freedom of religion. Many analysts argue that the USA is an anomaly among developed, Western countries, as many among its people are regarded

191

as religious, measured primarily by the proportion of Americans who regularly attend religious services (Green, 2000). Yet, in contrast to many Western European countries, such as Britain or Sweden, there are no universally accepted symbols of the polity in the USA, such as monarchy (for example, Britain) or State Church (for example, Sweden: The Church of Sweden, or *Svenska kyrkan*). Instead, as discussed below, the values and rituals of *civil religion* traditionally provided unofficial means of articulating national identity in the USA.

Religious voices from various Christian denominations are currently politically significant in the USA. Some groups of religious actors, notably conservative Christians gathered together under the rubric of the Christian or Religious Right, have been particularly important – not least because they were significant to the outcomes of the 2000 and 2004 presidential elections, contests that led to the election and re-election of a born-again Christian George W. Bush, and may be influential again in the 2012 presidential poll. In recent years, in addition, various Christian groups, including the conservative Protestants who mainly comprise the Christian/Religious Right, have had a growing foreign policy voice, influencing US policy in various ways (L. Taylor, 2005; Hehir et al., 2004; Haynes, 2008b; Patterson, 2011; Byrnes, 2011). In order to explain and account for the political significance of the Religious Right – in both domestic and international contexts – this chapter has the following structure. We start by looking at the general issue of religion and politics in the USA in order to understand why the Religious Right has recently become an important political actor. After that, we examine both the Religious Right and another group of influential Christians: US Catholics. Finally, we look at the influence of the Religious Right in relation to two recent and current foreign policy issues: (1) the conflict in Iraq and the 'War on Terror', and (2) an 'evangelised' foreign policy, involving an inter-religion coalition, led by the Religious Rights, which focuses on religious freedom in global 'black spots', including North Korea and Sudan.

## Religion and politics in the USA

In the USA, the allowable limit of 'religious expression by public authority' continues to generate a lively and continuing debate among Americans

(Wald, 1991: 238; Patterson, 2011: 1–15). The controversy is not new: the US political system has long presented a fertile environment for the expression of religious differences in the public realm, despite the official predominance of a secular political environment (Wald, 2003). Prospects for a religious presence in public life in America are, however, high owing to several factors: first, unlike most Western Europeans, a large proportion of Americans – said variously to be between 40 and 70 per cent, astonishingly high by Western standards (Norris and Inglehart, 2004) – regularly attend religious services, attesting to the high popular regard that many Americans have for religion in their personal lives.[1] Second, religious affiliation and ethnic identity have long been connected in the USA. Third, there is a remarkable diversity of religious opinion in the country. Because of these factors, religion is an important feature in defining terms of political competition in America (Wald, 2003).

According to Wald (1991: 241), religion in America has political significance 'through such diverse paths as the impact of sacred values on political perceptions, the growing interaction between complex religious organisations and State regulatory agencies, the role of congregational involvement in political mobilisation and the functionality of Churches as a political resource for disadvantaged groups'. This is not to imply that things have remained static: America's progress towards modernity has greatly affected its people's patterns of religious commitment. This is because modernity – according to Thomas (2005: 143), the USA is the most 'modern' country in the world – has long encouraged tendencies towards both religious *differentiation* – that is, there are a great many extant religions *and* divisions within religions – and religious *voluntarism*, that is, people increasingly feel that their religious choices are less an ascriptive trait, conferred by birth, and more a matter of choice and discretionary involvement (Wald, 2003).

To examine these issues, in this chapter we focus upon two significant religious organisations in the USA: the Religious (or Christian) Right and the Roman Catholic Church. Both have had influence on US foreign policy. We seek to answer three specific questions:

- *To what extent are religious actors politically important in the USA?*
- *Has religion recently gained increased political and social prominence?*
  For four decades – from the 1930s to the 1960s – there was little

**193**

consistent engagement in US politics from religious organisations. At this time, while the USA was characterised by high levels of piety, religion was effectively 'privatised', that is, without sustained public or political influence. Some groups however managed intermittent influence, for example, some Christian Churches played a significant part in the Civil Rights movement of the 1960s. One Christian leader, Dr Martin Luther King, was particularly prominent in this context; and he paid for it with his life: he was assassinated in 1968. King was both a Baptist minister and figurehead of the Southern Christian Leadership Conference. In addition, at the time of the Vietnam War in the 1960s and early 1970s, various Christian leaders – especially from the Catholic Church – were prominent in anti-war peace protests. Now, however, various religious actors, notably but not exclusively from among the Religious Right, are *consistently* involved in an array of socio-political issues.

- *What happens when there is religious involvement in America's foreign policy?*

## Civil religion and church–state relations

We start with an examination of the concept of *civil religion* and outline the main features of church–state relations in the USA.

### Civil religion

Robbins and Anthony define civil religion as the 'complex of shared religio-political meanings that articulate a sense of common national purpose and that rationalize the needs and purposes of the broader community' (Robbins and Anthony, 1982: 10). According to Coleman (1996: 27), 'American civil religion has a complex relationship with the polity – a relationship that reflects the history of the United States'. Traditionally, religious belief was not associated with any single political position in America; instead, the language of *civil religion* was intended to be used by all. From the 1970s, however, the contribution of religion to political culture and the judicial sphere underwent significant change. Not least, certain religious groups, notably the Religious Right, developed comprehensive political agendas consistently couched in religious terms (Reichley, 2002). In addition, over time religious cleavages did not disappear as America modernised. Instead, religious alignments were redefined, with group differences extending to new social and political issues.

## BOX 9.1 Rousseau and Bellah on civil religion

The American State historically attempted to create the concept of civil religion as a unifying ideology. The Swiss philosopher Jean-Jacques Rousseau (1712–78) first used the term *civil religion* in *The Social Contract*, originally published in 1762 (Rousseau, 2004). For Rousseau, civil religion referred to the religious dimension of a polity; over time, the term became an important concept in the sociology of religion, largely through the work of an American, Robert Bellah. In an influential article published in 1967, 'Civil religion in America', Bellah attempted to define the notion of a civic faith and assess its significance in the history of post-colonial America. To Bellah, civil religion is the *generalised* religion of the 'American way of life', existing with its own integrity alongside the more particularistic faiths of Judaism and the various Christian denominations. The concept of civil religion in America underpins the idea that a democratic United States is the prime agent of God in history, implying a collective faith that the American nation serves a transcendent purpose in history. While, as already noted, the political and religious spheres are differentiated structurally in America, civil religion nonetheless theoretically furnishes a symbolic way to unite the two.

Like Alexis de Tocqueville (2003 [1835]), who visited America in 1831, the contemporary American political scientist Robert Bellah saw civil religion in the USA as essential to restrain the self-interested elements of American liberalism, turning them instead towards public spirited forms of citizenship that allow republican institutions to both survive and thrive. Bellah argued that civil religion was a fundamental requisite for stable democracy in America, given the United States' highly pluralistic and individualistic culture. He also contended that civil religion made a positive contribution to societal integration by binding a fractious people around a common goal, imparting a sacred character to civic obligation. For Bellah, the generic concept of civil religion also provided an important public manifestation of religion, as opposed to the more privatised orientations of particular faiths. For him, of specific interest was the problem posed both by the increasing structural differentiation of private from public sectors and by growing religious diversity, which together made general acceptance of a shared conception of moral order and cosmos increasingly implausible. Bellah also claimed that civil religion in America was the medium through which people perceived common values in a society built, on the one hand, on ideals of mutual tolerance and unity and, on the other, on cultural and religious pluralism. Ironically, however, just as Bellah was relaying his views about civil religion in the late 1960s, things were beginning to change.

## BOX 9.2 Bellah's *The Broken Covenant*

In *The Broken Covenant* (1975 [1992]) Bellah's ideas about the unifying power of civil religion were undermined by the social changes that served to erode public confidence in the US 'project', significantly represented by the concept of civil religion and helping to weaken the shared religious tradition that traditionally had sustained faith in the republic. Over time, national reverses and scandals collectively shattered the erstwhile social consensus so central to the plausibility of civil religion as a concept. They included the Vietnam War (1954–75; USA involved, 1961–75) and the political scandal called 'Watergate' that led to the resignation of President Richard Nixon in August 1974. In addition, societal unity was undermined over time by societal fragmentation and various moral and ethical issues, including: the issue of decriminalisation of 'soft' drugs, such as cannabis; gender- and race-based discrimination; abortion rights; increased rates of male/female cohabitation, without marriage; permissiveness towards sexual expression in art and literature; reduced sanctions against homosexuality; and a Supreme Court decision prohibiting public prayers in school. For some, especially within the burgeoning Religious Right, these changes collectively reflected an abhorrent, fundamental, shift away from traditional Judaeo-Christian morality which fatally undermined civil religion as a unifying concept.

In sum, whereas civil religion was once widely viewed as a crucial component in an understanding of the USA as a unified society, held together by shared religious agreement about morality and ethics and considered of central importance to the health of American public life, over time things fragmented (Green, 2000). The civil religion ideal was seriously eroded by various national political setbacks and scandals from the 1970s, some of which had their roots in foreign policy reverses, such as the Vietnam War. Today, it is sometimes argued that the concept of civil religion in the USA is dead. Others maintain, however, that it is still a force with which to be reckoned. For Wald (1991: 256), 'if the core of the concept [is] the tendency to hold the nation accountable to divine standards, then the case can be made that US political culture has actually been revitalised by the rise of the "New Christian Right" (NCR)'. We turn to this point shortly.

## Religious fragmentation and politics

During the 1970s, the USA was greatly affected by both internal and external factors that significantly undermined the sense of national identity. Later, in the 1990s and the first decade of the 2000s, growing numbers of Americans were seriously afflicted by interlinked economic, political and cultural insecurities. Many angry white people blamed African-Americans and immigrants for taking their jobs, while unemployed African-Americans looked to blame the Hispanics. Out of a population of more than 300 million, around 40 million Americans – nearly one-tenth – had no health insurance, while the wages of working-class Americans fell in real terms by nearly 20 per cent compared to the 1970s. The impact of globalisation, was to 'downsize' the supply of middle management jobs, while manufacturing jobs were 'exported' to low-wage Asian countries – especially China and Vietnam – and to South America, notably Mexico, the USA's southern neighbour. Meanwhile, the richest 2 per cent of the US population controlled the majority of the wealth (Abramsky, 1996: 18). A single company, communications giant AT &T, shed 40,000 jobs, while its chief executive enjoyed a $5 million (£3.2 million) rise in the value of his share options. In short, the USA was racked by scapegoating and chronic insecurity in the 1990s. Then 9/11 occurred (Hassner, 2002).

In the 1990s, what was originally an ideological left–right *vertical* split in American politics became a *horizontal* split. On the one hand, there were the elites and the educated, who for the most part believed in the benefits of globalisation. On the other hand, there were many further down the socio-economic scale who feared globalisation for its apparent deleterious effects on jobs and security (Hacker and Pierson, 2005). What was the impact of globalisation on religion in politics in the USA? Once a speechwriter for Richard Nixon, the discredited president forced to resign in 1974 as a result of the Watergate scandal, Pat

Buchanan was able to gain some credible early victories in Republican caucuses and primaries in the presidential election campaign of 1996. He managed this not only by stressing his conservative religious views but also his economic nationalism: he claimed that, if elected, he would pull America back from the North American Free Trade Association and the World Trade Organisation. Given the manifest insecurities affecting many millions of Americans, it was unsurprising that such populism was widely appealing. Buchanan's economic guru was Ludwig Erhard, the architect of Germany's post-war economic reconstruction, who devised the thesis that economics is not simply a series of equations but a philosophy which takes note of the human soul, an idea enshrined in Buchanan's notion of 'conservatism of the heart'. In the 1996 presidential race Buchanan was initially able to attract many of the so-called 'Reagan Democrats', disaffected blue-collar workers who feared the loss of their jobs as a result of globalisation. Buchanan achieved his best results in areas of the country where politically and socially conservative Christian evangelicals were most numerous, notably the South.

Buchanan's short-lived electoral success, linked to his being voted for by many Christian conservatives, is not evidence that growing material insecurity persuaded Americans to *return* to religion, because they never left it. Rooted in a unique historical legacy, there is both religious pluralism and vibrancy in the United States. As Bruce notes, this is contrary to what the secularisation thesis proposes: religious pluralism is associated in the United States with increased – rather than diminished – religious adherence (Bruce, 1992: 5). To understand why this is the case, we need to bear in mind that, to a considerable degree, religious dissenters from Europe forged the fledgling American nation in the late eighteenth and early nineteenth centuries. Such people understood that elimination of state-established churches and a guarantee of religious freedom were the price of a reasonable degree of civil cordiality in a pluralistic society. Ironically, Christian churches thrived when cut loose from the paternalistic hand of government; evangelical activism became – and continues to be – a phenomenon of and force in society, boosted significantly by the activities of numerous 'televangelists' ('television evangelists'), including Pat Robertson, Oral Roberts and Kenneth Copeland.[2] Statistics measuring religiosity in the USA confirm the deep-rootedness and longevity of religious adherence, *not* its revival (Norris and Ingelhart,

2004). As a result, we can note that, like their parents and grandparents, most Americans are people who have religious beliefs, especially a belief in God: nearly three-quarters of Americans claim membership of a church, and more than 90 per cent express belief in God (Hertzke, 1989: 298).

Pollsters and scholars often focus on the politically salient religious cleavages in American society, in part because they seem to be changing fast. There is a traditional tripartite split among Christians. A 1978 poll indicated that Catholics comprised approximately 30 per cent of the population; 'mainline', that is, moderate or liberal, Protestant Churches – the Episcopalian (the US equivalent of the Church of England), the Lutheran and the Methodist – encompassed 35 per cent; and 22 per cent identified themselves as evangelical Christians. Jews accounted for 5–7 per cent, and Muslims, Hindus and Sikhs numbered about 4 per cent each, around 12 per cent in total. Nine per cent of Americans regard themselves as 'secularists' (Kepel, 1994: 104).

The 1978 poll was conducted in the middle of a 25-year decline in membership of the mainline Protestant denominations – which eventually led to a loss of one-third of members – that did not level off until the late 1980s. Theologically conservative evangelical churches, conversely, saw dramatic growth in the same period, reflecting a major restructuring of religious alignments. The evangelical Southern Baptist Convention, for example, is now by far the largest Protestant denomination in America with around 16 million members. Other fast-growing churches include the Assemblies of God, Nazarenes, Seventh Day Adventists, and the Mormons, while the fastest-growing church in the South is the New Covenant Fellowship, an evangelical interdenominational group. Sociologist Dean Kelley explains the trend towards such churches in the following way: 'While the mainline Churches have tried to support the political and economic claims of [US] society's minorities and outcasts, it is the sectarian groups that have had most success in attracting new members from these very sectors of society' (Kelley, 1986: xxv).

There are four distinct religious groupings in the USA, roughly comparable in terms of the numbers of those adhering to them: (a) mainline Protestants; (b) conservative, often evangelical, Protestant Christians; (c) Roman Catholics; and (d) 'others' (including Jews, Muslims, Sikhs, Hindus, atheists and agnostics) (Kohut and Rogers, 2002). Note, however, that patterns of religious adherence are not static. The proportion of both mainline Protestants and Catholics is declining, while that of conservative evangelical Christians and 'others' are increasing (Bates, 2006, 2008).

What does this imply for the relationship between religion and politics in the USA, both domestically and in relation to the country's international relations? We can note the following in relation to domestic factors. First, traditional, politically salient Protestant–Catholic divisions that once virtually defined US society have been replaced over time by a split between, on the one hand, mainly conservative evangelical Protestant Christians and, on the other, theologically liberal Christians (Hertzke, 1989: 298; Fowler et al., 2010). Until the 1940s, the politically salient division between early and later immigrants principally hinged on the fact that the former were solidly Protestant and the latter firmly Catholic (Casanova, 1994: 168). Yet division was not expressed in religious terms per se, rather it focused largely on questions about social welfare and labour policy; that is, the chief electoral issue was the clash between the 'haves' – in the main, mainline Protestants – and the 'have nots' – often recent Catholic immigrants. After the Second World War, the Democratic Party bound together most Catholics, Jews and evangelical Protestants – white and black alike – largely because they were outsiders, prompting them to form a de facto coalition to contest the electoral ground with their rivals: 'mainline' Protestant Republicans. Until about 1960 this electoral equation held; afterwards it was increasingly likely that Catholics, Protestants, and to a certain degree African-Americans and Jews, engaged politically under the banner of either party (Wald, 1991: 265; 2003).

In 1992 mainline Protestants voted narrowly for the Democratic challenger Bill Clinton against the incumbent Republican president, George H. W. Bush (42/37 per cent). Twenty per cent voted for the 'third force' maverick, Ross Perot. This closely reflected the overall national vote. Conservative born-again Christians provided core support for Jimmy Carter's presidential campaign in 1976, Ronald Reagan's in 1980 and 1984, that of the 'televangelist' Baptist preacher Pat Robertson in 1988, the conservative Catholic Pat Buchanan's in 1992 and 1996, and the campaigns of George W. Bush in 2000 and 2004. The psephological point is that even though numbers of mostly conservative evangelical Christians increased over time, until recently they did not exhibit high levels of electoral solidarity. Consequently, what might be called 'the right-wing Christian vote' was unable decisively to determine the outcome of presidential elections in the 1990s. But in both 2000 and 2004, conservative evangelical Christians were pivotal in George W. Bush's electoral triumphs (Green et al., 2005). In 2008, however, no one candidate was able to acquire the votes of this constituency, largely because neither of the candidates – Barack Obama and John McCain – were judged to be sufficiently 'Christian' or 'conservative' (Fowler et al., 2010).

'Moderate' American Roman Catholics, however, were by no means uniform politically; for example, they were not monolithically anti-abortion. For 40 years, following the Second Vatican Council ('Vatican 2') in 1965, US Catholics were divided between: (1) devout and regular worshippers who largely accepted the teachings of the Church on birth control and abortion, and (2) people whose Church attendance was more casual and who lived with little apparent regard to papal encyclicals. In 1992 and 1996, Catholics voted for Clinton over his Republican challenger, slightly more pro-Clinton than the national average. In the 2000 and 2004 elections, conversely, Catholics switched to George W. Bush in significant numbers (Duin, 2004). In the latter year, it is estimated that the president increased his vote by nine million, of which seven million were Catholics, even though his challenger – John Kerry – was himself a Catholic (Green et al., 2005). In 2008, an estimated 54 per cent of US Catholics voted for Barack Obama, a position 'at odds with the Church's stance on issues such as abortion and same-sex marriage, despite the urging of more than 50 heads of dioceses to support pro-life candidate' (Swanson, 2008).

The 'others' are a motley group: Hindus, Jews, Muslims, Sikhs and secularists, collectively the most loyal Democratic base. In 1992, they went for Clinton over Bush by a heavy margin of 63 to 26 per cent, with an additional 10 per cent voting for Perot (Walker, 1996). Whereas the Jews have traditionally been of political importance, 'exercis[ing] impressive influence through robust organisations, eminent leadership, and focused political agendas', they have recently been out of the political spotlight; instead, Muslims, have 'emerged as a visible political force', the result of both immigration and conversions of inner city African-Americans (Hertzke, 1989: 299). In the 2000 and 2004 elections, despite the hopes of the Bush campaign, only about a quarter of American Jews voted for George W. Bush (Besser, 2004; L. Taylor, 2005). In 2008, around three-quarters of American Jews voted for Obama ('2008 Jewish Vote for Obama Exceeds All Expectations', 2008).

Over time the traditional Protestant–Catholic division was replaced by a fragmentation of religious–political alignments: new patterns of group affiliation focusing primarily on moral and social issues, including, inter alia, recreational drug use, pornography, homosexuality, abortion and marital fidelity. The result was 'a pronounced attitudinal gap between practising Christians and non-believers', revealing distinctive religious preferences which do not conform to the historical dimension previously defining religious conflict on public issues (Wald, 1991: 265–266).

In the next section, we examine two influential religious constituencies – (1) the Religious Right, and (2) US Catholics – before turning to the issue of their significance for America's international relations.

## Politically significant religious groups in the USA

### The Religious Right

It used to be said that every four years at the time of the US presidential elections, American and foreign journalists rediscovered religion. This was the periodic occasion when the media scented the electoral possibilities of the influence on electoral outcomes of the Religious Right, the politically influential corpus of millions of mostly 'born again', socially and politically conservative Protestant Christians. This interest reflected the fact that the Religious Right has become a significant domestic political lobby group. An early classification, the 'New Christian Right', was used in the 1970s to refer to a surge in political activity among Protestant fundamentalists and conservative evangelicals. Over time, however, its usage has become more flexible, sometimes referring to a broad community of generic religious conservatives and at other times referring to a small subset of institutionalised organisations pursuing goals characterised by cultural, social and political conservatism. Prior to the 1970s, the US conservative evangelical movement was a subculture, largely keeping its distance from electoral politics. But with a new focus on social conservatism, around the time of the presidency of Ronald Reagan (1981–89), Republican Party strategists – together with neoconservatives and other right-wing ideologues – encouraged the politicisation of conservative evangelicals as part of the New Right fusionism that ushered Ronald Reagan into the presidency in 1981 and returned him to power in 1985 (L. Taylor, 2005).

---

## BOX 9.3 What the Religious Right believes

Despite ideological and political differences among the different organisations that make up the movement, most members of the Religious Right would believe that at home secularism poses a serious threat to liberty, democracy and pluralism. The Religious Right is 'radical' in that it advocates dramatic changes in society. It is 'religious' in that its members and leaders tend to base their ideologies upon religious doctrines drawn from the Bible. In the mid-2000s, it was estimated that those claiming identification with the ideas of the Religious Right in the USA comprised around 20 per cent (some 60 million people) of the overall 300 million plus population (Green et al., 2005; Bates, 2006). At home, the Religious Right seeks to uphold and perpetuate 'Christian values', regarding as anathema manifestations of what are regarded as manifestations of 'excessive liberalism', including: legal abortion, absence or downgrading of prayers in state-run schools, and science teaching that adopts a rationalist, rather than a 'Creationist', perspective (Halper and Clark, 2004).

---

From the 1980s, the Religious Right began to make common cause on many foreign policy issues with secular neoconservatives, serving to focus concerns more widely on countries where basic religious freedoms were suppressed, notably minority Christian and Jewish populations in some Muslim and communist nations. Overall, the key foreign policy goal was a generalised one: 'the spread of freedom', often directed against shadowy adversaries – 'international terrorism' and 'radical Islam'. Groups within the Religious Right especially concerned with foreign policy include: the National Association of Evangelicals, Empower America, and the Foundation for the Defense of Democracy. As we shall see later, the Religious Right interpreted 9/11 as 'an apocalyptic contest between good and evil', and a politician of the Religious Right, Pat Robertson, claimed that Islam 'is not a peaceful religion' (Halper and Clarke, 2004: 196; L. Taylor, 2005).

## US Catholics

America's largest church is the Catholic Church. In 2011, the church had an estimated 68.5 million members, around a quarter of all Christians in the USA.[3] Like the mainly Protestant Religious Right, the Catholic Church has also sought actively to influence policy via dialogue with political leaders, including successive presidents and their close advisors. Over the years, Catholic religious leaders have sought to influence federal policies and programmes in a number of areas, including: the legal right of women to have abortions, government policies for social justice concerns both at home and abroad, the nuclear arms race and deterrence, especially during the Cold War, and, most recently, the ethics of the 'War on Terror' and the US invasions of Iraq (http://www.usccb.org/index.shtml). As far as the abortion issue is concerned, some Catholics have allied themselves with the Religious Right, because its recent presidential candidates (Gary Bauer, Pat Buchanan and Pat Robertson) consistently stated their opposition to abortion under any circumstances. Yet, that issue apart, most Catholic opinion has traditionally been more liberal, to the political left of the Religious Right. For example, in 1992 Catholics voted for Bill Clinton over George W. Bush, Senior, by 44 to 36 per cent, slightly more pro-Clinton than the national average. They maintained a similar margin in favour of Clinton in 1996 (Walker, 1996; Reichley, 2002). In 2000, George W. Bush had narrowly lost among Catholics (Associated Press, 2004). However, Bush increased his vote by nine million in 2004, of which seven million were Catholics – even though his challenger John Kerry is a Catholic. Bush won 52 per cent of the Roman Catholic vote, with support of 56 per cent of white Catholics, defeating the first Catholic presidential candidate from a major party since John F. Kennedy. In 2008, as already noted, Obama received the vote of about 54 per cent of US Catholics.

Because mainline Protestant denominations now claim only a quarter of the US population, almost on a par with their fast-growing conservative evangelical competitors who make up 23 per cent of the overall electorate (Bates, 2008), Catholics, comprising about a quarter of Americans, hold a significant position in a keen cultural and political struggle with the Religious Right. Although once aliens in a Protestant land, the vast majority of Catholics now feel comfortable in

American society. However, there are political divisions between ordinary Catholics, reflected in their leaders' political pronouncements. On the one hand, bishops' pastoral letters on nuclear arms and the economy have given ammunition to social gospel liberals, while, on the other, anti-abortion pronouncements and support for public accommodation of faith buoy some cultural conservatives. Overall, the pluralism of American Catholicism helps both to shape and to constrain the Church's political influence.

---

### BOX 9.4 US Catholics: both American *and* 'Roman'

American Catholicism has been shaped by consecutive waves of immigration – Irish, Italians, Central and Latin Americans – to become a multi-ethnic, territorially organised national church. The Catholic Church underwent swift Americanisation after the First World War; within 50 years – that is, by the 1960s – assimilation of most American Catholics of Irish and Italian origin into the mainstream of US life was complete. However, the American Catholic Church has had to live with two specific sources of tension, the result of being a member of the universal Roman Catholic Church, that is, it is *both* Roman and American. As a result, it is caught between the traditional church principle of prescribed membership and the voluntary denominational principle dominant in the American religious environment. The result is conflict between the traditional episcopal, clerical and authoritarian governance structures of the church and the democratic, lay and participatory principles permeating America's polity (Casanova, 1994: 176).

---

In terms of church–state relations, American Catholicism has stood to the left and the right of government at different times. It has demanded more from a 'right wing' position than any administration in the 1980s, 1990s or early 2000s was able or willing to offer – that is, a constitutional amendment equating abortion with murder – while, from the left, it has been open in its opposition to US support for Latin American dictators in the 1980s, the continuing nuclear arms race, and, most recently, the war in Iraq and the War on Terror.

During the first half of the twentieth century, Catholic devotion became less communitarian and more privatised, moving towards progressively higher levels of generality: from the village to the ethnic neighbourhood to American Catholic community to American national community to world community. US Catholics learnt to compartmentalise rigidly two spheres of life, the religious and the secular. According to Casanova, Catholicism became 'restricted to the religious sphere, while Americanism was restricted to the secular sphere' (Casanova, 1994: 181). However, in the 1950s as the Cold War with the Soviet Union deepened, the associated anti-communist crusade served to end the tension of being both Catholic and American. Casanova explains that 'this was a crusade all freedom-loving people could join, those fighting for republican freedom and those fighting for the freedom of the Church. Rome and the republic could at last be allies' (Casanova, 1994: 183). By the late 1960s, however, many lay Catholics had become increasingly more dovish than many of their religious leaders, Protestants and the general population in relation to the Vietnam War. Only in 1971, long after many other religious leaders and ordinary Americans had unequivocally condemned the war, did the US Catholic bishops admit that it was no longer a 'just war' (Wald, 1991: 264).

Liberalising Catholic attitudes on a range of social issues stemmed to a large degree from the Second Vatican Council ('Vatican 2') which ended in 1965. Vatican 2 led to a radical transformation of American Catholicism, a radical reform from *above* coming from *abroad*, albeit moulded by the specific American political context. The consequence was that a new and activist intellectual stratum emerged within American Catholicism, manifested among bishops, priests, nuns and laity alike, and focused on greater concern for social justice, and in 'offer[ing] broader, more universalistic perspectives which challenged the nationalist particularism of the American civil religion' (Casanova, 1994: 178). Three discrete issues – abortion, nuclear weapons, and economic and social justice – exemplified the new type of public Catholicism that emerged after Vatican 2.

President Bush's controversial meeting with Vatican official Cardinal Angelo Sodano in 2004, when he reportedly asked for American Catholic bishops to become more politically aggressive on cultural, family and life issues, specifically gay marriage, is said to be evidence that Bush 'hoped the Vatican would nudge [US Catholics] toward more explicit activism' (Joyce, 2004). However, the US Catholic Church was one of the institutions that Bush is said to have 'thumbed his nose at in invading

Iraq' (Jackson, 2004). Shortly before his death on 2 April, 2005, the late Pope John Paul II asked rhetorically in his World Day of Peace Message ('Do Not Be Overcome By Evil But Overcome Evil With Good'): 'How can we not think with profound regret of the drama unfolding in Iraq, which has given rise to tragic situations of uncertainty and insecurity for all?' (http://www.vatican.va/holy_father/john_paul_ii/messages/peace/documents/hf_jp-ii_mes_20041216_xxxviii-world-day-for-peace_en.html).

In addition, Pax Christi, the US Catholic Peace Movement, strongly criticised the invasion of Iraq. Pax Christi noted that by late 2011, more than eight years after the occupation began, over 2,000 US soldiers were dead, and more than 10,000 seriously wounded. Tens of thousands of Iraqis had died as a result of the conflict and countless numbers were wounded. Iraqi resistance to the occupation had grown both in numbers and sophistication, waging daily attacks on both US forces and the Iraqi government (http://paxchristiusa.org/2011/11/28/take-action-turn-the-page-on-a-decade-of-war/).

The overall point is that while increased numbers of US Catholics voted for George W. Bush in 2004 compared to 2000, there were significant manifestations of Catholic institutional opinion expressed both in the US and internationally that articulated significant reservations in relation to US foreign policy in Iraq after 9/11. This could be one important reason why over half of US Catholics voted for Barack Obama in 2008, as he might have been expected to seek to end US involvement in both Iraq and Afghanistan, given his pronouncements on these conflicts during campaigning.

In conclusion, our discussion of two important religious constituencies in the United States – the Religious Right and US Catholics – underlines the following:

- Both became politicised from the 1960s and 1970s, although their core concerns differed over time.
- Both domestic and foreign policy issues have been a focus.
- In recent years, various foreign policy concerns – including those stimulated by 9/11 and including subsequent US-led wars in Iraq and against 'Terror', as well as others, including religious freedom and social justice issues – have become key issues of US foreign policy in which religious actors have an input.

## US foreign policy and religion: the conflict in Iraq, 'The War on Terror', and an 'evangelised foreign policy'

The events of September 11 2001 ('9/11') and the subsequent 'War on Terror' declared by the George W. Bush presidency were of pivotal importance for subsequent direction and focus of American foreign policy. The 11 September event led to a new, fearful, foreign policy climate for the USA, providing a tragic opportunity for George W. Bush and key neoconservative advisers and policy makers to attempt to redraw the political map of the Middle East towards democracy and 'freedom'. This in turn had a profound impact upon the USA's international relations more generally. Post-9/11 foreign policy was put into effect via the US-led invasions of Afghanistan and Iraq. In the former country, the goal was not merely to oust the Islamist government, the Taliban, from power and to kill or capture local al Qaeda leaders and personnel, or, in the latter, to eliminate Saddam Hussein and his regime and their alleged Weapons of Mass Destruction (Seipel and Hoover, 2004). Both policies were ideologically informed by the fusion of two mutually reinforcing sets of ideas: religious ones emanating from the Religious Right, dovetailing with influential neoconservatives' secular security concerns.

The then National Security Advisor Condoleezza Rice stated in April 2002 that 9/11 was an 'earthquake' that 'started shifting the tectonic plates in international politics' (Rice, 2002). Deputy Secretary of Defense Paul Wolfowitz opined in *Vanity Fare* magazine a year later on 9 May 2003 that:

> The most significant thing that has produced what is admittedly a fairly significant change in American policy is the events of September 11th ... If you had to pick the ten most important foreign policy things for the United States over the past 100 years [9/11] would surely rank in the top ten if not number one. It's the reason why so much has changed.

Two months after that, on 9 July 2003, in an address to the Armed Services Committee, Defense Secretary Donald Rumsfeld averred that Washington now viewed the world 'through the prism of 9/11' (Dinan, 2003). Collectively, these remarks from Rice, Wolfowitz and Rumsfeldt underline the importance of 9/11 for subsequent US foreign policy.

We noted in Chapter 1 that to date there has been relatively little systematic, comparative research on the impact of religious actors on foreign policy formation and execution. We saw in Chapter 2 that to wield influence, religious actors must be able to exercise what Joseph Nye calls soft power. How and under what circumstances might religious actors influence a state's foreign policy in the direction they would like? A starting point is to note that as 'religion plays an important role in politics in certain parts of the world' then it is likely that there will be 'greater prominence of religious organizations in society and politics' in some countries but not others (Telhami, 2004: 71). However, the ability of a religious actor to translate *potential* ability into *actual* influence on foreign policy depends on several factors. First, can it access and thus potentially influence foreign policy decision-making processes? This ability should not be understood only in terms of formal institutional access, important though this is, but it also depends on another, equally important factor: the ability to influence policy via other means, for example, the media. The USA has a democratic political system that offers accessible decision-making structures and processes. This potentially offers many sorts of actors – both religious and secular – opportunities to influence policy formation and execution, both domestic and foreign (Hudson, 2005: 295–97). However, the idea that religious actors must 'get the ear of government' by 'lobby[ing] elected representatives and members of the executive branch' directly is a very limited and traditional understanding of influence. In addition, 'interest groups can make campaign contributions, vote in elections, try to mould public opinion, etc' (Mearsheimer and Walt, 2006: 6; also see, Mearsheimer and Walt, 2008).

Yet religions are not just run-of-the-mill lobby groups. In addition, they may have a form of influence that while indirect is nevertheless instrumental in helping construct the mindset of those that have responsibility for making policy in relation to the issue in question. But what questions are raised? What issues are of concern? What terms are used? How are they thought about? And even if a religious actor gets access to formal decision-making structures and processes it does not *guarantee* their ability significantly to influence either policy formation or execution. To have a profound policy impact, it is often necessary to both build and consolidate close relations with key players in both society and politics, as well as to foster good relations with influential print and electronic media. Overall, religious actors' ability to influence state foreign policies is likely to be greatest when, as in the USA after 9/11, there is ideological empathy between key religious and secular leaders and power holders – that is, when religious actors can employ soft power to try to achieve their objectives. We can note the influence of the Religious Right in relation to US foreign policy in the Middle East, especially after 9/11. Leading figures included Gary Bauer, head of an advocacy group, American Values, and Republican presidential contender in 2000, Jerry Falwell, prominent Southern Baptist and televangelist, Ralph Reed, former executive director of the Christian Coalition and candidate to be Lieutenant Governor of Georgia in 2006, Pat Robertson, former Republican presidential candidate and televangelist, Dick Armey, former Republican congressman and co-chair of Freedom Works,[4] and Tom DeLay, a prominent member of the Republican Party. These men enjoyed close personal relationships with President George W. Bush and his key confidantes, including John Bolton, Robert Bartley, William Bennett, Jeane Kirkpatrick and George Will (Mearsheimer and Walt, 2006: 6; Mazarr, 2003; Bacevich and Prodromou, 2004). Some individuals, such as Michael Gerson, a Bush policy adviser, speechwriter (and a man who helped coin the phrase 'axis of evil') and former journalist, has links to both groups: Gerson is not only 'a member of an evangelical Episcopal church in suburban Virginia' but is also a driving force behind President Bush's 'emphasis on a global spread of what the president sees as God-given rights' (LaFranchi, 2006).

As Table 9.1 indicates, the current influence of religion on US foreign policy is not unique, as historically there has often been a link between US foreign policy goals and religious concerns.

To account for the influence of the Religious Right on US foreign policy, especially during the George W. Bush presidency, we need to take into account the general importance of norms, values and ideology in the making of foreign policy. As Finnemore and Sikkink (1998: 888) note, 'the ways in which norms themselves change and the ways in which they change other features of the political landscape . . . [make] static approaches to International Relations . . . particularly unsatisfying during the current era of global transformation when questions about change motivate much of the empirical research we do'. This highlights the importance of paying analytical attention to the relationship between *ideational* and *material* issues to account for changes in US foreign policy

**Table 9.1** US foreign policy and religion

| Period | Mission | Adversary | Means |
|---|---|---|---|
| Pre-revolutionary colonial America (1600–1776) | Millennium | Papal anti-christ | Example as 'city on the hill' |
| Revolutionary and founding era (1776–1815) | Empire of liberty | Old world tyranny, 'hellish fiends' (Native Americans) | Example, continental expansion, without entangling alliances |
| Manifest Destiny (1815–48) | Christian civilisation | Savages or 'children' (Native Americans) | Examples, continental expansion, without entangling alliances |
| Imperial America (1898–1913) | Christian civilisation | Barbarians and savages (Filipinos) | Overseas expansion, without entangling alliances |
| Wilsonian Internationalism (1914–19) | Global democracy | Autocracy and imperialism | International organisations and alliances |
| Cold War liberalism (1946–89) | Free world | Communism | International organisations and alliances |
| Bush and neoconservatism (2001–09) | Spread of freedom | International terrorism, radical Islam | Unilateral action with ad hoc alliances |
| Obama and an even-handed foreign policy approach (2009–) | To make the world a more cooperative, less conflict-prone environment | International terrorism, radical Islam | Collective action when possible, utilising both permanent and temporary alliances |

Adapted from J. Judis, 'The chosen nation: The influence of religion on US foreign policy', *Policy Brief*, no. 37, March 2005.

after 9/11. It reflects a shift from the predominance of secular foreign policy goals during the Cold War to a shift in emphasis in the 1990s whereby religious concerns became more significant. During the Clinton era (1993–2001), 'left-leaning [religious] activists' had access 'to top administration officials. After [George W.] Bush took office, evangelical Christian leaders were the ones able to arrange sessions with senior White House aides' (Page, 2005; Haynes, 2008b). During the Obama presidency, foreign policy officials sought to broaden the range of US religious actors with which the administration engaged (Seiple, 2011).

The influence of the Religious Right was pivotal – but not entirely novel. In the 1980s, during the presidency of Ronald Reagan, a man who shared many of their ideals and goals, the Religious Right began to consolidate itself as a significant lobby group (Haynes, 1998: 28–33; Halper and Clarke, 2004; 182–200; Judis, 2005). The second key component in the shift in US foreign policy after 9/11 was the influence of a group known as neoconservatives ('neocons'); their rise to political dominance coincided with the rise in the Religious Right's influence. Both groups shared common ground and beliefs and the alliance between them deepened following 9/11 (Oldfield, 2004). Lieven (2004) notes five key developments in the 1990s that led to their deepening association: (1) narrowing of Christian beliefs; (2) sense of being under threat from globalisation; (3) growing desire to resist external influences; (4) harking back to a golden age; and (5) readiness to use all available means to achieve successful policy outcomes in crucially important areas. Influential groups that can be located ideologically within the corpus of the Religious Right, include the National Association of Evangelicals,[5] Empower America and the Foundation for the Defense of Democracy. According to Halper and Clarke, such organisations interpreted 9/11 as 'an apocalyptic contest between good and evil', an interpretation shared by at least some neoconservatives (2004: 196). In addition, a leading member of the Religious Right, Pat Robertson, claimed after 9/11 that Islam 'is not a peaceful religion' (Halper and Clarke, 2004: 196). This concern dovetailed with a key foreign policy goal of the Religious Right: to spread religious freedom to parts of the world that were said to lack it, notably many communist and Muslim countries, including Sudan (Seipel and Hoover, 2004).

Over time, however, there has developed what LaFranchi calls an 'evangelized foreign policy' (LaFranchi, 2006). This policy is represented not only by a continuing focus upon Iraq but also incorporates other concerns represented in the following laws that have reshaped US foreign policy, including diplomacy towards key countries including China and Saudi Arabia:

- The International Religious Freedom Act (1998). This makes freedom of religion and conscience a 'core objective' of US foreign policy. It also established an office and an annual international religious-freedom report that grades countries on rights. The measure was lobbied for by 'a coalition of conservative Christians, Jews, Catholics, mainline Protestants, Tibetan Buddhists and others' (Page, 2005).

- The Trafficking Victims Protection Act (2000). This law seeks to do away with the international crime syndicates that dispatch children and women from the developing world into prostitution and sweatshops.
- The Sudan Peace Act (2002). Conservative evangelicals promoted this law, along with others outraged by the Khartoum government's attacks on southern Christians and animists. The law and its accompanying sanctions are credited with helping create the road map for the 2003 ceasefire and the peace treaty the following year.
- The North Korea Human Rights Act (2004). Korean Americans and conservative Christians lobbied for this bill. It aimed not only to focus US attempts to help defectors from North Korea but also to focus attention on the country's egregious human rights violations and its nuclear weapons programme.
- Conservative evangelical Christians' influence is also seen in the Bush administration's focus both on AIDS in Africa and in attacks on international family-planning activities (MacAskill, 2006).

The overall result, according to Alan Hertzke, author of *Freeing God's Children: The Unlikely Alliance for Global Human Rights* (2004), is that, since the mid-1990s, conservative evangelicals provided the most important influence in a new, highly significant, human rights movement emanating from the USA. In doing so, they helped create 'a new architecture for human rights in American foreign policy'. Hertze also contends that 'Without a determined constituency pressuring for engagement in international affairs, it would be likely that – given the difficulties in Iraq – you would have had the administration hunkering down a bit, and the American people with them . . . But instead, you have these substantial forces pushing on human rights causes and demanding intervention' (Hertzke quoted in Page, 2005). The overall result is that American conservative evangelicals have broadened their perspective and widened their agenda, focusing on a number of international human rights issues. This is to imply that domestic social issues have lost significance – but it does indicate that a concern with social welfare issues both at home and abroad have encouraged them to develop broader alliances in often unexpected ways – including with the Jewish community and mainline Christian organisations, as well as on college campuses and in traditional religious and secular human rights organisations – which have long been interested in such foreign causes (Green et al., 2003). According to LaFranchi,

> In just a few years, conservative Christian churches and organisations have broadened their political activism from a near-exclusive domestic focus to an emphasis on foreign issues . . . Even as many in Washington trumpet the return of realism to US foreign policy and the decline of the neoconservative hawks, the staying power of the evangelicals is likely to blunt what might otherwise have been a steep decline in Wilsonian ideals.
>
> (2006)

In sum, we have noted that the recent roles of religious ideas in foreign policy formation and execution can be seen during the later stages of the Cold War in the 1980s, the Clinton era of the 1990s, and the Bush administrations in the early 2000s. In each phase, various religious constituencies, especially the Religious Right, saw the USA to be involved in an international struggle between 'good' and 'evil'. During the 1980s this was a 'secular' evil (the USSR), while in the 1990s and early 2000s 'evil' was Janus-faced: Islamist terrorism and human rights denials; both in their different ways were opposed to core US values – democracy and individualistic human rights. Consequently, US political leaders were encouraged to exhibit a high level of moral courage and character, attributes said to be rooted in a range of 'American values', necessary requirements in order to speak out and act in defence of the claims of 'good' over 'evil'. For example, when President George W. Bush talked of how the Cold War was 'won' and how the 'War on Terror' would be won in the future, he focused upon a twin necessity: for America to show both moral courage and character. He linked such virtues – both implicitly and explicitly – to values derived from his religious beliefs. For example, in May 2001, Bush spoke in Warsaw of how, he claimed, communism had been humbled by 'the iron purpose and moral vision of a single man: Pope John Paul II' ('Remarks by the President in Address to Faculty and Students of Warsaw University', 2001). A year later, in Prague, he returned to this theme, stating that: 'in Central and Eastern Europe the courage and moral vision of prisoners and exiles and priests and playwrights caused tyrants to fall' ('President Bush Previews Historic NATO Summit in Prague', 2002).

Such concerns contextualise President Bush's claims not only to want to help establish 'freedom and democracy' in the Middle East region but also to improve human rights in a number of contexts around the world, including North Korea and Sudan. Such a virtue was also characteristic of President Reagan's concerns nearly two decades before about the moral imperative of overturning communism – and like President Bush, Reagan drew his inspiration in this respect from religious values and beliefs. This is not to claim however that either Bush or Reagan always privileged religious over secular values. Indeed, Hurd (2004) labels President George W. Bush a 'Christian secularist'. The justification for this seemingly contradictory – even oxymoronic – juxtaposition of terms is to be found in the fact that in the USA secularism is a deep-rooted political tradition that, like in some Western European countries, notably France, developed over a long period. In the USA, however, secularism is also linked in important ways to various religious traditions, notably Judeo-Christianity focused in the concept of civil religion, a fusing of ideas and values that provides US secularism with identifiably 'religious' values.

For example, President Bush calls for 'secular democracy' in both Afghanistan and Iraq. Note, however, that this is the same form of secularism that appears in the constitution of India; that is, no one religion is favoured over others, yet religion is theoretically and officially privatised, removed from the public domain. This situation is conventionally accepted – *theoretically and officially* – in many Western, especially Western European countries, not only the USA: separation of religion and politics is believed a necessary prerequisite for successful democracy. Yet, as we have seen in the case of the United States in this chapter, the official view does not accord with reality. As a result, when President Bush expresses evidence of a worldview strongly informed by conservative Christian values and norms, this is not necessarily deemed to be unacceptable by the great majority of Americans. When Bush claims, as he did in a 2003 speech, that 'liberty is both the plan of Heaven for humanity, and the best hope for progress here on earth' ('President Bush Discusses Freedom in Iraq and Middle East', 2003), there is no reason to believe that most Americans disagree with him.

Yet, this duality of religious and secular ideas appears on the surface contradictory: Bush appears to be *simultaneously* both secular *and* religious in his public statements. One way of dealing with the conundrum is to note that secularism can come in different forms, with potentially inconsistent effects. Nicholas Wolterstorff of Yale Divinity School suggests that Bush relies on what he (Wolterstorff) calls a 'theistic account of political authority' ('Pew Forum on Religion and Public Life', 2003). According to Wolterstorff, 'among the ways a theistic account of political authority is distinct from all others is that it regards the authority of the State to do certain things as transmitted to it from someone or something which already has that very same authority' (ibid.). Thus God is believed to be transmitting directly to the political power holder, in this case Bush. Through Bush's articulation of what he believes are God's imperatives, the state gains the theistically derived power and right to provide judgement in legislative and/or judicial forms. These concerns were also apparent when Bush mused in November 2002 that: 'Dwight Eisenhower said this of Radio Free Europe and Radio Liberty – "The simplest and clearest charter in the world is what you have, which is to tell the truth." And for more than 50 years, the charter has been faithfully executed, and it's the truth that sets this continent free' ('What World Leaders Say About RFE/RL', 2002). It seems highly unlikely that Bush's choice of words *unwittingly* plagiarised those of the evangelist John. Instead, it is much more likely that they were a *deliberate* restatement of words that clearly link what are to him two sets of 'truths': the 'truth' of liberal democracy and divinely revealed 'truth'. And, from what we have seen in this chapter, it is by no means certain that most Americans would disagree with him.

## Barack Obama, religion and foreign policy

It is widely understood that George W. Bush is an evangelical Christian whose personal beliefs fed into his pro-religious outlook in foreign policy during his presidency (Judis, 2005; Bates, 2008; Marsden, 2011). What of the presidency of Barack Obama? To what extent, if at all, was there continuity or discontinuity between the Obama presidency and that of George W. Bush regarding a religious focus in US foreign policy? In early 2009, Obama's secretary of state, Hillary Clinton, in the course of one of her first overseas trips, asserted that the United States would continue strongly to pursue a policy developed during the George W. Bush presidency: to press China's rulers, not only on Tibet and Taiwan, but also on human rights, including religious freedoms, a core concern of the evangelical lobby since the 1990s. However, the evangelical magazine *Christianity Today*[6] claimed in March 2009 that 'evangelicals and other human rights activists [are] feeling a distinct chill'. This seems to have been a response – at least in part – to what Clinton said to reporters accompanying her on her foreign trip: 'Successive administrations and Chinese governments have been poised back and forth on these issues, and we have to continue to press them. But our pressing on those issues can't interfere with the global economic crisis, the global climate change crisis, and the security crisis.' In addition, she stated that, 'It is essential that the United States and China have a positive, cooperative relationship' ('China's human rights in the red', 2009). For *Christianity Today*, this statement about what appeared to be of prime importance for Clinton seemed necessarily to reduce the importance of religious freedom in US foreign policy, a qualitative change from the George W. Bush presidency.

Clinton's timing was embarrassing for the Obama administration and discomfiting for 'house-church' Christians[7] and human rights activists inside China. In the same week in March 2009, Clinton's State Department issued its 2008 Country Reports on Human Rights Practices, in which it strongly criticised China for deteriorating human rights. The report noted that: 'The [Chinese] government's human rights record remained poor and worsened in some areas . . . During [2008] the government increased its severe cultural and religious repression of ethnic minorities in Tibetan areas – Other serious human rights abuses included extrajudicial killings, torture and coerced confessions of prisoners, and the use of forced labor, including prison labor.' Note, however, that this is a mere snapshot of the criticisms of China's human rights in 2008. Many other examples of what the US government saw as egregiously bad human rights in China could be quoted from the report, which extends for 40 pages (full report available at http://www.state.gov/g/drl/rls/hrrpt/2008/eap/119037.htm).

Noting that the persecution of house-church Christians in China also worsened in 2008, an advocacy group, China Aid, called Clinton's remarks 'a retreat on the priority of human rights issues in U.S.-China relations' ('China's human rights in the red', 2009). In an interview with *Christianity Today*, a leading human rights advocate Congressman Frank Wolf (Republican, Virginia) called Clinton's comments 'unbelievable'.[8] He averred that her words would have a dispiriting effect on human rights monitoring within the State Department. It did not bode well, he claimed, that the Obama administration also shows no signs of using influence on China to improve human rights in Sudan, one of China's major trade partners ('Wolf: China's Record on Human Rights is Abysmal', 2009).

In March 2009, a bipartisan group of 16 congressmen and women, including Frank Wolf, sent Clinton a letter urging her to refrain from divorcing human rights from other legitimate government concerns. The letter claimed that

> these complicated, multi-lateral issues will only be solved when the government and its people work together, with justice and mutual respect . . . These issues cannot and should not be separated from concerns about human rights and the rule of law. As long as practices of forced abortions, imprisonment of human rights lawyers, and persecution of unregistered churches continue, the people of China will be neither free nor safe.
>
> ('16 Members of Congress Urge Secretary Of State Clinton To Address Human Rights In China', 2009)

The concerns noted above about human rights in China do not begin and end with religious freedoms. The conservative Heritage Foundation, in its Annual Index of Economic Freedom, ranks states by their citizens' level of control over their own labour and property (view the annual reports at: http://www.hertage.org/Index/). For the Heritage Foundation, in a view doubtless shared by many conservative evangelicals, governments that allow their citizens vigorous economic freedoms are also likely to enable them to enjoy a good range of religious freedoms. While many conservative evangelicals would no doubt allow that the relationship between economics and religion is complex, they would likely not agree that the issue of religious freedoms – in China and elsewhere – should be sidelined or marginalised by a single-minded pursuit of trade and economic benefits. The Clinton view, however, appeared to roll back a fundamental tenet of the George W. Bush era foreign policy.

Human rights promotion, including that of religious freedoms, would henceforward be secondary in US foreign policy compared to economic goals. Note, however, that the Clinton view appeared to chime better with public opinion than the religious-freedoms-at-all-costs preference of the conservative evangelicals. A Pew Poll published in 2011 showed that public support for the notion that the USA should promote human rights abroad declined from 37 per cent in 2005 to 29 per cent in 2009. In addition, public support for the idea that the USA should promote democracy abroad also declined – by a smaller margin – from 24 per cent in 2005 to 21 per cent in 2009. Finally, the Pew Poll also showed a decline in the view that the US should seek to improve living standards in poor countries from 31 per cent in 2005 to 26 per cent in 2009. Overall, the three policies noted here – promoting human rights abroad, promoting democracy abroad, and seeking to improve living standards in poor countries – were bottom of the list of 11 US foreign policy goals (Pew Research Center, 2011).

In addition, on becoming president in early 2009, Barack Obama made an historic visit to Cairo, Egypt, where, in June of that year, he made a speech urging 'a new beginning between the United States and Muslims'.[9] President Obama's speech was aimed at Muslims across the world. The president defended his decision to increase US involvement in Afghanistan and did not apologise for the invasion of Iraq that led to the deaths of hundreds of thousands of people. On the Israel–Palestine conflict, while Obama did not call for a full Israeli withdrawal from the Occupied Territories, he did liken the Palestinian struggle to the US civil rights movement and said Israeli settlement building should stop. Finally, he acknowledged the US role in the 1953 overthrow of Iran's democratically elected government. This did not imply of course that the US government was content with Iran's nuclear capacity building programme and continued strongly to oppose it. It is not, however, clear in the three years since Obama's Cairo speech that much has been achieved in rebuilding links between America and the Muslim world. A July 2011 Zogby International survey of Egyptians found only 5 per cent had a favourable opinion of the USA, a lower proportion than during the George W. Bush administration. In addition, a Pew Research survey taken in early 2011 found that Egyptians overwhelmingly (82 per cent) disapproved of Obama's handling of the conflict between Israelis and Palestinians, while over half – 52 per cent – felt that Obama was not handling political change well in the Middle East during the time of the 'Arab Spring' (Maginnis, 2011).

## Conclusion

At the start of the chapter I posed three questions:

- *Is religion an important political actor in America?*
- *Has religion recently gained increased political and social prominence?*
- *What happens when there is religious involvement in America's foreign policy?*

We are now in a position to provide some answers. First, evidence suggests that religion is an intermittently important political actor: recently the Religious Right was able to enlist support from secular neoconservatives in relation to post-9/11 foreign policy towards Iraq and Afghanistan. In addition, since the 1990s a broad coalition of religious organisations, featuring but not always led by conservative evangelicals, has helped to focus US foreign policy under both Clinton and Bush on human rights and social welfare issues.

Second, more than two decades after the end of the Cold War and the collapse of the Soviet Union, the United States now pursues a range of foreign policies that significantly draw on often mutually reinforcing religious and secular ideas, norms and values, including the championing of human rights such as religious freedom, democracy and social welfare.

## Notes

1. In February and March 2002 the Washington-based Pew Research Council conducted a survey of 2,002 adults in the USA. Questions about religious preference were included. The results were as follows: Christian 84%, Jewish 1%, Muslims <1%, 'Other non-Christian' 1%, No religious belief 13%, Don't know 1% (Kohut and Rogers, 2002).
2. A list of more than 80 prominent US televangelists is available at: http://en.wikipedia.org/wiki/List_of_U.S._televangelists.
3. The *2011 Yearbook of American and Canadian Churches*, published by the National Council of Churches, lists 68,503,456 members.

4. Freedom Works was founded in 2004, following merger between Citizens for a Sound Economy and Empower America.
5. The NAE, led by Pastor Tom Haggard, represents 53 denominations with 45,000 churches and 30 million members across the USA (http://www.nae.net/).
6. 'Christianity Today International is a not-for-profit ministry. We are not affiliated with any particular denomination. Billy Graham started this organization (Christianity Today International) in 1956. . . . *Christianity Today* . . . delivers honest and relevant news from an evangelical viewpoint, with interviews, feature articles, challenging thought pieces, and the most complete news coverage of the Church in the world today' http://www.christianitytoday.com/free/features/magazines.html.
7. In China, 'house-churches' are religious movements of unregistered Christian assemblies, which operate independently of the government-run Protestant and Catholic organisations.
8. See a selection of Frank Wolf's human rights concerns and his attempts to try to redress them at http://wolf.house.gov/index.cfm?sectionid=108 &sectiontree=7108.
9. Full text of Obama's speech is at http://www.whitehouse.gov/the-press-office/remarks-president-cairo-university-6–04–09.

## Questions

- Examine and assess the political impact of the Religious Right on US politics under the presidencies of both George W. Bush (2001–09) and Barack Obama (2009–).
- What are the implications for international relations of US Catholics being part of a transnational religious movement concerned with social justice and welfare issues?
- What is an 'evangelised foreign policy' and how does it relate to the involvement of religious organisations in current US foreign policy?

## Further reading

S. Bates, *God's Own Country: Power and Religion in the USA: Religion and Politics in the USA*, London: Hodder, 2008. In recent years, the power and influence of right-wing evangelical Christianity has become an important component of political life in the USA. Bates explains how this affects American government policy at home and abroad: not least in Israel and the Middle East.

J. Green, *The Diminishing Divide: Religion's Changing Role in American Politics*, Washington, DC: Brookings Institution Press, 2000. Green focuses on religion's influence on American political attitudes and behaviour. The United States, a profoundly religious nation that nonetheless sought to build an impenetrable wall between church and state, is a country where religion and politics are tightly interwoven. Religion has been a powerful moral and cultural force since the nation's founding, but its influence on politics was more subtle in the past, when most presidents and other political leaders considered their religious beliefs to be private. Since the 1980s, however, presidents and presidential candidates have all been quick to express their faith in God. In addition, many citizens – both on both left and right – readily acknowledge the importance of religion in guiding their political beliefs and participation. The author argues that religion will continue to alter the political landscape in the current century, perhaps in unexpected ways.

M. Lewis Taylor, *Religion, Politics, and the Christian Right: Post-9/11 Powers in American Empire*, Minneaspolis, MN: Augsburg Fortress Publishers, 2005. Taylor analyses right-wing Christian movements in post-9/11 USA. He argues that militant Christian faith must be viewed against a backdrop of both American political romanticism and corporatist liberalism in the USA, both historically and at the present time. He presents an innovative framework for interpreting how Christian nationalists, Pentagon war planners and corporate institutions today are forging alliances in the USA that have significant impacts both at home and abroad.

E. Patterson, *Politics in a Religious World: Building a Religiously Literate U.S. Foreign Policy*, New York and London: Continuum, 2011. This book discusses the lack of religious understanding in US foreign policy, examining why successive US governments often choose to avoid or ignore religious aspects of international relations.

R. Seipel and D. Hoover, *Religion and Security: The New Nexus in International Relations*, Lanham, MD: Rowman & Littlefield Publishers, 2004. Many would agree that in the context of global security today, religion is not only part of the problem but also part of the solution. This book explores issues where religion and security interact, paying particular attention to the resources within the Abrahamic faith traditions of Judaism, Christianity and Islam that foster sustainable peace. It also seeks to place the role of the USA in this regard in a wider international context.

# 10 | Europe

There is broad agreement that in Europe,[1] especially the continent's western portion, religion has changed significantly over time, largely due to the compartmentalisation of societies and the reduced power of churches. While one school of thought believes that this is a continuous trend (Gauchet, 1985; Luhmann, 1989; Bruce, 2002, 2012; Wilson, 2003; Hirst, 2003), other theorists focus on the regional picture outlook, arguing that religion is still institutionally and politically powerful in many European societies (Casanova, 1994, 2005; Berger, 1999; Davie, 2000, 2002, 2007). In addition, many Europeans still perceive themselves to be differentiated or affected by religious and/or cultural criteria; some are of relevance to political outcomes, manifested in various ways (Davie, 2000, 2002, 2007). They include:

- *Catholic/Protestant divisions, in various countries, including (Northern) Ireland and Germany.* In the former, religious–cultural divisions are the main social basis of competing political parties, such as, the nationalist and Catholic Sinn Fein and the 'loyalist', Protestant-focused, Democratic Unionist Party and Ulster Unionist Party.
- *Religious differences – roughly along right-left political lines – internal to the main confessional traditions.* In Britain, for example, there is the cross-party, socially conservative Movement for Christian Democracy, while both France and Italy also have Christian political movements.
- *A variety of church–state relationships.*

However, while such concerns are intermittently important in some domestic European political contexts, they do not usually form part of the region's international relations. In this chapter, we examine a key issue in relation to Europe's current domestic and international concerns: Islam, with a focus on the following issues:

- *The impact of globalisation on the religious, political and social position of Europe's Muslim minorities.* For Europe's Muslims, Islam is an important basis of identity which can impact upon various social and political concerns.
- *European fears of Islamic extremism.* This issue came to the fore largely as a result of the 11 September 2001 New York and Pentagon attacks, and the Madrid and London bombings in March 2004 and July 2005 respectively.
- *Muslim Turkey's bid to join the European Union.* Fears of Islamic extremism encourage some Europeans to oppose Turkey's bid to join the European Union. Would Europe's 'Christian cultural identity' be diluted by the admission of Turkey, with its 80 million – mostly Muslim – people?

The chapter is divided into three sections. The first examines the social and political position of Muslims in Europe, focusing on the impact of globalisation. The second section looks at the impact of transnational Islamic ideas in relation to Britain and France, where two recent issues have highlighted the position of Muslims in both countries. In Britain, the issue was the 7 July 2005 London bombings. In France, a focus on Islam was provided by the Paris riots of October–November 2005. Some commentators claimed that the riots were indicative of a new trend in France: alienated youths from Muslim backgrounds did not see themselves primarily as French but as Muslims, part of the global Islamic *ummah*, empowered and radicalised by extremist ideas. In addition, former President Sarkozy's raising of the issue of *halal* meat – that is, animals are killed in a certain, prescribed, Islamically acceptable way – during the 2012 presidential campaign also helped to focus attention on France's Muslim population.

In the third section, we examine Turkey's continuing, controversial application to join the European Union (EU). We discuss the opposition of some EU member states, political leaders and populations to countenance the entry of Turkey to the EU – primarily because it would mean that a large Muslim country – Turkey has a population of around 80 million people, of whom 99 per cent are Muslims – would join the Union. The fear is that this would result not only in an 'unacceptable dilution' of the EU's claimed 'Christian' cultural characteristics but also further open up Europe to infiltration from Muslim extremism. The chapter's main conclusion is that in Europe, the religious, social and political importance of Islam is consequential in various ways for the region's internal and international relations.

## Globalisation and Islam in Europe

The extent to which globalisation weakens the power of national governments is a matter of debate. Many would, however, agree that despite significant changes in recent decades, in international relations the nation-state remains the chief wielder of power (Haynes et al., 2011). Hirst and Thompson (1999) define the legitimacy of the democratic nation-state as its ability to represent the people inhabiting its territory. The more ethnically diverse the people, the more potentially complicated this becomes. Through a high degree of cultural homogenisation, various peoples living together in a national territory are said to be able to identify with both the state and each other. Rosenau's (1997) concept of 'the Frontier' highlights a factor that potentially complicates homogenisation. This refers to a new or newly relevant divide emerging from the fact that many nations – including in Europe – now consist of citizens related to countries with which the nation has 'foreign affairs', including, in this context, the Middle East and North Africa. And, since domestic and foreign politics increasingly engage with the same issues, the result is that traditional distinction between the two previously autonomous spheres dissolves (Haynes, 2005a), in some cases replaced by a new dividing line between citizens.

In Europe, the concept of 'the Frontier' is said to be relevant to the relations between the Muslim minority and host populations. The issue came into sharp focus following the continuing US and British involvement in Afghanistan (from 2001) and Iraq (from 2003). Both events had serious political repercussions for the then leaders of both countries: President George W. Bush in the USA and Prime Minister Tony Blair in Britain. Especially in the latter country, many among Britain's nearly three million-strong Muslim community saw the actions as fundamentally 'anti-Muslim' (Pew Global Attitudes Project, 2005; http://features. pewforum.org/muslim/number-of-muslims-in-western-europe.html). Further problems emerged in 2005 following the publication of the

**225**

infamous 'Mohammed cartoons' in a Danish newspaper, *Jyllands-Posten* (in English, *The Morning Newspaper/The Jutland Post*).[2]

The *Jyllands-Posten* controversy erupted after 12 cartoons were published in the newspaper on 30 September 2005. Several of the cartoons portrayed the Prophet Mohammed and some seemed to equate him with terrorism. The purpose, the newspaper claimed, was to contribute to a continuing debate regarding criticism of Islam and self-censorship. The effect, however, was almost certainly not what the newspaper intended, as publication of the cartoons was followed by public protests from Danish Muslim organisations,[3] which helped to disseminate knowledge about them around the world. The controversy swiftly grew, with newspapers in over 50 countries reprinting some or all of the cartoons. The result was often violent protests in many countries, especially in the Muslim world. Both *Jyllands-Posten* – whose office received a bomb threat in January 2006 – and Denmark became a focus of Muslim anger. Demonstrators in the Gaza Strip (Palestinian territory) burned Danish flags, Saudi Arabia and Libya withdrew their ambassadors to Denmark, Danish goods were boycotted across the Middle East, and many Middle Eastern and Asian countries saw violent clashes, with demonstrators attacking the Danish and Norwegian Embassies in Tehran and thousands of protesters taking to the streets in Egypt, the West Bank, Jordan and Afghanistan (Bright, 2006). Overall, the main complaint expressed by critics of the cartoons were that they were both Islamophobic and blasphemous. Their purpose was to humiliate a marginalised Danish minority and more generally to insult Islam. In February 2006, Denmark's prime minister, Anders Fogh Rasmussen, announced that the Prophet Mohammed cartoons controversy was Denmark's worst international crisis since the Second World War ('70,000 gather for violent Pakistan cartoons protest', 2006).

In Egypt, a government-owned newspaper *Al-Gomhuria* stated on 2 February 2006: 'It is not a question of freedom of opinion or belief. It is a conspiracy against Islam and Muslims which has been in the works for years. The international community should understand that any attack against our prophet will not go unpunished'. From Jeddah, Saudi Arabia, a journalist, Amr Al-Faisal, writing in the pro-government *Arab News*, commented on 6 February: 'Muslims are not doing enough to stop the aggression of Western countries, shown by the incident of the Mohammed cartoons. This aggression stems from their weakness.' Al-Faisal proposed a gradual boycott of Western economies coupled with increased self-reliance on Muslim manufacturing capacity ('Muslims Voice Anger Over Mohammed Cartoons', 2006).

Supporters of the cartoons claim they illustrate an important issue in an age of Islamist religious terrorism; their publication exercises the right of free speech which the extremists abhor. In addition, the furore illustrated the intolerance of Muslims: similar cartoons about other religions are often printed, supporters claimed, illustrating that Muslims were not being targeted in a discriminatory fashion. In Amman, Jordan, a weekly tabloid newspaper, *Al-Shihan*, published three of the cartoons on 1 February 2006, accompanied by pleas for Muslims of the world to 'be reasonable'. Jihad Momani, the editor-in-chief, explained his decision to print because 'people are attacking drawings that they have not even seen'. His action was not, however, accepted in the spirit that he claimed: Momani was swiftly removed from his post and the newspapers withdrawn from the newsstands ('Muslims Voice Anger Over Mohammed Cartoons', 2006).

There were international attempts to dampen down the furore. The Organisation of the Islamic Cooperation (OIC) joined the United Nations and European Union in appealing for calm over the Prophet Mohammed cartoons. A statement attributed to the OIC secretary general, Ekmeleddin Ihsanoglu, along with the UN secretary general, Kofi Annan, and EU foreign policy chief, Javier Solana, said: 'We are deeply alarmed at the repercussions of the publication in Denmark several months ago of insulting caricatures of the Prophet Mohammed and their subsequent republication by some other European newspapers, and at the violent acts that have occurred in reaction to them' (statement quoted in Bilefsky, 2006).

However, Iran attempted to take the lead among Muslims in the controversy. European Union officials expressed concern that Iran, increasingly isolated over its nuclear programme in late 2005 and early 2006, was said to be seeking to exploit the crisis to try to unite the Muslim world against the West (Tisdall, 2006). Iran's *largest selling* newspaper, *Hamshahri*, announced it was sponsoring a contest to draw cartoons caricaturing the Holocaust in response to the publishing in European papers of caricatures of the Prophet Mohammed. It said that 'private individuals' would offer gold coins to the best 12 artists – the same number of cartoons that appeared in *Jyllands-Posten*. The purpose of the competition, according to the newspaper, was to turn the tables on the assertion that newspapers can print offensive material in the name of freedom of expression ('Muslims Voice Anger over Mohammed Cartoons', 2006).

This discussion emphasises that the Prophet Mohammed cartoons controversy focuses on how the issue of Islam and the position of Muslims in European countries generates intense debate both in Europe and around the world.

## Islam and identity in Europe

In many European countries, Islam is usually associated with communities of fairly recent immigrant origin. Increased Muslim immigration largely occurred in the 1970s and 1980s, a time of European regional economic recession and an international environment characterised by international friction between Muslims and the West following Iran's revolution (Cesari and McLoughlin, 2005). In recent years, Muslim numbers have continued to increase as a consequence of children born to Muslim immigrants, as well as conversions. Over time, many Muslims, especially among the second-generation, have become politicised, in part because of the impact of globalisation.

In his study of construction of Hong Kong identity after Hong Kong's incorporation into China in 1997, Mathews (2000) offers a useful methodological approach to globalisation and identity that can be applied to Muslims in Europe. Mathews distinguishes between the state as constructor of culture in the nationalistic sense of 'the people's way of life', related to institutionalised practices, and the global 'cultural supermarket' as producer of free-floating culture-items, objects of individual choice. Thus an individual constructs their self-identity in relation to both – and can choose between self-identity as an 'authentic national culture', or a 'completely different' culture, or 'something in between', by combining ethnicity and values. In the Hong Kong example, identity is Chinese ethnicity *plus* democracy/rule of law/human rights/ freedom/gender equality, 'plus' being values associated with 'international' British-ruled Hong Kong as opposed to authoritarian 'isolationist'

China. Simultaneously, mainland Chinese moving to Hong Kong identified themselves with the same values, to the incredulous chagrin of 'authentic' Hong Kong inhabitants (Mathews, 2000). Mobility and global culture-shopping also give rise to transnational communities whose values and identities are constructed in dialectical relation to both new countries and countries of origins, and therefore cannot be explained simply in terms of one over the other (Kennedy and Roudometof, 2002; Roy, 2004). From this viewpoint, it is possible to argue that ethnicity and culture constitute 'forms' of self-identity which can be filled with different 'value-contents'.

## BOX 10.1 Islam and identity in Europe

In the context of Muslims in Europe, the issue of identity is sometimes controversial among 'second' or 'third' generation' Muslims, usually offspring of immigrant parents or grandparents. Such people may experiment with ethnic and national identity in ways that differ from their parents' more fixed identities (Cesari and McLoughlin, 2005). This is especially apparent in recent years when the issue of 'European identity' has been widely discussed and debated, including in the context of Islam. It contrasts with the position a few decades ago when Islam was virtually unknown for most non-Muslim Europeans, with the faith physically manifested in only a few mosques in some major European cities. The situation began to change with the expansion of labour migration in the 1970s. Initially, Muslim immigrants were principally defined by the host society vis-à-vis their economic function (for example, in Germany where Turks were referred to as *gastarbeiter*, or 'guest workers'), their skin colour or their nationality, and only to a lesser extent by culture and/or religion. According to Nonneman, 'this reflected the migrants' own perception of their place in their European surroundings, and their relative lack of concern with opportunities for socio-religious expression within the context of the host society' (1996: 382).

The religious and cultural dimension of Islam emerged as an important social and political issue from the late 1970s. It was largely 'the unforeseen consequence of the drastic change in European immigration policy at the time of the 1972–4 recession' (Nielsen, 1992: 2). Although most European governments halted further labour immigration, many did allow family unification. The result was that the Muslim presence in Europe changed from one essentially of migrant workers to social communities in a fuller sense. Contacts and interactions between Muslims immigrants and host societies increased. By the late 1980s, there were collectively about five million Muslims in Britain, France and Germany – countries where the families of male Muslim 'guest workers' were allowed to join them. Many Muslims became increasingly politicised, especially those of the 'second generation', the offspring of migrant workers and their spouses. Born in Europe, they were familiar from the start with Western assumptions about political participation. In some countries – for example, Britain and France – it was relatively easy to acquire citizenship. An effect of the accompanying expectations on the part of these Muslims became apparent in their increased willingness to agitate for what they perceived as their social, political and economic rights.

## BOX 10.2 Islamic extremism and globalisation: the impact on Europe

Various international events and concerns involving Islam impacted upon Europe from the late 1970s, especially Iran's 1979 revolution which raised the issue of Islamic extremism. In addition, there was increasing focus more generally of Islamic involvement in politics, a development facilitated by globalisation which included increased media reporting on international issues. Partly as a result of real or perceived discrimination and insensitivity to cultural differences, some European Muslims – especially among the second generation born in Europe – identified with fellow Muslims' political causes in the Middle East, including the Palestinians' struggle for a homeland and the goals of the Iranian revolution. Sections of public opinion in the host societies reacted by focusing on the perceived excesses of 'Islamic extremism'; for example, in Iran or Saudi Arabia. The claim was that some European Muslims were a threat to political and social stability because they too were likely to be 'Islamic extremists'. This was also a time of relatively high unemployment in many European countries, a situation encouraging and generating hostility towards Muslims. The overall result was increasing friction between Muslim and host communities in various European countries (Amiraux, 2005).

Some Islamists – that is, people who believe that it is appropriate to link Muslim values to political outcomes – see Western individualistic liberalism as both unauthentic and antipathetic to their culture and religion (Marty and Appleby, 1997; Hirst and Thompson, 1999; Turner,

1994, 2000; Roy 2004, 2010). As a 'cultural authenticity-brand', Islamism is sometimes regarded as comparable to other global religious 'roots-movements', including New Age, Spirituality, neo-paganism and Occultism (Roy, 2004; Katz, 2005). A focus on Islamism also provides a useful illustration of the relation between research and identity. Although Islamism is a marginal type of religiosity, it now dominates research and public debate to the extent that in both Europe and the USA 'Islam' is often identified unthinkingly with Islamic extremism (Roy, 2004, 2010; Sen, 2006).

---

### BOX 10.3 Olivier Roy on Islamic extremism

French author and analyst of Islam Olivier Roy argues that to counter European constructions of Islam, which he sees as focusing upon what he calls 'Islamic fundamentalism', it is necessary significantly to raise public awareness of the majority of Muslims in Europe. According to Roy, many 'do all those things fundamentalists say Muslims should not do', including: selling and drinking alcohol, voting for secular parties, having non-Muslim friends, marrying non-Muslims – yet they still consider themselves to be good Muslims (Roy, 2004).

Roy's comments raise an important question: To what extent – if at all – is there an inevitable and unbridgeable incompatibility between Muslims-in-Europe, their values, norms and beliefs, and the secular organising principles of non-Muslim European societies? Esposito (2002), Ayubi (1991) and Piscatori (1986) contend that there is no real incompatibility because Islam is primarily pragmatic, with separation between, on the one hand, religious principles and institutions and, on the other, between the temporal ruler and the state. As a result, Piscatori (1986) contends, there are not only grounds for expectations of compatibility between Islamic precepts and the 'world of nation-states' but also no impracticable obstacles of principle to a reasonable degree of compatibility between 'Islamic' and 'Western' practices regarding citizenship and the nature of socio-political organisation. 'European Muslims' reactions (themselves varying strongly) may often be less a matter of "Islamic practice" than of a cultural minority's sense of discrimination leading to a search for rallying points' (Nonneman, 1996: 384).

---

This is not to suggest that Muslims in Europe are necessarily complaisant about the norms, values and practices they encounter. Muslim leaders often express concern for the development of their faith and its adherents, especially in relation to the moral wellbeing of the young.

For many Muslims, Western society is essentially meaningless, rootless, characterised by crime, juvenile delinquency, riots, collapse of marriages, and sexual promiscuity (Ahmed, 1992; Leiken, 2012). Some Muslims believe that Islam could provide an alternative and appropriate lifestyle satisfactorily contrasting with European secular societies' crass materialism and selfishness. In a bid to achieve this goal, some Muslims in Europe choose to pursue the goal of Islamicisation via what Roy (2004) calls 'neo-fundamentalism'. Others, according to Leiken (2012), take a different path: they pursue Islamic authenticity via extremism and even terrorism. Roy's term, 'neo-fundamentalism' refers to the idea of a transnational Islamic community emerging from Europe and constructed largely through the internet. It identifies Muslim identity as *Sharia*, but breaks with traditional Islamic jurisprudence in which Muslim minorities are obliged only to follow *Sharia* ritual, not its legislation (Roy, 2004). Within this parameter, the call for *Sharia* has widely different implications. The francophone Swiss Muslim intellectual and scholar Tariq Ramadan advocates liberal reform of *Sharia*, but nevertheless challenges existing European models of citizenship by explicitly making *Sharia* the guiding principle for Muslim citizens. Combined with his call for European Muslims to represent the oppressed South against Western neo-liberal imperialism, his message is potentially divisive (Ramadan, 2003: 172ff.)

Ramadan, who was named by *Time* magazine in 2000 as one of the 100 most important innovators of the twenty-first century, argues that Islam can and should feel at home in the West.[4] In *Western Muslims and the Future of Islam* (2003), Ramadan focuses on Islamic law (*Sharia*) and tradition in order to analyse whether Islam is in conflict with Western ideals. According to Ramadan, there is no contradiction between them. He also identifies several key areas where Islam's universal principles can be 'engaged' in the West, including education, inter-religious dialogue, economic resistance and spirituality. As the number of Muslims living in the West grows, the question of what it means to be a Western Muslim becomes increasingly important to the futures of both Islam and the West. While the media are focused on radical Islam, Ramadan claims, a silent revolution is sweeping Islamic communities in the West, as Muslims actively seek ways to live in harmony with their faith within a Western context. French, English, German and American Muslims –

both women and men – are reshaping their religion into one that is faithful to the principles of Islam, dressed in European and American cultures, and definitively rooted in Western societies. Let us examine Ramadan's ideas in relation to Muslims living in Britain and France.

## BOX 10.4 Tariq Ramadan on the 'Islamic state'

The goal of Swiss Muslim intellectual Tariq Ramadan, who is also a professor at Oxford University, is to create an independent 'Western Islam', anchored not in the traditions of Islamic countries but in the cultural reality of the West today. Ramadan urges a fresh reading of Islamic sources, in order to interpret them for a Western context. This would enable a new understanding of universal Islamic principles that could open the door to integration into Western societies. He then shows how these principles can be put to practical use. Ramadan also contends that Muslims can – indeed *must* – be faithful to their principles while participating fully in the civic life of Western secular societies. In his book *Western Muslims and the Future of Islam* (2003), Ramadan offers a striking vision of a new Muslim Identity, one which rejects once and for all the idea that Islam must be defined in opposition to the West.

## *Britain*

Britain is home to nearly three million Muslims, amounting to around 5 per cent of the total population of 60 million people. British Muslims have various roots, with communities in the UK comprising people originally from: Pakistan, Bangladesh, North Africa, sub-Saharan Africa, Cyprus, Malaysia, the Middle East and, most recently, Eastern Europe (primarily Bosnia-Herzegovina). Until the 1960s, Islam was a relatively obscure religion in Britain; there were only a few mosques in major cities, including Cardiff, Liverpool, Manchester, South Shields and London's East End. The situation changed with the expansion of Muslim labour migration in the 1970s. At this time, as a result of a change in immigration policy, British governments halted further labour immigration, while allowing family unification (Nielsen, 1992: 2). As a result, the Muslim presence in Britain changed from one of primarily migrant workers to social communities in a fuller sense. As a result, contacts significantly increased between Muslim families and the British host society.

During the 1980s, some Muslims – especially among the second generation, offspring of first-generation immigrants and their spouses – became increasingly politicised and in some cases politically active. Such people, with British citizenship and familiar with British assumptions about political participation, began to demand what they saw as their rights. At the same time, a backlash began against some British Muslims from some sections of existing British society. This was in part a consequence of increased fears of 'Islamic extremism', often linked to Iran's 1979 revolution, and more generally with increased Islamic militancy in many parts of the Muslim world. Some sections of British public believed that British Muslim communities were hotbeds of 'Islamic extremism', posing a threat to peace and social stability (McLoughlin, 2005; Leiken, 2012).

Some British Muslims, especially among the young, began increasingly to identify with struggles of fellow Muslims in Israel-controlled Palestine and elsewhere, with some radicals organising themselves into 'a huge web of Islamic associations of various shades of feeling and opinion' (Kepel, 1994: 37; also see, Ramadan, 2006 and Leiken, 2012). Such organisations included: the Young Muslims, *Al Muntada al Islami*, Muslim Welfare House, *Al-Muhajiroun*, and *Hizb ut Tahrir*; collectively they represented a range of Islamist positions. *Hizb ut Tahrir* is often regarded as one of the most radical of such groups (www.hizb.org.uk/). *Hizb ut-Tahrir*, an Arabic term that translates as 'the Party of Liberation', is a radical political organisation with members throughout the Muslim world and in countries – including, Britain – with significant Muslim populations. Taqiuddin an-Nabhani, an Islamic jurist, formed the organisation in Jerusalem in 1953.[5] *Hizb ut Tahrir* calls for separation of Muslims from Western society, while employing 'anti-Israel, anti-homosexual, anti-liberal rhetoric' (Dodd, 1996; also see the many relevant articles and postings at www.hizb.org.uk/).

According to Ansari, some young Muslims in Britain are attracted to *Hizb ut Tahrir* and other radical groups because of their deep sense of injustice. He argues that such sentiments have increased over time because of 'a huge rise in the number of attacks on Muslims in Britain, increasing threats to civil liberties in the name of security measures, a resurgence in the activities of the far-right in Britain and elsewhere in Europe, and a crackdown on refugees fleeing persecution' (Ansari, 2002:

1). Reflecting such concerns, many British Muslims are said to be primarily troubled about two main issues: one domestic and one external. These are, respectively, defence of Muslim culture and religion, especially in relation to their children's education in Britain. The second is linked to issues of terrorism and international security, especially prominent and focused following the US-British assault on Afghanistan in 2001, the campaign in 2003 to oust Saddam Hussein in Iraq, and the continuing but inconclusive bid to pacify the country's insurgency.

## BOX 10.5 Muslims and education in Britain

The education of their children is a key issue for large numbers of Muslim parents in Britain. In many cases this is linked to a firm desire to safeguard their religion and culture in a strongly secular society. Many British Muslims want segregated education – believed to be necessary in order to prevent young Muslims drifting away from their faith and culture (Travis, 2004). Many Muslim parents also demand that their children's school curriculum should include: teachings of Islam, with associated school prayer facilities; celebrations of the main Muslim festivals, *Eid ul Fitr* and *Eid ul Adha*; and exemption from what many see as inappropriate sex education for children. They also want schools to offer *halal* food and to allow wearing of appropriately 'modest' clothing, especially for girls (Goulborne and Joly, 1989: 92–94). But despite Muslim demands, which have been made over many years, these conditions are not met in British state schools. As a result, increasing numbers of Muslims now withdraw their children from UK state education, with numbers of Muslim schools in Britain growing from 24 in the mid-1990s to around 140 in 2011 (Abrams, 2011). These schools collectively educate well over 10,000 Muslim children (Ahmad, 2002; Abrams, 2011). A 2004 opinion survey of 500 British Muslims indicated that if available, nearly half would send their child to a Muslim school rather than a conventional – that is, secular – state school. Since only a small fraction of Muslim children are already in Muslim schools, this represents a huge latent demand for separate religious schooling. The demand is said to be greatest among men, younger families and the more affluent (Travis, 2004; Abrams, 2011).

An opinion survey in March 2004 found that many British Muslims expressed little desire fully to integrate with the host culture and people, a view partly founded in anti-Western resentment at US and UK involvement in Iraq, seen by many simply as a 'war on Islam'. The poll also showed that many British Muslims saw George W. Bush and Tony Blair's 'war on terror' also as a facet of a more general 'Western' conflict with Islam as a faith and Muslims as a group of people. Finally, nearly two-thirds (64 per cent) believed that Britain's stringent anti-terrorist laws were being used unfairly against Britain's Muslim community (Travis, 2004). While it is not fully clear what their motives were, it seems highly likely that Britain's home-grown Islamist bombers who struck on 7 July 2005 with four bomb attacks in London killing over 50 people were motivated at least in part by a deep sense of grievance and injustice at what they perceived as punitive Western policies against Muslims in Afghanistan, Iraq, Israel's occupied territories and elsewhere.

This section has described how the likelihood of the achievement of the kind of aims expressed by Tariq Ramadan for Western Muslims may be seriously undermined by the existence of grievances, both domestic and international. Unless they are resolved, Muslim criticisms of the status quo might significantly undercut chances of the development of a 'Western Islam' advocated by Ramadan and other figures, including Olivier Roy (2004, 2010).

## France

France is thought to have between five and six million Muslims, twice as many as the UK. It is thought that about half have French citizenship – although precise figures are unavailable. This is because the French state is officially secular and officials are forbidden to ask citizens questions about their religion or ethnicity. It is often asserted, however, that while still preponderantly Catholic, France now has more Muslims than Jews or Protestants, historically the country's most significant religious minorities. Overall, Islam is now almost certainly the country's second religion in terms of numbers of followers (Caeiro, 2005: 71).

Growth in the numbers of Muslims in France came, as in Britain, initially by immigration. Most came from France's former North African colonies, including Algeria and Morocco. Although a presence from around the time of the First World War, Muslims arrived in significant numbers in France only in the 1960s. At this time, the government granted asylum to hundreds of thousands of Algerians who had fought on the French side in Algeria's 1954–62 war of independence. During the same decade, France also invited immigrant manpower – including many Muslims – to meet the needs of the country's then booming economy. The economic boom soon fizzled out but by the 1970s there were substantial numbers of Muslims in most of France's main towns and cities.

Like Britain, France has had a policy of 'zero immigration' since the 1970s. However, France's Muslim population still increases because of relatively high birth rates, an unknown number of illegal entrants, particularly from North and sub-Saharan Africa, and a legal exception that allows the reunion of immigrant families. The purpose of the exception makes clear French policy in regard to its Muslims: to legitimise them in French society by integrating them into it. This policy contrasts with that of Britain, where governmental strategy has long been that of 'multiculturalism', that is encouraging development of separate cultures in an overall context of 'Britishness'.

Successive French governments have claimed to want to integrate the country's Muslims into French society. This implies reducing overt signs of 'Muslim-ness', especially particularistic forms of dress, such as the *hijab* ('Islamic veil'). Reflecting this concern, the so-called 'headscarves of Creil affair' erupted in late 1989, focusing on the desire of several young Muslim women to wear Islamic headscarves at school in the seaside town of Creil. The affair was portrayed in the French media as an attempt to introduce 'communalism' into schools, a traditionally neutral sphere. To explain the passion that this issue raised, it is important to note that France is the country where the Enlightenment began, leading to the presumption that the common ground for the French is their 'rationality', implying that religion takes a decidedly secondary position. Now, many French people are highly secular, perceiving visible signs of what they see as religious identity – such as the *hijab* – to be highly disturbing – because they believe it undermines basic French values of secularism (Caeiro, 2005: 78–80; also see Barras, 2012).

As in Britain, Islamic networks grew in France during the 1980s and 1990s. Members comprised mainly students and other young people, whose parents were mostly from Algeria or Morocco. Some Islamic activists wanted to stage a trial of strength by confronting the French state on the sensitive ground of *laïcité* (secularism) (Kepel, 1994: 40). The issue seemed to strike a chord with many French Muslims who, it appeared, also wanted 'positive discrimination' in favour of Muslim girls in French state schools. Student militants appointed themselves as the spokesmen of 'Islam', seeking to negotiate 'positive discrimination' for practising Muslims enabling them to withdraw, in some contexts, from French law and replace it with *Sharia* law. The Islamic militants found powerful allies in the campaign from other religious entities, including leaders of the Roman Catholic Church in France and some Jewish rabbis. These non-Muslims supported the campaign because they were also religious people, determined to seek protection of their faiths in the face of what they regarded as an increasingly strident *laïcité* (Kepel, 1994: 41). Eventually, despite the protestations of the religious groups, the French national assembly voted overwhelmingly in February 2004 in favour of a ban on the *hijab* and other 'conspicuous' religious symbols in state schools, despite warnings from religious leaders that the law would persecute Muslims and encourage 'Islamic fundamentalism'. The national assembly voted 494–36 in favour of banning 'conspicuous' religious symbols in schools.[6] The law, ratified by the senate in March 2004, came into effect the following September (Henley, 2004). Seventy-eight per cent of French people favoured such a prohibition (as did smaller majorities in Germany (54 per cent) and the Netherlands (51 per cent) (Pew Global Attitudes Project, 2005).

As in the UK, Muslims' domestic concerns in France overlapped with international issues, including the invasions of Afghanistan and Iraq in 2001 and 2003 respectively. Unlike the British government, however, that of France was strongly opposed to the invasion. Did France's large Muslim minority help determine French policy? Such a question is hard to answer, but it does seem clear that the then president – Jacques Chirac – welcomed (1) the renewed bond between the Muslim community and the rest of the French population that resulted from a common opposition to the war in Iraq, and (2) the boost to his personal popularity that he would no doubt gain from the anti-war stance.

Given this apparent meeting of minds between President Chirac and the Muslim communities of France over opposition to the invasions, how can we explain and account for the riots primarily involving youths of Muslim origin that erupted in Paris soon after, in October 2005, and spread to other towns and cities?[7] Two broad arguments have been expressed to explain why they occurred. One is linked to the perceived impact of globalisation, the other to domestic factors. According to Watson and Jones (2005),

> The world watches in trepidation as the wildfires of chaos sweep from France across Europe. We are witnessing the fruits of globalization. Rampant unchecked immigration policies and the enforced fusion of multi-culturalism form the backbone of the New World Order's systematic purge of the sleeping middle class.

This view expresses what might be called the 'clash of civilisations' argument, whereby the riots were seen in the context of a polarised conflict between 'Western civilisation' and 'Islamic extremism'. However, according to de Koning (2006), many of the rioters seemed more in tune with American rappers and spoke in French, not Arabic. Yet this did not prevent a number of prominent French people, including a well-known intellectual and academic, Alain Finkielkraut, and the then interior minister, Nicolas Sarkozy, claiming that the riots were linked to the 'inability' of Muslims to live according to French norms and values. In this view, those who believed that the source of the riots was to be found outside Islam were naïve.

Those who claimed that the 2005 French riots were rooted in domestic factors expressed a second view. Some argued that it was the result of unemployment, a consequence of the country's adhesion to the European Social Model with attendant high wages for those lucky enough to be in work, but also leading to high unemployment, especially among Muslim youths in the *banlieues* (suburbs) of major cities, including Paris (Astier, 2005). Few – certainly not from the peaceful majority in the suburbs whose cars and schools were torched – argued that violence was a legitimate way to express grievances. Yet what for many was beyond question was that the rioting was *not* an affirmation of a distinct religious or ethnic identity, buoyed by a transnational network of Islamist extremists. According to a French sociologist, Laurent Chambon, the riots were not about 'youth gangs inspired by radical Islam'. Instead, they were part of a movement against the 'precariousness' of everyday life in the French *banlieues*, that is, the riots were the product of alienation and existential angst not Islamist radicalisation (de Koning, 2006: 30).

Overall, few if any French commentators found plausible evidence for an ethnic or religious component to the protests. 'Very few in the suburbs are saying: black (or brown) is beautiful. Their message is the exact opposite: neither the colour of our skins nor our names should make us less than fully French' (Astier, 2005). Nor were the riots prompted by religion. However, many among the urban youths who rioted would define themselves as Muslims, in a way that they would not have done ten or fifteen years ago (de Koning, 2006). In addition, it may well be that the 2004 ban on the wearing of the headscarf in public schools – more accurately, the 'law on religious signs' (for the display of Christian as well as Muslim signifiers were prohibited) – was a factor. Nevertheless, very few French Muslims challenged the separation of church and state. Mohammed Elhajjioui, a youth in Lille, claimed that the headscarf ban negated the original, tolerant spirit of French-style secularism which guarantees religious freedom (Astier, 2005). Prior to 2004, courts had upheld the right of girls to wear headscarves in schools. Yet a sense of *religious* grievance was not in evidence during the period of unrest, a six-week time when nearly 3,000 rioters were arrested. Certainly, there was no call by French Muslim leaders, with virtually all mosques appealing for calm (Caeiro, 2006). In short, the *banlieues were* seething with anger, but that anger had little or nothing to do with a desire to be recognised as separate. Indeed, the separateness of the youths from mainstream French society appeared to be endured with resentment, certainly not proclaimed with pride. According to de Koning (2006), the riots and accompanying violence did not express a rejection of French ideals as such, rather a deep sense of frustration that those ideals were not being put into practice for such people. What seems clear was the exact opposite of what Alain Finkielkraut claimed: the violence of October and November 2005 revealed how *unsuccessful* extremist Muslim groups had been in significantly penetrating the urban youth culture of the *banlieues*. In short, Islam is not the problem; the problem is that the majority of the residents of the *banlieues* are Muslim and/or black and because of this many have been discriminated against for long periods, especially in the search for employment. The youths were rebelling because they still dreamt of being accepted as French, not because they wanted to separate themselves from mainstream French society. In other words, the riots were the result of a refusal to be marginalised, a manifestation of 'a deep acceptance of fundamental French values expressed in the "coupling of liberty and equality"'. However, if French society supported Sarkozy's 'push to crush the violence by cleansing the ghettos of their "troublemakers", the next "intifadah of the cities" could well be in honor not of Marianne, France's national emblem and the personification of liberty and reason, but of Musab al-Zarqawi and his successors' (LeVine, 2005).

---

### BOX 10.6 Alain Finkielkraut on the French riots of October and November 2005

The French philosopher Alain Finkielkraut stated in an interview with an Israeli newspaper, *Ha'aretz*, on 18 November 2005 that the riots were 'anti-white, anti-republican pogroms'. They constituted 'a revolt with an ethno-religious character . . . directed against France as a European country. Against France, with its Christian or Judeo-Christian tradition'. While the then interior minister, Nicolas Sarkozy, supported Finkielkraut, the latter was heavily criticised in France, leading him to apologise a week later in *Ha'aretz* for his outburst (Ben-Simon, 2005). But his analysis was very popular in the USA, Russia and the Netherlands, three countries that were all concerned in different ways with the issue of Islam and the integration of Muslims into society (de Koning, 2006: 30).

---

In conclusion, we can note that while many but not all rioters were Muslims, with origins in North and sub-Saharan Africa, 'Islamic extremism' was not a driving force, but anger, frustration, alienation and unemployment were. Few if any lessons appeared to be learnt by the French state from the 2005 riots. During the 2012 presidential campaign both the National Front candidate, Marine le Pen, and her rival, the incumbent president, Nicholas Sarkozy, vied with each other to make Islam and Muslims 'the problem' during outspoken comments about *halal* meat, which became a metaphor for wider concerns about the presence of millions of Muslims in France.

*Halal* meat became a topic of debate on 18 February 2012, when Le Pen made the erroneous claimed that all meat in the Paris region is now prepared according to Islamic methods. It is not labelled as such, she claimed, with the intention of misleading non-Muslim customers. The inference was that was a sop to French Muslims and an attempt to pull the wool over the eyes of non-Muslim French regarding the allegedly growing influence of Muslims and Islam in the country. Yet, as officials later confirmed, although Paris region abattoirs mainly supply local Muslim butchers, this does not imply that all or even most of the meat consumed Paris is *halal*; in fact, most comes from outside the region and is neither kosher nor *halal*.

Sarkozy initially criticised Le Pen for creating a 'false controversy', he was soon content to re-ignite the controversy, in what some saw as a cynical ploy to increase his electoral attractiveness to 'anti-immigration' voters ahead of the presidential election in April 2012.

## Conclusion

Our brief surveys of Britain and France indicate that Islamic extremism is a marginal tendency, seemingly of interest only to small groups of Muslim militants without much in the way of popular support. Figures including Tariq Ramadan and Olivier Roy make the point that Islam can be divided into 'good' and 'bad' versions, driving a more general call for an 'Enlightened' Islam. This implies a Muslim *aggiornamento* (liberalisation) as a prerequisite to the integration of Muslims into Western societies – setting the necessary conditions not for a privatisa- tion of the faith but for a public Islam (Ramadan, 2003; Roy, 2004, 2005, 2010; Peter, 2006).

## Turkey: 'European state' or 'Muslim country'?

French concern about the position of Muslims in France also finds a wider European focus in the issue of Turkey's long-running bid to join the European Union (EU). The issue inspires many comments from politicians and opinion formers to the effect that Turkey's entry into the EU would not only unacceptably dilute 'European identity' but also open up the region to increased threat from transnational Islamist networks (Gul, 2004; Haynes, 2012a). In the mid-2000s, two-thirds of French (66 per cent) and Germans (65 per cent) opposed Turkey's EU bid, as did a majority of the Dutch (53 per cent). European nations expressing support for Turkey's admittance to the EU included Spain (68 per cent) and Britain (57 per cent) (Pew Global Attitudes Project, 2005).

The Republic of Turkey connects Europe and Asia, bridging a divide between (mainly) Muslim Asia and (mainly) Christian Europe. Sharing a border with several Muslim countries – Iraq, Iran and Syria – Turkey is also a member of NATO, an organisation dominated by the United States and other Western countries. While the Muslim population of Turkey amounts to 99 per cent of the overall inhabitants,[8] the country emphatically rejected Islamic rule 80 years ago in favour of secular government. Now, however, Turkey's current government – under the control of the moderate Islamic party, the Justice and Development Party – finds itself caught on the horns of a dilemma: on the one hand, Western governments are often suspicious of Islam, a concern exacerbated in recent years by the continuing 'war on terror'; on the other hand, Turkey has an increasingly vocal Islamic constituency at home that dislikes Turkey's growing closeness towards what some see as a 'Christian club', the European Union (Gul, 2004; Walker, 2004).

## BOX 10.7 Stephen Kinzer on Turkey and Europe

Kinzer examines the social and political tensions generated in Turkey by the bid to join the European Union. In his 2001 book *The Crescent and the Star: Turkey Between Two Worlds*, he explores the cult of modern Turkey's founder, Kemal Ataturk, and the country's historical background rooted in Islam. Kinzer also examines Turkish oppression of the Kurds, as well as the long struggle to free Turkey's government from the grip of the military. He also highlights an issue of international significance: can Turkey survive as a secular state in the Islamic world? If not, how would other Muslim countries be able to make the transition to European-style modernity?

According to Kinzer, Turkey reached an important turning point on 17 August 1999. On that day, more than 18,000 Turks were killed in a massive earthquake. The inadequacy of the state's response to the earthquake led millions of Turks to question the entire power structure in Turkey. This was because the authorities had allowed thousands of death-trap buildings to be constructed and then stood by impotently when there was no disaster plan to put into operation when these buildings collapsed (Kinzer, 2001).

In addition, powerful forces of globalisation are said to be challenging popular faith even further in the 'powers that be' in Turkey. In 1999, the European Union announced that Turkey was an official candidate for EU membership. According to Kinzer: a wave of ecstatic self-congratulation washed over the country, accompanied by solemn newspaper commentaries declaring it the most important event in the history of the Republic. But the European Union then laid out the conditions under which Turkey could become a member, and the military and its civilian allies balked. To repeal limits on free speech, grant

every citizen the right to cultural expression, subject the military to civilian control, resolve social conflicts by conciliation, allow citizens to practise their religion
as they see fit – suggestions like these froze the generals into immobility (Kinzer,
quoted in 'Turkey, elections, and globalization' 2006).

Turkey's putative membership of the EU is controversial in Turkey, as it
is among current EU member states. Concerns over Islamic extremism
are reflected in some European opinions about Turkey's bid to join the EU.
However, attitudes towards immigration are even more strongly associated with views about Turkey's admission to the EU. As Table 10.1
indicates, more than two-thirds (68 per cent) of Turks strongly endorse
membership of the Union. An equally large majority in Spain (68 per cent)
also favours Turkey's admission, as do 57 per cent in Great Britain and
51 per cent in Poland. Elsewhere in Europe, however, majorities oppose
allowing Turkey to join the EU: 66 per cent in France, including 30 per
cent who strongly oppose; 65 per cent in Germany; and 53 per cent in
the Netherlands. The Pew Global Attitudes Survey 2005 adds that

> attitudes toward immigration are associated with these views. Those who
> consider immigration (from the Middle East and North Africa, or from
> Eastern Europe) to be a bad thing are more likely to oppose Turkey's mem-
> bership into the European Union. This pattern is particularly strong in the
> Netherlands, France and Germany. Similarly, those who are more concerned
> about Islamic extremism in their homeland are more likely to oppose having
> Turkey join the E.U., especially in Germany, France, and the Netherlands,
> but less strongly elsewhere.
>
> (Pew Global Attitudes Project, 2005: 3)

**Table 10.1** Turkey joining the European Union

|  | In favour % | Oppose % | Don't know % |
| --- | --- | --- | --- |
| Turkey | 68 | 27 | 5 |
| Spain | 68 | 21 | 11 |
| Britain | 57 | 29 | 14 |
| Poland | 51 | 22 | 27 |
| Netherlands | 44 | 53 | 2 |
| France | 33 | 66 | 1 |
| Germany | 32 | 65 | 3 |

Source: Pew Global Attitudes Project, 2005: 3

Questions about the political and social role of Islam in Turkey, as well as the impact of globalisation, find focus in the long saga of Turkey's bid to join the EU. The advance of European integration implied by the expansion of the EU in recent years is regarded in various ways by academic observers. For some, the EU is an example of 'turbo-charged globalization', while others regard it more as 'a protective shield against the negative "fall-out from" globalization' (Christiansen, 2001: 511–512). Both interpretations can be invoked to explain and account for the EU's recent – and likely future – expansion, not only into southern and eastern Europe but also to the periphery of the region, to include Turkey.

Until 2004, the EU was exclusively a Western European regional grouping of established democracies. However, in May of that year, it expanded both numerically and geographically, to welcome ten new members: Cyprus, Czech Republic, Estonia, Hungary, Latvia, Lithuania, Malta, Poland, Slovakia and Slovenia. In 2007, two further Eastern European, post-communist countries, Bulgaria and Romania, joined the EU. To some, the new, enlarged EU symbolises the end to Europe's artificial division at the end of the Second World War. Now the organisation is a pan-European Union of 27 states. However, the road to EU enlargement was a drawn out and complex process, dominating the politics of Europe's pan-regional relations for a decade prior to the actual enlargement. The process began with the first manifestations of Euro-enthusiasm from Poland and Hungary in the early 1990s, a time when both countries were emerging from decades of communist rule. In 1993, the EU officially set out its definition of membership criteria in response to requests to join: aspirant countries must have democratically elected governments, a good human rights regime and liberal economies without 'too much' state control. Shortly after, in early 1994, the first formal EU accession applications were submitted, from Hungary and Poland. Applications then followed from Slovakia, Romania, Bulgaria, Estonia, Latvia, Lithuania, Slovenia, and the Czech Republic (Bardi et al., 2002: 227). Following the EU announcement in 1999 that Turkey was an official candidate for EU membership, at the Helsinki Summit in the following year, Turkey was given the status of being a candidate country for full EU accession.

Political and economic criteria that the EU attaches for putative members were important factors in encouraging both democratisation (and the consolidation of democracy) and the marketisation of their economies. Pridham lists six 'broad types of influence exerted by the EU on democratization in applicant countries' (Pridham, 2000: 299). This amounts to a combined 'carrot-and-stick approach'. It features the use of political and economic 'conditionality' in order to encourage putative new members to implement satisfactory political economic policies. The chief incentive for putative members was a 'clear timetable for quick accession to the EU' and 'generous aid, credit and direct investment flows from the member to the candidate countries' (Yilmaz, 2002: 73). However, some observers claim that for the new members the objective of joining the EU goes beyond expected economic benefits; it is also seen as emblematic of a rediscovered, shared 'European-ness'. For Hettne, the 'question "what is Europe?" can only be answered by the political process of self-recognition. It is a social construct, . . . an idea rather than a territory'. It implies that 'the content of "European" can be defined normatively by: a strong role for civil society, various institutionalized forms such as parliamentary decision making, and a democratic culture stressing above all individualism and human rights inherent in the individual human being' (Hettne, 2001: 38–39).[9] For our concerns, the issue and application of 'European-ness' is important as it sheds light not only on the question of Turkey's bid for EU membership but also on the larger *problematique* of 'European identity' and where the region's Muslims fit in.

EU membership was the touted reward – *if* Turkey both democratised and made progress towards a human rights regime 'acceptable' to the Union. Turkey's political system is sometimes referred to as a transitional democracy, because the country only relatively recently emerged from decades of strong military political involvement. The EU sought to use both political and economic conditionality[10] to encourage Turkey's government to reform politically and to improve its human rights regime. Turkey's case illustrates, however, that the application of conditionality can lead to a variety of outcomes. While Turkey, on the periphery of Europe, has long aspired to join the EU, for years the country's relatively poor human rights record gave the EU a defensible reason not to progress Turkey's membership application. In recent years, however, Turkey's democratic and human rights record has demonstrably improved – to the extent that EU membership may now be a realisable ambition.[11] There is however another important dimension to note. After 9/11, many EU governments seemed to believe that it was better to have Muslim Turkey in the EU rather than, potentially, part of the anti-western 'axis of evil'. As a consequence, in early 2003, the European commission recommended that aid to Turkey should be doubled – from €0.5bn to €1.05bn – in 2004–06. This can be seen as a calculated attempt both to encourage Turkey's moderate Islamic government to refrain from military intervention in Iraq as well as concrete encouragement to continue with domestic political and human rights reforms (Osborn, 2003).

Some senior European figures were, however, openly opposed to Turkey's membership bid. For example, in September 2004, Frits Bolkestein, then the EU single market commissioner[12] and former leader of the Dutch Liberal Party, warned that 'Europe's Christian civilisation' risked being 'overrun by Islam'. In addition, he claimed, the EU was in danger of 'imploding' in its current form if 80 million Turkish Muslims were allowed to join. Thus, according to Bolkestein, Turkey's entry could undermine Europe's 'fragile' political system, ending all hopes for the continent's integration. Bolkestein claimed at a speech at Leiden University, the Netherlands, in September 2004 that demography was the 'mother of politics', that is, 'while America had the youth and dynamism to remain the world's only superpower, and China was the rising economic power, Europe's destiny was to be "Islamised"'. Quoting the Orientalist American author Bernard Lewis, Bolkestein warned Europeans that in a few decades Europe could become an 'extension of North Africa and the Middle East'. He also compared the EU to the former Austrian-Hungarian empire, which included so many different people from various cultures that it eventually became ungovernable. Bolkestein did however imply that a closer relationship between Turkey and 'Europe' would be desirable – under certain conditions:

> Although a secular state, Turkey is still rooted in Islam. As such she could spearhead a cultural continent with its Arab neighbours and thus become the main actor of a culture with its own identity but with whom others can share common humanist values. This idea does not oppose close and friendly association and collaboration with Europe; instead, it could foster a common front against all forms of fundamentalism.
>
> ('Turkey-European Union', 2004)

247

Cardinal Joseph Ratzinger (now Pope Benedict XVI) appeared to agree with Bolkestein's views. In an August 2004 interview with the French newspaper *Le Figaro*, Ratzinger commented on Ankara's application to join the EU. He claimed that 'Europe is a cultural and not a geographical continent. Its culture gives it a common identity. In this sense, Turkey always represented another continent throughout history, in permanent contrast with Europe'. It would be wrong, he believed, to equate the two sides for 'mere commercial interests' as it 'would be a loss to subsume culture under the economy'. Like Bolkestein, Ratzinger urged Turkey to assume leadership of the Muslim world, spearheading dialogue with the West (Kay, 2005).

Such controversial interventions encouraged a Turkish response. In December 2004, Turkey's then Foreign Minister Abdullah Gul claimed the 'carrot' of EU membership had been a key component of Turkey's 'process of political and economic reform that has been remarkably successful and has received widespread popular support'. Gul also claimed that Turkey was demonstrating strong commitment to internal political, social and economic restructuring that merited recognition by both the European and the global community. Moreover, he averred, the numerous requirements for membership had now been addressed and thus fears expressed by figures such as Bolkestein appeared unwarranted. According to Gul, Turkey's Muslim identity would neither be a handicap nor 'political time bomb'. Instead, 'positive EU-Turkey relations will show that shared democratic values and political unity prevail, sending the message that a "culture of reconciliation" within Europe is at hand' (Gul, 2004).

The EU Commission was at the time of the interventions of Ratzinger and Bolkestein working on a report on the issue of Turkish accession to the Union. The EU enlargement commissioner, Gunther Verheugen, put forward a broadly positive verdict in numerous interviews. He suggested that Turkey now met various basic tests for EU membership, including a free market economy and pluralist democracy, conditions that had progressively strengthened since 2002. Moreover, the death penalty has been abolished and the Kurdish language recognised (Walker, 2004). In 2005, EU accession talks finally began with the intention of finding a *modus operandi* for Turkey to join the Union. But because of the controversy about Turkey's application, the talks are lengthy, without certainty of success. By the time of writing (mid 2012), there is no concrete progress and Turkey's membership of the EU still seems a long way off (Haynes, 2012a).

## Conclusion

In this chapter we examined the following topics:

- The political and social position of Muslim minorities in Europe.
- The threat of Islamic extremism in Europe.
- Muslim Turkey's problematic bid to join the European Union.

In relation to the first issue, we saw that from the 1970s the issue of Muslim assimilation into European societies became a controversial social and political issue, reflecting both domestic and international concerns and issues. From the 1980s, globalisation – and its tendency to facilitate transnational networks – suggested to some that the disaffected among Muslim communities in Europe were a Trojan Horse for the infiltration of 'Islamic fundamentalism' into Europe. However, evidence emanating from the French riots of 2005 appeared to belie the claim that Islamic extremism would find fertile ground in Europe.

Second, the events of 9/11 and subsequent bomb attacks on Madrid (11 March 2004) and London (7 July 2005) helped further to focus popular, governmental and academic concerns on social, religious and political questions in relation to Europe's Muslim communities. The terrorist attacks were widely perceived as a significant turn for the worse in relations between Muslims and non-Muslims in Europe, reinforcing perceptions of the Muslim 'Other' in what for some commentators appeared to be an emerging 'clash of civilisations' between Islam and the West. Others, however, saw the attacks as the acts of international terrorists who unjustifiably used Islam as a bogus vehicle for their murderous escapades.

Our brief surveys of Britain and France indicated that Islamic extremism was in both countries a controversial and marginal tendency, apparently engaging the allegiance of only small groups of Muslim militants with little popular support. We found that Islam can be divided into 'good' and 'bad' versions, a concern driving a more general call for an 'Enlightened' Islam, necessitating, according to some analysts, a general

Muslim *aggiornamento* (liberalisation) as a prerequisite to the integration of Muslims into Western societies. This would also set the necessary conditions not for a privatisation of the faith but for a public Islam (Ramadan, 2003; Roy, 2004, 2005; Peter, 2006).

Third, acceptance in principle of Turkey's application for membership of the EU, announced in 2000, appears further to polarise opinion. On the one hand, for some such as former EU Commissioner Frits Bolkestein and Cardinal Ratzinger (now Pope Benedict XVI) it threatened Europe's sense of cultural identity. For others, however, Turkey's membership of the EU would be useful in helping drive a further wedge between 'Islamic fundamentalists' and moderate Muslims – by showing the latter an important example of what moderation can achieve.

## Notes

1. In this chapter we are primarily concerned with Western Europe, but for reasons of brevity I will sometimes use the term 'Europe'.
2. *Jyllands-Posten*, based in a suburb of the city of Aarhus, is Denmark's biggest selling daily newspaper, with a week day circulation of approximately 150,000 copies.
3. Denmark is home to approximately 150,000 Muslims, amounting to less than 3 per cent of the overall population of 5.4 million. Around a quarter are of Turkish ethnic origin. Earlier migrants came primarily for economic reasons; most later ones, from the 1980s, came as refugees. Currently about 40 per cent of all Muslims in Denmark have a refugee background. Most Muslims live in Denmark's larger cities; most inhabit Copenhagen (http://euro-islam.info/pages/denmark.html).
4. Many of Ramadan's recent articles – in English – can be found at: http://www.tariqramadan.com/rubrique.php3?id_rubrique=43&lang=en.
5. In August 2005, British prime minister Tony Blair announced plans to ban the Islamist group *Hizb ut-Tahrir*, in a crackdown in the wake of the 7 July bomb attacks. The plans, however, were not implemented and at the current time (April 2012) Hizb ut-Tahrir operates legally in the UK.
6. Banned religious symbols also included the Christian cross.
7. The riots began following the deaths of two boys of Malian origin – Bouna Traore, aged 15 years, and 17-year-old Zyed Benna. A third boy, Muhittin

Altun, also 17, of Turkish Kurdish origin, was severely injured. All three were electrocuted by a transformer in an electric substation, after they ran away thinking that the police were chasing them, after demanding their identity documents.

8. Most Turkish Muslims are Sunnis, although a few belong to the Twelver Shia sect. The remaining 1 per cent of the population includes Christians, Jews and Baha'is.

9. Hettne defines civil society as 'inclusive institutions that facilitate a societal dialogue over various social and cultural borders', while 'identities and loyalties are transferred from civil society to primary groups, competing with each other for territorial control, resources and security' (Hettne 2001: 40).

10. Yilmaz defines conditionality as the 'effectiveness, visibility and immediacy of external punishments and rewards'. The EU has employed conditionality since the 1980s to achieve certain foreign policy goals – including, good governance, democratisation, better human rights, the rule of law, and economic liberalisation – in numerous transitional democracies and non-democracies (Yilmaz, 2002: 83).

11. The American non-government organisation Freedom House reported that 'Turkey [had] registered forward progress as a result of the loosening of restrictions on Kurdish culture. *Legislators made progress on an improved human rights framework, the product of Turkey's effort to integrate into European structures.* At the same time, political rights were enhanced as the country's military showed restraint in the aftermath of a free and fair election that saw the sweeping victory of a moderate Islamist opposition party' (emphasis added; Freedom House, 2002: 12).

12. A spokesperson for the European Commission stressed that the Dutch commissioner 'was speaking in a personal capacity' (http://www.rferl.org/featuresarticle/2004/09/fdc6f2b0-c615–4ee1-a913-ca182c355a43.html).

## Questions

- Why is Western Europe so secular?
- Examine and assess the comparative political impact of 'moderate' and 'extremist' Islam in *one* European country.
- To what extent does the post-9/11 'War on Terror' influence Muslim perceptions of Europe?
- What caused the French riots of November 2005?
- To what extent is the issue of Turkey's entry to the EU about religion and culture?

# Further reading

J. Cesari and S. McLoughlin (eds) *European Muslims and the Secular State*, Aldershot: Ashgate, 2005. The starting point for this book is the question of Islam's institutionalisation in Europe. The editors argue that secularisation represents much more than the legal separation of politics and religion in Europe; for important segments of European societies, it has become the cultural norm. The consequence is that for some, Muslim communities and their claims for the public recognition of Islam are perceived as a threat. The book examines current interactions between Muslims and the more or less secularised public spaces of several European states, assessing the challenges such interactions imply for both Muslims and the societies in which they now live. It is divided into three parts: state–church relations; 'Islamophobia'; and the 'War on Terrorism. Overall, it evaluates the engagement of Muslim leaders with the state and civil society, and reflects on both individual and collective transformations of Muslim religiosity.

G. Davie, *Religions in Modern Europe: A Memory Mutates*, Oxford: Oxford University Press, 2000; *Europe: The Exceptional Case. Parameters of Faith in the Modern World*, London: Darton, Longman and Todd 2002; and *The Sociology of Religion*, New York: Sage, 2nd revised edition, 2007. These books are collectively concerned with the sociology of religion, with a particular emphasis on (a) currents of religion outside the mainstream churches, (b) the significance of the religious factor in modern European societies, and (c) parameters of faith in the modern world. Davie is interested in what she calls 'European exceptionalism'. That is, European patterns of religion that are not a prototype of global religiosity, but peculiar to the European continent. It follows that the relatively low levels of religious activity in modern Europe are not simply the result of early modernisation; they are part of what it means to be European and need to be understood in these terms. In *Religion in Modern Europe: a Memory Mutates*, she examines this theme from within Europe itself. In *Europe: the Exceptional Case. Parameters of Faith in the Modern World*, she looks at Europe from the outside, asking what forms of religion are widespread in the modern world but do not occur in most parts of Europe. Pentecostalism is an obvious example.

T. Ramadan, *Western Muslims and the Future of Islam*, Oxford and New York: Oxford University Press, 2003. Ramadan argues that Islam can and should feel at home in the West. In this book, he focuses on Islamic law (*Sharia*) and tradition in order to analyse whether Islam is in conflict with Western ideals. According to Ramadan, there is no contradiction between them. He also identifies several key areas where Islam's universal principles can be 'engaged' in the West, including education, inter-religious dialogue, economic resistance and spirituality. As the number of Muslims living in the West grows, the question of what it means to be a Western Muslim becomes increasingly important to the futures of both Islam and the West. While the media are focused on radical Islam, Ramadan claims, a silent revolution is sweeping Islamic communities in the West, as Muslims actively seek ways to live in harmony with their faith within a Western context. French, English, German and American Muslims – both women and men – are reshaping their religion into one that is faithful to the principles of Islam, dressed in European and American cultures, and definitively rooted in Western societies.

O. Roy, *Globalised Islam. The Search for a New Ummah*, London: Hurst, 2004; and *Holy Ignorance*, London: Hurst, 2010. The 2004 book is the sequel to Roy's *Failure of Political Islam* (first published in French in 1992 and in English in 1994), in which he argued that the conceptual framework of Islamist parties was unable to provide an effective blueprint for an Islamic state. In *Globalised Islam*, Roy examines the prejudices and simplifications used in much popular culture and media in the West regarding Muslims. He explores how individual Muslims are reacting to (not necessarily against) globalisation and Westernisation. Overall, the book is an extremely useful introduction to the politics of Islam in the Middle East, Europe and the United States. The follow-up book, *Holy Ignorance*, argues that the modern disconnection between faith communities and socio-cultural identities provides a fertile space for religious Islamic extremism to grow.

# 11 | The Middle East

This chapter focuses on the region commonly known as the 'Middle East', an area that for many people is one of the first that comes to mind when thinking about interactions between religion and politics, both domestically and internationally. Centring on the eastern Mediterranean basin, the Middle East is, however, a geographical region without clear or obvious borders, unlike, for example, sub-Saharan Africa, bounded on east, west and south by oceans and to the north by the Sahara desert. The lack of obvious boundaries for the region of the Middle East has led to at least four extant versions of its geographic extensiveness, involving between 5 and 25 countries. First, in its most restricted form it comprises just five countries: Syria, Lebanon, Israel, Palestine and Jordan. A second, slightly more expansive, version adds Cyprus, Turkey, Egypt and Iraq, making a total of nine countries. A third entity is larger still, and includes: Iran, Kuwait, Saudi Arabia, Bahrain, Qatar, United Arab Emirates, Oman and Yemen (17 countries in all). The fourth and largest version adds various North African countries, including: Libya, Tunisia, Algeria, Morocco, Mauritania, Sudan, Eritrea, Djibouti and Somalia, amounting overall to a Middle East region of 26 countries. In this chapter we focus on: Israel, Saudi Arabia, and Iran, implying that the third version is our overall focus. This is for three main reasons. First, it enables us to examine the impact of three of the region's most important religious traditions in three of its leading countries: Israel (Judaism), Iran (Shia Islam) and Saudi Arabia (Sunni Islam). Second, in each of these countries, various religious actors seek to influence foreign policies via the application of soft power, often in tandem with hard power wielded by the state in the form of military and economic leverage. Third, these countries are a key source of international focus because of their importance to the stability of the Middle East, a concern underlined by the significant involvement of the United States in each country's foreign policy and international relations.

The religious context of this chapter is that, uniquely among regions of the world, the Middle East was the birthplace of 'three main world religions: Judaism, Christianity and Islam' (Korany, 2005: 72). Partly for this reason, and partly because there have been many recent examples of the interaction of politics and religion in the region, including the Iranian revolution in 1979 and the rise to power of Hamas in the Palestinian National Authority in 2005, many people now routinely associate the Middle East region with religious competition, tensions, and clashes, especially between Islam and Judaism. In this chapter, we examine the significance of religion in the foreign policies and international relations of Israel, Saudi Arabia and Iran. In each case, we shall see attempts to influence foreign policy through wielding religious soft power, whereby groups of domestic actors seek to encourage their governments to apply religious principles, values and ideals to foreign policy aims, goals and outcomes. Thought of in this way, this notion of 'religious soft power' is in line with what Fox and Sandler have noted: '[R]eligion's greatest influence on the international system is through its significant influence on domestic politics. It is a motivating force that guides many policy makers' (Fox and Sandler, 2004: 168).

For many people, the relationship of religion and politics in the Middle East is contextualised by two key events: the 1948 founding of Israel as a homeland for the Jews and Iran's 1979 Islamic revolution. The latter was internationally significant in three main ways. First, unlike earlier globally resonant revolutions – such as the French Revolution (1789) and the Bolshevik Revolution in Russia (1917) – the dominant ideology, forms of organisation, leading personnel, and proclaimed goals of the Iranian Revolution were religious in both appearance and inspiration. Second, in Iran the key ideological sources and 'blueprint' for the post-revolutionary period were all Islamic, derived from the Muslim holy book, the Qur'an, and the *Sunnah* (the traditions of the Prophet Mohammed, comprising what he said, did, and of what he approved). Third, there were fears expressed by Western governments – emphasised by the fact that, following the revolution, approximately 70 US hostages were held in Tehran for 444 days by student militants – that Iran's revolutionary regime would now aggressively attempt to utilise an Islamist revolutionary ideology to try to export revolution to radicalise further already restive Muslims in the Middle East and elsewhere.

Earlier, another key event in the Middle East to do with religion and politics was the founding of the State of Israel in 1948 as a homeland for the Jews. This followed the horrific, genocidal policy of attempted national extermination of Germany's Jews undertaken by the Nazis. Since its founding over six decades ago, Israel's sense of identity has consistently been based on its 'Jewishness' (Korany, 2005: 72), although, as Smith (2005: 220) notes, within Israel 'factions have always differed on what lands were essential to constitute the state of Israel'. The issue of the extent of the geographical area of Israel is at the centre of the continuing dispute with the Palestinians, a conflict that over the last six decades has become inexorably internationalised, involving external involvement from various states and international organisations. The conflict began as a 'conventional', secular security issue yet evolved over time into an unresolved political battle with significant national *and* religious dimensions.

In this chapter we focus on the following issues. First, we examine the political role of religious Jews in Israel. We also examine the influence of the 'Israel Lobby' and of a group of people known as 'Christian Zionists' in the United States who are said to be collectively significant in influencing US foreign policy towards Israel in a pro-Israel direction. Second, we examine the soft power of religion in Saudi Arabia, with special reference to the country's foreign policy and international relations. Finally, we consider Iran's Islamic revolution, its post-revolutionary international relations and foreign policy, and the influence on the latter of influential religious actors, with special focus on Iraq and the competition with Saudi Arabia to try to achieve an influential regional and global position.

Voll (2006: 12) seeks to contextualise these issues in wider changes to international relations since the end of the Cold War in the late 1980s. He suggests that 'the structure of world affairs and global interactions is in the middle of a major change. Both in terms of actual operations and the ways that those operations are conceived and understood by analysts, the old systems of relationships are passing rapidly'. Arquilla and Ronfeldt (1999: ix) note that these changes particularly affect 'political, economic, and military areas, [with] international "soft power" . . . taking precedence over traditional, material "hard power"'. Often, however, in discussions of soft power, religion does not get much attention. For example, the US international relations expert Joseph Nye, who originally coined the term 'soft power' over a decade ago, only briefly notes that 'for centuries, organized religious movements have possessed soft power' (Nye 2004a: 98). Most of his attention, however, is on secular sources of soft power.

As we have already seen in earlier chapters, we can no longer ignore the soft power of religion in international relations (see Haynes, 2012b for further discussion of this issue). For example, in the Middle East, much attention is devoted to militant transnational Islamist movements, including, but not restricted to, al Qaeda. As Voll notes, 'the growing importance of soft power enhances the strength of these militant movements' (Voll, 2006: 15). Less often noted, however, is another use of religious soft power in the Middle East: attempts by domestic religious actors and organisations to influence their government's foreign policy and, more widely, their country's international relations. In this chapter we examine this issue in relation to Israel, Saudi Arabia and Iran.

## Politics and religion in Israel: domestic and international factors

### Religion, identity and Zionism

Israel is an ethnically and religiously majority Jewish country, the only such state in the world. Other religions, including Islam and Christianity, are also respected. More than 75 per cent of Israelis classify themselves as Jews and 16 per cent characterise themselves as Muslims. The remainder – less than 10 per cent of the overall population – include Christians, Druze[1] and the religiously unclassified. Since the country's founding in 1948, successive governments have striven to maintain this aspect of Israel's character (Sandler, 2006). It is important to note, however, that Israel is not a theocracy.[2] Secular institutions predominate in government and in the state more widely.

Since Israel's founding in 1948, there has been much controversy over whether the country is a modern, Western-style, essentially secular state – that is, where secular institutions dominate, as in, for example, Britain, France and Germany – or whether Israel is a *Jewish* state, that is, where Judaist laws and customs would necessarily take precedence over secular ones. In 1969, Luckmann described the state of Israel as characterised by a process of bureaucratisation along 'rational business lines'. This implies not only that Luckmann regarded Jewish religious interests as politically unimportant, unable to determine major issues of public policy, but also that he believed that four decades ago there was overall a state commitment in Israel to an explicitly 'secular', 'Western' way of life (Luckmann, 1969: 147). Luckmann was implicitly referring to the well-known classificatory schema of the celebrated German socio-logist Max Weber (1864–1920). Using Weber's terminology, Luckmann characterised Israel as both a 'modern' and a 'rational' state with the following institutions: (1) a representative legislative body (the Knesset) to enact laws; (2) an executive authority – the government – to conduct the state's affairs; (3) a disinterested judiciary to enforce the law and protect individuals' rights; (4) a rational bureaucracy (civil service) to regulate and organise educational, social and cultural affairs; and (5) state-dominated security services – including, the police and the armed forces – to protect the state from both external and internal attack (Weber, 1978: 56). In 1969, none of these institutions looked to religious bodies or organisations to fulfil their roles and duties.

Over time, however, Luckmann's conclusions would be increasingly contested. Today, is it still correct to describe Israel as a Western-style, secular state? One key source of doubt in this regard is the increased public role of Judaism in Israel (Sandler, 2006). This is partly due to the fact that numbers of religious Jews have grown in recent years. Now Israel's Jews are almost evenly divided between the 'religious' and the 'secular'. Just under half – 49 per cent – classify themselves as 'religious'. Of these, 6 per cent define themselves as *haredim*, that is, 'ultra-Orthodox', 9 per cent classify themselves as 'religious', 34 per cent as 'traditional-ists', that is, they strictly adhere to *halakha* (Jewish law). The remaining 51 per cent of Israeli Jews regard themselves as 'secular', although half of them still profess to 'believe in God' (Elazar n.d.; Ben Porat, 2012).

Some secular Israeli Jews no doubt regard Israel's religious Jews as dangerous, intolerant fanatics, an opinion emphasised in November 1995 when the then prime minister, Yitzhak Rabin, was assassinated by Yigal Amir, a 25-year-old religious Jew. Amir killed Rabin because of the latter's willingness to negotiate with the Palestine Liberation Organisation (PLO) to try to end the decades-long conflict between Israel and the

Palestinians, a deal that involved allowing the Palestinians to control some of the land in the Gaza Strip and the West Bank (of the River Jordan) that Israel has occupied since its victory in the Six-day War of 1967. For many religious Jews – including Amir – willingness to hand over territory to the Palestinians was unacceptable because they believed that it was God's will that present-day Israel should conform to the geographically larger size of the biblical entity, *Eretz Yisrael*. For many non-religious Jews, Rabin's murder appeared to be a clear manifestation of the willingness of 'Jewish fundamentalists [to] attack Jews with secularist leanings' in pursuit of their religious goals (Bealey, 1999: 140).

## BOX 11.1 Religious Jews and 'Jewish fundamentalism'

Religious Jews are sometimes referred to as 'Jewish fundamentalists', characterised by their determination to follow the 'fundamentals' of Judaism and to work to get them observed in both private and public life (Silberstein, 1993). Contemporary Jewish fundamentalism – manifested by organisations such as the banned terrorist organisation *Gush Emunim* (see below) – has roots in Israel's remarkable victory (in just six days) over several Arab armies in the June 1967 war (Sprinzak, 1993; Ben Porat, 2012). For religious Jews, this was a particular triumph as it led to the regaining of the holiest sites in Judaism from Arab control, including Jerusalem, the Temple Mount, the Western Wall, and Hebron. The victory was taken as a sign of divine deliverance, an indication of impending redemption. At the time, even some secular Jews spoke of the war's outcome in theological terms (Sander, 2006).

The nature of Jewish identity has long been understood as an overlapping combination of both religion and nation (Ben Porat, 2010). Many Israelis, especially those who are religious Jews, think of themselves as a nation inhabiting a *Jewish* state created by their covenant with God. This interpretation of the covenant and its implications gave rise to the characteristic beliefs and practices of the Jewish people. Vital to this covenant was the promise of the land of Israel. Following historical dispersions under first the Babylonians and then Romans, Jews prayed for centuries for the end of their exile and a return to the 'promised land': Israel. Except for relatively small numbers, Jews lived for centuries in exile, normally in separate communities. Awaiting divine redemption to return them to their homeland during the diaspora, many Jews' lives were defined by *halakha* (religious law), which served as a core, national component of their Jewish identity. Overall, the Jews' historical suffering during the diaspora was understood as a necessary continuation of their special dedication to God (Chazan, 1991).

Over time, a feeling grew among many Jews that they should seek to acquire their own national homeland. A mobilising political ideology reflecting this aspiration – Zionism, focus of the endeavour to create a national home for the Jews – emerged in the second half of the nineteenth century. Fundamental to Zionism is the recognition of the national identity of the Jews, the rejection of exile and belief in the impossibility of assimilation with non-Jewish, often hostile, communities where the Jews found themselves living in exile. While the Jewish holy book, the Torah, is central to secular Zionists as a 'historical' document, many are uncertain about both the centrality of religious elements in Jewish cultural history and the extent of rejection of orthodox Jewish practices. As a result, the secular Zionism of Theodor Herzl's World Zionist Organisation, founded 1897, was condemned as 'idolatry' by religious Jews, who believed that it sought to replace reverence for God and the Torah by secular nationalism and the 'worship' of the land. In response, religious Jews founded both the *Mizrahi* party (*Merkaz Ruhani* or Spiritual Centre in 1902) and *Agudat Israel* (Association of Israel, founded 1912), although many also supported Zionist efforts to establish a Jewish state. The result was that by the late 1930s and early 1940s there was growing support for the idea of the state of Israel even among religious Jews, stimulated by knowledge of the anti-Jewish Holocaust in Nazi-controlled Germany, during which the Nazis murdered around six million Jews.

Having established the religious and nationalist background to the formation of the state in Israel, next we examine religious Jews influence on Israel's domestic and foreign policies.

## Politics and religion in Israel

Since the country's founding in 1948, state policy in Israel has traditionally favoured the political centre ground; this means that neither religious nor secular political ideas have routinely been able to dominate the political agenda. Over time, however, religious Jews have become an increasingly significant political voice. They have not been collectively strong enough to govern alone via various political parties, although they have often been important components of successive coalition governments, the norm in Israel over time, reflective of the country's fragmented political society. Religious Jews are especially vocal in opposition to the policy of conceding parts of biblical Israel to the Palestinians, especially the West Bank of the River Jordan. The topic is a subject of intense controversy that divides the country. It has dominated the political agenda since the early 1990s, focused in the divisive Oslo peace accords of 1993, Prime Minister Rabin's assassination in 1995 and, following US pressure, the handing over of the Gaza Strip to the Palestinians a decade later, in 2005 (Smith, 2005; Ehteshami, 2002; Ben Porat, 2010, 2012).

In national-level elections in recent years, explicitly religious parties have achieved significant electoral success. In elections since the mid-1990s, religious parties have typically gained more than 20 seats of the total of 120, around 17 per cent. This has often been sufficient to give them a role in government. The current Knesset, elected in February 2009, has only 23 members overall from religious parties: *Shas* (11), National Union (4), and The Jewish Home (3), Torah and Shabbat Judaism (5). This means that 15 per cent of Knesset seats are currently (mid-2012) in the hands of religious parties.

## BOX 11.2 Religious political parties in Israel

Religious parties first entered government in 1949, but it was not until 1967 that they managed significantly to influence Israel's political life. Israel's decisive victory in the Six-day War in 1967 suggested to many religious Jews that the messianic age had begun, leading inexorably to the recreation of the biblical kingdom of Israel. Various Jewish religious–political organisations, including *Edah Haredit* (God Fearful Community), *Neturei Karta* (Guardians of the City) and *Gush Emunim* (Bloc of the Faithful), also emerged at this time. *Gush Emunim* was formed in early 1974 in the West Bank settlement of Kfar Etzion. Its main concern was to achieve conquest and settlement of what it regarded as the biblical land of Israel (*Eretz Yisrael*). Over the next decade, *Gush* grew rapidly, especially after the 1978 Camp David agreement between Israel and Egypt that led to the return to the latter of the Sinai desert – grabbed by Israel in the 1967

> war. Not only *Gush*, but also other such organisations, including the late Rabbi Meir Kahane's organisations, *Kach* ('Thus') and *Kahane Chai* (Kahane Lives; founded after Kahane was assassinated in 1990), argue on religious grounds against giving back territory not only to Egypt but also to the Palestinians or any other non-Jewish entities. This is because they regard such a policy as in contradiction of God's will expressed in the Torah.

Religious zealots – organised in various movements, such as *Kach* and *Kahane Chai* – have been mouthpieces of the mostly religious Jewish settlers who tried to influence Israeli policy in relation to both Egypt and the Palestinians: not to hand back land to non-Jews. Following the 1993 Oslo Peace accords with the Palestinians, involving the latter receiving autonomy in the Gaza Strip from August 2005 and a still to be ascertained area around the West Bank city of Jericho, religious opposition to the accord with the Palestinians was manifested in mass murder. A Jewish religious zealot, Baruch Goldstein, linked to both *Kach* and *Kahane Chai*, murdered 29 people and injured approximately 100 more in a dawn attack on a mosque in the West Bank town of Hebron in February 1994. Following the massacre, the Israeli government, in a sign of its commitment to crush Jewish extremist groups systematically using violence to try to achieve their objectives, banned both *Kach* and *Kahane Chai*.

The political significance of religious parties and movements on policy making in Israel is unlikely soon to fade for several reasons. First, the basis of both nationality and the creation of the state of Israel remains a sense of religious identity, making the issue consistently vulnerable to the influence of religious Jews, some of whom are also political extremists. Second, there has been strong growth in numbers of religious Jews since the early 1970s. Now, it is claimed that up to a half of Israeli Jews 'respects the religious commands', while one in ten belongs to the *haredi* (ultra-orthodox) community. Around 60 per cent of the *haredi* population is under 25 years of age – and the proportion of the ultra-orthodox will grow because many have large numbers of children (Bhatia, 1996; Ben Porat, 2010). Many such people form the core support and activist bases of the – sometimes extremist and banned – religious movements and parties. Third, the latter will continue to have a major political influence because of the nature of the country's political system based on proportional representation. As a result, such parties have the ability to acquire political rewards in return for supporting either of the three main secular political parties, Kadima, Likud and Yisrael Beitenu, in the context of the formation of coalition governments. Finally, in recent years there has been a dovetailing of secular security concerns (concerned with Israel's regional national interests and power) and religious interests (aversion to handing over land to the non-Jewish Palestinians, as it is believed to be against God's will). In tandem, the two constituencies amount to a powerful coalition of interests, often able to apply significant pressure on Israel's government both via the ballot box and other forms of leverage, including interaction with what Mearsheimer and Walt (2006, 2008) have identified as an extremely influential 'Israel Lobby' in the United States.

## The Israel Lobby in the USA

How and under what circumstances might Israeli religious actors influence the foreign policy of the USA in relation both to Israel and, more generally, to the Middle East? According to Telhami (2004: 71), 'religion plays an important role in politics in certain parts of the world' with 'greater prominence of religious organisations in society and politics' in some countries compared to others. As we have already noted in relation to Israel's domestic political scene, over time religious parties have been consistently influential. This means that they are also likely to have a voice in the country's foreign policy. However, religious actors' potential ability to wield such influence is not the same thing as saying that they will consistently be able to influence foreign policy, as their ability will depend on various factors. First, even if a religious organisation or individual gets access to formal decision-making structures and processes, it does not guarantee influence on either policy formation or execution. To have a policy impact, it will also be useful to establish and develop relations with key players in both society and politics, including influential print and electronic media. Second, as Mearsheimer and Walt (2006: 6) suggest, various 'interest groups', including religious ones, can acquire influence by lobbying elected representatives and members of the executive branch, making campaign contributions, voting in elections and trying to mould public opinion in various ways.

According to Mearsheimer and Walt (2006: 1), the Israel Lobby influences US policy towards the Middle East so significantly that 'the thrust of US policy in the region derives almost entirely from [US] domestic politics, and especially the activities of the "Israel Lobby"'.[3] Mearsheimer and Walt employ the term 'the Israel Lobby' as a shorthand expression to refer to a 'loose coalition of individuals and organisations who actively work to steer US foreign policy in a pro-Israel direction'. 'Hardliners' include the American-Israel Public Affairs Committee (AIPAC) and the Conference of Presidents of Major Jewish Organisations, important entities that support Israel's expansionist policies, while 'softliners' include Jewish Voice for Peace, bringing together groups that are inclined to make concessions to the Palestinians. Yet, despite their differences, according to Mearsheimer and Walt (2006: 6) both 'moderates' and 'hardliners' 'favour giving steadfast support to Israel'. The Israel Lobby does not include only Jewish Americans but also conservative Christian evangelicals, such as Gary Bauer, Jerry Falwell, Ralph Reed, Pat Robertson, Dick Arney and Tom DeLay, as well as various 'neoconservative gentiles', including John Bolton, Robert Bartley, William Bennett, Jeanne Kirkpatrick and George Will (Mearsheimer and Walt, 2006: 6). Some among the latter are also 'Christian Zionists', people who believe that Israel's rebirth in 1948 was the fulfilment of biblical prophecy and support the government's expansionist agenda, as to do otherwise would be going against God's will (Clark, 2003). This belief is commonly, although not exclusively, associated with conservative evangelical Protestants in the USA. Christine Zionists also believe that the maintenance of a Jewish state in Israel is a precondition for the Second Coming of Christ, and as a result, advocate unwavering US support for the State of Israel. Finally, Christian Zionists consider that the return of the Jews to the Holy Land, and the establishment of the State of Israel in 1948, was in accordance with biblical prophecy, a necessary precondition for the return of Christ to reign on earth (Halper and Clarke, 2004). Note that Christian Zionist beliefs are different from those of Zionism, that is, the general principle that the Jews have a right to a national homeland in Israel. Christian Zionism is a specifically theological belief, not necessarily involving overt sympathy for the

Jews, either as a national or a religious group. Christian Zionists believe that the Jews must eventually accept Jesus as the Messiah for biblical prophecy to be fulfilled. As a result, some Jews view Christian Zionism as a form of anti-Semitism.

Many Israelis recognise the Christian Right's political clout in the USA, especially during the period of the presidency of George W. Bush (2001–09). For example, since 2001, 'Gary Bauer has met with several Israeli cabinet members and with [former] Prime Minister Ariel Sharon'. Another 'former prime minister Benjamin Netanyahu claimed that, "We have no greater friends and allies" than right-wing American Christians' (Zunes, 2004). It is not the case, however, that Israel's foreign policy is directed from outside by Christian Zionists in the USA or any other external group. Instead, as Chazan (1991: 83) explains, Israel's foreign policy and more generally the country's international relations are also strongly influenced by three domestic factors with significant religious elements: (1) the 'structure and composition of political institutions'; (2) 'social differentiation and the concern of specific groups'; and (3) 'substance of political debates and their relations to fundamental ideological concerns'. She also notes a key implication of these factors: Israeli reactions to stimuli from outside the country are 'filtered through a domestic political lens which operates according to its own distinctive rules'.

Such an arrangement is quite common: foreign policy in at least some states – including, but not restricted to, the USA, India, Iran, and Saudi Arabia – is affected, sometimes considerably, by domestic religious constituencies and organisations. In Israel, religious Jews' political significance derives from three main factors: (1) the nature of the country's political system   proportional representation, giving an influential voice to an array of small parties, including religious ones; (2) the ethnically and religiously fragmented nature of society; and (3) the country's conflict-ridden, ideologically diverse, political party system. When we add to the mix the fact that Israel's public life also reflects the consistently influential voice of public opinion, then we can conclude that Israel's foreign policy is heavily affected by the views of religious Jews. At times, this influence is significantly bolstered by the support of both secular nationalist constituencies within Israel and that of the 'Israel Lobby' in the United States, which brings together both Jewish American organisations and Christian Zionists (Walt, 2005; Mearsheimer and

Walt, 2006, 2008; Halper and Clarke, 2004; Marsden, 2008; Zunes, 2004; Clark, 2003).

Overall, the ambitions of religious Jews in Israel are strongly supported by various lobby groups in the USA, including various Jewish American entities and non-Jewish Christian Zionists with strong representation in Congress. Yet such people were collectively unsuccessful in seeking Israeli retention of Gaza and removal of the Palestinians from both Gaza and the West Bank 'in order to fulfil Old Testament prophecy' (Smith, 2005: 220). This suggests that the combined soft power of Christian Zionists and Jewish American groups, while a major factor in current US Middle East policy, was insufficient to tip US foreign policy in the direction of not supporting Israel's pull out from Gaza in August 2005.

In conclusion, in this section we have seen that the political involvement of religious Jews in Israel had an important impact over time on the country's policies, both domestic and foreign. However, it would be incorrect to see the issues in both contexts as simply reducible to religious concerns; it would be correct to see them as involving an interaction of secular security and religious concerns expressed in a variety of political forms and contexts.

In the next section, we shift emphasis to examine religion's significance in the international relations and foreign policies of two important Middle Eastern Muslim countries: Saudi Arabia and Iran. We will see that in both cases significant political issues – respectively the 1990–91 Persian Gulf War and the 1979 revolution – led to a refocusing of the role of religion in politics, with important international ramifications. We also learn, however, that this did not necessarily imply that religious concerns dominated secular security concerns consistently in relation to either country. As with Israel, we conclude that in both Saudi Arabia and Iran, while religious actors and goals were politically significant, in terms of international relations this did not mean that religious concerns will always dominate secular concerns.

## Saudi Arabia: religion, foreign policy and international relations

The monarchy is the central political institution in Saudi Arabia. The king's powers are in theory limited within the confines of Islamic

(*Sharia*) law and other Saudi traditions. He – never she – is chosen through a two-stage, informal process: the royal family chooses a candidate, and the decision is subsequently endorsed by the *ulama* (Muslim religious scholars trained in Islam and Islamic law). The current king is Abdullah ibn Abdulaziz al-Saud (born 1 August 1924), who ascended to the throne in 2005, following the death of his brother, King Fahd.

## BOX 11.3 Saudi Arabia: the king's political role

In Saudi Arabia, the ruler should aim to rule in a consensual way in order to retain the support of important societal elements, especially the royal family and *ulama*. The overall political policy is enshrined in the Basic Law adopted in 1992, which declared: (1) Saudi Arabia is a monarchy ruled by the sons and grandsons of King Abd Al Aziz Al Saud, and (2) the Muslim holy book, the Qur'an, is the country's constitution, and the basis of government is Islamic law (*Sharia*). In addition, there have been several new laws in recent years, deemed necessary to seek to regulate the increasingly complex functions and concerns of modern Saudi society. However, the new laws are in addition to the *Sharia*, and must not run counter to it. No political parties or national elections are allowed in Saudi Aarbia, although a consultative council, the Majlis ash-Shura, with 150 members exists, albeit with little concrete power. Overall, the king enjoys absolute power, although the support of senior Islamic scholars (the *ulama*) is central in upholding the legitimacy of his rule.

According to Hinnebusch (2005: 169), the king's position over time has grown stronger relative to the *ulama*. Thus, while Saudi 'decision makers cannot wholly ignore political Islam in foreign policy making, no Islamisation of foreign policy has resulted'. In addition, no influential international Islamic alliance has developed under Saudi auspices. There is a parallel here with an earlier, international ideology of significance in the Middle East: pan-Arabism. Several factors – including the autonomy of separate state structures, the disorder of the international states system, the lack of economic interdependence involving Islamic countries, and the dependence of many on the most powerful countries in international relations, especially the USA – served collectively to undermine the ability of pan-Arabism to serve as an effective international mobilising ideology for the Arab states of the Middle East. The contemporary successor to pan-Arabism is pan-Islam. Pan-Islam originally emerged as a transnational Muslim movement during the second half of the nineteenth century. It called for Muslims around the world to come together, drawing on a belief not only that Muslims shared common interests based on religion but also that the great majority were being forced to live under European colonial rule. The idea of pan-Islam is often credited to an individual, Jamal al-Din al-Afghani, a key founder of 'Islamic modernism' (Milton-Edwards, 2006). However, the concept of pan-Islam was short-lived as, around the time of the First World War, it was replaced by secular Arab nationalism, which quickly became more important among Arab governments and nations than the idea of transnational Muslim unity, without regard for modern state formation, advocated by Afghani (Kamrava, 2011a).

In recent years, however, there has been a resurgence of interest among many Muslims in the idea of pan-Islam, with numerous transnational groups forming. However, pan-Islam is a useful idea for both rulers and their challengers. Many among the former, including the government of Saudi Arabia, have used it to try to solidify their rule. The Organisation of Islamic Cooperation (OIC) is an important contemporary vehicle of pan-Islam. The OIC seeks to act as the main conduit of international Muslim concerns. However, the ability of the OIC to act in this leadership role is undermined by the fact that its leading members, including Saudi Arabia and Iran, use the organisation as a competitive vehicle for their national foreign policy concerns. In addition, the OIC's cohesiveness is also impeded by the global fact of sometimes contentious rivalry between Shia and Sunni interpretations of Islam. Finally, counter-elite revolutionary challengers, including al Qaeda and its offshoots and imitators, find the concept of pan-Islam to be a useful ideological referent when seeking to mount challenges to the status quo both internationally and in respect to various domestic governments, including that of Saudi Arabia. Groups such as al Qaeda do not support the OIC, seeing it as an organisation of governments who are united against 'true' Islamisation of their societies (Haynes, 2005c).

## BOX 11.4 Wahhabism and foreign policy in Saudi Arabia

Saudi Arabia is run ideologically under the aegis of Wahhabism, a very puritanical form of Sunni Islam that seeks to spread influence internationally by funding construction of mosques and Qur'anic schools around the world. Since the 1970s, the Saudis have sponsored an estimated 1,500 mosques and 2,000 schools worldwide, from Indonesia to France. As Nye notes, this Saudi funding is immensely important as a way of spreading its soft power. It is almost impossible to estimate accurately the extent of this Saudi financial largesse, which emanates from both state and private sources. Nye estimates that the Saudis have spent around $70 billion on aid projects since the 1970s' oil price hikes, channelled through both radical Islamist groups and mainstream Islamist charities. Nye also notes that even if this amount is heavily inflated, it still 'dwarfs the $150 million that the U.S. spends annually on public diplomacy in the Islamic world' (2004b). The implication we can draw from this is that US soft power loses out to Saudi soft power partly because the latter is bolstered by much greater financial clout.

Like that of Israel, Saudi Arabia's foreign policy is partially based on religious considerations; for example, for religious reasons, the government opposed both 'Jewish' Israel and atheist Soviet Union. During the 1990s, as a result of both domestic and international pressures, the Saudi government, again like that of Israel, sought to re-orientate its foreign policy. Partly as a result of US government encouragement, Israel turned its attention to trying to find a political solution to the 'Palestinian problem'. The Saudi government was also encouraged by the USA to seek to redevelop its foreign policy towards a more 'pro-Western' focus – and this implied a reduction in religious influence and content of foreign policy, especially the funding of radical Islamist groups. This was a major shift in emphasis, as the religious component of Saudi foreign policy had been consistent for decades, in various ways, both financially and institutionally. As noted above, especially since the onset of enhanced oil prosperity from the early 1970s, the kingdom has donated tens of billions of dollars in a strategy which it views as necessary both to support the spread of Sunni Islam and to back various Muslim nations and groups, especially those that adopt the Saudi religious ideology of Wahhabism (Hinnebusch, 2005: 156). Second, Saudi Arabia has consistently sought to exploit its position as guardian of the most holy places in Islam – Mecca and Medinah – strongly encouraging Muslims around the world to make the pilgrimage (*hajj*), while also expanding arrangements to house and transport the millions of pilgrims who arrive annually. Third, Saudi financial contributions have played a major role in building the Muslim World League (MWL), a religious-propagation agency founded in 1962 with headquarters in Mecca. According to Novikov, following scrutiny of MWL documents published in Arabic on the MWL website in 2005, Wahhabi clerics, backed by Saudi Arabia, 'are increasingly targeting Europe as an ideological recruiting ground' (2005: 8).[4]

Saudi foreign policy was encouraged partially to change direction in the early 1990s. At this time, Saudi Arabia was faced with what appeared to be the strong possibility of invasion by Iraq, whose government had demonstrated aggressive intent by occupying Kuwait. It was by no means certain that a massive United States military presence in Saudi Arabia would deter Iraq from invading Saudi Arabia or to withdraw from Kuwait. Consequently, the Saudi government was faced with a clear choice: openly side with the US government or risk invasion from Iraq on its own. In choosing the first option, the Saudi government was compelled to join the United States-led anti-Iraq alliance to try to force Iraqi withdrawal from Kuwait. In response, Iraq tried to play the 'Islamic card', calling for Arab and Islamic solidarity against the United States and its allies. The Saudis noted, however, that a claimed shared Islamic orientation did not forestall Iraq's invasion of Kuwait. During the fighting, Iraq directed missiles against Saudi territory, with several striking both the capital Riyadh and several other population centres. Overall, the outcome of the war demonstrated to the Saudis that it was implausible to try to base the country's foreign policy solely on their vision of the spread of Islam. Instead, the king and his advisers became convinced that the kingdom's security interests necessitated a balancing of both secular security concerns and religious considerations (Hudson, 2005; Kamrava, 2011a, 2011b; Gause III, 2011). As a result, Saudi policy shifted from its earlier focus – propagation of Sunni Islam and attempted containment of Shia Iran – to side with the US in the anti-Iraq coalition.

The change in Saudi foreign policy orientation had serious political ramifications domestically. It resulted in a continuing political crisis that has divided the country's ruling elite. On the one hand, there is King Abdullah – the leader of a group of reformers – who seeks closer links with the West, especially the USA, for security purposes. On the other side of the ideological divide was the crown prince, Prince Nayef (1933–2012), leader of the decidedly anti-American Wahhabi *ulama* (Ziyad, 2003). Internationally, the king has a higher profile, but domestically the prince was very influential. The division between the two men drew attention to the institution of the Saudi monarchy which had traditionally functioned as intermediary between two distinct political communities: a Westernised elite that looks to Europe and the United States as models of economic and to some extent political development, and a Wahhabi religious establishment convinced that its interpretation of Islam's golden age serves as the country's most appropriate religious and ideological guide, including the view that giving a political voice to non-Wahhabis is idolatrous (Doran, 2004). The *ulama* – backed by Prince Nayef – strongly supports the principle of *Tawhid* (monotheism), epitomised by the ideas of Mohammed ibn Abd al-Wahhab, the eponymous founder of Wahhabism. The goal is to project an emphatically monotheistic version of Islam against the Wahhabi enemies, 'polytheists' and 'idolaters', including: Christians, Jews, Shi'ites and even insufficiently devout Sunni Muslims. These four entities are collectively regarded as a grand conspiracy whose goal ultimately is to destroy 'true Islam' – that is, the Wahhabist form of Sunni Islam. The United States, referred to as the 'Idol of the Age', is said to lead the anti-Wahhabi conspiracy. This is because the US: (1) attacked Sunni Muslims in both Afghanistan and Iraq, on both occasions making common cause with Shi'ites; (2) supports Israel against the mainly Sunni Muslim Palestinians; (3) allegedly promotes Shi'ite interests in Iraq; and (4) encourages the Saudi government to de-Wahhabise the country's educational curriculum. More generally, US and Western culture is said to undermine Saudi societal values through its control of various media – including cable television and the internet. According to Saudi Wahhabists, this tide of idolatry finds a focus in 'ultra-liberal', permissive attitudes towards sex, informed by Christian values, and supportive of previously unheard of female freedoms in Saudi Arabia (Ayoob and Kosebaleban, 2008).

> ### BOX 11.5 *Tawhid* and *jihad*
>
> The ideas of *Tawhid* are closely connected to *jihad* or holy war – that is, the struggle by some Muslims – 'sometimes by force of arms, sometimes by stern persuasion' (Doran, 2004) – against idolatry. For many among the *ulama* there is little or no difference between seeking to eradicate what they regard as un-Islamic cultural, social and political practices at home and supporting *jihad* against the US in Afghanistan and Iraq. The position of the *ulama* on these issues is important in Saudi Arabia as the canon of *Tawhid* ensures they enjoy a uniquely important political status – because of their privileged position, deriving from the fact that they alone have had the necessary education and training to identify and do away with anti- or un-Islamic behaviour and entities (Freeman, 2002; Ayoob and Kosebaleban, 2008). This underlines that *Tawhid* is not merely a set of religious ideas but also a set of political principles. Until his death in 2012, Prince Nayef, crown prince, deputy prime minister, and interior minister, was a strong supporter of the principle and practice of *Tawhid* and of the *ulama* as a religious and political entity. The prince strongly defended Wahhabi puritanism in part because he depended politically upon the support of the conservative *ulama*. In foreign policy, Nayef's support for *Tawhid* included championing *jihad*, and this was manifested in a concrete way through his control over the Saudi fund for the support of the Palestinian intifada (which the *ulama* perceive as a defensive jihad against a global anti-Islam, anti-Palestinian, Zionist-Crusader alliance) (Doran, 2004; Korany, 2005: 73).

Since 9/11 the battle for dominance in Saudi Arabia between 'moderates' and 'hardliners' has acquired a new international focus. There are the moderates, led by King Abdullah, supported by the United States. The government of the latter sees itself engaged in a continuing war of ideas for the hearts and minds of moderate Muslims and Arabs. To win that war, according to Nye (2004d), the USA is going to have to become more accomplished in wielding soft power, especially in the Middle East. The biggest challenge to the United States in terms of soft power comes from radical Islamist ideologies, which in Saudi Arabia emanates from Wahhabist ideas, increasingly significant internationally in recent years (Novikov, 2005; Ayoob and Kosebaleban, 2008). According to Nye, 'radical Islamists are expert in the use of soft power, attracting people to their ranks through charities that address basic needs and through religious institutions that form the backbones of communities' (2004d).

This highlights how difficult it is to control soft power, as Saudi Arabia's ruler has discovered. It can have unintended consequences – including attracting people to what many in the West see as intensely malevolent religious organisations and networks, including al Qaeda.

Yet the soft power of Wahhabism is not a resource that the Saudi king and his allies can be sure of controlling, much less banking on to obtain favourable foreign policy results. Many among the *ulama*, as well as ordinary Saudis, regard the royal family as corrupt and in league with Western infidels. For some, the aim is to replace the current regime with a more authentically Islamic one, and some zealots are clearly not averse to the use of terrorism to try to achieve this goal, as attacks in 2003 on residential compounds and the bombing that ripped apart a police headquarters in Riyadh a year later indicate. In June 2011, a 'specialized criminal court [began] hearings against 85 people accused of terrorism' (The Royal Embassy of Saudi Arabia, 2011). In sum, according to Nye, 'the royal family's bargain with the Wahhabist clerics backfired because the soft power of Islamic radicalism has flowed in the direction of Osama bin Laden and his goal of overthrowing the Saudi government' (2004d).

Saudi Arabia's future ideological direction can ultimately be reduced to a single issue: can the state reduce the domestic and international soft power of the radical *ulama* and their Wahhabist ideas? We have seen that in Saudi Arabia, where such Islamists had access to the levers of power via Prince Nayef, they have not so far been able to direct Saudi Arabian foreign policy uniformly along the lines they would prefer. King Abdullah and his allies know that such a foreign policy direction would likely lead to serious conflict with the US government. Consequently, out of deference to Washington, the moderates aimed to block Prince Nayef's support for al Qaeda and other radical Islamists – albeit so far with limited success. Fear of offending Washington also prevented a Saudi/OIC stand against US sanctions against Iran and Pakistan for their development of nuclear capacities (Haynes, 2005c; Kamrava, 2011b).

## Iran: Islamic revolution and foreign policy

In this chapter we draw parallels between Saudi Arabia and Iran because both are regional states that have adopted and developed explicitly

Islamic approaches to government, the state and foreign policy. Note, however, that this does not imply that the countries choose the same policies or pursue similar goals. Both states are 'Islamist' but, beyond that, they are very different. Iran's Islamic Republic is a revolutionary state, which has sought to employ a religious ideology with the goal of transforming both domestic and international orders in the Middle East region and beyond (Ehteshami and Zweiri, 2012). Saudi Arabia, however, is profoundly conservative although, as we have seen, there is debate and competition between leaders pursuing different Islamist interpretations (Gause III, 2011). In Iran, after more than 30 years, the Islamic Revolution is also energetically debated and a source of significant controversy. Over time, Islamism in Iran has been profoundly delegitimised, at least among certain influential sections of society, including many among the educated and the middle class, to the extent that it is claimed that Iranian society has been *secularised* to a profound degree after three decades of living under an Islamist revolutionary regime (Takeyh, 2009; Kamrava, 2011b).

The overthrow of the Shah of Iran in 1979 was one of the most significant, yet unexpected, political events of recent times, because of the pivotal role of Islamic actors in his downfall. Unlike earlier revolutions in other Muslim majority countries, such as Egypt, Iraq, Syria and Libya, Iran's was not a secular, leftist revolution from above, but one with massive popular support and participation from below that ended with an Islamic theocracy in power, with the state dominated by Muslim clerics under the overall leadership of Ayatollah Khomeini. It was also surprising that the Islamic revolution displaced the Shah's regime so easily, as it was not a shaky, fragile monarchy – but a powerful centralised autocratic state possessing a strong and feared security service (*Sazeman-i Ettelaat va Amniyat-i Keshvar*, National Organisation for Intelligence and Security, known as SAVAK) and an apparently loyal and cohesive officer corps. The point, however, was that the forces that overthrew the Shah were united in their goal, derived from all urban social classes, the country's different nationalities and religious groups, and ideologically dissimilar political parties and movements. Following infighting that saw Muslim clerics eventually triumphant, an Islamic Republic was declared, with the Islamic Republican Party coming to power before promulgating an Islamic constitution.

## BOX 11.6 The international significance of Iran's 1979 revolution

The Iranian revolution was internationally significant in three main ways. First, it was the first modern revolution where the dominant ideology, forms of organisation, leading personnel and proclaimed goals were all religious in appearance and inspiration. Second, the guiding principles of the revolution were derived from both the pages of the Muslim holy book, the Qur'an, and the *Sunnah* (the traditions of the Prophet Mohammed, comprising what he said, did, and of what he approved). While economic and political factors played a major part in the growth of the anti-Shah movement, the religious leadership saw the revolution's goals primarily in terms of building an Islamic state, publicly rejecting both 'Western' materialism and liberal democracy. Third, there were immediate fears from Western governments that Iran's revolutionary regime would attempt to 'export' its revolution to radicalise already restive Muslims in the Middle East and elsewhere.

Radicals within Iran's ruling post-revolution elite lost ground following the death of Ayatollah Khomeini, the revolution's charismatic leader, in June 1989, a few months after the end of Iran's war with Iraq (1980–88). Iranians, like people everywhere, hoped for improving living standards. It was becoming increasingly clear to elements in the government that if Iran was to achieve this aim, the country urgently needed foreign investment, technology and aid. A clear lesson was emerging: a successful *Islamic* revolution would struggle to succeed when globally isolated. Over time, it also became apparent that many – perhaps most – Iranians were not content with the policy of Islamicisation, a process that for many amounted to little more than severe political and social repression – especially for women and non-Muslims – behind a religious facade (Ehteshami 2002; Takeyh, 2009). Reflecting the weight of such concerns, a self-proclaimed reformer, President Khatami, was elected as president in a landslide victory in 1997. On taking office, Khatami found himself caught between two sets of demands: on the one hand, there were those wanting social and political liberalisation, in effect to move away from a strictly Islamist interpretation of revolutionary change, and, on the other, a powerful, entrenched, highly conservative set of religious actors who wished to maintain the status quo, not least because they personally benefited from it (Takeyh, 2009: 129–160). Ultimately, President Khatami was unable to assert himself sufficiently, and the result was stalemate between reformers and conservatives, with the latter eventually returning to political pre-eminence (Barnes and Bigham, 2006; MacAskill and Tisdall, 2006; Tisdall, 2006). Now, over three decades after the revolution, religious conservatives are still in power. The costs, however, are high: the government has lost much of its initial popularity, failed satisfactorily to develop the country economically despite vast oil wealth, not managed to build a viable model of Islamic administration and, finally, unwittingly overseen a process of secularisation with many Iranians equating the revolution with an acceptably draconian form of power allowing little in the way of freedoms and ability meaningfully to debate the problems of the day (Barnes and Bigham, 2006; Sohrabi, 2006; Ehteshami and Zweiri, 2012; Dalacoura, 2012).

What has been the impact of the Islamic revolution on Iran's foreign policy and international relations more generally? The first thing to note is that few if any nations at the present time have so clearly articulated an official religion-based ideology and view of the state as an instrument of that ideology, as has Iran. Second, like Saudi Arabia, Iran's post-revolution foreign policies and activities have been the focal point of competition for influence by both Islamist and secular factions. As a result, Iran's foreign policy has fluctuated between a focus on traditional foreign policy concerns – such as, security and economic goals – and Islamic revolutionary goals regionally and internationally. From 2005, President Mahmud Ahmadinejad led a partial reassertion of Islamist concerns in Iran's foreign policy, without neglecting traditional, security issues, most notably, 'Iran's right to civil nuclear power, Iran's regional interests, [and] its attitude to the United States and Europe' (Barnes and Bignam, 2006: 33; Kamrava, 2011b: 186–88).

## BOX 11.7 Public opinion, religion and foreign policy in Iran

In the West, it is often assumed that Iran is a closed society with little ability for citizens to discuss political, social and economic issues. It comes as a surprise then to learn that in fact both domestic and foreign policy debates are featured in Iran's newspapers, while foreign policy is also a frequent topic of open deliberation in the Iranian parliament, the Majlis (Sarioghalam, 2001; Takeyh, 2009). The Ministry of Foreign Affairs is the main promoter of Iran's secular state interests. In contrast, religious hardliners in Iran, like in Saudi Arabia, advocate Tehran's championing of Islamic causes and expressions of Muslim solidarity with coreligionists beyond Iran's borders frequently attacking the Foreign Ministry's policies, especially in the pages of the Iranian daily *Jomhuri-ye Islami* (Afrasiabi and Maleki, 2003). This indicates that religion may have an impact on foreign policy – especially when the country's rulers find it useful to bolster support for a policy that it advocates, such as seeking to increase Iran's influence in neighbouring Iraq. This includes more generally propagation of (Shia) Islam and advancing the cause of other Muslim peoples. But such policies' significance will fluctuate dependent on the views of significant personnel, within government and outside it, both religious and non-religious, and their ability to influence government decisions (Afrasiabi and Maleki, 2003; Ehteshami and Zweiri, 2012).

Following Ahmadinejad's initial election as president in 2005, the former president, Mohammad Khatami, publicly criticised 'the "powerful organization" behind the "shallow-thinking traditionalists with their Stone-Age backwardness" currently running the country'. This was believed to be a covert reference to a radically anti-Bah'ai and anti-Sunni semi-clandestine society, called the Hojjatieh, which Katami said was rapidly 'reemerging in the corridors of power in Tehran' ('Shi'ite supremacists emerge from Iran's shadows', 2005).[5] According to Barnes and Bigham (2006: 2), the chief ideologue of Hojjatieh is Ayatollah Mohammad Taqi Mesbah-Yazdi, a hardline Shi'ite cleric and key inspiration to Iranian 'messianic fundamentalists' Ayatollah Mesbah Yazdi is a close ally of President Ahmadinejad, a claim supported by the fact that Mesbah-Yazdi issued a *fatwa* urging all two million members of the *bassij* Islamic militia[6] to vote for Ahmadinejad in the 2005 presidential elections ('Shi'ite supremacists emerge from Iran's shadows', 2005). This is evidence to bolster Sarioghalam's (2001: 1) claim that 'Iran's foreign policy is shaped, not mainly by international forces, but by a series of intense post-revolutionary debates inside Iran regarding religion, ideology, and the necessity of engagement with the West and specifically the United States'. Until the 2005 election of Ahmadinejad, there was often agreement that when the material interests of the state conflicted with commitments to 'Islamic solidarity', then Iran's government would usually give preference to secular security and economic considerations. Iran sought to use religion in pursuit of secular state interests – as a way of contending with neighbouring regimes or trying to force changes in their policies. For example, Iran's government has long promoted Islamic radicals and anti-regime movements when official relations with a Muslim country are poor, such as with Uzbekistan or Azerbaijan, but does not work to undermine secular Muslim regimes such as Turkmenistan if that regime's relations with Tehran are good (Kemp, 2005; Ramazani, 2004).

But the election of Ahmadinejad appears to have led to a change in the power balance in Iran, whereby religious soft power has emerged as an influential component of Iran's foreign policy especially in relation to Iraq and the continuing competition there with Saudi Arabia for influence (Barnes and Bigham, 2006; Byman, 2011; Gause III, 2011: 177, 180; Ehteshami and Zweiri, 2012). Iran is 90 per cent Shiite and Iraq is between 60 and 65 per cent Shiite, while about one-third of Iraqis are Sunnis. These factors have facilitated the ability of Iran to achieve considerable power and influence in Iraq since the fall of Saddam Hussein in March 2003. Iran has actively supported the position of the United States in advocating elections in Iraq. The main reason was that by the use of its cultural and religious soft power, Iran had a practical way to try to facilitate the political dominance of Iraq's Shiite majority and, as a result, the government hoped to achieve an influential position in relation to the country's political future. The post-2003 position contrasts with the approach Iran adopted in the immediate aftermath of the 1979 revolution when the government focused efforts on hard power strategies, for example, seeking to export the revolution 'through the funding of Shiite resistance groups'. Now, however, 'current circumstances encourage Iran to use soft power to help create some sort of Islamic government in Iraq' (Kemp, 2005: 6). However, the use of Iranian soft power to appeal to coreligionists comes up against a bid from Saudi Arabia to extend its influence in Iraq. Both sides use a mix of hard and soft power, including religion. Iran is said to have a good intelligence presence and a better organised military capability in Iraq, while Saudi Arabia seeks both to use its financial largesse and to exploit the dissatisfaction of Iran's Sunni minorities. Iran's Sunni minorities live in some of the least-developed provinces and are under-represented in parliament, the army and the civil service. Iran's Kurds, who are Sunni, have rioted in the north, while the ethnic Arab south is another location that has suffered both riots and bombings since the fall of Saddam (Kemp, 2005; Barnes and Bigham, 2006; Byman, 2011).

In Iraq, the government of Iran is seeking to win the hearts and minds of ordinary Iraqis, the majority of whom are Shiites (Haynes, 2008a). While Iran is believed to have a better intelligence presence in the country, Saudis are said to account for the majority of suicide bombers active in Iraq. Writing in *Newsweek* in August 2005, a former Central Intelligence Agency agent, Robert Baer, quoted an unnamed senior Syrian official who told Baer that more than 80 per cent of the 1,200 suspected suicide bombers arrested by the Syrians in the two years following the invasion of Iraq in March 2003 were Saudis. Baer then quoted Iran's Grand Ayatollah Saanei who responded by describing the Saudi Wahhabi suicide bombers as 'wolves without pity'. Iran, he declared, would 'sooner rather than later . . . have to put them down'. Saudi Arabian interests are thought to be behind the suicide bombing campaign. Saudi Arabia is also reported to be active in Iran in other ways, especially in the ethnically Arab, oil-rich south of the country. Riyadh is said to have offered financial incentives for local people to convert from Shi'ite to Sunni Islam (Baer, 2005; Kamrava, 2011b).

Overall, it is probable that Iran will continue to promote democratic structures and processes in Iraq – as a strategy to help consolidate a strong Shiite voice in Iraq's government and thus likely to help Iran increase and maintain its influence in the country. Iran is also likely to seek to continue to use its soft power as a key short and medium term means to try to facilitate its main objectives in Iraq: political stability and an accretion of Iran's influence. However, Iran's involvement in Iraq is also part of a long-term strategy that may involve exercise of both soft and hard power. Since the fall of Saddam a decade ago, Iran has opted for intervention through primarily soft power and religious ties, but retains the capabilities to be a significant and active (and violent) player should its strategic interests be challenged (Dalacoura, 2012). 'Iran's capacity, capability, and will to influence events in Iraq are high in terms of both hard power and soft power' (Kemp, 2005: 7).

## Conclusion

In this chapter, we have focused on the international significance of the interaction of religion and politics in the Middle East, with specific examination of Israel, Saudi Arabia, and Iran. We have emphasised the following:

- In each of the country contexts we examined – Israel, Saudi Arabia and Iran – there were various issues of analytical significance linking both religion and politics and also religion, foreign policy and international relations.
- In the three countries under scrutiny, normative variables – such as, the concept of 'greater Israel', Sunni Islamic proselytisation (Saudi Arabia) and a revolutionary Islamist foreign policy (Iran) – interact with secular national interest concerns to produce foreign policy outcomes characterised by both 'religious' and 'secular' concerns.
- In each of the three countries, secular security concerns interact with religious issues in ways that are also linked to various expressions of religious soft power.

We have seen that to understand the dynamics of the regional and international involvement of religion and politics in the Middle East, it is necessary to take into account how secular structures and processes interact with religious ones. We saw that the political involvement of religious Jews in Israel is important in helping to mould the country's policies in relation to both the Palestinians in the Occupied Territories and the government of the United States. This emphasises that over time secular Zionist concerns have been augmented by religious Jews' concerns about the desirability of as large an Israel as possible in order to accord with God's will. However, it is incorrect to see political struggles reducible to religious terms and issues; rather, they reflect dynamic interaction of secular security and religious concerns. We saw this in relation to contemporary interactions between the governments of Saudi Arabia and Iran. In both countries, various issues – including respectively the 1990–91 Persian Gulf War and the continuing impact of the 1979 Islamist revolution – have led to a refocusing of the role of religion in foreign policy and more generally international relations. More recently, however, the post-2003 conflict in Iraq, the election to power of President Ahmadinejad in 2005 and again in 2009 and a corresponding rise in the influence of some religious individuals and organisation, as well as recent attempts by Saudi religious interests to increase the country's influence in Iraq, all indicate that the soft power of religious interests in both countries, but especially Iran, is currently in the ascendant.

## Notes

1. The Druze are a numerically small but distinct religious community. There are about 1 million Druze worldwide; most live in various Middle East countries – including Lebanon, Israel, Syria, Turkey and Jordan – while smaller communities live elsewhere, including the USA and Western Europe. Linguistically and culturally, the Druze are closely linked to Arabs and many Druze actually consider themselves to be Arabs (http://www.dailytimes.com. pk/default.asp?page=story_1-2-2004_pg3_5), although some Israeli Druze do not (http://news.bbc.co.uk/1/hi/world/middle_east/3612002.stm). However, the Druze are not judged to be followers of Islam by most Muslims in the Middle East, although many Druze insist that their faith is actually authentically Islamic.

2. Theocracy is government by or subject to religious authority, where religious figures exercise political power, and where religious law is dominant over civil law. For example, led by Ayatollah Ruhollah Khomeini (1979–89), Iran was a theocracy under the Muslim Shi'ite clergy.

3. The views of Mearsheimer and Walt were criticised by many following their publication in the *London Review of Books* in March 2006. The chief criticisms were that: they were being anti-Semitic, placing too much import-ance on Israel as a source of US foreign policy in the Middle East, and that Islamist terrorism was not only in response to US support for Israel but also linked to other, more global factors to do with the colonial background, when British and French interests dominated the Middle East region. For a selection of critiques from the Letters page of the *London Review of Books*, where a short version of their argument appeared on 23 March, 2006, go to: http://www.lrb.co.uk/v28/n07/letters.html. The original, and much longer, version of the piece, amounting to 82 pages, was a Working Paper (RWP06–011) published in March 2006 under the joint auspices of the University of Chicago and Harvard University, the institutions where Mearsheimer and Walt respectively were at the time employed. The definitive, book-length version of their argument was published in Mearsheimer and Walt (2008).

4. The Muslim World League's UK website is at http://www.mwllo.org.uk/.

5. Bah'ia is a religion founded in 1863 in Persia that emphasises the spiritual unity of all humankind.
6. These are Islamic vigilantes who are loyal to Iran's Supreme Leader, Ayatollah Ali Khamenei.

## Questions

- Is religion an important factor in the Middle East's international relations?
- Does the involvement of religion in the region's international relations make compromise more difficult to achieve in issues of competition and conflict?
- What is the role of religion in Israel's foreign policy?
- To what extent is it correct to see Saudi Arabia's foreign policy as a focal point of competition between 'moderates' and 'radicals'?
- Why was Iran's revolution so significant internationally?

## Further reading

A. Ehteshami and M. Zweiri (eds), *Iran's Foreign Policy: From Katami to Ahmadinejad*, New York: Ithaca Press, 2012. This collection of papers sheds new light on the foreign policy of Iran over the last decade or so. The contributors examine the interaction of secular and religious concerns that is characteristic of foreign policy under both Katami and Ahmadinejad.

L. Fawcett (ed.), *International Relations of the Middle East*, Oxford: Oxford University Press, 2005. This textbook offers a historical framework and up-to-date analysis of contemporary events in the Middle East. The editor has brought together leading scholars in the field, and the book overall presents a balanced and comprehensive assessment of the international relations of the region.

M. Kamrava (ed.), *International Politics of the Persian Gulf*, New York: Syracuse University Press, 2011. The Persian Gulf has long been at the centre of the Middle East region's strategic influence, while also being wracked periodically by political instability and tension. Adopting a country focus, this book examines the foreign policies of regional countries, including the influence of religion.

C. Smith, *Palestine and the Arab-Israeli Conflict*, New York: St Martin's Press, 6th edition, 2010. This book is perhaps the most highly regarded volume on this topic. It analyses the role of both religious and secular issues in the evolution of the conflict between Israel and the Palestinians.

S. Telhami and M. Barnett (eds), *Identity and Foreign Policy in the Middle East*, New York: Cornell University Press, 2002. This book focuses upon how the formation and transformation of national and state identities among Middle Eastern countries affects their foreign policy behaviour.

# 12 | Sub-Saharan Africa

The purpose of this chapter is to examine how religion affects the international and transnational relations of sub-Saharan Africa.[1] Africa is a huge region of 45 states, nearly a quarter of all the world's countries. There is a huge variety of languages, cultures and traditions found throughout the region. However, almost all African countries share a history both of European colonial control and of concerted proselytisation from Christianity and Islam that led to the current situation: hundreds of millions of adherents of both religious traditions are found throughout Africa. However, despite the general societal importance of religion in Africa, very few African countries – Sudan is one example – have state policies which are closely linked to religious ideas or principles. But what is of widespread significance throughout the region are various transnational networks, both Christian and Islamic. Reflecting this, we focus upon African transnational religious networks: from Christianity, transnational Roman Catholic and Protestant networks, and from Islam, both a moderate transnational organisation, *Tablighi Jamaat*, and several 'extremist' Islamist networks, including Boko Haram in Nigeria. Finally, we examine the impact of the 'evangelisation' of US foreign policy in relation to Sudan's recently ended civil war between the Muslim north and the Christian and animist south of the country.

## The spread of Islam and Christianity in Africa

During the first half of the twentieth century, the pace of growth of Christianity in Africa outstripped that of Islam. Numbers of Christians increased from around 10 million in 1900 to more than 250 million by the early 2000s. Over the same period, the total number of African Muslims grew from about 34 million to nearly 300 million (Barrett et al., 2001). While Christians are spread throughout the entire region, the location of Muslims is more fragmented. Millions of African Muslims live north of the Saharan desert, in the North African countries of Morocco, Algeria, Tunisia, Libya and Egypt. In addition, Africa is predominantly Muslim above the tenth parallel, which cuts through the northern regions of Sierra Leone, Côte d'Ivoire, Ghana, Togo, Benin, Nigeria, Cameroon, Central African Republic, Ethiopia and Somalia. The same line roughly separates Muslim from non-Muslim in Sudan and Chad. Above the tenth parallel, the Gambia, Senegal, Mali and Niger are preponderantly Muslim.

---

### BOX 12.1 The spread of Christianity in Africa during the colonial period

During the colonial period in Africa (c.1880–1960), conversion to Christianity and Islam was facilitated among Africans for various reasons. For many Africans, conversion to Islam was a manifestation of antipathy to European colonialism, an alternative modernising influence opposed to the influence of European Christian missionaries. Islam provided converts with an alternative modernising worldview, not defined by the colonial order and its foreign norms, but by a perceived 'indigenous' culture that many Africans perceived to be authentically closer to their existing cultures than the 'alien' creed of Christianity. Other Africans, however, saw conversion to Christianity, as a means not only to acquire spiritual benefits but also to gain access to both education and welfare, a key means to acquire 'upward mobility'. During the colonial period, education and welfare provision were under the almost exclusive control of foreign Christian missions.

---

While various parts of Africa received more proselytisation from one faith or the other, Islam and Christianity were only rarely in direct competition. In the Muslim areas, colonial authorities discouraged Christian missionaries from proselytising. This was because the European-introduced system of rule typically relied on good relations between colonial authorities and local Muslim rulers. The best example of a mutually beneficial relationship in this regard was between Europeans and local Muslim rulers in northern Nigeria. There Lord Lugard's system of indirect rule (actually first developed in Uganda, following Britain's Indian colonial experiences) owed much of its success to the fact that it tampered hardly at all with pre-existing socio-political structures and cultural norms. The local, slave-owning Fulani elite became intermediaries with the colonial administration as a reward for putting down an Islamist revolt in Satiru in 1906. Fulani leaders were able to enlarge their sphere of influence – and to convert more people to Islam – by extending their supremacy over groups of previously autonomous non-Muslims, notably those in what eventually became Plateau and Borno states.

Until colonial rule was firmly established in Africa, roughly by the time of the First World War, Christian missions often made relatively little headway in their conversion attempts. Nevertheless, the social influence of early missionaries was important. They were aware that teaching a love of Christ was insufficient on its own, realising that many Africans regarded themselves as in need of material as well as spiritual assistance. It was, therefore, in the missionaries' interest to seek to improve the material knowledge, skills and wellbeing – via African converts' ability to read, write and have access to Western methods of health protection. In this way, Africans would develop into more useful members of Christian society. Over time, a class of educated Africans emerged, people who owed their upward mobility to the fact that they had converted to Christianity and been able to absorb the benefits of a mission education. By and large, the leaders of post-colonial Africa were drawn from among the ranks of such people.

## BOX 12.2 The spread of Islam in Africa

Islam spread from North Africa southwards from the seventh century CE, predating European colonialism by hundreds of years. Its diffusion was multi-directional. Over time, Islam strongly established itself – reflected in both socio-political organisation and religio-cultural developments – among many communities in much of western and, to a lesser yet still significant degree, eastern, Africa. Consequently, attempts at mass Christian conversion in those areas in the late nineteenth and early twentieth centuries were, on the whole, singularly unsuccessful. However, Islam made much less progress during the colonial era in central-southern and southern Africa. Its relatively late arrival from the north came up against the rapid spread of European Christianity from the south in the last decades of the nineteenth century; as a result, Islam's influence was minimised.

Where they existed, the progress of Islam followed pre-existing trade routes, such as the North African and Indian Ocean ways. Conversions were also made via *jihad* ('holy war') during the late nineteenth and early twentieth centuries. In the late nineteenth century, the wider Muslim world experienced the slow demise of the Ottoman empire and the near contemporaneous emergence of Saudi Arabia as champion of Wahhabist reformist ambitions. The growth of the Sufi brotherhoods and their reformist rivals were two developments in African Islam more or less contemporaneous with the consolidation of European rule, while others included: (1) the extension of Muslim networks throughout much of Africa and beyond, and (2) the introduction of new, modernising ideas. Many Muslims joined Sufi brotherhoods to further their own commercial networks, and were often receptive to the reformist ideas of the Wahhabiya and of pan-Islamic ideals – in the context of urbanisation and development of ethnically orientated Muslim associative groups. Sufi brotherhoods prospered under colonial rule in, inter alia, Senegal, Mauritania, Northern Nigeria, Tanganyika, Sudan and Somaliland (Haynes, 1996: 23–50).

The outcome was that various 'versions' of Islam established themselves in Africa, both north and south of the Sahara. In both regions, Africans have long belonged to Sufi brotherhoods. In addition, many ethnic groups, especially in West and East Africa, converted to Islam en masse before and during the colonial era, giving religious belief among such people an ethnic dimension. Some of them would also be members of Sufi brotherhoods, so the latter may also have an ethnic aspect. However, orthodox conceptions of Islam – nearly always Sunni in Africa – are the province of the religious elite, the *ulama* (religious/legal scholars), who look down on the 'uneducated' followers of Sufi Islam who practise 'degenerate' or 'impure' versions of the faith.

Differing manifestations of Islam point to the fact that the faith in Africa covers a variety of interpretations of what it means to be a Muslim. Away from the Arab countries of the north, Islam in south of the Sahara can be divided into distinct categories, corresponding to extant social, cultural and historical divisions. The first includes the dominant socio-political and cultural position of Islam in the emirates of northern Nigeria, the lamidates of northern Cameroon and the shiekdoms of northern Chad. In each of these areas, religious and political power is fused in a few individuals; over time, a class structure developed based on religious differentiation. Second, there are the areas where Sufi brotherhoods predominate, generally in West and East Africa, and especially in Senegal, the Gambia, Niger, Mali, Guinea, Kenya and Tanzania. Third, in a number of African states, Muslims, fragmented by ethnic and regional concerns, are politically marginalised. This is the situation in a number of African countries, including: Ghana, Togo, Benin and Côte d'Ivoire.

In Sudan, however, recent rulers sought to utilise Islam as an ideology of conquest and of Arabicisation. This policy is primarily directed against the Dinka, the Nuer and other southern Sudanese peoples. Many among the latter took part in a long civil war against the northern Arab-Muslim-dominated state. As we shall see later, this attempt to Islamicise and Arabicise received the attention from US Protestant evangelicals, some of whom encouraged the US government to introduce a law in 2000 that is credited with helping end the civil war in Sudan in 2005.

The long-running campaign by Sudan's government to Islamicise the country is but one manifestation of political Islam, or Islamism in Africa. There are two broad types of Islamist groups found in sub-Saharan Africa. First, there are 'moderate' groups, such as *Tablighi Jamaat*. Second, there are 'radical' groups, such as al Qaeda and its affiliates, active in the region. *Tablighi Jamaat* is a transnational Islamic missionary movement, which originated in India, encourages greater religious devotion and observance. Its founder, Mawlana Mohammed Ilyas, strove for a purification of Islam as practised by individual Muslims through following more closely the rules established in the Sunnah. Over the years, the *Tablighi Jamaat* has grown into what Janson (2006: 44) describes as probably the largest Islamic movement at the current time. Yet, few scholars have paid attention to this fact, preferring in many cases to focus upon radical vehicles of Islam, such as Boko Haram in Nigeria. Yet *Tablighi Jamaat* is highly significant in many African countries, an expression of moderate Islam that attracts a wide variety of people. As we shall see below, both radical and moderate Islamic groups in Africa seek to attain the same broad goals:

improvement in both spiritual and material wellbeing through closer application of religious tenets. The same point could also be made in relation to many African Christians who, like their Muslim counterparts, often look to transnational religious networks to help them fulfil their goals. In Africa, as in many other regions that we examine in this text, transnational religious actors seek to achieve goals through the inauguration, embedding and development of cross-border associations, building links with like-minded groups via transmission and receipt of inter-personal and inter-group exchanges of information, ideas and/or money. Often encouraged by globalisation, such actors inhabit a 'globalising social reality' where previously significant barriers to communication have considerably diminished. As a result, they can construct national, regional, continental or, in some cases, global networks of like-minded people, a development that may serve to increase their influence.

## The Roman Catholic Church: liberation theology in South Africa

The Roman Catholic Church is a highly important transnational actor in contemporary international relations. The Church is important in Africa partly because of the large numbers of Africans who are baptised Catholics – around 120 million people, one-fifth of Africa's population – and partly because it is the only regional religious institution which is also a self-financing transnational organisation, a fact that gives the Church considerable societal influence.

Diamond notes the Church's political significance in relation to democratisation outcomes in both South Africa and Kenya in the early 1990s. At this time, the Church was at the forefront of societal demands to 'oppose, denounce, frustrate and remove authoritarian regimes' (Diamond, 1993: 49). Leading local Roman Catholics were involved in national conferences in the early 1990s concerned with the post-authoritarian political way forward in various French-speaking African countries, including: Chad, Congo-Brazzaville, Gabon, Mali, Niger, Togo, and Zaire (now Democratic Republic of Congo (DRC)). Overall, however, outcomes were variable; for example, in Congo-Brazzaville a new government was democratically elected, although the political situation remained tense for many years. In Togo, Chad, Gabon and Zaire/DRC, however, national conferences did not lead, in the short term, either to new constitutions or democratically elected governments. In DRC and Togo, the outcome was initially stalemate, as opposition forces were initially too weak to unseat these authoritarian leaders. Later, however, dictators in both countries left power under pressure from civil society, including that from the Roman Catholic Church.

In addition to the Church's role in democratisation in several African countries, it was also a key actor in the demise of apartheid rule in South Africa in the early 1990s, and the country's subsequent democratisation. Although the Roman Catholic Church is a minority church in South Africa – only around 7 per cent of South Africans belong to it – it is appropriate to call the Church in South Africa a 'significant player' in relation to the end of apartheid and subsequent democratisation, because of the Church's ability to apply transnational, institutional and moral pressure against the National Party government of President de Klerk (Haynes, 1996: 96–97, 148–152). During the apartheid era (1948–94), the white-dominated state looked to its main religious ally, a Protestant church, the Dutch Reformed Church (NGK), for religious justification for its policy of 'separate development'. Over time, however, things began to change – in response to both internal and external developments – with other non-Afrikaner churches – especially the Roman Catholic Church – becoming increasingly bold in challenging apartheid on both religious and moral grounds. In the mid-1980s, the South African Council of Churches came under black leadership, the ecumenical vanguard for a radical 'Black theology'. Its best known – and probably most influential expression   was the 'Kairos document', a publication that included both social and contextual analysis to describe the struggle for salvation from public sin. The overall importance of Christian, including Roman Catholic, opposition to white minority rule was clear at the end of the 1980s, when the premises of leading church organisations were fire-bombed by right-wing groups (Harris et al., 1992: 466). In sum, Christian anti-apartheid institutional opposition – especially from the Roman Catholic Church – was influential in encouraging South Africa's government to reform apartheid and begin a process of democratisation.

## BOX 12.3 Liberation theology in South Africa

The impact of transnational ideas linked to Catholicism can be seen in South Africa, where the application of liberation theology and the founding of Latin American-style Basic Christian Communities (BCCs) were politically significant from the 1980s. Both developments significantly informed the advance of 'Black theology'. BCCs first emerged in Latin America in the 1960s, orientated towards community development through the application of group effort. An essentially biblical radicalism, often melded with facets of Marxism–Leninism, the tenets of liberation theology stimulated numerous Roman Catholic priests in Latin America to champion the concerns of the poor. The contemporaneous development of liberation theology focused attention on socio-political divisions and associated political struggles in Latin America. Liberation theology is an intensely political concept, essentially a radical religious response to poor socio-economic conditions. Central to the idea is the notion of dependence and underdevelopment; the use of a class struggle perspective to explain social conflict and justify political action; and the exercise of a political role to achieve both religious and political goals. In the 1960s, the Church in Latin America was radicalised by influential theologians and religious thinkers – such as Gustavo Gutierrez and Paulo Freire – whose ideas were put into effect by mainly younger priests, serving to help develop a socially progressive Catholicism. BCCs were the most concrete sign of the spread of liberation theology concerns in Latin America. The political effects of liberation theology in Latin America are widely believed to have contributed to the democratisation of the region from the 1970s (Haynes, 1993: 95–109).

Socially progressive Catholics in South Africa, both black and white, were encouraged by their own ideas of radical Christian theology of liberation to demand fundamental political reforms. Radical Christian theological interpretations gained ground in the 1970s and 1980s, with significant political ramifications. The Institute for Contextual Theology (ICT) declared in 1984 that it wanted to encourage formation of BCCs in South Africa because it saw them as a key vehicle of 'conscientisation'.[2] To this goal, the ICT worked to develop 'contextual theology', that is, liberation theology, programmes for study by South Africa's emergent BCCs. Father Albert Nolan, a member of the ICT staff from 1984, published a book with Richard Broderick that quickly became known as *the* 'manual for contextual theology' in South Africa (Nolan and Broderick, 1987). Members of BCCs were encouraged to interpret the

Bible for what it says about political oppression and liberation, to seek conscientisation through social analysis, and to arrive at an understanding of the need for major structural changes in society. What this amounts to is that Latin American-style liberation theology was being applied to the South African context in order to further the chances of political liberation. In South Africa, liberation theology was known as 'Black' or 'contextual' theology in order to differentiate South Africa's particularistic political environment – with its specific type of race and class exploitation, wide range of Christian, Islamic and traditional religious cultures – from those of Latin America. But the overall aim was the same: political liberation, beginning from an awareness of and a positive approach to what it meant to be a black African Christian during apartheid rule.

Black theology identified 'the concept of salvation with liberation, which leads (it) to justify and support active struggle by (Christian) believers against social exploitation and oppression', involving, when appropriate, class-based political struggle (Schoffeleers, 1988: 186). More generally, the social polarisations which apartheid rule entailed convinced many ordinary Christians in South Africa that the struggle against it was necessarily both theological and political. Ryall (1994) notes that, in effect, the mainstream Christian churches, with the exception of the Roman Catholic Church, had been absorbed into the structures of white dominance during the decades of apartheid rule. None offered a lead to those striving for liberation. Gradually, however, more and more Christian professionals emerged from a condition of conforming to the norms of the apartheid culture, yet for a long time they were 'not so much the servants of God as of temporal power' (Walshe, 1992: 33). Nevertheless, several Anglican priests, including Trevor Huddleston and Michael Scott, campaigned vigorously against apartheid; the former was recalled to England, the latter imprisoned and later expelled from South Africa.

Black theology's development had its origins in the 1960 Cottesloe Conference of the World Council of Churches, which condemned apartheid as an evil system which had led to such atrocities as the Sharpeville massacre. Over the next 20 years, opposition to the racist government grew steadily worldwide. Within South Africa itself, the focal points of opposition were black township councils, formed explicitly to control and tax urban black people, and the tricameral, racially based constitution of 1983 which sought to divide and rule non-white people, to separate 'Indians' and 'coloureds' from black people by giving the two former groups limited representation, while denying it to the latter. This was the political context that led to the growth of Black theology, which served as an ideology of support for black political struggles that paved the way for the eventual collapse of apartheid and South Africa's democratisation process.

## US Protestant evangelicals and the growth of African Independent Churches

Africa was on the receiving end of two waves of Protestant evangelisation from the United States. The first occurred between the 1920s and the 1950s, and comprised various US churches (Hoekema, 1966: 24–31). The Seventh Day Adventists were especially successful with an estimated 2,000 missionaries in the field by the 1950s, while the American Assemblies of God had about 750 (Wilson, 1985: 309). By the early 1960s, the Full Gospel Businessmen's Fellowship International, founded in 1952 and with headquarters in Los Angeles, had established international chapters in Southern Africa (Hoekema, 1966: 33). It aimed, along with other groups, such as Campus Crusade, Youth With A Mission, and Christ for the Nations, to focus a message of redemption to higher education campuses, particularly West African institutions, where mass conversions took place. A second wave of foreign evangelical penetration of Africa occurred from the 1970s, a result of the success of various American television evangelists, including Pat Robertson, Jim and Tammy Bakker, Jimmy Swaggart and Oral Roberts – who focused upon Africa as a benighted continent crying out to be saved (Gifford, 1994, 2004; Freston, 2001, 2004).

The spread of US Protestant evangelical churches to Africa was greeted with concern by leaders of several of the established churches, who often saw their followers leaving for the foreign churches. Sponsored by American television evangelists and their local allies, thousands of conservative mainly foreign Protestant evangelical crusaders promoted American-style conservative Christianity in the 1980s. Ardently anti-communist, they worked to convert as many Africans as possible to their type of Christianity and in the process, it is argued, to promote American foreign policy goals of anti-communism (d'Antonio, 1990).

Pieterse alleges that a new religious and political hegemony developed in Africa as the result of the impact of the US churches. He claims that they were able to gain the cultural leadership of Christianity because of their social prestige and personal persuasiveness. Norms, beliefs and morals favourable to American interests were in turn disseminated as a fundamental aspect of the religious message. What this amounts to, according to Pieterse, was that African converts to the US conservative evangelical churches were victims of manipulation by the latest manifestation of neo-colonialism. The objective was not, however, to spirit away Africa's material resources, but rather to deflect popular political mobilisation away from seeking structural change of the society and the economy, in order to serve either American strategic interests and/or financial objectives of US transnational corporations (Pieterse, 1992: 10–11).

Yet, as Mbembe and other have argued, successive waves of foreign Christian proselytisation in sub-Saharan Africa resulted not in foreign imposition of an alien doctrine but instead indigenisation of Christianity (Mbembe, 1988: 181; Ellis and ter Haar, 2004; Freston, 2004: 1–2). During the colonial era, European-style Christianity tried unsuccessfully to appropriate the richness of the autochthones' imagination and beliefs, in order better to convert and to dominate. But the outcome was different to what was anticipated: African independent churches emerged, while the former mission churches were Africanised. There are now thought to be well over 20,000 African independent churches (AICs). Their growth has been swift in a number of countries, including: Nigeria, Kenya, Ghana, Liberia, Malawi, Zimbabwe and South Africa. From small beginnings, some have now reached an impressive size. Among them are Benson Idahosa's Church of God Mission in Nigeria, which has more than 2,000 branches. Others, including Andrew Wutawunashe's Family of God Church, Ezekiel Guti's Zimbabwe Assemblies of God Africa (both Zimbabwe), Mensa Otabil's International Central Gospel Church, and Bishop Duncan-William's Action Faith Ministries (both Ghana), have also grown swiftly (Gifford, 2004; Freston, 2001).

African independent churches offer a distinctive reinvention of an externally derived innovation, moulded and adapted to offer spiritual re-birth, potentialities for material improvements, and the growth of a

293

new community spirit among followers. Regarding their theology, while adhering to the Bible as an unimpeachable theological source, many such churches also preach the effectiveness of experiential faith, the centrality of the Holy Spirit, the spiritual gifts of glossolalia ('speaking in tongues') and faith healing, and the efficacy of miracles. Their worldview is also often informed by personal conversion as a distinct experience of faith in Christ as Lord and Saviour (being 'born again' in the sense of having received a new spiritual life), and in helping others have a similar conversion experience. Rather than relying on foreign donations, as many of the former mission churches still do to some degree, most African independent churches are primarily reliant on members' donations for their upkeep (Gaiya, 2002: 1–7).

Members of AICs often have a strongly moralistic worldview: lying, cheating, stealing, bribing (or being bribed), adultery and fornication are frowned upon. Because members of the churches conceive of a clear division between what is right and what is wrong, they tend to be opposed to public corruption. There is a strong sense that the wellbeing of society is highly dependent upon good standards of personal morality. The nature of social interactions within some of the AICs also helps to re-orientate traditional gender relations and, in the process, transform sexual politics. While some of the churches continue to promote a doctrine of female submissiveness, many do not. This appears to be one of the main attractions of such churches for young, urban women in Lagos, capital of Nigeria. It is particularly in the spheres of marriage, family and sexuality that one finds doctrines and practice in some AICs transforming gender relations quite dramatically.

Millions of Africans have joined AICs in recent years because of the intensity of the prayer experience they offer, the attraction of a simple and comprehensible message that seems to make sense out of the chaos which many perceive all around them, a moral code that offers guidance and the resuscitation of community values, as well as a sense of group solidarity exemplified in the way that individual followers often call each other 'brother' and 'sister'. In addition to spiritual and social objectives, members of AICs often seek material goals. For some, the hope of prosperity is one of the churches' main attractions, leading to charges that their message of hope is little more than a mindless and self-centred appeal to personal material wellbeing.

Although it would be misleading to try to standardise these churches and to assume that they are all the same, some things are clear. First, such churches often function as an alternative for those seeking a religious and social experience that the former mission churches often appear unable to offer. Many AIC members formerly belonged to the Roman Catholic Church and various Protestant denominations. Second, many of their followers are young people. Third, regarding their theology, while there is a need for more research, it is clear that the faith gospel of 'health and wealth' is central to many, perhaps most. In Lagos, Nigeria, for example, AIC members run their own catering companies, hospitals, kindergartens and record companies. Employment is offered first to co-religionists because they are considered likely to be honest and to work hard (Corten and Marshall-Fratani, 2001).

The faith gospel was originally an American doctrine devised by the media evangelists in the 1950s and 1960s. Yet much of Africa's traditional religion has always been concerned with fertility, health and plenty. It is by no means clear to what extent such a gospel is still an identifiably American doctrine or whether it has now been thoroughly Africanised. The class make up of the AICs is diverse: they do not simply minister to the poor or the middle classes or some other identifiable societal group, but find adherents from among all social classes. Another key theological feature is the understanding of spirits in the churches. Like the notion of 'health and wealth', spirits are an essential part of African religious culture. It is by no means clear what the relationship is between this traditional thinking and the demonology of Western Pentecostalism.

Followers of AICs are often concerned with social issues, involving a communal sharing of fears, ills, jobs, hopes and material success. Earthly misfortune is often perceived to be the result of a lack of faith; God will reward true believers. Such believers appear to estimate that people's redemption is in their own hands (or rather in both God's and the individual's hands), and expectations that government could or should supply all or even most of people's needs and deal with their problems is misplaced.

In sum, AICs challenge the Christianity of the former mission churches both intellectually and materially. Such is the concern with the haemorrhaging of followers, that the mainline Christian churches attack them on two fronts. On the one hand, AICs are accused of being little (if anything) more than Trojan horses of American conservative evangelical churches (Corten and Marshall-Fratani, 2001). On the other hand, the fact that some AICs are patronised by wealthy foreign (especially North American) pastors, probably helps confirm to many followers the desirable association between religion and personal prosperity. At the same time, many mainline churches have rushed to incorporate glossolalia, faith healing and copious biblical allusions into their services (Haynes, 1996; Gifford, 1994, 2004).

The key point to emerge from our brief survey of attempts by US conservative evangelical churches to spread their influence in Africa was that their significance was overall diminished by the fact that their religious messages were invariably Africanised, often leading to the founding of distinct African churches. Yet this was not a trait of Christianity alone – indigenisation also characterised historically how Islam was received in many African countries.

## Transnational Islam in Africa

The historical characteristics of the Arab-Islamic–African connection make the relationship between the two regions easy to trace but difficult to assess. Interactions between Islam and Africa began with the intrusion of Arabs and the process of religious conversion. This was a process reflective of the 'dominant Arab/dominated African' relationship which was to become an unhappy component of Africa's historical development, as we shall see below when we examine Arab/non-Arab relations in Sudan. In general, given the historical significance of slavery in Africa, the role of the Arabs in the region was hardly auspicious. This is not to diminish the impact of effects of European colonial rule, for it tended to forge a closer link between the Arabs and the Africans, especially during the post-independence period as both regions fought the struggle against imperialism. The years of colonial rule underlined the fact that divisions widely existed between Muslim Africans, often powerful in their communities, favoured and patronised by some colonialists, and non-Muslim Africans who, often deeply resenting the burden of European colonial control, produced the great majority of African nationalist leaders after the Second World War.

In the post-colonial era, the sometimes-uneasy relationship between Muslims and non-Muslims significantly informed political developments not only in Sudan but also in other countries, including: Kenya, Tanzania, Nigeria, Chad and Uganda. Religious rivalry was often informed by two main issues: first, African involvement in the wider Islamic community, including the Organisation of Islamic Cooperation (OIC) and, second, the role of Arab oil wealth in Africa's economic and social development.

The transnational influence of the OIC has been muted by the inter-organisational rivalry between its leading members. In addition, Africa has been a focus of competition between oil-rich, non-African Muslim countries that have sought to pursue foreign policy goals in Africa, connected to their control of oil wealth and associated attempts to increase regional significance. The governments of Iran, Saudi Arabia and Libya have all been active in Africa since the 1970s, seeking to pursue strategic foreign policy goals that often had the, no doubt unintended, impact of helping to stir up local Muslim discontent. Decades of buoyant oil revenues gave such states the financial ability to prosecute aggressive foreign policies in Africa, where separation of political, diplomatic and religious goals is often difficult to draw. It is clear, however, that Iran's biggest drawback – it is predominantly a Shiite country where most African Muslims are Sunni – was partially offset for some African Muslim radicals – for example, in Nigeria during the 1980s – by its obvious revolutionary credentials. Some African Muslim radicals were attracted to Iran's revolutionary message for two main reasons: first, it gave them an immediately recognisable radical programme to try to appeal to politically marginalised and alienated people in their country; and, second, it offered Muslim radicals a political platform from whence to launch attacks on conservative Muslim elites, often close to ruling regimes. Like Iran, Libya also pursued radical goals in Africa, while Saudi Arabia's concerns included trying to counter the influence of Libya and Iran in Africa.

A further focus of the international and transnational impact of Islam in Africa has been the growth of militant Islamic networks in several parts of the region, notably East Africa, close to the Middle East and centres of Islamic radicalism, including Saudi Arabia and Yemen (Overton, 2005). America's post-9/11 'war on terrorism' focused, inter alia, on East Africa, although the attacks on the Twin Towers and the Pentagon were not the start of US interest in the region. Earlier, in the early 1990s, a US military mission had failed to pacify insurgents in Somalia. The latter were Islamist organisations, with significant sponsoship and encouragement from Saudi Arabia, which had grown in numbers and influence from the 1980s. They were also conduits of radical Islamist ideologies, a development that led the US and other Western governments to label them 'terrorist' organisations. Such a concern was justified when it became clear that Islamist extremists linked to al Qaeda were responsible for deadly embassy bombings in 1998 Kenya and Tanzania, as well as the unsuccessful attack on an Israeli jet in Mombasa (Kenya) in 2002. But before turning to focus on the emergence and development of radical Islamic networks in East Africa, we examine the significance of a 'moderate' transnational Islamic actor, the *Tablighi Jamaat*.

## *The* Tablighi Jamaat: *a moderate transnational Islamic network*

*Tablighi Jamaat* is a pan-Islamic movement founded in 1927 in the Mewat province of India by Mohammed Ilyas. Tablighi means 'revitalisation' in Arabic (Rudolph, 1997b: 252). The aim of *Tablighi Jamaat* is 'to deliver (the message)' of Islam, in the belief that this is the first duty of all Muslims. Tablighi activities are normally limited to Muslim communities, as the key aim is their spiritual awakening.

To achieve this goal, the movement encourages Muslims to spend both time and money in pursuit of a spiritual journey (called *gasht*) both to acquire religious knowledge (*taleem*) and to promote the faith. During scheduled journeys for the purpose of trying to achieve these goals, members of each travelling group (called *jama'ats*) exchange information about basic tenets of the faith from each other. In addition, a list of the desired qualities of the *sahabah* (the companions of the Prophet Mohammed) are studied and practised. They are:

• Conviction of faith and belief in the oneness of God. This is understood to include the idea that 'the creation cannot do anything without the will of God, but God can do everything without the creation'. It also includes the belief that complete success in this world and the hereafter is only achievable by following as closely as possible the way of life shown by the Prophet Mohammed. Every other course of action is believed to lead inevitably to failure in this world and the hereafter.

- Humility and devotion in *salah*. This refers to the idea of perfection in observance of prayers (*salah*).
- Acquiring knowledge and remembrance of God.
- Good behaviour towards both Muslims and non-Muslims. It implies sacrificing one's own needs in order to fulfil another's and also involves respecting ones elders and showing kindness to younger people.
- Purity of intention. This means that all good actions should be solely for the pleasure of God.
- Inviting to God. This is a concern with spending both time and money in the 'Path of God, that is, calling people towards God, just as the Prophet Mohammed did' (http://www.tariqjamil.org).

Janson reports on the recent spread of the movement in the West African country, Gambia. She emphasises that the *Tablighi Jamaat* is a transnational missionary movement that encourages greater religious devotion and observance. In Gambia, *Tablighi Jamaat* missionaries insist that it is the duty of all Muslims – not only the few learned scholars – to carry out Tablighi work. Janson also emphasises that pan-Islamic missionary work has been a characteristic of Tablighi since its founding nearly nine decades ago (Janson, 2006: 44).

However, despite the fact that the *Tablighi Jamaat* is almost certainly the largest contemporary Islamic movement, there has been little scholarly attention paid to it. This is surprising because, as Gaborieau notes, the movement has a worldwide influence on the lives of millions of Muslims. The explanation for this is not only because Africa is often seen, unjustly, as the periphery of the Muslim world but also because by far the greatest attention is paid to radical transnational Islamic movements that often seem to threaten Western security (Gaborieau, 1999: 21).

Some observers contend, however, that the *Tablighi Jamaat* is actually a radical organisation linked to various expression of 'Islamic terrorism'. Alexiev argues that the *Tablighi Jamaat* is not a benign missionary movement. Instead, he claims, '*Tablighi Jamaat* actions and motives [have] serious implications for the war on terrorism'. He also asserts that Tablighi has 'always adopted an extreme interpretation of Sunni Islam, but in the past two decades, it has radicalised to the point where it is now a driving force of Islamic extremism and a major recruiting agency for terrorist causes worldwide', with al Qaeda allegedly recruiting its cadres from among the ranks of the Tablighi movement (Alexiev, 2005: 4).

## Militant Islamic networks in East Africa

For observers such as Alexiev, the alleged radicalisation of the Tablighi can be seen in the context of the recent growth of Islamic extremism in parts of Africa, including East Africa. Al Qaeda bomb attacks in Kenya and Tanzania in 1998 ushered in a new era of security concerns in East Africa linked to the perceived growth and interaction of domestic and transnational expressions of militant Islam. Since then, both local and Western governments and policy makers have frequently expressed concern over the potential of East Africa to be a new focal point for Islamic militant organisations, including al Shabaab in Somalia. Sizeable Islamic communities live in the hinterlands and coasts of a broad band of East African countries – from Sudan to Tanzania. Earlier, developments in Somalia – involving serious clashes in 1993 between local Islamic militants and US troops – underlined the potential for growth in influence of transnational Islamic militancy, especially al Qaeda, which built contacts with local warlords and is today widely reckoned to be in alliance with al Shabaab.[3] Al Qaeda was also implicated in the killing of 18 American peacekeepers in 1993, leading to the withdrawal of all US forces from the region. From this time, Somalia became a haven for Arab fighters expelled from Pakistan, where many underwent religious and guerrilla training. During the early 2000s, an Islamist movement, the Islamic Courts Union, came to power in parts of the country, including the capital, Mogadishu. With the subsequent rise to prominence of al Shabaab, many observers believe that Somalia has developed into a 'beach-head' for al Qaeda, with consequential concerns for Western security (Tisdall, 2006; Rice et al., 2006).

## BOX 12.4 Islamist militancy in Somalia

During the 1990s, Somalia was a key entry point for Islamist militants into East Africa. Infiltration was facilitated by the fact that Somalia has a lengthy border with Kenya, and an extensive, unguarded coastline with the Red Sea. At the same time, there was growth in expressions of Islamist militancy in, inter alia, Kenya, Tanzania and Uganda. Each of these countries is characterised by: widespread political repression, economic crises, rapid social change, uneven industrialisation and swift urbanisation; each country also experienced extensive economic, social and political problems. Many Kenyans, Tanzanians and Ugandans, including members of their minority Muslim communities, are at or near the bottom of the economic and political hierarchies, and some harbour deep feelings of disappointment and disillusionment in relation to economic and political outcomes (Haynes, 1996, 2005d). According to Dagne, 'From 1991, when Osama bin Laden was based in Sudan, al Qaeda has been building a network of Islamist groups in both the Horn of Africa (Eritrea, Ethiopia and Somalia) and East Africa (Kenya, Tanzania and Uganda)' (Dagne, 2002: 5). Dagne also believes that, as in Afghanistan and Pakistan, al Qaeda was able to exploit extant circumstances of widespread poverty, ethnic and religious competition and conflict, poorly policed state borders, and often corrupt and inefficient governmental officials to create a regional 'terror centre' in East Africa.

The most recent manifestation of this development is the growing significance of Somalia's al Qaeda-affiliated al-Shabaab movement. Al-Shabaab was formed in 2006 following the collapse of the Islamic Courts Union which fought Somalia's transitional government to control the country. Al-Shabaab is thought to comprise several thousand fighters, including foreigners from outside of the region, including: Afghanistan, Pakistan, the Gulf states, the USA and Britain. Having been forced out of Mogadishu by African Union troops, al-Shabaab has managed to establish and exercise control over large areas of the country, including south towards the Kenyan border, where it imposes *Sharia* law. In February 2012, the leader of al Qaeda, Ayman al-Zawahiri, formally welcomed al-Shabaab to membership of al Qaeda's network (Laing and Flood, 2012).

Concern with the growth of regional Islamic militancy was expressed by various sources, including the CIA: since 9/11 in particular, the Agency has taken the threat of Islamic militancy in East Africa very seriously – to the extent of withdrawing from Asia some of its best agents in charge of observing Islamist movements and reposting them to various countries in the sub-region (Tenet, 2002). Following the London bombings on 7 July 2005, UK security agencies also paid more attention to the 'Islamist threat' believed to emanate from East Africa (Laing and Flood, 2012). Kenya, Uganda and Tanzania are targets for the expansion of transnational Islamic militancy, seeking to exploit novel spaces for growth (McGrory et al., 2005). Ronfeldt and Arquilla (2001) contend that East Africa is the focal point for a 'war of networks', rather than a Huntingtonian 'clash of civilisations'. That is, rather than a traditional army, hierarchical political parties or guerrillas groups, there is instead a loose network of militant Islamic movements at work, whose operations are encouraged by the ease of communications provided by and via the internet. For Marchesin (2001), such Islamic networks comprise an important new realm of threats, especially to incumbent, unrepresentative governments: non-military phenomena of general, vague and flexible forms, embodied in a plethora of 'informal organisations', typically autonomous cells acting without any imperative contacts with an organisational head.

As already noted, this is not to claim that 9/11 was the starting point for such Islamic networks. Prior to 11 September, there is evidence that both Kenya and Tanzania were already targets of transnational Islamic terrorism. For example, on 7 August 1998, al Qaeda operatives used truck bombs against the US embassies in Nairobi, Kenya and Dar es Salaam, Tanzania. The explosions killed 240 Kenyans, 12 Tanzanians, and 11 Americans, and injured over 5,000 people, mostly Kenyans. Four years later, on 28 November 2002, two simultaneous attacks were conducted against Israeli targets in Mombasa, Kenya. Suicide-bombers drove a truck into an Israeli-owned hotel, killing 10 Kenyans and 3 Israelis, and injuring over 20 Kenyans. Around the same time, terrorists tried to shoot down an Israeli aircraft using surface-to-air missiles; had they succeeded they would have killed more than 200 passengers on board.

In sum, recent expressions of Islamic militancy in East Africa – primarily involving local operatives such al Qaeda-affiliated al-Shabaab– are judged both by local governments and by Western security agencies and governments to be a significant and growing threat to stability and Western interests in the East African sub-region. Kenya and Tanzania – both countries attract hundreds of thousands of Western tourists each year – represent soft targets for such attacks, with several factors – including poor security, inadequate border controls and the ability to 'blend in' to local populations – facilitating the infiltration of foreign Islamic militants, including al Qaeda operatives (McGrory et al., 2005).

Further, there are suggestions – and, according to both government and academic sources in East Africa (see below), firm evidence – that some among the burgeoning number of transnational and local Islamic NGOs aid and abet the growth of Islamic militancy in the sub-region. They pursue this goal by blurring distinctions between social, economic, political and religious functions and goals in directions that are commensurate with the objectives of the militants. Typically, the goals of Islamic NGOs active in East Africa include:

- provision of relief and humanitarian assistance to poor (Muslim) communities during emergencies, natural disasters (prolonged drought and floods), famine and epidemics;
- improvement of medium- and long-term development outlooks, with a focus on community development, improving agricultural yields, clean water, and improved provision of health and education, especially in the least-developed African Muslim countries;
- *da'wa* (that is, Islamic call, an equivalent to Christian evangelism) and conversion to Islam;
- publishing, broadcasting and disseminating Islamic teaching and values.

Salih argues that some Islamic NGOs in East Africa 'have been used as a vehicle for spreading political Islam at an accelerated rate combining faith and material rewards among the disfranchised Muslim poor . . . becoming cronies to militant Muslim groups, including an emergent tide of indigenous African Islamic fundamentalist movements' (2002: 1–2). Ghandour (2002) contends that the characteristics of such Islamic NGOs include not only an exclusive reference to Islam and an often-powerful social legitimacy, but also sometimes ambiguous bonds with militant Islamists. This may place them in conflict relationships with African governments, as well as Western NGOs and states. In addition, he also claims that some Islamic NGOs act as intermediaries between

> Islamic financiers and recipients operating in the environment of Islamist activists. It is extremely difficult for Western intelligence services to identify, localise and block the financial flows towards violent [Islamic] groups, because the NGOs are very active mediators that cover their tracks. Practically there are no direct relationships between powerful Islamic financial backers and Islamic activist organisations.
>
> (2002: 129)

Following the August 1998 Nairobi bombing, Kenya's government banned five Islamic NGOs – Mercy Relief International, the Al-Haramain Islamic Foundation, Help African People, the International Islamic Relief Organisation and Ibrahim Bin Abdul Aziz Al Ibrahim Foundation – because of their (1) alleged sympathies towards the aims of local 'Islamic fundamentalists', and (2) alleged mediatory role in relation to the financing of local militant Islamic organisations (Achieng', 1998; Salih, 2002: 24–25). In addition, Kenyan police and FBI agents from the US raided the offices of Mercy Relief International. According to John Etemesi, director of the Co-ordinating Board for Kenya's NGOs, the government's actions were necessary as the NGOs had allegedly been 'working against the security interests of Kenyans' (quoted in Achieng', 1998).

Following 9/11, there was a clampdown on numerous Saudi Arabian, Sudanese and Gulf charities, businesses and NGOs in Tanzania; all were said to have active links with al Qaeda. In late 2001, the country's central bank froze 65 bank accounts of such companies (Kelley, 2001). Sources in the banking industry in Dar es Salaam said the accounts belonged to several banks on the initial post-9/11 list issued by the US government of 20 globally sought-after international companies said to be al Qaeda owned and run businesses. Most of the companies were said to have branches in both Tanzania and Kenya, having moved there when bin Laden left Sudan in 1996 (Jamestown Foundation, 2003b). In addition, Tanzania's government also expressed concern about what it regarded as several 'questionable' Islamic NGOs. These included the African Muslim Agency (a Kuwaiti organisation) – engaged in the construction of mosques, schools and hospitals – and the Community Initiative Facilitation Assistance Development Group (a joint Tanzanian-Saudi investment venture established in 1995), whose activities include a focus on gender-related poverty (Jamestown Foundation, 2003a: 3–4; Intermediate Technology Development Group-Eastern Africa, 2002).

As in Kenya and Tanzania, Islamic NGOs have also been active in Uganda, with similar concerns, including: relief assistance to refugees and homeless people; founding and running orphanages, health centres and vocational training centres; and dealing with displaced persons and victims of natural disasters. The International Islamic Relief Organisation (IIRO) is one of the most active Islamic NGOs in Uganda; it also operates in Kenya. The IIRO was established in 1978 as a humanitarian

NGO to provide assistance to victims of natural disasters and wars all over the world, because some 80 per cent of refugees and victims, it claims, are Muslims. The IIRO claims that its relief programmes are directed solely towards the provision of medical, educational and social support for those in desperate need. It also aims to encourage local entrepreneurs by sponsoring viable economic projects and small businesses that can help victims find employment and earn a living. To fulfil these objectives, the IIRO has established a wide network of national and international contacts with various Islamic and non-Islamic relief organisations, institutions and individuals, operating in several countries in Europe, Asia and Africa. The major part of IIRO's financial contributions comes from private donations in Saudi Arabia, and an endowment fund (Sanabil Al-Khair) was established to generate a stable income to finance IIRO's various activities. The NGO has several departments, including: Urgent Relief and Refugees; Health Care; Orphans and Social Welfare; Education; Agricultural Affairs; Architectural and Engineering Consultancy; and the 'Our Children project' (www.islamic-knowledge. com/Organizations.htm). The European Intelligence Agency contends that assistance to Ugandan Islamists – from both al Qaeda and the government of Sudan – was provided through various Islamic NGOs, including the IIRO, the Islamic African Relief Agency, the World Islamic Call Society, the International Islamic Charitable Foundation, Islamic African Relief Agency, and the Africa Charitable Society for Mother and Child Care (European Intelligence Agency, *Al Qaeda Infrastructure in Sudan*, p. 21, quoted in Marchesin, 2003: 4). Table 12.1 lists the Islamic NGOs that are alleged to be supportive of Islamic militancy in Kenya, Uganda and Tanzania.

Many academic and Western intelligence sources agree that the growth of Islamic militant networks in East Africa is facilitated and promulgated by a shared sense of transnational Islamic identity that stems from long-established historical, cultural, linguistic and trade ties to the Arab world. They also accept that proselytising of various Islamic militants – including but not restricted to bin Laden and his then second in command, now al Qaeda leader, Ayman al-Zawahiri – seeks to exploit popular dissatisfaction that has developed following decades of undemocratic rule, endemic and serious corruption, and growing poverty and developmental disappointments (Salih, 2002; Jamestown Foundation 2003a, 2003b).

**Table 12.1** Islamic NGOs in Kenya, Uganda and Tanzania that are alleged to support Islamic militancy and terrorism

| Islamic NGO (home country in brackets) | Where in Africa the NGO is active |
| --- | --- |
| The Africa Charitable Society for Mother and Child Care (Sudan) | Uganda |
| Help African People (Kenya) | Kenya |
| Islamic African Relief Agency* (Sudan) | Kenya, Uganda |
| Muslim World League* (Saudi Arabia) | Kenya, Tanzania, Uganda |
| World Islamic Call Society (Libya) | Uganda |
| International Islamic Charitable Foundation (Kuwait) | Kenya, Tanzania, Uganda |
| International Islamic Relief Organisation (Saudi Arabia) | Kenya, Uganda |
| Ibrahim Bin Abdul Aziz al Ibrahim Foundation (Saudi Arabia) | Kenya |
| Mercy Relief International (USA) | Kenya |
| Al Haramain Islamic Foundation* (Saudi Arabia) | Kenya, Tanzania, Uganda |
| The African Muslim Agency (Kuwait) | Tanzania |
| Community Initiative Facilitation Assistance Development Group (Saudi Arabia) | Tanzania |

Source: Salih, 2002.

* These organisations were on the list of 25 Islamic charities and NGOs that, in January 2004, the US Senate Finance Committee asked the US Internal Revenue Service (IRS) for records on their activities (for a complete list, go to http://www.danielpipes.org/blog/164). This inquiry was part of an investigation into possible links between Islamic NGOs and terrorist financing networks. Committee Chairman Charles Grassley and senior Democrat Max Baucus stated in a contemporaneous letter to the IRS that 'many of these groups not only enjoy tax-exempt status, but their reputations as charities and foundations often allows them to escape scrutiny, making it easier to hide and move their funds to other groups and individuals who threaten our national security' (http://usinfo.state.gov/ei/Archive/2004/Jan/15–147062.html).

Concern with the influence of external militant Islamist groups was a key reason for the US-sponsored East African counter-terrorism initiative (EACTI), announced by President George W. Bush in June 2003. The stated purpose of EACTI was to root out local manifestations of 'Islamic terror groups' and to destroy their regional networks.[4] The inauguration of EACTI underlines how the US government believed that in recent years East Africa had become a 'safe haven' both for Middle East-based Islamic terrorist groups, and for indigenous militant Islamic organisations. EACTI has been continued under the Obama presidency (Ploch, 2010).

In sum, explanations for the increase in Islamist militancy in East Africa suggest that its increased prominence is linked to the increased influence of regional networks with headquarters in various Arab countries that are known to be logistical hubs of Islamist militancy, including: Kuwait, Saudi Arabia, Yemen and United Arab Emirates (Marshall, 2003; Salih, 2002). Various countries in the East African sub-region – including Kenya, Tanzania and Uganda – provide new opportunities for the recruitment and mobilisation of new members for militant Islamic organisations, including al Qaeda, its affiliates and off-shoots. Second, much of East Africa offers favourable grounds for the spread of transnational Islamic militancy, as a result of highly porous land and sea borders, widespread corruption, largely dysfunctional structures of law enforcement, endemic organised criminality (involving everything from drugs and people smuggling to weapons trafficking) and growing numbers of weak and failed states. These factors imply multiplication of 'grey zones' where state power is at best fragmentary.

## Religious identity and conflict in Sudan and Nigeria

### Civil war in Sudan: religious and international factors

Some African countries, including Sudan, Mauritania, Mali, Niger, Nigeria, Somalia, Chad and Eritrea, share a controversial issue: the relative religious, social, and political positions of Muslims and non-Muslims. These African countries are located on the 'periphery' of Arab centres of political and commercial power, places that historically experienced long periods of Arab political and commercial dominance. They straddle an African geographical and cultural Arab/non-Arab division, located approximately 15–20 degrees north of the Equator. In this section, we look first at the issue of religious identity in Sudan's long-running, but now concluded, civil war. Second, we examine the recent rise of an Islamist terror group, Boko Haram, in Nigeria. Nigeria has a long history of Muslim–Christian discord and the terrorist tactics of Boko Haram – including murders and bombings – has done nothing to decrease the historic tensions.

The question of national identity and the socio-political role of Islam has long been a key focus of political competition and conflict in

307

Sudan. Sudan is unique among African countries south of the Sahara, because it is only there that until recently Islam had the status of state ideology. Sudan has long been associated with a poor human rights regime, with certain non-Arab, partially Christian, ethnic groups – such as, the Dinka, Nuer and Nuba – victimised by successive regimes whose policy appeared to be both Arabicisation and Islamicisation of the entry country (Haynes, 1996: 157).

## BOX 12.5 Islamic government in Sudan

Sudan achieved independence in 1956. Its population is about 40 per cent Arab, living mostly in the north. The remaining Sudanese are black Africans, living mostly in the south. Sunni Muslims overall comprise about 70 per cent of the population, Christians about 5 per cent, and the remainder (about 25 per cent) comprising followers of various local traditional religions. Until 2005, the National Islamic Front (NIF) government was in power, a northern- and Arab-based regime. Founded by Muslim Brotherhood leaders (particularly Hassan al-Turabi, who, as the late President Numeiry's attorney general in the 1980s, played a key role in introducing *Sharia* law), the NIF was the main political force behind the 1989 military coup that brought the NIF government to power. The National Congress, created in early 1999 by President Al-Bashir, served as a front for the NIF and NIF members dominated the government until the change of regime in 2005.

Following the accession to power of the NIF regime, an Islamist government took over. Its stated ambition was to bring about a radical transformation of public life throughout north-eastern Africa, a notoriously unstable region long riven by multiple civil conflicts and traditional rivalries. During the 1990s, the Islamist regime helped create community associations, many of which were able to deliver much-needed welfare and social services. Yet the regime also had fatal ideological flaws: it was too rigid and one-dimensional, lacking sufficient constructive direction to form an appropriate basis to rule a modern nation-state (de Waal, 2004). Instead, the lure of apparently permanent *jihad* was strong – leading the Sudanese government into a tragically pointless civil war with various ethnic groups, mainly in the south of the country, as well as destructive relations with its neighbours, including Uganda, to try to win that war.

Sudan's civil war began in the early 1970s, and over the next three decades more than two million people died, and over four million were displaced from their homes. The background to the long-running conflict was that at the time of Sudan's independence in 1956, the country's nationalist leaders did not regard Islamic ideas as progressive. They were primarily motivated by the fervour of anti-colonial success, looking to modernist, temporal ideologies, especially socialism, to express and convey national unity even in Sudan, a predominantly Muslim country. In other words, the preferred developmental model was not indigenously derived but drew on European models, whereby secularisation was an integral part of developmental strategy. As a result, Islam remained culturally, socially and historically important, not judged to be significantly progressive to form a basis for the ideological, political and developmental advancement of post-colonial Sudan.

Things began to change in the early 1980s, following the failure of the country's post-colonial development programme. From this time until recently, governments attempted to emphasise their power by underlining what they saw as Sudan's Arab-Muslim identity, involving a concentrated process of attempted Arabicisation. The then state president, Ja'far al-Numeri, adopted Arab-Islamic dress in public, with the *jellabiya* (robe) and *anima* (turban) worn for many public appearances. This served to jettison the military uniform that Numeri had previously preferred to wear in public. Numeri also supervised the issue of new currency at this time, with bank notes depicting him as resplendent in his new persona. In addition, *Sharia* law was adopted as the country's national law from 1983 (although it was never made to stick in the largely non-Arab, partially non-Muslim, south). Such acts, Bernal notes, served to bolster 'Sudan's Muslim and Arab identity while associating Islam with power and nationalism' (1994: 48). Underlying the move towards Arabicisation and Islamicisation were both foreign and domestic pressures. In terms of the former, Sudan's then chief aid provider was the government of Saudi Arabia.[5] The Saudi government joined forces with the country's most important domestic Islamic movement, the Muslim Brotherhood, to demand more dynamic manifestations of Islam in public life. The result was that political discourse in Sudan became increasingly phrased in Islamic terminology, while Numeri's political opposition also adopted the language of Islam to press their case. Following Numeri's overthrow, the military-Islamic regime of Omar Hassan al-Bashir, which achieved power following a military coup d'etat in June 1989, sought to juxtapose a form of Islamic social control by use of the military's organisational skills. It attempted to use the *Sharia* in a way reminiscent of communist states' use of Marxist–Leninist dogma to justify policy.

The attempt at domination by mainly northern Arab-Muslims in Sudan, striving for control of the non-Arabs of the south was often portrayed as that rare phenomenon in Africa, a religious war. However, it is more appropriate to see the conflict as primarily informed by attempts by northern Arabs to dominate southern non-Arabs, not a conflict about religion as such, but with ethnic and cultural competition as the key focal point. In other words, the conflict was de facto a struggle for Sudan's national identity – should it be one based in Arab-Islamic domination or should it be secular and multi-ethnic pluralism? We can see this issue coming to the fore in the case of Sudan's Nuba people, non-Arab but mostly Muslim. The Nuba live in the area of the Nuba mountains in the north of the country, and have been consistently victimised by the Arab north for not being 'real' Muslims. However, the most significant issue is that the Nuba are not Arabs, but black Africans (Flint, 1993).

These factors – involving northern Arab attempts to Arabicise the south, including attempted countrywide imposition of *Sharia* law; non-representative, authoritarian governments, backed by the military; and significant cultural differences between the Arab north and the predominantly non-Arab south – form the backdrop to Sudan's three-decade civil war. For 30 years, armed resistance to the state in the south was focused in the two wings of the Sudan People's Liberation Army (SPLA), led respectively by the late Colonel John Garang de Mabior and Riek Machar Teny-Dhurgon. The civil war dragged on for so long because while both sides could avoid defeat, neither was strong enough to impose its preferred outcome. The SPLA could prevent the victory of the Arab-dominated Sudanese army – but it could not defeat it. Similarly, the army could keep the SPLA confined to its strongholds but not beat it through force of arms. The result was stalemate, until January 2004 when both the government and the SPLA signed a peace deal following foreign, especially, US pressure.

There was extensive foreign involvement in negotiations to end the conflict. Earlier, in the late 1990s and early 2000s, the civil war, once confined to the south, had spread to Sudan's north-east border with Eritrea. Sudan government forces encountered not only several thousand soldiers of the SPLA but also six other opposition armies, which had recently organised themselves to fight together under a single command. This threat of a wider regional conflict prompted peace initiatives from Libya and Egypt, and from Africa's intergovernmental Authority for Development. Later, in November 2002, a peace envoy from the US government, John Danforth, visited Sudan and met leaders of both the government and the SPLA. Danforth not only proposed a series of confidence-building measures to bring the warring parties together but also managed to broker a ceasefire allowing aid agencies to airlift supplies to the beleaguered Nuba mountains. However, as Danforth admitted, years of mutual distrust between the warring parties made reconciliation especially difficult.

It took 15 months of extensive negotiations, until January 2004, before Sudan's government and rebel leaders signed a peace deal that appeared to mark the end to one of Africa's longest civil wars of modern times. It was expected that the south would henceforward enjoy considerable political autonomy, with an administration to be called the 'government of southern Sudan'. The late SPLA leader John Garang was not only to lead the southern government but also to become a national vice president. Garang was, however, killed in an air crash in August 2005. Immediately following his death, 36 people died in riots in Sudan's capital, Khartoum. Many of those involved were southern Sudanese living in Khartoum who believed that the crash was suspicious, probably carried out by the government in order to eliminate Garang and his influence. Most southerners hoped that he would be able to lead them in the future, putting into effect policies to change their lives and end discrimination in favour of Arabs. Following Garang's death, Sudan's president, Omar al-Bashir, said he was determined to continue the peace process in which John Garang had played such a central role, ending more than 20 years of civil war.

## Boko Haram and Islamist terror in Nigeria

Boko Haram is an Islamist religious sect. Its name means 'Western education is a sin'. Since 2009, Boko Haram has violently targeted

**311**

Nigeria's police, rival Muslim clerics, politicians and public institutions. Boko Haram is said to be leading an armed revolt against several targets, including: governmental corruption, abusive security forces, strife between the disaffected Muslim north and Christian south, and widening regional economic disparity in an oil rich, yet impoverished, country. It may be that Boko Haram's actions go beyond narrowly religious issues to include socio-economic concerns which Nigeria's government has shown little capacity to resolve in the country's disaffected Muslim north, a region of deep poverty and limited opportunities for improvement. In August 2011, Boko Haram's alleged bombing of a United Nations building in the capital, Abuja, and claims that it has ties with al Qaeda, led to new Western fears of Boko Haram's growth and influence (Johnson, 2011).

Boko Haram was established in 2002 in Maidugiri, capital of the north-eastern state of Borno, by Mohammad Yusuf, a radical Islamist cleric. The aim of Boko Haram is to establish an Islamic state in all Nigeria, not just the northern part of the country which has a majority Muslim population. Paul Lubeck, a University of California professor studying Muslim societies in Africa, says Yusuf was a trained salafist, a school of thought often associated with jihad, while being heavily influenced by Ibn Taymiyyah, a fourteenth-century legal scholar, often considered as a 'major theorist' for radical Islamist groups in the Middle East and sub-Saharan Africa (Lubeck is quoted in Johnson, 2011).

While, as already noted, Boko Haram is usually translated in the West to mean 'Western education is a sin', the group actually calls itself Jama'atul Alhul Sunnah Lidda'wati wal jihad, meaning 'people committed to the propagation of the prophet's teachings and jihad'. It may be that Boko Haram is an outgrowth of the Maitsatsine political upheavals of the 1980s, which also centred on demands for an Islamic state led by a radical Islamic preacher. According to Johnson, 'many Nigerians believe Yusuf rejected all things Western'. However, Lubeck argues that 'Yusuf, who embraced technology, believed Western education should be "mediated through Islamic scholarship", such as rejecting the theory of evolution and Western-style banking' (Lubeck is quoted in Johnson, 2011).

In July 2009, Boko Haram members refused to follow a motorbike helmet law, leading to heavy-handed police tactics that set off an armed uprising in the northern state of Bauchi and spread into the states of Borno, Yobe and Kano. The incident was suppressed by the army and left more than eight hundred dead. It also led to the televised execution of Yusuf, as well as the deaths of his father-in-law and other sect members, which human rights advocates consider to be extra-judicial killings. In the aftermath of the 2009 unrest, 'an Islamist insurrection under a splintered leadership' emerged, says Lubeck (quoted in Johnson, 2011). Boko Haram began to carry out a number of suicide bombings and assassinations from Maiduguri to Abuja, and staged an ambitious prison-break in Bauchi, freeing more than seven hundred inmates in 2010.

In November 2011, the group staged its most deadly attacks so far, with more than 150 people killed, according to the Nigerian newspaper *The Nation* (http://www.thenationonlineng.net/2011/index.php/news/25500-boko-haram-exodus-in-yobe-as-death-toll-hits-150.html). Targeting Maiduguri as well as Damaturu and Potiskum, Boko Haram attacked churches, mosques, banks and police stations. The November attacks received wide international condemnation from various organisations, including: the head of the Organisation of Islamic Cooperation, the Pope, the United Nations (UN) Security Council, and the UN secretary general. Further bombings followed on Christmas Day in 2011 targeting churches and killing dozens, raising fears about the possibility of another spate of religious conflict between Muslims and Christians (http://www.reuters.com/article/2011/12/27/us-nigeria-blast idUSTRE7BQ0DE20111227).

## Conclusion

The following points have emerged in this chapter, concerned with the role of religion in Africa's international and transnational relations:

- Both Christianity and Islam are of immense importance, informing many domestic and international political issues.
- In the late 1980s and 1990s religion's political role in Africa – notably the influence of the Roman Catholic Church – was particularly manifested in involvement in democratisation moves in several regional countries, including South Africa.

- US evangelical churches were important influences in founding thousands of American Independent Churches, although the latter mainly developed over time as indigenous churches with African characteristics.
- Both 'moderate' and 'extremist' transnational Islamic movements are active in Africa.
- The end of Sudan's long-running civil war in 2004 was due in large part to the influence of US evangelical Christians who were influential in encouraging the Bush administration to enact a law in 2002 designed to punish severely Sudan's Islamist government if it did not make serious efforts to seek to end the conflict.
- The emergence of new radical Islamist groups – such as al-Shabaab in Somalia and Boko Haram in Nigeria – are the consequence of interlinked domestic and external factors.

Overall, what emerged from the chapter was that external religious movements and traditions are of great significance in understanding Africa's transnational and international relations, in both historical and contemporary contexts. This should not, however, be taken to imply that such external actors were simply able to impose their policies and programmes on Africans. We saw important processes of indigenisation of external religious traditions and ideas, which in some cases, leads to both an Africanisation and a radicalisation of extant religious faiths. The overall conclusion is that Africans are far from being passive acceptors of foreign religious ideas, preferring instead to develop their own religious vehicles.

## Notes

1. Our focus in this chapter is on sub-Saharan Africa, that is, Africa below the Sahara Desert, which divides North Africa from the rest of Africa. However, for reasons of brevity, we shall often use the term 'Africa' in the chapter to refer to sub-Saharan Africa.
2. According to the Brazilian educator, Paulo Freire (1921–97), conscientisation is a process enabling people to develop an objective distance from reality, to conduct a critical analysis of that reality, and as a result fashion necessary the conditions enabling them to act upon and seek to change that

reality. Freire did not claim that gaining critical awareness *necessarily* leads to positive social action, merely that it is an *essential* prerequisite for making that movement. For Freire, the final aspect of conscientisation involves action towards the transformation of reality (Freire, 1999).

3. Infiltration of al Qaeda into Somalia was said to be facilitated by the fact that the country had become a collapsed or 'failed' state by this time; that is, a polity without an effective central government and with a generalised break down of law and order.

4. A US Department of Defense official, Vincent Kern, told more than 120 senior African military officers and civilian defence officials gathered at the Africa Center for Strategic Studies (ACSS) seminar on 10 February 2004 that in June 2003, 'President Bush announced a $100 million, 15-month Eastern Africa counter-terrorism initiative under which the United States is expanding and accelerating [US] counter-terrorism efforts with Kenya, Ethiopia, Djibouti, Uganda, Tanzania and Eritrea'. The programme, Kern said, was designed to counter terrorism by focusing on coastal and border security; police and law enforcement training; immigration and customs; airport/seaport security; establishment of a terrorist tracking database; disruption of terrorist financing; and 'community outreach through education, assistance projects and public information'. Kenya, for example, was to receive training and equipment for a counter-terrorism police unit aimed at 'building an elite Kenyan law enforcement unit designed to investigate and react to terrorist incidents' (http://japan.usembassy.gov/e/p/tp-20040212–24.html).

5. Following the rupture of Sudan's relations with Saudi Arabia during the Gulf war of 1991, Iran became Sudan's most important patron and aid provider.

## Questions

- To what extent does religion influence international relations in Africa? Illustrate your answer by reference to *one* religion
- Assess the impact of various kinds of transnational Islamic networks on Africa's international relations.
- Describe and account for the significance of transnational ideas associated with Catholicism in relation to political change in South Africa from the 1980s.
- Was the civil war in Sudan a religious war?
- Why is it said that the activities of al-Shabaab and Boko Haram are not only religious but also include political and socio-economic issues?

# Further reading

A. Corten and R. Marshall-Fratani (eds), *Between Babel and Pentecost: Transnational Pentecostalism in Africa and Latin America*, Bloomington, IN: Indiana University Press, 2001. This book focuses on extraordinary recent growth of the Pentecostal movement in Latin America Africa. The contributors both focus on its transcendental dimension, expressed through doctrine and the religious experience it produces, and assess Pentecostalism's sociological and political impact in various countries, including Ghana, Nigeria, Kenya, Brazil and Peru.

S. Ellis and G. ter Haar, *The Worlds of Power: Religious Thought and Political Practice in Africa*, London: Hurst, 2004. The starting point of this book is that religious thought and political practice are closely intertwined in Africa. African migrants in Europe and America send home money to build churches and mosques, African politicians consult diviners, guerrilla fighters believe that amulets can protect them from bullets, and many ordinary people seek ritual healing. All of these developments suggest the frequent application of religious ideas to everyday problems of existence, at every level of society. Far from falling off the map of the world, Africa is today a leading centre of Christianity and a growing field of Islamic activism, while African traditional religions are gaining converts in the West.

P. Freston, *Evangelicals and Politics in Asia, Africa and Latin America*, Cambridge: Cambridge University Press, 2001. This book is a pioneering comparative study of the political aspects of the new mass evangelical Protestantism of sub-Saharan Africa, Latin America and parts of Asia. Freston examines 27 countries from these regions, examining specificities of each country's religious and political fields. He also looks at implications of evangelical politics for democracy, nationalism and globalisation. This uniquely comparative account of the politics of global evangelicalism will be of interest to many students of international relations.

P. Gifford, *Ghana's New Christianity: Pentecostalism In A Globalising African Economy*, Bloomington, IN: Indiana University Press, 2004. This book explores Ghanaian charismatic Christianity (or neo-Pentecostalism) in relation to economic and political processes. It has two goals: (1) to identify this new Christianity and its religious vision, and (2) to analyse its socio-political role in effecting modernity in Ghana, a country that in recent years has been developing relatively quickly, in part because of its willingness to take advantage of globalisation in various ways. Gifford's study focuses on the country's capital, Accra, and assesses the range and diversity of the capital's new churches. Gifford's study is both extremely rich in data – on leaders, adherents, theology, discourse, practices, Bible use, media activities, music, finances and organisation – and broad in range. It addresses the whole charismatic spectrum, from prophets and healers who focus on deliverance from demonic forces to teachers who stress human responsibility. It is of interest to international relations students as Gifford demonstrates that the original American-style Pentecostal is transformed into a recognisably Ghanaian form of religion.

G. Joffe, *Islamist Radicalisation in North Africa: Politics and Process*, London: Routledge, 2011. In the current chapter, we have paid quite a bit of attention to Islamist radicalism. Although Joffe's book concentrates on North Africa, it will still be of interest to those focusing on sub-Saharan Africa. His book focuses on the current issues and analytical approaches to the phenomenon of Islamist radicalisation. Taking a comprehensive approach to the subject, it looks at the processes that lead to radicalisation, as well as the often-violent outcomes.

# 13 | South Asia

The South Asian region comprises five countries: Bangladesh, India, Nepal, Pakistan and Sri Lanka. They differ greatly in terms of size, geography, religious and cultural traditions, economic and political structures, forms of rule, and relations with external powers. The region's countries have had variable political histories since their emergence from British colonial rule in the late 1940s: long-running monarchical, latterly democratic, rule in Nepal; a lengthy civil war in Sri Lanka between the (Hindu) Tamil minority and the (Buddhist) Sinhalese majority which ended in May 2009; alternating military and civilian regimes in Bangladesh; periodic democratic interludes in Pakistan, with growing influence for Islamist political parties and movements; and a long-established, secular democracy in India, significantly influenced in recent years by Hindu nationalism. In this chapter we focus on India, Pakistan and Sri Lanka. This is because in all three countries various religious actors are important politically – both domestically and in relation to regional foreign policies and international relations. For each of these three South Asian countries, we conclude that: (1) domestic structures and processes have thrown up politically influential religious actors – which often seek to influence international outcomes, and (2) religious goals do not take precedence over secular security concerns in these South Asian states' foreign policies.

## Religion and international relations: India, Pakistan and Sri Lanka

South Asia has been greatly affected by a changing international context in recent years, including: increasing influence of globalisation, the end of Cold War in the late 1980s, the ramifications of 11 September 2001, and the subsequent 'war on terror' led by the United States. These factors interacted with domestic concerns – notably an increased political significance for various religious actors – in our three featured South Asian countries: India, Pakistan and Sri Lanka. The impact of both the end of the Cold War and increased influence of globalisation can be seen in Rizvi's (1995: 84) observation, that the 'democratic transformation of South Asia in the aftermath of the Cold War has been breathtaking'. In addition, as Kumaraswamy (1999: 175) notes, the 'end of the Cold War and the emerging new international order' were important factors in South Asia's recent international relations. In particular, there was increased pressure from the US government directed against Pakistan's government to take a fuller full role in the post-9/11 'war on terror' against both al Qaeda and Afghanistan's erstwhile rulers, the Taliban, for India to improve relations with Pakistan, and for Sri Lanka's rulers to rebuild the country after decades of debilitating civil war.

## *India*

From independence in 1947, India enjoyed long periods of democratic stability, initially under the rule of the secular Congress Party. However, India experienced sharpening political disputes from the late 1970s, characterised by a general decline in political stability and fragmentation of the hitherto stable political party system. At this time, numerous new parties emerged. Many sought to represent constituencies that until then were politically marginalised, including various religious (especially Hindu and Muslim), ethnic, caste and regional interests. The rise to political prominence of what is often referred to as Hindu nationalism dates from this time. The electoral success of the Hindu nationalist Bharatiya Janata Party (BJP; 'Indian People's Party') began in the early 1980s, starting a process that saw the BJP become the most electorally significant party in India from the mid-1990s to the mid-2000s. During this time India had successive coalition governments led by the BJP. The increased political domestic influence of the BJP was built on a Hindu religious ideology known as Hindutva ('Hindu nationalism') (Bhatt, 2001). The concerns of Hindutva were reflected in both a pronounced 'Islamophobia' and a move away from international non-lignment towards closer relations with Israel and the USA. The influence of Hindutva was also reflected in relation to two specific foreign policy issues: the continuing dispute with mainly Muslim Pakistan over the Indian state of Kashmir and the now-ended civil war in Sri Lanka between Buddhist Sinhalese and Hindu Tamils. In short, Hindutva influenced India's foreign policy under BJP rule, although this was not the only factor of significance.

As Ganguly (2003/4: 41) notes, 'the end of the Cold War and of the Soviet experiment shattered the long-cherished assumptions of India's foreign policy establishment and forced a radical realignment of its foreign policy'. Reflecting this, the late Narasimha Rao, a Congress prime minister between 1991 and 1996, was the chief proponent of India's post-Cold War 'New Look' foreign policy. This emerged as a result of two contemporaneous international developments which together greatly affected India's international relations and foreign policy:

- transformed global environment after the Cold War;
- collapse of India's key ally, the former Soviet Union, with subsequent impact on India's perceptions of the international power balance

The BJP was in power between 1996 and 2004. Its tenure coincided with a phase of international relations which Kapila (2005) claims was characterised by the rise of 'United States unilateralism and new American policies of pre-emption and military intervention in global affairs without restraint'. In addition, the disintegration of the Soviet Union and the generally changed international environment as a consequence of globalisation led to a reorientation of India's foreign policy. There were, however, competing influences. On the one hand, there was Hindutva, a powerful domestic factor, and, on the other, there was the impact of globalisation and the power of the USA. Indian governments from this time understood the desirability of forging new alliances and foreign policy directions. As a result, when the BJP came to power in 1996, there was not an abrupt shift in foreign policy direction, rather there was continuity, albeit with a significantly different ideological component: from international non-alignment to Hindutva. This was reflected in the BJP's foreign policy focus which was concerned with 'US-India strategic cooperation, normalising and enlarging cooperation with both China and Israel' and a commitment 'to bring the "old foe", Pakistan, to the dialogue table' (Kapila, 2005).

## Pakistan

Like India, the political situation in India's neighbour, Pakistan, was also characterised by both volatility and the pronounced influence of religious organisations – in this case, various Islamist entities. In the 1980s and 1990s, short-lived, democratically elected civilian governments followed each other rapidly. Then, in October 1999, the military stepped in and terminated the democratic system. This was, however, a generally popular move that reflected a widespread view in Pakistan: when civilians are in power they tend to rule both poorly and corruptly. Many Pakistanis, disgusted at the inability of successive civilian governments to control the scale of corruption, were said at this time to be 'disillusioned, apathetic, weary . . . indifferent to the fate of the venal politicians . . . so busy lining their own pockets that they had little time to ponder the welfare of the country and its people' (Ali, 1999). Despite the unconstitutional nature of the military takeover, some prominent citizens openly called for a political system that would give the armed forces a permanent, institutionalised, 'supervisory' political role. The sustained political prominence of the military in Pakistan eventually gave way to an elected civilian government in 2008. The rule of the military was bolstered by the support of influential Islamist parties and movements that, like their counterparts in India, the Hindu nationalists, sought to influence Pakistan's foreign policy and international relations. This was especially apparent in relation to the disputed Kashmir region, a bone of contention between India and Pakistan since the creation of Pakistan in 1947.

## Sri Lanka

Sri Lanka's recent political history was long dominated by the country's civil war which finally came to a conclusion in May 2009. The conflict, fought between the majority Buddhist Sinhalese and the minority Hindu Tamils, was characterised by Reoch (2001) as the 'No Mercy War'. This was not only because the conflict involved multiple suicide bombings but also because overall it was fought with little apparent concern for civilian casualties; during the conflict there were more than 65,000 deaths on both sides. In addition, there were serious human rights abuses by both sides, while an estimated one million people were displaced from their homes (Reoch, 2001). Although the war only intermittently received much attention from outside the region, when the conflict intensified in April 2000, it took on an international dimension with several external governments, including those of India, the USA and Norway, becoming involved in efforts to forge peace. India in particular was consistently involved in the civil war, although not always on the side of the Hindu Tamils. This preference might have been expected, given the religious make up of India – over 80 per cent Hindu – and the nationalist BJP-led government.

## Religion and politics in India

India achieved independence in 1947 under the aegis of the Congress Party. Politically dominant for three decades, Congress later experienced serious electoral decline. From the mid-1970s, its hegemony was undermined by the rise of various identity-based parties. During the 1980s and 1990s, the number of political parties increased from a handful to around 450 (Kohli, 1994: 89). Many of the new parties based their electoral appeal on various identity factors, notably religion, ethnicity and caste. During this time, communal tensions between, on the one hand, Sikhs and Hindus, and on the other, Hindus and Muslims, spread from the urban into the rural areas where they were hitherto largely unknown. They became pronounced in various southern parts of the country, such as Tamil Nadu, as well as in the north, including Punjab and Jammu-Kashmir. The conflict between Sikhs and Hindus came to a head in the 1980s, rooted in the Sikh demand for their own state in Punjab (putatively to be called 'Khalistan'), characterised by various terrorist acts perpetuated by militant Sikhs, including the assassination of the then prime minister, Indira Gandhi, in 1984. There followed widespread destruction of Sikh-owned property and the murders of Sikhs in several northern Indian cities, perpetrated by Hindu gangs. Eventually, however, due to a combination of strong-arm tactics on the part of the state and the political division of the Sikhs into various factions, Sikh demands for Khalistan diminished. From the 1990s, however, tensions developed between India's Muslim minority – some 11 per cent of the population, around 130 million people – and various Hindu nationalist movements.

## Hindu–Muslim relations and the rise of the BJP

> India has its own homegrown brand of religious militancy – Hindu national-
> ism – which also enjoys close government ties. This militancy threatens to
> undermine the religious impartiality (commonly known in India as 'secular-
> ism') upon which India's democratic constitution is based.
>
> (Center Conversations, 2003: 1)

The issue of Hindu–Muslim relations is a key political topic in India.
The concern is highlighted by the significance of Hindutva, a political
ideology based on a particular political representation of 'Hinduness'.
An Indian nationalist, Vinayak Damodar Savarkar, coined the term in
his 1923 pamphlet, *Hindutva: Who is a Hindu?* Today the term refers to
a number of movements, primarily in India, which collectively advocate
Hindu nationalism. The BJP, the ruling party in India between 1996
and 2004, is closely linked with a variety of organisations and movements which collectively promote Hindutva. Their collective name is
the Sangh Parivar ('family of associations'), and leading associations
include the Rashtriya Swayamsevak (RSS), Bajrang Dal, and the Vishwa
Hindu Parishad (VHP) (Brass, 2005).

### BOX 13.1 What is Hindutva?

Hindutva is an extreme right-wing ideology that grew in political and religious
prominence during the twentieth century (Chiriyankandath, 2006). However, it
did not play an important role in Indian politics until the late 1980s. From that
time, largely because of two events, it attracted many formerly mainstream
Hindus. The first was the decision by the Congress government of Rajiv Gandhi
to employ his large parliamentary majority to overturn a Supreme Court verdict
with which many conservative Muslims disagreed (known as the Shah Bano
case (Mullally, 2004)). Second, there was a major quarrel between Hindus
and Muslims over ownership of a sixteenth-century Mughal Babri mosque in
Ayodhya, Uttar Pradesh. Some Hindus maintained that it was both birthplace
and site of the original temple of Rama, a figure that Hindus believe was an
avatar of God. Following growing frictions between Muslims and Hindus, the
mosque was destroyed by a Hindu mob in 1992, leading to riots across India.

The overall aim of the Sangh Parivar is to increase the societal, political
and cultural predominance of Hinduism in India through various means,
including violence and terror (Human Rights Watch, 2002: 39–41;

Ram-Prasad, 2000: 184). The Hindutva agenda includes attempts to suppress or drive out Muslims and Christians, who together total around 17 per cent of India's population. This is because, for the Sangh Parivar, they are alien faiths, historically introduced into India by external conquerors. Islam was introduced by the Muslim Moghuls in the sixteenth century CE and Christianity by the British in the nineteenth century. At independence in 1947, the electorally victorious Congress Party reluctantly accepted partition (between India and Pakistan), yet decisively rejected the ideology of Hindutva. Later, however, in the 1980s, India saw tensions increase between Muslims and Hindus, a situation that facilitated the electoral rise of the BJP. The BJP is now a major force in the Indian political arena, a party that consistently emphasises the ideology of Hindutva, leading to a serious challenge to traditional Indian understandings of, and commitment to, secularism (Chiriyankandath, 1996).[1]

## BOX 13.2 The political rise of the BJP

The background to the rise of the BJP was that the party was initially a northern-based phenomenon popular only in certain Hindi-speaking areas, especially among particular urban constituencies, notably middle-class traders. Its political rise began in 1989 when the BJP won 85 seats in parliament (15.5 per cent of the total). Over the next decade the BJP built growing political support. It achieved a political breakthrough in the 1996 general elections, winning the most parliamentary seats of any party (161 of 545; 29.5 per cent). Falling well short of an overall majority, the BJP nevertheless headed the resulting short-lived coalition government. The BJP leader, Atal Bihari Vajpayee, became prime minister, but the new government soon fell after losing a confidence vote. However, this setback did not prevent the BJP from gaining the largest number of parliamentary seats in national elections in both 1998 and 1999; again it formed governments with Vajpayee as prime minister. From then, the BJP remained in power until losing the May 2004 elections to the resurgent Congress Party. In the most recent general elections, held in April/May 2009, the BJP won 116 seats, just over 21 per cent of the total of 543, making it the second largest political party behind the Congress Party, which won 206 seats.

During its decade in power, the BJP energetically promoted economic reforms and avidly sought development goals, welcoming into the country as much foreign investment as possible. However, the BJP continued to be regarded as a serious challenge to traditional Indian understandings of, and commitment to, secularism. Marshall observes that in power the BJP remained close to the RSS and other Hindu nationalist organisations collected in the Sangh Parivar, effectively functioning as its 'political wing'. Prime Minister Vajpayee publicly praised the RSS and regularly attended its functions. Other high-level BJP figures, including former Home Affairs Minister L. K. Advani, also had close links with the RSS. In power, the BJP sought to pursue the objectives of Hindutva – that is, to try to 'Hindu-ise' Indian politics and society, by various methods, including: 'propaganda, the manipulation of cultural institutions, undercutting laws that protect religious minorities, and minimizing or excusing Hindu extremist violence. At the state level its functionaries have abetted and even participated in such violence' (Marshall, 2004).

Regarding what it sees as 'foreign' religions – notably, Christianity and Islam – as serious social and cultural threats, BJP officials not only sought to restrict minority religious groups' international contacts but also to reduce their domestic rights to build places of worship. The BJP government passed anti-conversion laws, as well as changing personal laws governing marriages, adoptions and inheritance. In addition, it practised legal discrimination against Christian and Muslim Dalits (the so-called 'Untouchables'), but not against those among the latter who classified themselves as Hindus. Marshall reports that 'with BJP support, laws were adopted in Tamil Nadu and Gujarat states restricting the ability of Hindus to change their religion, and proposals for national restrictions' were made. In June 2003, the late pope, John Paul II, described these developments as 'unjust' and said they prohibited 'free exercise of the natural right to religious freedom' (Marshall, 2004; Human Rights Watch, 2002).

Earlier, inter-communal relations between Hindus and Muslims had taken a serious turn for the worse. In December 1992, Hindu extremists, many of whom were said to be connected to various Hindu organisations, including the RSS and BJP, destroyed a historic mosque at Ayodhya (Chiriyankandath, 2006; Lall, 2005). Widespread communal riots followed, with huge loss of human life and destruction of property. Ten years later, in February 2002, Muslims in Gujarat experienced serious violence when between one and two thousand Muslims were massacred after Muslims reportedly set fire to a train carrying Hindu nationalists, killing several dozen people. Many of the victims were burned alive or dismembered while police and BJP state government authorities were said to have stood by or joined in the violence (Brass, 2005). The mobs are said to have had with them lists of homes and businesses owned by Muslims, lists that they could have acquired only from government sources. After the massacre, state BJP officials were accused of impeding the investigation into the events (Amnesty International, 2003).

Following the violence, a prominent Mumbai-based politician, Bal Thackeray, leader of the Shiv Sena, a political party based in Mumbai and allied to the BJP, stated that, 'Muslims are cancer to this country . . . Cancer is an incurable disease. Its only cure is operation. O Hindus, take weapons in your hands and remove this cancer from the roots' (MacFarquhar, 2003: 51). Gujarat's chief minister, Narendra Modi, a BJP member, called upon his supporters to 'teach a lesson' to those who 'believe in multiplying the population', implicitly referring to Muslims. Other Sangh Parivar officials were even more explicitly threatening (*The Times of India*, 2002). VHP International President Ashok Singhal described the Gujarat carnage as a 'successful experiment' and warned that it would be repeated all over India. After the December 2002 BJP election victory in Gujarat, VHP General Secretary Pravin Togadia declared, 'All Hindutva opponents will get the death sentence, and we will leave this to the people to carry out. The process of forming a Hindu rule in the country has begun with Gujarat, and VHP will take the Gujarat experiment to every nook and corner of the country' (Vyas, 2002).

In addition, to anti-Muslim violence and outbursts, Christians were also targeted by Hindu militants, responsible for violent attacks in the late 1990s on Christian minorities in various states, including Gujarat, Madhya Pradesh and Orissa (Brass, 2005). The BBC reported at this time that

India's Home Ministry (internal security) and its National Commission for Minorities officially list over a hundred religiously motivated attacks against Christians per year, but the real number is certainly higher, as Indian journalists estimate that only some ten percent of incidents are ever reported. These attacks include murders of missionaries and priests, sexual assault on nuns, ransacking of churches, convents, and other Christian institutions, desecration of cemeteries, and Bible burnings.

('South Asia: Attacks on Indian Christians continue', 1998)

In order to maintain the political coalition that enabled it to rule at the national level, the BJP government sought to downplay such events and to portray itself as a moderate party. However, chiefly because of the anti-Christian attacks noted above, the US Commission on International Religious Freedom proposed in 2004 that India be included on the State Department's official shortlist of the worst religious persecutors for its 'egregious, systematic, and ongoing' violations of religious fights (Marshall, 2004).

In sum, India's commitment to secularism, written into the country's constitution after independence from British rule, appeared to many observers to be under serious threat due to the rise in prominence and significance of the Hindutva ideology. During the 1990s and early 2000s, there were numerous attacks on religious minorities, especially Muslim and Christians and evidence of an increasingly overt and strident Hindu fundamentalism which seriously affected India's domestic politics (United States Commission on International Religious Freedom, 2004: 81–84). In October 2011, the Vatican sent a message to Hindu leaders in India requesting them 'to resist "hateful propaganda" against Christians and allowing Christians to practice their faith in peace'. As noted above, a principal cause of conflict is the conversion to Christianity of Dalits or 'untouchables.' According to Walker (2011), 'aggression against Christians stretches across much of India, from the eastern state of Orissa to the southwest state of Kerala'.

## Hindutva and foreign policy

To what extent, if at all, is the ideology of Hindutva projected into India's foreign policy and international relations, especially during BJP rule? According to Katalya, following independence in 1947, India's foreign policy was characterised by both moderation and pragmatism, including:

- dialogue with Pakistan;
- expansion of trade and investment relations with China;
- strengthening of ties with Russia, Japan, Western Europe, and the United States;
- attempts to help construct a regional organisation, the South Asian Association for Regional Cooperation (Katalya, 2004).

## BOX 13.3 India's foreign policy changes

Ganguly argues that there was a change in emphasis in India's foreign policy from the 1990s. This was not so much to do with the impact of Hindutva as the changed international circumstances of this time – including the end of the Cold War and the impact of globalisation – which, he claims, was most important in explaining the shift in emphasis in India's foreign policy. Until this time, the main emphasis was on non-alignment between the two superpowers, the USA and the USSR, implying even-handed dealing with the governments of both countries. India also sought to project itself as a defender of the world's poor and powerless. In pursuit of the latter objective, India's political leaders demanded a 'global foreign aid regime designed to redistribute the world's wealth, an international trading order that favored the needs of the developing world, and the restructuring of such global institutions as the World Bank and the International Monetary Fund so as to give the weaker states a greater voice. These efforts produced little of substance' (Ganguly, 2003/4: 42).

The end of the Cold War and the deepening of globalisation coincided with the rise to power of the BJP and more strident assertion of the ideology of Hindutva. What impact was there on India's foreign policy and international relations? MacFarquhar (2003) states that under the BJP, India's foreign policy shifted focus from a concern with non-alignment and development injustices to a pronounced concern with 'Islamist terrorism'. This implied a more abrasive stance towards Pakistan, which the Indian government claimed was the main sponsor of 'anti-Indian', Muslim terror groups fighting to wrest Muslim-majority Kashmir from Indian control (see below). More generally, the BJP government 'criticized nonalignment and advocated a more vigorous use of India's power to defend national interests from erosion at the hands of Pakistan and China. The BJP also favored the overt acquisition of nuclear weapons' (Federal Research Division of the Library of Congress, 1995).

Overall, Thirumalai claims that, following the BJP's ascent to power in the mid-1990s, 'the role of religion in India's foreign policy cannot be exaggerated. Hindus claim to be the most tolerant of all religious groups. But this claim has been continuously shattered, resulting in certain adverse reactions among various nations.' As a result

India has to come to grapple with the fact that Hinduism is more or less a single nation religion, whereas Islam, Christianity and Buddhism are religions practiced and encouraged in many and diverse nations. The view the practitioners of other religions hold regarding Hinduism and Hindus certainly influences the foreign policy of these nations towards India. India's insistence on its secular credentials may be appreciated in the academic circles all over the world, but India continues to be a Hindu-majority nation, a Hindu nation, in the minds of lay Christians, Muslims, and Buddhists all over the world. The foreign policy formulations of other nations do not fail to recognize that India is a Hindu nation, despite India's claims to the contrary.

(Thirumalai, 2001)

According to Marshall, perceptions of India as a Hindu nation were reinforced as a result of many incidents of Hindu extremism and terrorism. Globally since 9/11, much attention has been paid to Islamic extremism and terrorism but relatively little attention to what some commentators see as increasingly violent trends towards Hindu extremism among groups advocating Hindutva, including the RSS and VHP (United States Commission on International Religious Freedom, 2004: 81–44). Such extremism, Marshall (2004) contends, was supported by 'allies in the Indian government, which until mid-2004 was led by the BJP'.

Bidwai suggests that 'if the ideologues of India's Hindu-supremacist Bharatiya Janata Party and key policy makers in the coalition government it leads in New Delhi had their way, they would bring into being just such an alliance or ' "Axis of Virtue" against "global terrorism" ', involving the governments of India, USA and Israel (Bidwai, 2003). India's then national security adviser, Brajesh Mishra, advanced the 'Axis of Virtue' proposal on 8 May 2003, in Washington. Mishra was addressing the American Jewish Committee (AJC) at an event where there were also many US Congressmen and women present. Mishra emphasised his desire to help fashion an 'alliance of free societies involved in combating' the scourge of terrorism. Apart from the fact that the US, Israel and India were all 'advanced democracies', each 'had been a significant target of terrorism. They have to jointly face the same ugly face of modern-day terrorism'. The proposed 'Axis of Virtue' would seek to 'take on international terrorism in a holistic and focused manner . . . to ensure that the global campaign . . . is pursued to its logical conclusion, and does not run out of steam because of other pre-occupations. We owe this commitment to our future generations' (Mishra quoted in Embassy of India, 2003). A month later, also in Washington, Deputy Prime Minister Lal Krishna Advani spoke in glowing terms about the proposal. He stressed 'similarities' between India and the US, calling them 'natural democracies'. He praised the relationship 'developing between our two countries [that is, India and the USA], which is powerfully reflected' in President Bush's latest National Security Strategy document. Obliquely referring to Pakistan, he added, 'it is not an alliance of convenience. It is a principled relationship' (Advani quoted in Bidwai, 2003). According to Biswai, 'The BJP's ideology admires people like [the then Israeli prime minister, Ariel] Sharon for their machismo and ferocious jingoism. It sees Hindus and Jews (plus Christians) as "strategic allies" against Islam and Confucianism. Absurd and unethical as it is, this "clash-of-civilisations" idea has many takers on India's Hindu Right.' Overall, according to Biswai, there were three main reasons why the BJP wished to move India closer to Israel and its ideology of Zionism:

- a wish to build closer relations with Israel's main ally, the USA, and thus try to isolate Pakistan;
- shared 'Islamophobia' and anti-Arabism;
- shared commitment to an aggressive and dynamic nationalism (Bidwai, 2003; also see Primor, 2011).

Due to a change of government in India in May 2004, the 'Axis of Virtue' proposal did not make it past the planning stage. Following the election, the Congress Party and its allies had the largest number of seats in parliament (216, compared to the BJP's 186) but it did not achieve enough to rule with an overall majority (273 seats). As a result, the new Congress government had to heed the wishes of its main coalition partners, the Communists and the Muslim League, while the Congress government itself featured committed secularists away from the 'Axis' proposal. In the next section we turn to examine India's major regional rival, Pakistan, and the political influence of its Islamist actors both at home and abroad.

# Religion and politics in Pakistan

As a country, Pakistan is an entirely artificial creation. It was created as a homeland for India's tens of millions of Muslims following serious communal conflict in the late 1940s that left an estimated one million people dead. Carved out of India, initially in two territories (East and West Pakistan) separated from each other by thousands of kilometres, the country became independent in August 1947. A republic was established in 1956. Fifteen years later Pakistan's national territory was confined to former West Pakistan following the de facto independence of Bangladesh (formerly, East Pakistan). After a military coup in July 1977, martial law was in operation until 1985 when a semi-democracy emerged. Constitutional democracy followed in 1988, surviving until October 1999 when a military government took over (Nasr, 2001).

Pakistan started life with a number of inauspicious structural characteristics that militated against the establishment of a workable democratic system. In addition, there was no sustained external encouragement to democratise. This was largely because Pakistan was a key regional ally of the USA during the Cold War, a time when American governments preferred stable allies rather than democratic ones with pronounced instability. In other words, the long-term support of US governments for 'stable' – that is, in Pakistan's case, military – governments not only undermined chances of democratisation in Pakistan but later encouraged Islamist groups in a bid to counter the influence of secular political parties that wanted democratic rule.

In 1997, 50 years after independence, Diamond characterised Pakistan as being at 'the edge of political chaos, with massive political corruption and heavy-handed presidential intervention forcing out one elected government after another' (Diamond, 1999: 29). At this time, many Pakistanis were very condemnatory of their political leaders, a position explained in part by recent corruption scandals involving senior politicians (Robinson, 1998; Diamond, 1999: 92). Sizeable majorities of the Pakistani public considered that the country lacked an impartial judiciary (62 per cent), freedom of the press (56 per cent), or a government free of corruption (64 per cent). 'The bottom line: nine years into civilian government, half do *not* consider Pakistan a democratic state (about a quarter do)' (Diamond, 1999: 50). Diamond described the extant political system a 'hollow democracy, rife with semiloyal and disloyal behavior on the part of important political actors. No one should confuse its persistence with consolidation or with liberal democracy' (1999: 73). This dismal political context helps to explain the rise of numerous Islamist movements and political parties in Pakistan from the 1990s. Part of their popularity was that many Pakistanis saw such entities not only as relatively incorrupt but also untainted by earlier failures of secular – civilian and military – governments (Mian and Nayyar, 2008).

## Islamism in Pakistan

Pakistan was founded on the idea that the Muslims of India formed a secular nation and, as a result, they were entitled to a territorial homeland of their own, in much the same way that the Jews (and especially Zionists) in the diaspora considered that they could only flourish within their own nation state: Israel. Initially, Pakistan was constituted in two halves – East and West – separated by India, and with practically no history of shared national unity. The members of the Pakistani 'nation' did not speak a common language, have a common religion (although most were Muslims), homogeneous culture, or share the same geographical or economic space. As a result, Pakistan was emphatically not a nation in the traditional Western sense of a group of people living in a contiguous territory believing they have the same ethnic origins, and sharing linguistic, religious and/or other cultural attributes. Over time, lack of shared characteristics proved fatal to the pursuit of national unity: following a civil war, the independent state of Bangladesh (initially, East Pakistan) was created in 1971 with India's help (Nasr, 2001).

At the time of the establishment of East and West Pakistan, the country's rulers faced two main problems: first, how to create a sense of national identity to suit the reality of the new boundaries and, second, how to devise a workable system of government for a populace divided by huge geographical distances, as well as religious, ethnic, cultural, regional, economic, linguistic and ideological differences. Initially, it was assumed that the umbrella of a presumed common 'Muslim identity' would take care of these differences. Consequently, the new political leaders espoused an Islamic form of nationalism as the country's unifying symbol. The appeal to their heterogeneous people's shared Muslim heritage was initially enough to overcome the immediate differences – but not sufficient over time to suppress or eradicate within the new state contradictions of Muslim religious feeling, regional nationalisms and class antagonisms. As Lapidus (1988: 742) puts it: 'Pakistan was born as an Islamic state to differentiate it from the rest of the [Indian] subcontinent, but Muslim identity [did] not prove adequate to unite the country internally.' In sum, the founding circumstances of Pakistan were not conducive to long-term national, political or religious unity.

Initially, after the schism from India in 1947, Pakistan's leaders enjoyed a high degree of popular, albeit 'inverse legitimation'. That is, the new government was widely regarded as legitimate primarily because it was the regime that came to power following what most Pakistanis no doubt saw as unconscionable and incomprehensible Indian aggression (Nasr, 2001). But the benefits of the honeymoon period soon disappeared. Governmental legitimacy declined due to: poor economic performances, the use of political repression to stifle opposition forces, and serious state-level corruption. Democracy did not become institutionalised in the early years of independence and, as a result, it became impossible to establish a workable democratic system.

## BOX 13.4 Pakistan's political system

Pakistan's political system is notable for personalistic, rather than institutional, wielding of power, facilitated by three developments. First, Pakistan's federal system was designed to supply provincial legislatures and governments to check the power of the state at the national level. However, these important checks and balance soon became filled with cronies of figures at the centre and, as a result, the ability to check the power of the national government, diminished. Second, religious, ethnic and regional divisions helped make Pakistan's politics both volatile and violent. Third, when the Muslim League government gained power after partition it was at the cost of abandoning its political hinterland in Northern India, a development that served, more generally, to blight the growth of a competitive party system. Instead, political leaders, both civilian and military presided over a political system rooted in populism, with power heavily personalised and frequently abused (Diamond, 1999).

Pakistan failed to develop a viable political party system. Under military rule in the late 1950s, all political parties were banned, and even during the periods they were allowed to function, the state sought closely to control them. Following a brief period of relative freedom of operation in the 1970s and first half of 1980s, the then military dictator, General Zia, banned political parties again, claiming that the very concept of pluralistic parties was 'non-Islamic'. When they are allowed to operate, political parties in Pakistan are essentially sectional – that is, based on ethnic, religious, or regional concerns. They are typically ineffectual at mobilising citizens and prone to enter – and quickly leave – unstable multiparty alignments. In sum, the characteristics of Pakistan's political system, reflecting the characteristics of its inauspicious founding and alternating between military and civilian rule, are not encouraging for the development of democracy, instead encouraging a focus on political issues with religious or ethnic connotations (Siddiqi, 2012).

Following General Zia's death in a still unexplained aeroplane crash in 1988, an event that precipitated a return to democracy, numerous political parties and groups emerged or re-emerged. The main contenders for political power at this time were two broad-based coalitions: one dominated by secular, the other by religious, parties. The former was the Pakistan Democratic Alliance (PDA), dominated by the left of centre Pakistan People's Party (PPP), led by Benazir Bhutto, which was allied to several smaller parties. The PPP's main opponent was the Islam-e-Jamhoori Ittehad (IJI; Islamic Democratic Alliance), a coalition led by the Pakistan Muslim League and the Jamaat-i-Islami (Pakistan Islamic Assembly). Other significant parties at this time included Altaf Husain's MQM, representing the *mohajir* community in Sind, that is, refugees from India who entered Pakistan in the late 1940s, and the regionally based Awami National Party, with roots in the North-West Frontier Province and northern Baluchistan. The overall point is that these coalitions comprised parties representing a variety of sectional interests, including ethnic, religious and regional interests. However, their very diversity meant that the winning coalition would comprise a conglomerate of competing groups whose main aim would be to acquire as much power as possible and to deny their rivals it (Haynes, 2001a: 124–132; United States Commission on International Religious Freedom, 2004: 85–87; Siddiqi, 2012).

## Islamism and foreign policy

Although Pakistan emerged as a homeland for India's Muslims, this did not mean that there was only one concept of the idea of a Muslim state; in fact, there were at least two. On the one hand, the secularised political elite considered Islam a communal, political and national identity that could be stripped of its religious content. On the other hand, a sizeable segment of the populace, led by Muslim religious leaders, expected – and later, when it was not forthcoming, demanded – a state whose constitution, institutions and routines of daily life would be governed by Islamic law and norms. The importance of the struggle – over both the political role of Islam and the ethnic and regional rivalries between West and East Pakistan – can be gauged by the fact that no constitution could be devised until 1956, a decade after the founding of the state. The constitution declared Pakistan to be 'an Islamic state', and made all parliamentary legislation subject to review by an Islamic Research Institute.

Following a successful military coup in 1958, the constitution was abolished and the Republic of Pakistan was declared. The main aim of the military government was to try to curb the power of Islamist leaders and their organisations. Over the following decades, however, the issue of the nature of the state in Pakistan was not resolved. Various rulers, such as General Zia ul-Haq (1977–88), sought to Islamicise the state further. Secular civilian political leaders, such as Zulfikar Ali Bhutto (prime minister, 1972–77) tried to reduce Islam's political influence. Later, attempting to increase support from the conservative Islamic establishment, the government of Nawaz Sharif (1988–93) achieved passage of an Islamic law bill in 1991. While for many religious Muslims the law did not go far enough in seeking to Islamicise the country, many secular-minded Pakistanis feared that a theocracy was being established (Cohen, 2004; Malik, 2002).

In foreign policy terms, the political significance of Islam in Pakistan is reflected in the existence of a number of influential Islamist organisations whose chief focus is the Indian state of Kashmir, the only one in India with a Muslim majority population. While Islamist organisations have existed in Pakistan since independence, their numbers grew during General Zia's rule (1977–88). Zia encouraged the growth of Islamist organisations, which he saw as a useful political instrument in support of his rule; this policy led to both growth in numbers and rise in political significance of various Islamist entities. Three main Islamist groups explicitly seek Kashmir's 'liberation' from India: Lashkar-e-Taiba, Jaish-e-Mohammed and Harakat ul-Mujahidin. Lashkar-e-Taiba (LeT) (English, 'Army of the Righteous') is the armed wing of Markaz-ud-Dawa-wal-Irshad, a pro-Sunni, anti-US Islamist group founded in 1989. LeT fights India in the disputed territory of Kashmir. In recent years, several LeT operatives were convicted of terrorist charges by the United States government. In November 2008, LeT was responsible for the siege of the Taj Hotel in Mumbai, which led to the deaths of more than 170 people (Tankel, 2009). A second group, Jaish-e-Mohammed ('The Army of Mohammed') was formed in 1994. It is a militant Islamist group based in Pakistan but largely funded from the United Kingdom, especially Birmingham. Like LeT, JeM carries out armed attacks on Indian armed forces and civilians in the Indian state of Jammu and Kashmir. Both JeM and LeT are said to canvass 'for supporters at British universities and mosques', and have done so for decades. 'Although both are outlawed in Britain they still collect around £5 million a year from UK donors, most of whom believe they are giving to humanitarian causes in Kashmir when some of that money is diverted to terror cells.' Ahmed Omar Sheikh, a former English public schoolboy, was one of their more notorious recruits. He 'abandoned his degree course at the London School of Economics in 1992' (McCarthy, 2002) and at the time of writing (mid-2012) is on death row in Islamabad allegedly for masterminding the kidnap and murder of Daniel Pearl, a *Wall Street Journal* reporter.

The third organisation, Harakat ul-Mujahidin (HUM, 'Movement of Holy Warriors'), is an Islamist militant group based in Pakistan but operating primarily in Indian-controlled Kashmir, where it undertakes insurgent and terrorist activities. In mid-February 2000, the deputy leader of the HUM, Farooq Kashmiri, a well-known Kashmiri commander, replaced the organisation's head, Fazlur Rehman Khalil. The group has a presence in several Pakistani cities, including Rawalpindi and Muzaffarabad, as well as in Afghanistan. It is believed that HUM has a few thousand, mostly armed followers, situated primarily in Azad Kashmir (part of the former princely state of Jammu and Kashmir now controlled by Pakistan), Pakistan, and the Kashmir and Doda regions of India. Due to defections to Jaish-e-Mohammed, HUM lost some of its membership, although it is said still to be capable of carrying out operations in Kashmir against both Indian troops and civilian targets. HUM has also been linked to an indigenous Kashmiri Islamist group, al-Faran, which in 1995 kidnapped and murdered five Western tourists in Kashmir. In addition, in December 2000, HUM was involved in hijacking an Indian airliner. Several of its militant followers managed to gain agreement for the release of Masood Azhar. Azhar had been imprisoned by the Indian government in 1994, for terrorist activities; he had led the HUM's forerunner, the Harakat ul-Ansar. On his release, Azhar chose to form a new group – the Jaish-e-Mohammed (see above) – rather than return to the HUM (Katzman, 2002).

## BOX 13.5 Similarities in worldview between Hindutva organisations in India and Islamist entities in Pakistan

There are similarities in the strategic worldview of Pakistan's Islamist groups described above and those of some of India's Hindutva organisations, including the RSS and VHP. Each is concerned with three overlapping areas of concern: the local, the regional and the global. The advocates of Hindutva see the world in bifurcated terms – that is, a universe essentially divided between themselves and Others, that is, non-Hindus – while Pakistan's Islamists see the world as polarised between Muslims and non-Muslims. Followers of Hindutva identify a key enemy: Pakistan, said to be the main supporter of militant Islam not only in India generally but also in Kashmir in particular. For Pakistan's Islamists, the governments of India and the United States are the main enemies, followed by those of Israel and Russia: all are perceived as inherently 'anti-Muslim' (Council on Foreign Relations, 2003). The United States and India are the main adversaries for the following reason. The government of the United States is believed to have a clear and aggressive anti-Muslim strategy, manifested in punitive actions in Afghanistan and Iraq since 9/11, where co-religionists – that is, Sunnis – have been on the receiving end of US military actions. India, on the other hand, especially under BJP rule, is regarded as being in general terms 'anti-Muslim', but especially excoriated for its unwilling to concede control of Kashmir to the Muslim majority population, for reasons associated with its ideology of Hindutva (Chiriyankanadath, 2006).

Finally, within Pakistan, the United States government was heavily criticised by Islamist organisations for being willing to ally itself with the 'corrupt' regime of General Musharraf, which stood down in 2008 – in order, it is claimed, to try to dominate the region. As a result, Pakistan's Islamist militants believe that every 'good Muslim' should join a holy war against both the United States and its local allies in Pakistan. The Islamists want an Islamic state, looking to the model established by the Taliban in neighbouring Afghanistan during their period in power (1996–2001). Overall, Pakistan's Islamists seek Pakistan's international relations characterised by the following: (1) abandonment of Pakistan's association with the United States and replacement by a strategy of enhancing links with Muslim countries in order to achieve 'strategic depth'; (2) a deepening of confrontational relationship with India in order to force a resolution of the Kashmir issue; and (3) the use of Kashmiri Islamist militants to try to undermine India's resolution to hold on to Kashmir, as it is accepted that Pakistan's military capability cannot match that of India's (Council on Foreign Relations, 2003; Tankel, 2009).

As noted above in the late 1970s and the 1980s, General Zia's government encouraged the formation and development of some of Pakistan's Islamist entities, including, Sipah-e-Sahaba and the Shia Tehrik-e-Jafria. The US Council on Foreign Relations claimed in 2003 that the Islamist groups had 'achieved substantial autonomy'. Indeed, since 9/11 and the subsequent global 'War on Terror', successive governments in Pakistan have repeatedly promised to crack down on Pakistan's domestic Islamist groups *if* they support the use of terror to achieve their objectives – although it is not clear that much progress has been made (Harrison, 2001). Following the war in Afghanistan (2001–) and the US-led invasion and subsequent occupation of Iraq in March 2003, Pakistan's Islamist groups became increasingly vociferous both in their anti-US and anti-government statements. In recent years, Pakistan's Islamist entities have sought to form linkages and networks with similar groups in other countries, and to work towards a proposed Islamic state that extends beyond the territorial borders of the present Pakistan state (Council on Foreign Relations 2003; Yousuf, 2012).

## Religion and the India–Pakistan dispute over Kashmir

In this section, we focus upon Kashmir. It is the key issue for both Pakistan's Islamists and followers of Hindutva in India.

At the heart of the current conflict between nuclear-armed India and nuclear-armed Pakistan is religious militancy. If South Asia is a nuclear powder keg, religious militancy is the match that threatens to set it off. As is widely known, militant Islamic groups that Pakistan has long supported and is only now beginning to restrain attacked India's Parliament in December 2001 and attacked a Christian church in Islamabad, Pakistan's capital, in March 2002. Then in May 2002 Islamic militants slaughtered more than thirty Indians, most of them women and children, in the disputed state of Kashmir, precipitating a renewal of severe tensions between these two nuclear powers and longtime rivals.

(Center Conversations, 2003: 1)

Conflict over Kashmir has involved the governments of India and Pakistan for more than six decades. During British colonial rule, Kashmir was an anomaly: a Muslim-majority state ruled by a Hindu prince. The origin of the dispute is that at the time of British withdrawal in 1947, the departing colonialists did not leave a precise prescription for how to divide the roughly 500 princely states of British India – including Kashmir – between India and Pakistan. In many cases, there was no problem as such states were usually physically located clearly within the borders of post-colonial India or Pakistan. But the Kashmir valley, part of the state of Jammu-Kashmir, was a particularly intractable issue between the two countries. This was because Muslims were a clear majority in the Kashmir valley, although ruled by a Hindu prince.[2] Following the division of India in 1947, hostilities broke out between the two sides over the issue who would rule in Kashmir, leading to the involvement of the United Nations (UN) in – so far unsuccessful – efforts to arrive at a resolution of the 'Kashmir question'. Now, 65 years on, the UN position is still that the political status of Kashmir should be settled by a referendum among its people. Yet, the vote has never been held, due to prevarication by the Indian government, which fears that it would lose the vote and thus lose Kashmir to Pakistan.

Conflict between India and Pakistan over Kashmir has not, however, been continuous. During the late 1970s and early 1980s there was a period of relative calm and stability. It was, however, during this period that Pakistan's government under the leadership of General Zia-ul-Haq came to power in a *coup d'état*. Zia was instrumental in helping to create the Islamist groups discussed above. Over time, however, they

339

achieved a high degree of independence. Contemporaneously, in India, the Congress governments of Indira Gandhi and her son, Rajiv, began to shift the country away from secular nationalism towards Hindu nationalism, a policy later pursued by the BJP regimes of the 1990s and early 2000s (Haggerty, 2002). The impact on the Kashmir question was not only to sharpen the conflict in general terms but also to make religion – rather than nationalism – the key issue at stake in the status of Kashmir (Smock, 2006).

In 1989 there was a local revolt in Kashmir led by local Muslims directed against both the Indian government and the Hindu ruler of the state, which attracted both political and material support from Pakistan. Since that time, there has been an inability to resolve the Kashmir issue, alternating between periods of relative calm and outbreaks of conflict. Haggerty notes that from the late 1990s the Kashmir issue became complicated by the fact that both India and Pakistan were nuclear weapons possessors, a situation that led to 'a vastly increased level of international interest and involvement' (Haggerty, 2002). This was also a time of growing political salience in India of Hindutva and in Pakistan of Islamism.

## BOX 13.6 Hindutva and the Kashmir conflict

The rise of Hindutva in India influenced the country's conflict with Pakistan over Kashmir in two main ways. First, Hindutva became a significant issue in relation to India's domestic concerns, especially during BJP rule. Second, Hindutva was an influential factor in relation to India's foreign policy in two main ways: (1) the relationship with Pakistan, and (2) more generally in relation to Muslim countries and fears of Islamic extremism. While Ram-Prasad notes that in India in recent years 'religious ideology in itself has played virtually no *direct* role in major political and economic decisions' (my emphasis; Ram-Prasad, 2000: 153), it seems clear that as a soft power factor – especially in relation to Kashmir – Hindutva has been important, in tandem with traditional secular nationalist concerns (Chiriyankandath, 2006; Ram-Prasad, 2000). Note, however, that this implies salience of Hindutva soft power especially when it is linked to hard power. Ram-Prasad (2000: 188) claims that 'there is very little even in a "hard" Hindu nationalism which could translate into an ideology of expansion'. Yet as we have seen, when Hindutva ideas are linked to hard power, it bolsters India's resolve not to allow Kashmiri Muslims – in association with the government of

Pakistan – to control the state, regarded by many Indians as the 'jewel in the crown' of 'Hindu India'. This underlines what we have repeatedly noted in this text in relation to various other countries, including the USA, Iran and Israel: a nation's foreign policy does not takes place in isolation from a combination of domestic factors – including 'geo-strategic location, economic health, military strength and domestic stability' (Kapila, 2005), and, we might add, in some cases the soft power of religion.

## Religion and conflict in Sri Lanka

Following our focus on religion in politics and foreign policy in both India and Pakistan, we finish the chapter with a shift in focus to Sri Lanka, a country beset by a bloody civil war for decades until 2009. First, we examine the extent in which Sri Lanka's civil war was informed by religious factors. Second, we look at reasons for India's frequent interventions in the civil war. Did India intervene for religious and ethnic reasons, to support the claim of Sri Lanka's Hindu Tamil minority for a separate state, carved out of the existing political territory of Sri Lanka? Sri Lanka's civil war attracted the attention of successive Indian governments, for two main reasons: the conflict (1) was regionally destabilising, and (2) centrally involved Tamils, millions of whom live in India (Allen, 1992; Jayawardena, 1992; Weiss, 2011).

Ceylon became independent in 1948, changing its name to Sri Lanka (in Sinhalese: 'resplendent land') in 1972. In 1978, the country's legislative and judicial capital was moved from Colombo to nearby Sri Jayewardanapura Kotte, and the national flag was also changed: orange and green vertical bars were added, representing the Hindu Tamil[3] and Muslim minority populations. Despite this attempt to indicate that Sri Lanka was not solely a Buddhist nation, it remained the case that 'Buddhist nationalism' played a pre-eminent political role in Sri Lanka, serving as a unifying force among the Sinhalese majority (Young, 2000). Buddhist Sinhalese comprise three-quarters of the population, while Hindu Tamils make up around 18 per cent of the population. The remaining people – less than 10 per cent – are mainly Muslims and Christians (Jayawardena, 1992).

## BOX 13.7 Religion, ethnicity, and civil war in Sri Lanka

The civil war in Sri Lanka set Sinhalese Buddhists against Tamil Hindus. It was a conflict about identity, an issue that includes both ethnicity and religion. As Young notes, 'religion plays a role in the conflict, [although] most Sri Lankans view its origins more in ethnic rather than religious terms'. There was also a pronounced developmental dimension to the war. Sri Lanka was once hailed for its impressive developmental indicators, including 'a high literacy rate and life expectancy, and low rates of infant and maternal mortality.' As a consequence, however, of the civil war – which erupted in 1983 – these indicators deteriorated sharply. Overall, the civil war had a 'devastating impact . . . on demography, health, education, and housing', while highlighting 'wide disparities within ethnic and regional groups' (Young, 2000: 1). Believing that they would not ever get a fair deal because of demographic reasons, many Tamils fought for their own independent state, a demand which diminished after the civil war ended (Weiss, 2011).

Many Sri Lankans and foreign commentators regarded the conflict in Sri Lanka as having roots in the British colonial period, with inherited political and economic grievances following independence in 1948 that were not adequately addressed by successive governments (Young, 2000). Following the end of British rule, Sinhalese majority governments in Ceylon/Sri Lanka sought to overturn what they regarded as British colonial favouritism towards the Tamil minority, especially in relation to both education and distribution of government jobs. As a result, successive Sinhalese-majority governments introduced policies that favoured the Sinhalese over the Tamils, including giving the Buddhist religion a privileged position constitutionally. Over time, Tamil grievances grew, escalating to the point that civil war broke out in 1983 following the killing in the city of Jaffna of 13 mostly Tamil soldiers. Over the next quarter century the conflict was often extremely violent, a wide-ranging struggle between the two ethnic/religious groups over political, developmental, religious and ethnic concerns. The civil war resulted in over 65,000 deaths on both sides (Young, 2000: 1).

During the 1980 and 1990s, successive governments officially did away with some of the policies discriminating against Tamils and, in addition, recognised Tamil as one of the country's official languages. But for many

Tamils this was inadequate and fighting continued between Sri Lanka's armed forces and those of the Liberation Tigers of Tamil Eelam (LTTE). After 9/11, the Tamil Tigers found their international support diminishing. Various influential governments – including those of India, the USA, Britain, Canada and Australia – declared the LTTE to be a terrorist organisation. This meant that henceforward the Tigers found it very difficult to find international support for their struggle.

A ceasefire was declared in 2001 although this did not lead immediately to the end of the conflict, despite attempts led by the government of Norway to resolve the parties' concerns (Støre, 2006). Several major obstacles to peace remained, notably:

- intense rivalry between the two main (secular) Sinhalese political parties, the Peoples Assembly (PA) and the United National Party (UNP);
- fierce opposition from sections of the Buddhist clergy, opposed to any accommodation to the Tamils and their grievances, concessions which they viewed as threatening to the dominant position of Buddhism in Sri Lanka;
- governmental reluctance to accept the mediation of external parties;
- apparent unwillingness of the LTTE to entertain any settlement short of a separate state (Young, 2000).

From this list of barriers to a settlement to the conflict, we can also add both secular nationalist and religious concerns. This combination of factors made the situation impossible to resolve without severe bloodshed. As a result, the period from the time of the signing of the ceasefire in 2001 built to a crescendo when in 2008 the government's forces finally crushed the Tamil Tigers with pronounced ferocity. In May 2009 the Tamil Tigers accepted defeat.

We noted above that the Sri Lankan civil war was a conflict that drew the attention of successive Indian governments, and which at times led to India's overt involvement in the war. India's government was keen to resolve the conflict, for three main reasons:

- to underline India's credentials as South Asia's leading regional power;
- to try to undermine the claims of India's own Tamils for autonomy or independence, through denial of the demands of Sri Lanka's Tamil separatists;

- to emphasise the Indian government's stated belief that Sri Lanka's Tamils were unacceptably discriminated against by the Sinhalese majority (Pal, 2006).

The major point to emphasise, however, is that there was no knee jerk support of the Sri Lankan Tamils simply because they were in the main Hindus, in common with over 800 million Indians. In fact, Indian involvement in the civil war was mainly linked to secular national interest concerns, because of India's close geographical position to Sri Lanka. This point can be illustrated by reference to the 1970s and early 1980s, a period when India was often controlled by secular Congress governments led by Indira Gandhi. At this time, India's key foreign policy goal in relation to Sri Lanka was to prevent its government building closer ties not only with various Western countries, including Britain and the USA, but also with neighbouring countries, including Pakistan and China (Pal, 2006). For the Indian government this posed an unacceptable challenge to India's position as South Asia's chief regional power. According to Krishna (2001), on various questions, including 'the Soviet invasion of Afghanistan [1979], declaring the Indian ocean a zone of peace, the issue of broadcast facilities to the Voice of America, the use of Trincomalee harbour, [and] membership in ASEAN [Association of South East Asian Nations]', the prime minister, Indira Gandhi, believed that, in relation to India, Sri Lanka's government was acting too independently and provocatively. Seeking an issue to help her focus India's concerns and as a result to deal with Sri Lanka, she focused upon the situation of the Tamil minority in Sri Lanka. She declared that the Tamils' fate was a crucial issue for India's national security. In sum, at this time, India's foreign policy under Mrs Gandhi was pursued 'for reasons having to do with assertion of India's hegemony over Sri Lanka' (Pararajasingham, 2004). India trained and armed Tamil militants, not in order to achieve a Tamil state ('Tamil Eelam'), but to complement diplomatic pressures already being exerted on Sri Lanka's government to compel it to toe the line and bend to India's will.

In the late 1980s, following unsuccessful attempts to get Sri Lanka to bend to India's will, India's government negotiated an agreement with the government of Sri Lanka on the Tamils' behalf – but without consulting the Liberation Tigers of Tamil Eelam (Jayawardena, 1992). India promised Sri Lanka's government military support if needed to enforce Tamil compliance with a deal that gave the Tamils a few political concessions – including Constitutional changes to grant them more local power – but certainly not the independence being demanded. Perhaps unsurprisingly, the initiative did not resolve the conflict – although it did achieve India's foreign policy of bringing Sri Lanka's government firmly under its influence if not control. Later, in 1991, when a government led by Indira Gandhi's son, Rajiv, tried to flex India's muscles by intervening in Sri Lanka militarily – both to exercise India's new-found influence and to overturn the earlier policy to arm the LTTE – he was assassinated by a Tamil extremist. This suggests that India seriously underestimated the depth of feeling underpinning Tamil nationalism in Sri Lanka that by this time had grown to be a major force of such potency that even applied Indian firepower could not obliterate it. Indeed, as Bose (1994) argues, India's physical intervention appears to have achieved the opposite effect to that intended: it served significantly to help consolidate Tamil nationalism in Sri Lanka. Overall, however, the situation was made more complex by a lack of agreement among Indian governments over the direction and thrust of India's policy. Under Congress Party rule the issue was viewed in secular nationalist and national interest terms. The government consistently supported Sri Lanka's (Sinhalese) government – as it was seen as the best means to curtail regional instability because of the war. BJP administrations, however, saw the conflict more through a Hindutva focus. This led them to make statements supporting the Tamils on religious grounds, a stance that also gained the backing of the regional government of Tamil Nadu, which had long backed the LTTE on ethnic grounds (Shankar, 2006).

## Conclusion

In this chapter we focused on the influence of religion in the international relations of South Asia, with particular focus on India, Pakistan and Sri Lanka. We saw that:

- in each of the three countries, various political issues have long been associated with religious factors;
- this was often in the context of competition or conflicts over identity, land or other resources;

- in each case, identifiable religious constituencies – including, Hindu fundamentalists in India, Islamists in Pakistan, and Sinhalese Buddhists and Tamil Hindus in Sri Lanka – sought to influence their country's foreign policy and international relations.

Our surveys of the political roles of religious actors in the three countries enable us to conclude that: (1) religious actors' influence in relation to the international relations of India, Pakistan and Sri Lanka is at times significant. Their chief tactic is to try to influence government policy, augmented, when they are available, by attempts to build transnational networks of religious believers; for example, in relation to Kashmir. This implies more generally that the soft power of religion is a variable that should not be overlooked. However, this is not to suggest that religious soft power is *always* the most influential factor in the region's international relations. But it does underline how in each of the regional countries we examined, domestic structures and processes throw up politically influential religious actors that seek to influence international outcomes, although they are by no means guaranteed success. They are, however, likely to be most successful when religious soft power works together with 'secular' hard power.

## Notes

1. According to Marshall (2004), 'Until the nineteenth century, the word "Hindu" had no specific religious meaning and simply referred to the people who lived east of the Indus River, whatever their beliefs. (The Indian Supreme Court itself has held that "no precise meaning can be ascribed to the terms 'Hindu' and 'Hinduism.'") It was only when the census introduced by the British colonial authorities in 1871 included Hindu as a religious designation that many Indians began to think of themselves and their country as Hindu.'
2. Mahmud (2005) explains that the state of Jammu-Kashmir, of which the Kashmir valley is a part, is not religiously homogeneous. Jammu is two-thirds Hindu and one-third Muslim, while the Kashmir valley is about 80 per cent Muslim. Azad Kashmir (the Pakistan-controlled) portion is 'almost entirely Sunni Muslim, including 1.5 million refugees settled in various cities of Pakistan'.
3. Tamils are an ethnic group, predominantly Hindu, whose language is also Tamil, a Dravidian language. In Sri Lanka, Tamils are mostly located in the country's Northern and Eastern provinces. Tamils are in the majority in the

Indian state of Tamil Nadu State, in the south-east of the country; there are strong links between the two communities. Some Tamils are indigenous, others are descendants of estate labourers imported under British colonial rule.

# Questions

- To what extent has the end of the Cold War and deepening globalisation affected the role of religion in conflict in South Asia?
- What is 'Hindu nationalism' and how does it affect political outcomes in India?
- 'Pakistan is a Muslim state and so we should expect a leading role for Islam in both domestic and foreign policy'. Discuss.
- Was the civil war in Sri Lanka a conflict between competing religious groups?
- To what extent has international involvement in South Asia helped to resolve religious conflicts?

# Further reading

C. Bhatt, *Hindu Nationalism: Origins, Ideologies and Modern Myths*, Oxford: Berg, 2001. Bhatt's book is clearly written and stimulating. It is both reasoned and succinctly argued, an analysis that delves into the history of the phenomenon and provides an illuminating account of the issues that will shape it in the future.

Paul Brass, *The Production of Hindu-Muslim Violence in Contemporary India*, Seattle: University of Washington Press, 2005. In recent years, serious Hindu–Muslim rioting in India created a situation where communal violence became a common event. Brass, one of the world's pre-eminent experts on South Asia, looks back at more than 50 years of riots in the north Indian city of Aligarh. Brass exposes the mechanisms by which endemic communal violence is deliberately provoked and sustained. He offers a compelling argument for abandoning or refining a number of widely held views about the supposed causes of communal violence, not just in India but also throughout the rest of the world. An important addition to the literature on Indian and South Asian politics, this book is also an invaluable contribution to our understanding of the interplay of nationalism, ethnicity, religion and collective violence, wherever it occurs.

Subrata Mitra, *Politics in India: Structure, Process and Policy*: London, Routledge, 2010. Mitra provides a comprehensive analysis of the broad spectrum of

India's politics, including key features of politics in India in a comparative and accessible form. The book is illustrated with relevant maps, life stories, statistics and opinion data. A comparative political approach is adopted, with a focus on anti-poverty measures, liberalisation of the economy, nuclearisation and relations with the United States and Asian neighbours such as Pakistan and China.

S. Nasr, *The Islamic Leviathan: Islam and the Making of State Power*, Oxford: Oxford University Press, 2001. Nasr manages to balance sophisticated political theory and effective historical analysis in his case studies of Pakistan and Malaysia. He challenges the prevailing assumption that Islam is against or is incompatible with secularism and modernisation.

Gordon Weiss, *The Cage: The fight for Sri Lanka & the Last Days of the Tamil Tigers*, London, Bodley Head, 2011. Weiss delivers a striking account of ruthless terror experienced by both sides during the civil war. This is the first comprehensive, factual account of the civil war's mass killing and Weiss explains why the United Nations was powerless to prevent it.

# 14 | Pacific Asia

Pacific Asia comprises 14 states: four in East Asia (China, Japan, Korea and Taiwan) and ten in South East Asia (Brunei, Cambodia, Indonesia, Laos, Malaysia, Myanmar (Burma), the Philippines, Singapore, Thailand and Vietnam). As McCargo (2001: 141) notes, 'unlike the more ambiguous phrase "Asia-Pacific", "Pacific Asia" clearly excludes Australia and North America'. Several of the world's major religions are commonly found in the Pacific Asia region, including: Buddhism (both Theravada and Mahayana),[1] Confucianism (in various forms, often mixed up with Taoism[2] and/or Buddhism), Islam (Indonesia is the world's most populous predominantly Muslim country, with a population of more than 200 million people), Christianity (often Catholicism, primarily in the Philippines, although both China and South Korea also have significant Catholic minorities), Hinduism (principally in Bali, an Indonesian island), Taoism, Shintoism (Japan),[3] as well as numerous localised traditional religions. In short, the Pacific Asia contains a large number of religious faiths and this complicates our understanding of the relationship between religion, politics and international relations.

Religious diversity is augmented by economic, historical and political differences. Economically, Pacific Asia ranges from 'the high tech capitalist economies of Taiwan and Singapore, to the predominantly agricultural societies of Laos and Vietnam' (McCargo, 2001: 141). Historically, the region has a complex and dissimilar colonial background and influences: no colonial control in Thailand or China, and British administrations in Burma, Hong Kong (now part of China), Malaysia and Singapore. In addition, the Dutch controlled Indonesia and the French controlled 'Indochina' (today, three separate states: Cambodia, Laos and Vietnam). Moreover, the Spanish had a long-term colonial presence in the Philippines, and the Japanese in Korea and Taiwan. Some regional countries (Cambodia, China and Japan) have very old civilisations, while others (such as the Philippines) were created quite recently. Finally, there are many kinds of political systems in Pacific Asia. These include an absolute monarchy in tiny Brunei, a constitutional monarchy in populous Thailand and a long-established military regime in Myanmar, which now appears to be tentatively democratising. There are also well-established regional democracies, including Japan, South Korea and Taiwan. In addition, Indonesia and the Philippines democratised over the last quarter century, while Malaysia and Singapore have well-established 'illiberal democracies', that is, political systems with both democratic and authoritarian characteristics (McCargo, 2001: 141–142).

## BOX 14.1 Pacific Asia and 'Asian Values'

Pacific Asia is a region with religious, economic, historical and political diversity. In recent years, there has been a continuing debate between two groups – 'Orientalists' and 'reverse Orientalists' – over what are the region's most politically and culturally important characteristics. While the Orientalists refer to the region's various indigenous forms of authoritarian rule which are said to be 'culturally appropriate', reverse Orientalists cite various recent rulers – including Mohammed Mahathir (Malaysia) and Lee Kuan Yew (Singapore) – who, it is claimed, turn old stereotypes into useful claims of cultural distinctiveness (Barr, 2002). This issue has been a key factor in the continuing controversy over whether there are, in fact, distinctive 'Asian Values'. Some contend that 'Asian Values' are actually linked to some of the region's religious traditions, leading 'value system[s] most congruent with Oriental authoritarianism' (King, 1993: 141). For example, Fukuyama (1992: 217) sees Confucianism as both 'hierarchical and inegalitarian', characteristic of 'the community-orientedness of Asian cultures'. The overall concern here is that, according to the proponents of a distinctive 'Asian culture', including former rulers and current intellectuals, such as the Chinese Jiang Qing, liberal democracy is 'culturally alien' to the Pacific Asia region (Ommerborn, n.d.). This is said to be because many regions have political cultures and histories that, while differing from country to country in precise details, nevertheless reflect an important factor: a societal emphasis on the collective or group, not the individual. This in turn emphasises 'harmony', 'consensus', 'unity' and 'community', all cornerstone values of Confucianism – that are said to differ significantly from 'Western culture' and its allegedly individualistic, self-seeking values, including liberal democracy (Deegan, 2005: 26).

In this chapter we focus primarily on two religions, Confucianism in relation to China, and Buddhism in relation to Thailand, Myanmar and

Cambodia. For comparative purposes, we also examine the role of transnational Islam in relation to religo-ethnic struggles for political autonomy in Thailand and the Philippines. The structure of the chapter is as follows: first, we examine Confucianism in relation to China, focusing on what is called the country's 'post-communist' foreign policy, characterised as 'New Confucian' or 'neo-Confucian' (the two terms are used synonymously). Second, we consider the political impact of Buddhism in relation to Thailand, Myanmar and Cambodia, three Buddhist-majority regional countries. We discover that there are no influential regional Buddhist networks that influence those countries foreign policies or international relations more generally. This is because in each country, nationalism has 'secularize[d] national identities that were historically rooted in religion'. This implies that 'each nation adopted [Buddhism] in a unique way according to its national characteristics' (Tepe, 2005: 287, 297). For example, unlike Cambodia or Myanmar, Thailand was never colonised by a Western country. As a result, Buddhism developed as the core of the country's national ideology. In recent years, 'new Buddhist movements' have emerged – some with overtly political goals and aspirations – emphasising that Buddhism is still of great importance in Thailand. In Myanmar, there was a different position regarding the social and political role of Buddhism. Buddhist monks (*sangha*) played a leading role in the country's attainment of freedom from British colonial rule after the Second World War. However, more recently there has been intermittent political conflict between some sections of the *sangha* and state, with the former in some cases key political opponents. In addition, the key political dissident and pro-democracy campaigner Aung San Suu Kyi is said to be strongly influenced by her Buddhist values and philosophy ('Buddhism through Buddhist Eyes', n.d.). Note, however, that Aung San Suu Kyi rarely if ever makes any overt link between Buddhism, politics and international relations and this helps confirm that the political role of Buddhism is mostly to be observed in Myanmar in domestic concerns related to the demands of the Buddhist *sangha*, not international issues. Unlike in Thailand or Myanmar, in Cambodia, Buddhism had to contend in the 1970s with serious attempts to snuff it out. During five years of rule by the murderous Khmer Rouge, the regime tried energetically to exterminate all religion – including Buddhism – while killing millions of Cambodians. However, following

351

the Khmer Rouge's overthrow in 1979 by a Vietnamese invasion, an initially hesitant state recognised the continuing popular appeal of Buddhism and today allows it an important voice in national affairs.

Overall, the chapter makes the following points:

- While both Buddhism and Confucianism have political roles in Pacific Asia, it is only in relation to China that we see a significant role for religion in foreign policy and international relations.
- The Chinese government emphasises what it describes as a 'culturally authentic' 'New Confucianism' as a prescriptive policy to try to balance the power of the USA and to achieve greater cultural and moral influence for China.
- Buddhism does not play a significant international or transnational role in Pacific Asia's politics.
- Important regional networks of dissident Muslim minorities are in conflict with the state in Thailand and the Philippines.

## China: Confucianism and foreign policy

Confucianism is an ancient religious and philosophical system. It has developed over the last 2,500 years from writings attributed to a Chinese philosopher, Confucius (the latinised version of Kung Fu-tzu (that is, Master Kung), a teacher in China who lived between c.551 and 479 BCE). His key teachings were concerned with principles of good conduct, practical wisdom, and 'proper' social relationships, and focused upon relationships between individuals, between individuals and their families, and between individuals and general society. The German sociologist Max Weber (1969: 21) noted that, in China, Confucianism was historically 'the status ethic of prebendaries, of men with literary educations who were characterized by a secular rationalism'. This underlines how important it was in China to belong to the *cultured* stratum; if one did not, he (much less she) did not count, and an adhesion to Confucian values was an important element. As a result, Confucianism was a status ethic of the 'cultured' stratum that in turn not only helped determine the way of life in China itself but also influenced neighbouring areas that historically came under Chinese influence or control, including present-day Korea, Japan, Singapore, Taiwan and

Vietnam. In Korea, for example, Confucianism grew in significance from the seventh century CE to become not only the traditional ideological core of the governing system but also of 'a religious or philosophical system which affected the social and cultural aspects of the nation's life' (Barr, 2002: 157–174).

Over time, however, countries influenced by Confucianism diverged politically. On the one hand, China, North Korea and Vietnam are three of the few remaining communist countries. On the other hand, from the time of the Cold War, which began in the late 1940s and ended 40 years later, Japan, South Korea, Singapore and Taiwan were closely allied with the USA and more generally the West. This suggests that while these countries may share cultural characteristics that highlight the importance of the community or the collective over the individual, a shared background in Confucianism does not dictate similar political developments or international relations. In China, Confucian cultural and religious factors can be seen today in relation to a 'post-communist' ideology that emphasises certain patterns of living and standards of social value, while also providing an important backdrop to recent developments in political thinking and foreign policy (Barr, 2002: 46–63; Feng, 2007; Kim, 1998; Ross and Johnston, 2006; Hoare-Vance, 2009).

## BOX 14.2 Confucianism: The core of Chinese civilisation?

A leading Chinese intellectual, Jiang Qing, argues that the 'Confucian religion is the core of Chinese civilisation, including political, cultural and religious aspects'. As the de facto Chinese state religion, he claims that 'it should be the cultural consensus and spiritual belief of the whole nation' ('Confucianism will never be religion', 2006). For Jiang Qing, government is legitimate only when it clearly reflects the values associated with the community's cultural traditions and principles and in China, he contends, this is Confucianism. He also claims that the so-called 'universal' appropriateness of Western-style, political and social values is simply wrong – as he believes it inevitably leads to undesirable outcomes, including 'social Darwinism or poverty of the third world etc' (Ommerborn, n.d.). Instead, national political institutions and practices in China should reflect local cultural values ('Confucianism will never be religion', 2006). Critics contend, however, that Jiang Qing 'negate[s] the generalisation of Western principles like democracy, freedom, and human rights etc' (Ommerborn, n.d.).

These concerns have risen to prominence in response to the stresses and strains that globalisation places on China's hitherto inward-looking political, social and developmental concerns (Barr, 2002: 46–63; Feng, 2007). To try to deal with the domestic impact of globalisation, China's rulers seek to draw ideologically on Confucian ideas and values. The government seeks now to emphasise its Confucian – no longer explicitly communist – approach to foreign policy and international relations (Jacques, 2006). This was evident in the visit of China's leader, Hu Jintao, to the USA in May 2006 when, in a speech at Yale University he set out – for the first time in such a forum – the Chinese view of 'a harmonious world based on the idea of Chinese civilisation'. This Confucian focus dovetails with an important strand of domestic policy established in the mid-1990s: an interlinked social, political and economic programme designed to 're-educate' and 'reinform' the Chinese people in the advantages of living according to 'harmonious' Confucian values. The campaign was accompanied by officially sponsored excursions into political philosophy with Confucianism harnessed to desirable prescriptions for politics and economic growth, based on principles of harmony, consensus and order. The overall aim is to try to eliminate or at least reduce the kinds of adversarial activity associated by at least some of China's leaders with economic liberalisation characteristic of economic globalisation (Yu Keping, 2004; Hoare-Vance, 2009).

As a result of the government's initiative, Hwang (2005) notes, 'the dormant seeds of a long-buried debate are beginning to sprout in China, with implications that could shape the future of the world's most rapidly developing society'. Both scholars and state officials are now busy re-examining China's Confucian past, attempting to devise strategies to deal both with domestic internal social and political conflicts, as well as to help provide a suitable, post-communist ideological content for the country's foreign policy and international relations. These 'New Confucianist' or 'neo-Confucianist' ideas significantly inform the current debate 'about values and morality, expressed in questions about how the country should legitimately be ruled'. In the likely continued absence of meaningful domestic democratic reforms, the Chinese government appears to be experimenting with Confucianism as a state ideology of control. The government's aim is probably to try to reinforce its hold on power through a focus on the cultural and societal appropriateness of Confucianism as a way of uniting the Chinese at a time of growing economic, social and political polarisation (Tamney and Hsueh-Ling Chiang, 2002; Adler, 2011).

This is not to suggest that the government's current focus on Confucianism is entirely cynical or self-serving. As Naím (2005) notes, Confucian ideas have 'long persist[ed] in the minds of Chinese politicians'. A noted China scholar, John King Fairbank, wrote in 1948 that even at the time of the communist revolution, Confucian ideas informed the ideas of revolutionary leaders, including Mao Zedong. This was because 'Confucianism began as a means of bringing social order out of [political] chaos. . . . It has been a philosophy of status and consequently a ready tool for autocracy and bureaucracy whenever they have flourished' (Fairbank quoted in Naím, 2005). Over 60 years later, China's current leaders are again seeking to draw on 'whatever Confucian instincts remain in the population to contain the social upheaval that is coming with the country's rapid modernization' (Pan, 2004). Social and political stresses and strains are reflected in official data, indicating that there were around 87,000 protests and incidents of social unrest in China during 2005 – an average of more than 230 a *day*, an increase of 6.6 per cent on 2004 (Watts, 2006). By 2010 this had doubled to over 180,000 such incidents (Orlik, 2011). Many of the clashes between 'the masses' and the police have their roots in either property disputes, 'pollution' or 'corruption' issues, while others focus on 'deadly ethnic' conflict, especially in Central China and Western China (Orlik, 2011). Key problems occur when the state tries to take land from local people for major developmental projects. During 2003, for example, 'tens of thousands of rice farmers fighting a dam project staged a huge protest in the western part of the country. The same day, authorities crushed a strike involving 7,000 textile workers . . . The Communist Party has indicated it is worried that these outbursts of discontent might coalesce into large-scale, organized opposition to its rule' (Pan, 2004). Despite these clear manifestations of popular protest, the government seems unwilling to establish democratic reforms – while seeking to try to contain popular agitation in other ways. These include trying to make the ruling Communist Party more accountable and popularly based, giving in to some protests but cracking down hard on others, and trying strictly to control the flow of information which has increased as a result of globalisation, including via the internet and email. However, growing popular access to foreign news media, coupled with greatly increased ownership of mobile telephones in recent years, makes state attempts at censorship increasingly difficult (Tamney and Hsueh-Ling Chiang 2002; Feng, 2007).

Part of the problem, the government acknowledges, is that China is strongly affected by both globalisation and wider changes in the post-Cold War world, including China's often-problematic relationship with the USA (Ross and Johnston, 2006; Feng, 2007). After the Cold War ended in the late 1980s, the US government sought to get to grips with China by advancing a policy of what it called 'constructive engagement'. This sought to portray the USA as the only remaining superpower, albeit with benign intentions, whose main goal was to find common ground with the (then mostly authoritarian) countries of Pacific Asia, including China. China's government saw the US initiative as useful because it implied a lessening of the need to respond to external pressures in areas where it was vulnerable: democracy and human rights. And, along with US 'constructive engagement', there seemed to be a growing international willingness to accept the belief that there was something called 'the Asian way' that justified different, less than fully democratic, development patterns (Kim, 1998). As already noted, such ideas are currently linked in China both to traditional Confucian ideas and to its modern expression, 'New' or 'Neo' Confucianism.

Ideas associated with New Confucianism dovetail neatly with US views on economic development: both share a belief that capitalism and free markets – the 'theology of the marketplace' – will solve the world's developmental problems, including those of China. President Clinton embraced this principle in 1996, declaring that 'freer enterprise will fuel the hunger for a more free society'. For many authoritarian leaders in Pacific Asia, including the government of China, this was a comforting thought, 'since even the most dictatorial regimes in Asia now embrace free-market capitalism' (Miller, 1997: 1–2). However, as Zhou notes,

> there is no doubt that different political systems are the essential reason for the conflicts between the United States and China. However, more profound causes of the disagreement between the United States and China on human rights issues lie in the different levels of economic development and the divergent cultures and basic values of the two countries. The notion of the responsibility of the state for individuals, the lack of the concept of rights in

traditional Chinese thought, and humiliation in recent history and corresponding sensitivity to sovereignty, count for the ordinary Chinese attitudes toward US policies on human rights towards China.

(2005: 105)

This suggests that, since the mid-1990s, a shared belief in the dogma of capitalism has not been sufficient to remove sources of friction between the USA and China, especially in the latter, the issue of political and religious freedoms. A focal point is the persecution of the Falun Gong religious sect. Falun Gong (also known as Falun Dafa) means 'Law of the Wheel Breathing Exercise', and is a largely spiritual movement that incorporates Buddhist and Taoist principles, Qigong (body, mind and physical exercises), and healing techniques. The aim is to cleanse both mind and body and simultaneously make better moral character through a regime of exercises, meditation and study. Falun Gong exercises are believed to be both relaxing and energising, with practitioners often performing them as a group. Li Hongzhi, also known as 'The Master' or 'Master Li', introduced Falun Gong to China in 1992. His teachings and philosophy are set forth in two books, *Falun Gong* and *Zhuan Falun* (*Turning the Law Wheel*), available in a variety of languages. Falun Gong is practised all over the world and Li Hongzhi claims to have a following of more than 100 million people.

## BOX 14.3 Falun Gong in China

Followers of Falun Gong in China experienced high levels of persecution in (Human Rights Watch, 2002; Beaumont, 2009). The Chinese government initiated a general campaign against assorted spiritual and religious groups in 1999, including Falun Gong. As a result, in April 1999, some 10,000 Falun Gong practitioners took part in an unauthorised silent protest against the Chinese government actions outside Zhongnanhai, the Chinese leadership's official residence. Three months after the protest, the Chinese government reacted by outlawing Falun Gong because it allegedly practises 'evil thinking' that threatens China's social stability. Since then, Falun Gong practitioners have been persecuted throughout China. Many are interrogated and forced to sign letters rejecting Falun Gong. The Chinese government has also destroyed more than two million Falun Gong books and instructional tapes and has placed Li Hongzhi on a list of wanted criminals (Human Rights Watch, 2002: 15–18.)

China's rulers have various concerns linked to international attention on the lack of religious freedoms in the country (Fox, 2008: 189–191). The government has 'uneasy connections with foreign religious groups active in China', including various Christian churches – both Catholic and Protestant. Reacting to China's religious repression, the Vatican seats its ambassador in Taipei, Taiwan, not Beijing (Waldron, 1999). In addition, the influence of conservative Protestant evangelical groups on US government's foreign policy (see Chapter 8) serves to increase pressure on the Chinese government, which faces tough questions 'on matters of religious persecution' (Waldron, 1999; Fox, 2008: 189–191). Collectively, these issues emphasise that China's rulers must now deal with several serious problems simultaneously: demands for religious and political freedoms; developmental concerns, including how to feed and employ the vast – and growing – population of more than one billion people; maintenance of the considerable flow of foreign investment; and, above all, how in the long run to retain their hold on power. In this context, the government regards New Confucianism as an important ideological referent in relation to both domestic and foreign policy. As Waldron (1999) notes, however, 'religion may well turn out to be a more important factor in foreign policy than in domestic policy'.

Chinese intellectual Jiang Qing contends that China, 'challenged by Western civilization in its broadest sense', should now seek to deal with current political and social problems by reference to the 'Confucian religion' ('Confucianism will never be religion', 2006). For Jiang 'remaking the Confucian religion' would 'enable Chinese people to launch a "dialogue between Chinese civilization and Western civilization"', that is, including a 'dialogue between the so-called Confucian religion and Christian religion' ('Confucianism will never be religion', 2006). Raja Mohan explains that 'besides providing the ethical glue at home, Confucius has become the emblem of a new Chinese foreign policy initiative'. In recent times, the Chinese government has begun 'offering support to build "Confucius institutes". The purpose of the Confucius institutes is to teach Chinese language and culture to the world'. This is an attempt, Raja Mohan contends, to support China's position as arguably the second most globally powerful country behind the USA, a recognition of the importance of 'soft power'[4] – that is, the power of attractive ideas – to underpin and extend China's 'growing hard power. The British

Council, Alliance Francaise and Max Mueller Bhavan might as well make space for the new cultural juggernaut from China. Beijing hopes to set up at least a hundred Confucius institutes around the world in coming years' (Raja Mohan, 2005). However, by late 2010, there were 322 Confucius Institutes in 94 countries, an indication of the importance China's government places on attempts to extend its soft power internationally ('316 Confucius Institutes established worldwide', 2010).

The background is that since 2003 and the coming to power of China's current leaders, Hu Jintao and Wen Jaibao, the country has sought to alleviate international concerns about its increasing economic, diplomatic and military power with a new policy slogan: 'China's Peaceful Rise' that evolved into 'China's Peaceful Development', in case the word 'rise' was seen as a threat both to China's neighbours and the USA (Schmitt, 2006). According to Jain and Groot (2006), this is manifested in China's current '"soft power" offensive'. The concept of soft power advocacy is said to have made a strong impression in China, especially after 'some agitation by at least one Shanghai think-tank' to influence China's Communist Party leaders to try to enhance China's soft power and thus China's global and regional influence.

China's New Confucian values in relation to its foreign policy provide a useful foundation for construction of a post-communist ideological framework. In November 2005, on the occasion of the opening of the first Confucius Institute in Japan, Wang Yi, Chinese ambassador to Japan, defined New Confucian values in relation to current Chinese foreign policy, what he called 'an independent foreign policy of peace'. The concept of peace, he asserted, was seen in Chinese foreign relations, in 'friendly neighboring policy', 'virtuous treatment' and happy relation with close neighbours and distant friends alike' (http://english.hanban.edu.cn/market/HanBanE/426610.htm).

Such concerns are undoubtedly a factor in the government's declared aim to underpin China's 'peaceful rise' to great power status, seeking through the use of New Confucian tenets not only to balance the United States globally but also regionally in relation to both Japan and India. The policy is rooted in a strategy of increasing civilisational dialogue, which for the Chinese government is an attempt to underpin and extend its attempts to help build world peace (Pan, 2004). Such concerns were manifested at a national conference in August 2005 in Beijing, devoted to a focus on the contemporary salience of Confucian ideas.[5] Shandong University professor Ding Guanzhi argued that 'the Confucian concept of seeking the "golden mean" meant keeping a balance. A righteous government should use power to maintain the mean, he said, and power between nations should be kept in balance' (Hwang, 2005). The implication seemed clear: China's international economic and military rise was henceforward to be focused on what the government regarded as a fundamental geopolitical imbalance. In this view, the position of the United States as the sole global superpower needed rectifying, and Confucian ideas were useful to inform China's rise to a comparative level of power and influence. At the same conference, Ren Ziyu, 'a scholar on world religions and the recently retired director of the [Chinese] National Library', averred that 'Confucianism lasted for 2,000 years because new content was constantly added . . . The core teachings had undergone two major waves of change in history . . . Today, with economic globalisation and cultural polarisation, it is time for a third surge of Chinese culture. Not just academic thought, we both need conscious power' (Hwang, 2005). In sum, it is clear that both the Chinese government and various scholars now seek to focus New Confucian ideas in a novel foreign policy focus that would not only build more productive international relations, but also improve relations with the USA, and more generally, to help build 'world peace'. Attempting to use ideas associated with China's oldest and most famous philosopher – Confucius – has the added advantage of avoiding overt reference to the USA's traditional *bête noire*: the continuing official state ideology in China – Marxism–Leninism. It is also especially useful that Confucius, both teacher and quasi-religious figure, is best known for championing peace and harmony and unsurprising that China's government now proclaims adherence to similar values, eager to try to dispel regional and international concerns about its rapid global economic rise.

In sum, it is useful to think of China's soft power in the context of recent and current attempts to win influence by persuasion and appeal rather than by expressions of hard power, that is, economic leverage and (threats of) military force. Elizabeth Economy, director of Asian Studies for the US-based Council on Foreign Relations,[6] contends that Chinese soft power is a mix of 'culture, education and diplomacy', while Bruce Gilley (quoted in Pan, 2006), expert on contemporary Chinese politics at New School University, contends that China wields soft power alongside hard power, such as its military threat and ability to impact, especially in the developing world, on other nations' political and/or economic security.

## Buddhism and politics in Pacific Asia: Thailand, Myanmar and Cambodia

At the beginning the chapter we noted that Pacific Asia has a variety of religions. As we have seen, New Confucianism influences both China's contemporary foreign policy and international relations, although opinions differ regarding how this should be understood in terms of the balance between the country's soft and hard power. Like Confucianism, Theravada Buddhism is a very significant religious tradition in Pacific Asia.[7] The use of the Pali term 'Theravada' (Doctrine of the Elders) to define the particular school reflects the fact that Theravadins present themselves as belonging to the branch of Buddhism which they believe preserves the 'orthodox' or 'original' teaching of the Buddha, Prince Siddhartha Gautama, born 2,500 years ago in what is now northern India. Theravada Buddhism (henceforward referred to in this chapter as 'Buddhism') is the Buddhist culture which is highly significant in Sri Lanka's religious, political and social life, as examined in Chapter 13 on South Asia. In Pacific Asia, Theravada Buddhism is the leading religion in Myanmar (Burma), Thailand and Cambodia.

---

**BOX 14.4 Buddhism in Thailand, Myanmar and Cambodia**

Buddhism has permeated the life of the nations of the region's Buddhist countries, leaving its distinctive mark on social, cultural and individual activity. The result is that, as in relation to Confucianism in China, Buddhism has long served as one of the main socialising, acculturating and unifying forces in several Pacific Asia countries. As a result, Buddhism has profoundly influenced the cultural, economic and political development of several Pacific Asia nations, and at the current time it continues to influence many regional people's cultural, social and political values. Buddhism is the root from which national identity and political and social heritages have for centuries developed in many regional countries.

---

During the post-Second World War era, a period characterised for many Pacific Asian countries by an assault from two separate secularising influences – Western-style modernisation and communism – Buddhism has shown both tenacity and adaptability. However, like many other religious traditions, Buddhism has also found itself increasingly subject to the eroding influences of foreign secular ideas. Both secularism (the idea that the government, societal morals, education and so on, should be independent of religion) and secularisation (a significant decline in the prestige and influences of religious institutions, personnel, and activities and a change in the overall character of human thought and action, such that they become less governed by mystical or transcendental criteria) are important in this context. Taken together, secularisation and secularism have significantly undermined traditional Buddhism-orientated worldviews in Pacific Asian countries. In response, Buddhist practitioners strive to shore up Buddhism's traditions, institutions, scriptural integrity, monastic discipline and moral values. As a result, both Buddhist renewal and reform are present, significantly involving sustained activism on the part of the Buddhist laity in several countries, including: Thailand, Myanmar and Cambodia (Haynes, 1998: 188–206). In addition, many Buddhist monks (the *sangha*) also find it necessary to reinterpret traditional Buddhist teachings to seek to appeal to increasingly modernised, urbanised and educated citizens (McCargo, 2009).

This train of events began after the Second World War, when foreign colonial rule was overthrown in the Pacific Asia region. In the regional national struggles for independence, Western notions of equality, liberty, self-determination and so forth were commonly employed by nationalist leaders seeking to legitimise their quest for national freedom with unifying ideas that were also seen as attractive and modern (Acharya and Stubbs, 1999: 118). Notions of representative government were particularly important here, forming a focal point of political attacks on traditional religious-political modes of government. The result was that by the time of the Second World War there was a small but influential group of Western-educated elites who had developed comprehension of, and commitment to, new secular values. Later, however, attempts to impose secularisation on traditional cultures and societies often led to tensions and conflicts and tensions (McCargo, 2001: 143–145; Cady and Simon, 2006).

Post-colonial state policies towards religion in Buddhist Thailand, Myanmar and Cambodia[8] were shaped not only by rulers' goals of Western-style modernisation but also by their need to legitimate their rule and to unify often ethnically and religiously divided peoples. Their main problem was that the two goals – modernisation and building nation-states – were often mutually exclusive. This is because while striving for modernisation entails rejection of those aspects of a society's traditions deemed impediments to a rationalised bureaucratic order, often including religious principles, nation-building depends on the very opposite. What is necessary here are successful attempts to identify what is basic to national identity, which might well include religion, and more generally community values rooted in a common history. Under prevailing circumstances of conflict and tension, political leaders in Thailand, Myanmar and Cambodia eventually (re)turned to religious values for assistance. The concept of 'national religion' – in each case, Buddhism – was invoked to try to initiate, explain and legitimise political actions, institutions and programmes, albeit with varying degrees of success (Stuart-Fox, 2006).

## BOX 14.5 Buddhist 'passivity' and politics in Pacific Asia

It is sometimes alleged that Buddhist countries are characterised by political 'passivity' (Huntington, 1991; Fukuyama, 1992). Critics of this view point to various high-profile political struggles involving Buddhists in Thailand, Myanmar and Cambodia, in recent years (Barr, 2002; Stuart-Fox, 2006). In addition since the 1970s, there have been frequent popular protests against authoritarian rule both in Thailand and, most prominently, in Myanmar, where Aung San Suu Kyi is the most notable political dissident and pro-democracy campaigner.[9] There has also been the rise and fall of the murderous Khmer Rouge regime in Cambodia. Overall, this political volatility significantly undermines claims of 'passivity', said by some to be central to Buddhist beliefs and worldview.

Claims of 'Buddhist passivity' are especially prominent when commentators refer to the alleged political proclivities of rural dwellers in the Buddhist countries of Pacific Asia (McCargo, 2001). However, it is by no means certain that it is their Buddhist culture that impels such people towards political passivity. Apparent Buddhist 'passivity' may merely reflect both a general lack of political influence for the mass of ordinary people and a rational response to heavy-handed, often military-based, state power. 'Passive' Buddhists may sensibly decide that it would be foolhardy openly to confront the state, assessing that realistically they have no chance of success in such a confrontation. But this is hardly a unique trait of rural Buddhist people! In other words, rather than alleged passive Buddhist culture being the cause of political passivity, it may well be much more important that powerful, unrepresentative governments, often closely backed by the military, create and embed political passivity by showing ordinary people that resistance to state power is not only futile but also highly dangerous. The implication is that the religion of such 'politically passive' people is not that important; yet, we never read of 'Muslim' or 'Christian' passivity in, for example, the Middle East or Africa. It is just as likely, however, that often powerless rural people in both regions are just as politically 'passive' as their counterparts in the Buddhist countries of Pacific Asia when confronted by overwhelming state power underpinned by the power of the military.

## Pacific Asia: religious networks and international relations

We saw in earlier chapters that some religions expressions – notably, Protestant evangelicals of various kinds, Roman Catholics, and various interpretations of Islam, including 'moderate' and 'extremist' entities – have developed geographically extensive transnational religious networks. In some cases, they have been politically and/or developmentally significant (Haynes 2012b). We have noted various examples, including the influence of Roman Catholics in helping countries to democratise in eastern Europe, Latin America and Africa, the role of US Protestant evangelicals, credited with 'evangelising' US foreign policy under President George W. Bush, leading to more emphasis on development and religious freedom goals and, in relation to Islam, the centripetal influence of 'moderates' and 'extremists'. So far in the current chapter, we have examined the international relations and foreign policy influence in China of New Confucianism. We saw there is a coming together of both soft and hard policy concerns in the Chinese government's reorientation of foreign policy away from communism, in response to changing international conditions, including the influence of globalisation (Yahuda, 2005). There are, however, no notable regional or international Confucian networks independent of government that would enable us to identify transnational or international dimensions to New Confucianism's current significance in China.

Turning to Buddhism, however, we have already noted not only that it is the most significant religion in three regional countries – Thailand, Myanmar and Cambodia – but also that it has a presence in several other regional countries, including Laos, Vietnam, Singapore, Japan and Taiwan. This suggests that potentially there are necessary conditions for the development of transnational religious networks of the kind that we have seen in relation to Islam and Christianity; that is, followers of a religion that are in contact with coreligionists in foreign countries. In the next section we focus on two questions:

- Does Buddhism inform the foreign policies of regional countries with significant Buddhist populations?
- Are there politically influential transnational Buddhist groups?

What would a Buddhist foreign policy look like? We noted above in relation to China's New Confucianist foreign policy that one of the key goals is said to be 'world peace'. A key Buddhist religious goal is 'universal peace' ('The Common Goal of Universal Peace in Buddhism and the Baha'i Faith', 1990). So, if Buddhism was a key component of a regional country's foreign policy, we might expect to see signs of it in a pronounced focus on regional and international peace. However, the lack of significance of such a key tenet of Buddhism in regional countries' foreign policies and international relations can be shown negatively: researching for this text, I could find very few relevant analyses highlighting Buddhism's foreign policy significance. One of the very few attempts that I found to examine a Buddhist country's foreign policy was not concerned with a Pacific Asian country but the tiny Himalayan kingdom of Bhutan, where three-quarters of the population is Buddhist (Priesner, 2008). According to Upreti (2005: 5), foreign policy in Bhutan 'is an important instrument of Gross National Happiness, the alternative model of development that Bhutan has pursued over the last two decades . . . A balanced foreign policy approach is required to attain the objectives of GNH'. This intriguing idea does not, however, appear to manifest itself in anything more profound than a statement regarding the importance of attempting to engage with globalisation and foreign influences in such a way as not to undermine Bhutan's existing Buddhist culture while increasing the country's economic and human development. In addition, Bhutan's government seeks to 'regulariz[e] foreign policy in a way that the external influences do not affect [Bhutan's] traditional cultural fabric'. In sum, there is little significance in Upreti's account that would enable us to ascertain concrete Buddhist ingredients to Bhutan's foreign policy.

Mongolia is another Asian country with a Buddhist majority, in relation to which the influence of Buddhism in foreign policy has been briefly noted (US Library of Congress, 1986; Sabirov, 2008). During the Cold War, Mongolia's Buddhist beliefs were thought to encourage a certain foreign policy direction: to try to link the communist and non-communist states of Asia, including Pacific Asia. Mongolia's capital, Ulan Bator, was at this time headquarters of the Asian Buddhist Conference for Peace (ABCP), an organisation that held conferences for Buddhists from various Asian countries, including Japan, Vietnam, Cambodia, Sri Lanka and Bhutan. It also published a journal for international circulation, while maintaining contacts with such groups as the Christian Peace Conference, the Afro-Asian People's Solidarity Organization, and the Russian Orthodox Church. The Asian Buddhist Conference for Peace also sponsored the Dalai Lama's visits to Mongolia in 1979 and 1982. Finally, the ABCP, headed by the abbot of the Gandan Monastery in Mongolia, was said more generally to support the foreign policy goals of the Mongolian government, which during the Cold War were in accord with those of the Soviet Union (US Library of Congress, 1986). Since the demise of the Cold War, however, both the influence of the ABCP and an alleged Buddhist focus of Mongolia's foreign policy seem to have diminished.

In relation to mainly Buddhist Thailand's foreign policy, a theme of regional and international cooperation has also been periodically highlighted. Thailand participates in various international and regional organisations, including the Association of South East Asian Nations (ASEAN), whose member states, in addition to Thailand, include: Indonesia, Malaysia, the Philippines, Singapore, Brunei, Laos, Cambodia, Myanmar and Vietnam. ASEAN foreign and economic ministers hold annual meetings, with cooperation focused on economic, trade, banking, political and cultural matters. In neighbouring Myanmar during the Cold War, foreign policy was notable not for regional cooperation but for a pronounced neutrality. Since the end of the Cold War, however, Myanmar has been less isolationist, attempting to strengthen regional ties. Like

Thailand it is a member of both ASEAN and BIMSTEC (Bangladesh, India, Myanmar, Sri Lanka, and Thailand). But neither country appears to have a demonstrable Buddhist element to foreign policy goals.

Our brief survey of the few extant references to Buddhist inputs to foreign policy among regional Buddhist countries in Asia makes it clear that there is not anything particularly 'Buddhist' in the foreign policies of Bhutan, Mongolia, Thailand or Myanmar (Cady and Simon, 2006). This observation underlines the fact that Buddhism lacks a unifying ethos that can transcend the influence of regionally more dynamic ideologies, especially that of nationalism. In the case of all the Buddhist Asian countries, we have noted in this regard, the post-colonial ideology of nationalism has been much more influential than Buddhism in focusing attentions of both governments and citizens (McCargo, 2001; Stuart-Fox, 2006). While as we have noted Buddhism has periodically played an often important *domestic* political role, when it comes to regional countries foreign policies and international relations its influence seems at best negligible and more often non-existent. This is partly because Buddhism lacks an institutionalised church which, as we saw in the case of Roman Catholicism, was crucial for development of both regional and international networks under the aegis of the Pope in the Vatican and which was able to link together the numerous national churches in pursuit of shared goals. In addition, certain non-religious factors significantly, perhaps fatally, undermine the ability of Buddhists to form and develop transnational networks: Pacific Asia is a disparate region, perhaps the world's 'most complex and diverse region', with numerous languages, civilisations, ethnicities and races (McCargo, 2001: 142). Collectively, these factors undermine the likelihood of Buddhism playing a significant role in the international relations of Pacific Asia, not least because regional Buddhists lack a lingua franca to communicate.

Before closing, however, it is important to examine a significant regional radical Muslim network because of its influence on domestic politics in both Thailand and the Philippines as well as in the wider context of the post-9/11 US-led 'war on terror'. Islamist networks developed in the Pacific Asia region, in the context of the anti-Soviet Union war in Afghanistan in the 1980s, which also led to the growth of al Qaeda and other radical groups in many parts of the Muslim world (Frost et al., 2003; Abuza, 2005). During this conflict, *mujahidin* guerillas supported

367

by the government of USA fought the Soviet occupation forces. In the 1990s, a nucleus of Islamist fighters in Afghanistan formed the first cadres of a network that developed in Pacific Asia. Frost et al. (2003) note several important factors in relation to its development:

- *The Afghan experience was central to the recent development of more radical Islamic groups in South East Asia.* Like Muslims nearly everywhere, most of Pacific Asia's more than 200 million Muslims (around one-fifth of the global total) are characterised by their moderate and tolerant views. This has typically enabled them to live in relative harmony with other religious groups and secular institutions. Now, however, more aggressive and anti-pluralist versions of Islam have been imported from various centres of Islamic militancy, including Saudi Arabia, Pakistan and Afghanistan. While extremist Islamic arguments have only appealed to small but often significant minorities in the region, some Muslims from Pacific Asian countries joined the anti-Soviet resistance in Afghanistan in the 1980s. In addition, many leaders of the region's radical Islamic groups served or trained in Afghanistan. Others studied in *madrasas* (religious schools) either within the region or in foreign countries, including Pakistan; in such cases, many individuals came into contact with radical interpretations of Islam.
- *The Afghanistan conflict added a new dimension to already existing demands for autonomy or independence from some Muslim minority peoples in the some Pacific Asian countries.* The influence of aggressive and/or extremist versions of Islam was noticeable in relation to some already disaffected regional Muslim ethnic groups in some Pacific Asian countries, including in southern Thailand, Aceh in Indonesia, and the southern Philippines. The Afghanistan war afforded many both additional religious and ideological inspiration as well as in some cases foreign assistance and/or funding.
- *Socio-economic factors have encouraged regional radical Islamic groups to organise and develop strategies to try to achieve their goal of independence.* Most such radical Islamic groups demand independence, an outcome strongly resisted by central governments of affected countries. Even when demands for autonomy falling short of independence were accepted, for example, in relation to Muslim demands

in the southern Philippines, they were not properly put into effect. In addition, the 1997 Asian financial crisis led to new or increased economic and financial pressures on all regional governments; as a result, state spending on sensitive welfare areas – including education – was often cut back. This helped lead to an increase in Muslim schools, which in turn were sometimes focal points for independence demands. Finally, often well-funded Islamic radical movements were in a position to offer and provide financial support when those they recruited were killed in combat. This was an attraction for many poor Muslims already enthused by the religious programmes of the radical groups.

- *Regionally, national borders are often porous with weak immigration controls.* For example, until recently, Malaysia did not require an entry visa for entrants from Muslim countries that are members of the Organisation of Islamic Cooperation (OIC), while the Philippines has an underdeveloped, ineffective immigration system which can often be circumvented by the use of bribes. Such circumstances facilitate the entry of people – including Islamic radicals – into regional countries.

- *Long-standing economic and trade links between South East Asia and Middle Eastern and South Asian countries.* Many such links operate outside state-controlled channels and governments find them difficult to monitor and control. Such networks can facilitate the transfer of funds from the Middle East and South Asia to regional radical Muslim groups.

Muslims in Pacific Asia no doubt see themselves as part of the global Muslim community, the *ummah* (Esposito, 1987). In some cases, they also identify themselves as disadvantaged minorities who see their membership of the *ummah* as an opportunity to draw upon its strengths in relation to various issues, including in some cases autonomy or independence demands (Hooker, 1997; Islam and Chowdhury, 2001). For example, the Philippines is home to more than 100 ethnic groups. Most Filipinos are Roman Catholics, and the country's Muslim minority is concentrated in the southern islands, amounting to more than four million people in the southern population of over 14 million, that is, about 5 per cent overall. Thirteen ethno-linguistic groups comprise the country's Muslim population, among them are the Tausugs, Maranaos and Maguindanaos; all are active in a Muslim secessionist movement. The Muslim separatists contend that their people have been forcibly included in a state that is dominated both by domestic Catholics and by foreign and domestic capitalists (Encarnacion and Tadem, 1993: 152). But the Muslim separatists of the Philippines are divided among themselves in relation to both tactics and organisational matters. The largest separatist group, the Moro Islamic Liberation Front (MILF), had to deal with other groups with differing agendas. During the 1980s, the Muslim struggle for autonomy in the Philippines became internationalised, with Libya supplying military equipment to the MILF. Later, in the 1990s, the MILF adopted an effective cease-fire and maintained it until 2000 when renewed heavy fighting broke out. However, in 2001 the MILF signed a cease-fire with the authorities, leaving only the Abu Sayyaf group still fighting ('Attention Shifts to Moro Islamic Liberation Front', 2002).

## BOX 14.6  Abu Sayyaf: Religious terrorism in the Philippines

Abu Sayyaf ('the sword bearer') was formed in 1990, with seed corn money from the then leader of al Qaeda, Osama bin Laden. The organisation is mainly based in the islands of Jolo and Basilan, south-west of Mindanao in the southern Philippines. Abu Sayyaf has and attracts a fluctuating number of recruits, usually numbering between 250 and 600 people (Country Reports on Terrorism, 2004). The Philippines authorities suspect that Abu Sayyaf receives funds from Islamist groups in the Middle East (Council on Foreign Relations, 2005). From April 1992, the group unleashed a number of terrorist assaults beginning with a hand grenade attack on the Roman Catholic cathedral in Iligan city that killed five and wounded 80 people. Three years later, in 1995, 200 alleged Abu Sayyaf activists attacked the southern town of Ipil, killing 53 people. In 2000, Abu Sayyaf militants were implicated in the kidnapping of a party of foreign tourists, most of who were freed by the end of the year following the payment of large ransoms. Later, 'in February 2004, the group planted a bomb in a passenger ferry docked off the coast of Manila killing more than 100 people'. Following this incident, the Philippines government conducted a sustained military offensive against 'Abu Sayyaf rebels in the south in efforts to quell the group's attacks against civilians' (Council on Foreign Relations, 2005). Over time, the group's activities increasingly included kidnapping of foreigners to hold for ransom to raise funds for its operations. In 2012, 'seven foreigners, including a Dutch man, a Swiss national, an Australian, two Malaysian traders, an Indian married to a Filipina and a Japanese man – are believed to still be held by the Abu Sayyaf' ('Muslim extremists seize Philippine health worker', 2012)'. Abu Sayyaf's activities led to US troops being based in the southern Philippines since the early 2000s, in a so far unsuccessful attempt to crush the organisation.

As in the Philippines, both religion and ethnicity have played a crucial political role in the demands of Muslim separatists in southern Thailand. Many among the Malay-Muslim minority – around three million people or 4 per cent of the national population of over 70 million – are alienated from the mainstream of predominantly Buddhist Thailand, because of their 'strict adherence to Islam' and their perception that Thailand is a Buddhist state (Encarnacion and Tadem, 1993: 153). Muslim estrangement is exacerbated by the fact that many among the Malay-Muslim minority engage in non-lucrative small-scale farming which serves to marginalise and impoverish them in a national economic situation dominated by Thai Buddhists and ethnic, non-Muslim, Chinese (Braam, 2006).

One result of Muslim alienation is intermittent armed conflict between Islamist radicals and the state. During several decades, Islamist Muslim rebels have fought Thai authorities in a still unresolved conflict. Two groups, the Pattani National Liberation Movement and the Path of God, have long been at the forefront of separatist demands. Over time, many Muslim militants have been incarcerated – usually around 200 at any one time. In the late 1990s, the Thai authorities claimed that there were less than 200 Muslim fighters in the field compared to around 2,000 some 20 years earlier. The government also claimed that it had tried to meet the Muslim demands by increasing government services and by greater local participation in state political activities. It asserted, however, that its attempts had been thwarted because of encouragement from foreign Muslim governments to the Muslim separatists, including those of Iran and Libya, which has helped to keep the flame of revolt alive (Russell and Jones, 2004). Indeed, after a brief lull, militant Islamist activity was resurgent from the early 2000s. Abuza notes the existence of four distinct organisations, 'two of importance, while two others are more fringe groups'. The most significant organisations are 'the Gerakan Mujahideen Islamiya Pattani (GMIP) and the outgrowth of the old Barisan Revolusi Nasional (BRN) organisations now known as BRN Coordinate (BRN-C)'. There are also two smaller fringe groups: Jemaah Salafi and New Pulo (Abuza, 2005: 5).

The GMIP was founded in 1986 but quickly degenerated into a criminal gang until 1995 when two Afghan veterans consolidated power. Since then, the rural-based GMIP has led attacks on police and army outposts. The group has close relations with a Malaysian militant organisation, the Kampulan Mujahideen Malaysia (KMM), also founded by Afghan war veterans in 1995. The Thai National Security Council acknowledged that there is 'a new Islamic grouping' which, 'through increasing contacts with extremists and fundamentalists in Middle Eastern countries, Indonesia, Malaysia and the Philippines, they have metamorphosed into a political entity of significance [*sic*]' (cited in Crispin, 2004). A key concern for the Thai government is whether any of these new Islamic groups have established contact with the notorious Jemaah Islamiyah of Indonesia. A series of bombings took place in southern Thailand on 31 March 2012, leading to 16 deaths and more than 320 injuries. Although no group claimed responsibility, there was much speculation that GMIP was involved, perhaps with additional involvement of Jemaah Islamiyah (Roughneen, 2012).

---

### BOX 14.7 Jemaah Islamiyah and regional religious terrorist networks

Jemaah Islamiyah ('Islamic Group' or 'Islamic Community') is often abbreviated to JI. It is a militant Islamic separatist movement in Indonesia, suspected of killing hundreds of civilians, dedicated to the establishment of an Islamic state in South East Asia, to include Indonesia, Singapore, Brunei, Malaysia, and the south of Thailand and the Philippines. Analysts have identified financial and organisational links between Jemaah Islamiyah and other terrorist groups, such as Abu Sayyaf and al Qaeda (Crispin, 2004). It is likely that JI cadres undertook the Bali car bombing of 12 October 2002 when suicide bombers killed 202 people in a nightclub and wounded many others. Following this outrage, the US Department of State designated JI as a foreign terrorist organisation. Jemaah

---

Islamiyah is also alleged to have perpetrated further bombings, including the Zamboanga and the Metro Manila explosions, as well as the bombing of the Jakarta Embassy in 2004. However, the Thai government denies that there are links between local groups and JI. A Thai foreign ministry spokesman said that, 'The causes of the situation [are] domestic. It's not part of any international terrorist network but of course we are concerned about the introduction of extremist ideologies among the youths. We are concerned about the possibility of extremist groups in the region connecting together and this could become a serious problem [sic]' (Abuza, 2005: 5).

In conclusion, Islamist groups in both the Philippines and Thailand justify anti-government struggles by use of a similar argument: they are coerced into conforming to the requirements of the dominant religious/national groups in each country and are regarded as second-class citizens, with no legitimate way to improve their condition under the present circumstances. In other words, Muslim separatists in both countries do not see themselves as part of the nation, instead believing their ethnic, religious, political and economic rights are consistently and comprehensively violated. However, none of the separatist groups were powerful enough to achieve their objectives and were eventually encouraged to seek peace with the state authorities. But since the end of the war in Afghanistan in the late 1980s, development of a regional Islamist militant network has manifested itself. The result appears to have been to stiffen the resolve of some Muslim militants to seek independence or at least significant levels of autonomy for Muslim minorities. In addition, al Qaeda has sought to exploit and benefit from pre-existing disaffection of Muslim minority peoples in both countries, not only in relation to their national governments but also to the perceived aggressive intrusion of Western capitalist interests (Abuza, 2005; Russell and Jones, 2004). As a result, there is now a collection of regional Islamist groups that while for the most part operate relatively autonomously, are collectively informed by shared ideological convictions deriving from the ideas of various figures, including Sayyid Qutb, one of the key ideological figures informing al Qaeda. As Frost et al. (2003) note:

It is increasingly evident that Southeast Asia has become an important arena for international terrorism, notably Al Qaeda. Al Qaeda is a highly decentralised and elusive transnational terrorist network that is difficult to identify and combat. . . . In Southeast Asia, Al Qaeda's activities appear to have been concentrated in the Philippines, Malaysia, Singapore and Indonesia. Al Qaeda established contacts in Southeast Asia from 1988 and established a logistics base in the Philippines in the early 1990s.

## Conclusion

This chapter makes the following general points:

- Both Buddhism and Confucianism are politicised in Pacific Asia but only the latter in relation to China has a significant role in the country's foreign policy and international relations.
- The Chinese government emphasises a 'culturally authentic' 'New Confucianism', regarded as a prescriptive policy to balance the power of the USA, to increase Chinese influence and, more loftily, to try to build world peace.
- Buddhism does not play a significant international or transnational political role in Pacific Asia.
- There is a regional network of dissident Muslim minorities. Some cadres draw on the radical ideas of al Qaeda, which are linked to ethnic demands for autonomy or independence in what are seen as unrepresentative and illegitimate states. Our examples were from Thailand and the Philippines, where restive Muslim minorities have engaged in political conflict with the state for decades.

In the chapter, we focused on two religious expressions: New Confucianism in relation to China, and Buddhism, especially in the context of Thailand and Myanmar. We saw in relation to China that New Confucianism supplies a clear ideological focus to foreign policy that informs China's external interactions both regionally and in relation to the USA, as well as the government's stated aim to help build 'world peace'. Second, we considered the political impact of Buddhism in relation to the foreign policies of various Asian Buddhist countries, including Bhutan, Mongolia, Thailand and Myanmar. We noted that there does not appear to be any significant input from Buddhism in relation to any of them. In addition, there are no transnational Buddhist networks with regional political significance. The main reason for this is the importance for regional countries of singular nationalist ideologies. This secular ideology has created and maintained national identities that in many cases have deep historical roots. In this context, it is not surprising that each regional country has in its own way adopted and adapted religious traditions in accordance with national characteristics and state policies, and has been uninterested in creating and developing transnational networks of religious believers. Finally, we briefly examined the regional impact of radical Islamist networks that are able to draw on religious, ethnic, social and political grievances which collectively impact on the region's religious, political and social stability.

## Notes

1. Lacking a god to worship, Buddhism is often regarded as a philosophy based on the teachings of the Buddha, Siddhartha Gautama, rather than a religion. Siddhartha Gautama lived between c.563 and 483 BCE. Buddhism began in India, and gradually spread throughout Asia to Central Asia, Tibet, Sri Lanka and South-East Asia, as well as to China, Mongolia, Korea and Japan in East Asia. Buddhism is both a philosophy and a moral practice, whose purpose is to work towards the relief of suffering, characteristic of human existence, by ridding oneself of desire. In the early 2000s, there were an estimated 350 million Buddhists around the world, divided into three main schools: Mahayana (56 per cent), Theravada (38 per cent) and Vajrayana (6 per cent).
2. Taoism (sometimes written as Daoism) 'refers both to a Chinese system of thought and to one of the four major religions of China (with Confucianism, Buddhism, and Chinese popular religion)' (http://www.questia.com/library/religion/asian-religions/taoism).
3. Shintoism is a religion which is native to Japan. It is characterised not only by a lack of formal religious dogma but also by widespread veneration of nature spirits and ancestors by millions of Japanese.
4. Employed in international relations, 'soft power' is used to describe ability of both states and non-state entities indirectly to influence what other states and non-state actors do through cultural and/or ideological measures. An international relations scholar, Joseph Nye, coined the term in 1990.
5. According to Hwang (2005), over 200 'scholars gathered at a Beijing hotel for a two-day conference sponsored by the government-backed China Confucian Foundation and three other organizations'.

6. According to its website, the Council on Foreign Relations is a 'nonpartisan resource for information and analysis' (http://www.cfr.org/).

7. Theravada Buddhism of South East Asia differs both from Mahayana Buddhism – of Mongolia, Tibet, Bhutan and various East Asian countries – and the Tantric Buddhism of parts of Central Asia The overall purpose and aim of Buddhist practice is to liberate the individual from suffering (*dukkha*). While some interpretations stress stirring the practitioner to the awareness of *anatta* (egolessness, the absence of a permanent or substantial self) and the achievement of enlightenment and Nirvana, others (such as the 'Tathagatagarbha' sutras) promote the idea that the practitioner should seek to purify him/herself of both mental and moral defilements that a key aspect of the 'worldly self' and as a result break through to an understanding of the indwelling 'Buddha-Principle' ('Buddha-nature'), also termed the 'True Self', and thus become transformed into a Buddha. Other Buddhist interpretations beseech bodhisattvas (that is, enlightened beings who, out of compassion, forgo nirvana in order to save others) for a favourable rebirth. Others, however, do none of these things. What most, if not all, Buddhist schools also encourage followers is to undertake both good and wholesome actions, and consequently not do bad and harmful actions. There can be very large differences between different Buddhist schools of thought.

8. Thailand is over 90 per cent Buddhist, as is Myanmar and Cambodia.

9. The military dictatorship in Myanmar detained Aung San Suu Kyi, a Nobel Prize-winning peace activist, periodically since 1990, when her party, the National League for Democracy, won the country's only democratic election. She is the daughter of Burmese General Aung San, a popular hero instrumental in helping to win national independence from the British in 1948. Recently, however, the government's position appears to have relented. Following elections, which Aung San Suu Kyi's party won resoundingly, she was allowed to visit both Norway and the UK in 2012, her first trips abroad in many years.

## Questions

- Are transnational religious networks in Pacific Asia politically important?
- To what extent is China's foreign policy now characterised by New Confucianism?
- Why is Buddhism in Pacific Asia largely confined to individual countries?
- Are separatist movements in Thailand and the Philippines motivated more by ethnic demands than religious grievances?
- To what extent is Jemaah Islamiyah a regional equivalent of Al Qaeda?

# Further reading

L. Cady and S. Simon (eds), *Religion and Conflict in South and South-East Asia: Disrupting Violence*, London: Routledge, 2007. This book seeks to advance comparative and multidisciplinary scholarship on the issue of the alignment of religion and violence in the contemporary world, with particular attention to South and South East Asia. Both regions are characterised by: recent and emerging democracies, a high degree of religious pluralism, the largest Muslim populations in the world, and several well-organised terrorist groups, making understanding of the dynamics of religious conflict and violence particularly urgent. The contributors ask whether there is an intrinsic connection between religion and violence. Is religious terrorism rooted in religion, or is it cloaked by religion? Is religious violence a misnomer, an indication that authentic religion has been hijacked? What difference, if any, does this make for policy interventions? Bringing scholars together from religious studies, political science, sociology, anthropology and international relations, the book brings a sustained focus on the role of religion in fostering violence in both regions.

Huiyun Feng, *Chinese Strategic Culture and Foreign Policy Decision-Making: Confucianism, Leadership and War*, London: Routledge, 2007. This book usefully examines important current academic and policy debates over China's rise and related policy issues.

R. Ross and A. Johnston (eds) *New Directions in the Study of China's Foreign Policy*, Stanford: Stanford University Press, 2006. This book brings together several generations of specialists in Chinese foreign policy to present readers with current research on both new and traditional topics. The authors draw on a wide range of new materials – archives, documents, memoirs, opinion polls and interviews – to examine traditional issues such as China's use of force from 1959 to the present, and new issues such as China's response to globalisation, its participation in several international economic institutions, and the role of domestic opinion in its foreign policy. The book also offers a number of suggestions about the topics, methods and sources that the Chinese foreign policy field needs to examine and address if it is to grow in richness, rigour and relevance.

M. Yahuda, *The International Politics of the Asia Pacific*, London: Routledge, 3rd revised edn, 2011. Yahuda's book is a useful survey of the region's international relations, tracing its development in terms of both historical and contemporary concerns, including globalisation and the post-Cold War order.

# 15 | Conclusion

Compared with the past, international relations scholars now take religion seriously. There are two generic kinds of religious actors in international relations: states and non-state actors. We examined both kinds in this text. We saw that very few governments – or states, the two terms are used synonymously in the international relations literature – claim consistently and purposively that religion is a central component of either their domestic or foreign policies. However, it is undeniable that 11 September 2001 (9/11) was an event of crucial and continuing importance in raising not only scholarly but also governmental and public awareness of how religion can affect international relations. Put another way, without 9/11, our interest in 'religion in international relations' would be far less today than it actually is. More than a decade after 9/11, books and other forms of academic output continue regularly to appear. Many start from the premise that 9/11 changed things in internationally relations fundamentally and, in the process, served more generally to highlight the issue of religion in world politics. For example, a very recent book, edited by three of America's foremost scholars of religion and international relations, Timothy Samuel Shah, Alfred Stepan and Monica Duffy Toft (2012), begins with the following words:

> Four guided missiles packed with explosive material hurtled into the morning sky. Though the day was brilliant blue and cloudless, no one saw them coming. They were aimed at a nation that did not see itself at war. Moreover, it was a nation convinced that missiles fired in anger no longer posed a serious threat to its security. The weapons were conventional in the strict sense: they did not carry nuclear warheads.
>
> (Shah, 2012: 1)

Yet, despite Shah's evocative prose, it is important to recognise that 9/11 was but one, albeit highly important, fact which changed how we understand and analyse religion in international relations. The al Qaeda attacks on the USA on 9/11 were collectively a murderous assault by a transnational religious extremist organisation on the world's most conventionally powerful country, the USA. But this unexpected attack, indicative of a wider and continuing conflict between the USA – and by extension, the West – and extremist Islamists, does *not* by any means exhaust all the ways that religion now affects outcomes in contemporary international relations. The purpose of this text is to present a more holistic view and, in effect, to be a counter-argument to that of scholars like Shah, Stepan and Duffy: 9/11 was *not* Year Zero and what has occurred since then in relation to religion and international relations does not begin and end with the attacks on the Twin Towers and the Pentagon.

In the text, we examined two key ways that religion affects outcomes in international relations: (1) state policy guided by religious concerns, and (2) activities of transnational religious actors. In the first category, we examined state actors that use religion significantly to influence foreign policy, including the governments of Iran and Saudi Arabia. In relation to the second category, we focused upon various transnational religious actors, including Islamist and Christian cross-border networks, which collectively bring an important yet variable set of issues, concerns, focus and strategy to the study of religion in international relations.

Because of the potentially vast subject matter with which this text is concerned, it was not possible to examine each and every area where religion has an impact on international relations. Instead, having established that religion affects international relations in two key ways – via state policy and non-state actors' actions – I focused analysis on what I contend are the key issues for understanding the significance of religion in international relations: democratisation and democracy, human development, conflict, conflict resolution and peacebuilding.

The overall starting point of the text was not 9/11. Instead, we began with the fact of a fast-changing international relations environment, which has been occurring at least since the end of the Cold War in the late 1980s. The last quarter century in international relations is characterised by: widespread religious resurgence, a deepening of globalisation, and a shift in the balance of international power, with new significant actors appearing, including India, China and Brazil. In addition, new security issues have emerged, including Iran's nuclear programme and the fears of some, including key members of the Israeli government (Hasan, 2012), that Iran is seeking to develop nuclear weapons, as well as aggressive, extremist Islamist transnational networks which, despite the assassination of Osama bin Laden in May 2011, continue to threaten Western security. The collective impact of these developments is that we must examine religion's variable, sometimes subtle, international influence.

What are the implications for international relations of religious resurgence in many parts of the world? To start to answer this question, we noted that there are two main ways by which religion can be internationally significant. First, religious actors might seek to pursue objectives via transnational networks, a development that has received increased attention over the last 25 years. The overall result of the end of the Cold War and the deepening of globalisation is that 'the structure of world affairs and global interactions is in the middle of a major change. Both in terms of actual operations and the ways that those operations are conceived and understood by analysts, the old systems of relationships are passing rapidly' (Voll, 2006: 12). Significant changes in this regard are ubiquitous, influencing 'across many political, economic, and military areas, [where] international "soft power" is taking precedence over traditional, material "hard power"' (Arquilla and Ronfeldt, 1999: ix). Second, there are attempts by various religious actors to influence state foreign policies in many countries, sometimes successfully, sometimes not. The overall result, according to Fox and Sandler (2004: 168), is that 'religion's greatest influence on the international system is through its significant influence on domestic politics. It is a motivating force that guides many policy makers'. What unites these two ways of thinking about religion in international relations – the effect on both state policy and various religious actors' transnational activities – is that religion, lacking conventional hard power, must seek to make the most of its undoubted soft power. It can do this, for example, by encouraging policy makers, as well as supporters and followers, to strive to apply and embed religious principles, values and ideals into their behaviour.

Yet, despite the burgeoning interest in how religion engages with international relations, it is surprising that to date very few discussions of soft power in international relations have focused on religion (Haynes, 2008a, 2012b). The American international relations scholar Joseph Nye (1990) originally coined the term 'soft power' over 20 years ago. But

Nye only briefly refers to religion, when he notes that 'for centuries, organized religious movements have possessed soft power' (Nye, 2004a: 98). Normally, his analysis focuses on secular sources of soft power and subsequent effects on international relations. In particular, Nye has employed soft power over the years especially in relation to the waxing and waning of US soft power:

> The basic concept of power is the ability to influence others to get them to do what you want. There are three major ways to do that: one is to threaten them with sticks; the second is to pay them with carrots; the third is to attract them or co-opt them, so that they want what you want. If you can get others to be attracted, to want what you want, it costs you much less in carrots and sticks.
>
> (Nye 2004b)

This suggests that a useful way to understand the concept of 'soft power' is to perceive it as the capability of an entity, not necessarily a state, to influence what others do through direct or indirect influence and encouragement. Nye's claim is that soft power co-opts people – it does not coerce them. Certain attributes – such as, culture, values and ideas – represent different, not necessarily lesser, forms of influence compared to 'hard' power; that is, often more direct, forceful measures typically involving (the threat or use) of armed force and/or economic reward and/or coercion. Conventionally in international relations, a country's power is believed to be measurable through quantitative measures, usually derived from various material attributes, including: gross national product, military capability and natural resources. However, seeking to measure a country's potential hard power assets is not necessarily a good guide to understanding whether it will be able to achieve its foreign policy goals. The problem is that even when a country seems to have sufficient relevant material assets 'to get the job done' *and* the will to use them, this does not always translate into foreign policy success. For example, the United States, by far the most powerful country in the world when measured in terms of conventional power resources, was not able to achieve its main goal in the Vietnam War (1954–75) – to prevent a communist regime taking power. In addition, the USA's post-9/11 ventures in the Middle East – which has centrally engaged the attentions of three administrations and two presidents since 2001 – have shown that even massive conventional power is not necessarily enough to get desired outcomes in two complex and problematic countries – Afghanistan and Iraq. In both countries, the government of the USA wants benign, secular, pro-Western regimes, built on secure democratic foundations; yet these goals are *not* being achieved after a decade of sustained efforts, the deaths of thousands of US troops, and the expenditure of tens of billions of dollars. Utilising its undoubted hard power with such little success may well suggest to at least some US foreign policy makers that a different approach may now be necessary; and that hard power is not enough on its own to achieve foreign policy goals in parts of the world imperfectly understood in Washington, DC, and Virginia (home of the Pentagon).

Soft power is neither 'sticks' nor 'carrots', but a 'third way' of seeking to achieve objectives. Soft power is more than influence, since influence can also rest on the hard power of (military or diplomatic) threats or (financial) payments. However, while soft power is not entirely synonymous with cultural power, it is the case that 'exporting cultural goods that hold attraction for other countries can communicate values and influence those societies' (Nye, 2004c) – for example, US efforts during the 'third wave of democracy' in the 1980s and 1990s to undermine authoritarian governments in many parts of the world (Haynes, 2001a).

*Economic strength is usually not soft power.* This is because responding to an economic incentive or sanction is not the same as aligning politically with a cause that is admired or respected. We can see this in relation to the influence of foreign aid donors, collectively of great importance in encouraging some economically poor authoritarian regimes to democratise in the 1980s and 1990s. This followed significant oil price rises in the 1970s and associated international indebtedness among many developing countries, when the ability of many such regimes to maintain adequate programmes of political and economic development dropped sharply in the 1980s and 1990s. The result was that it became increasingly difficult – especially for many developing countries without oil – to balance their budgets. Many became increasingly dependent on loans and aid from the West. Aid donors argued that the situation would be remedied by democratisation, part of a general process of improving governance. Increasingly, the continuity of foreign aid was made dependent on aid-hungry regimes agreeing to democratise. In this way, many economically poor, authoritarian regimes were encouraged to shift to democracy via the use of a range of inducements, including both sticks and carrots. In addition, in a linked move, several Western governments – including those of the USA and Britain – encouraged the installation of market-based economic programmes to the extent that they were 'intrinsic' to democratic openings in economically impoverished Africa and Central America (Haynes, 2001a). In short, recent external encouragement to democratise – linked to the supply of aid and loans – was often of major significance for poor countries – but it was not soft power because normally overt economic leverage was used.

*Soft power is not necessarily humane.* For example, the soft-power activisms of various significant political figures, including the late Indian nationalist Mohandas 'Mahatma' Gandhi (1869–1948), the US civil rights leader Martin Luther King (1929–1968), and South Africa's anti-apartheid activist par excellence Nelson Mandela (b. 1918), were uniformly informed by universal humanist and/or religious ideas. However, those of some others were not, including the German Nazi leader Adolph Hitler (1889–1945), the Russian Communist head Josef Stalin (1878–1953), and the mastermind of the 9/11 attacks Osama bin Laden (1957–2011), are said by Nye (2000c) to be reliant on twisting people's minds. Nye's claim suggests that the exercise of soft power does not only rely on persuasion or the capacity to convince people by argument but also is a sign of an ability to attract, and attraction often leads to acceptance of associated ideas. As Nye puts it:

> If I am persuaded to go along with your purposes without any explicit threat or exchange taking place – in short, if my behavior is determined by an observable but intangible attraction – soft power is at work. *Soft power uses a different type of currency – not force, not money – to engender cooperation. It uses an attraction to shared values, and the justness and duty of contributing to the achievement of those values.*
>
> (emphasis added; Nye, 2004c)

*Religion may be a form of soft power.* We can see this in relation to the post-9/11 'war on terror', a central component of US foreign policy during the presidency of George W. Bush (2001–09). During this time, competing conceptions of soft power vied for supremacy and rival sets of religious values – evangelical Christianity vs 'extremist' Islamism – were central to this competition. Lacking an influential soft power, hearts-and-minds policy that would demonstrably persuade all Muslims not to follow extremist groups such as al Qaeda who encourage and advocate violence, US foreign policy under George W. Bush found it impossible to convince many Muslims that its objectives in both Afghanistan and Iraq were not either self-serving or 'anti-Islam' (Shlapentokh et al., 2005). In addition, post-9/11 both 'extremist' and 'moderate' Islamic ideas and movements compete for the support of ordinary Muslims by offering different soft power visions. Several scholars – including, Casanova (2005), Voll (2006), Appleby (2006) and Haynes (2005c, 2005d, 2012b) – have recently examined the international impact of various Muslim transnational networks. Their collective conclusion is that some – al Qaeda is an obvious example because of the events of 11 September 2001 – can have a greater impact on the world stage and receive more foreign policy attention from the great powers than many 'weak' states in the international system.

Turning to state foreign policy, it may be that Iran's judicious mix of hard and soft power is a more effective strategy to build and deepen its influence in post-Saddam Iraq compared to the one-dimensional – hard power – approach, utilised by the government of the USA for a decade in relation to both Afghanistan and Iraq (Haynes, 2012b). Yet our account in Chapter 11 suggests that so far at least this is clearly not the case. This is because while inter-elite links between senior religious and governmental figures have developed, Iran's central position in post-Saddam Iraq is not popular with most Iraqis. Following the overthrow of Saddam and the US-led invasion in March 2003, Iran has sought to develop what Nye (2004c) calls 'smart' power, that is, is it a winning strategy?

Today, Iran seeks to spread its influence in Iraq through several channels. Tehran encourages its Shia religious allies in Iraq to get fully involved in the political process, the better to influence it. Given its political, economic and cultural, including religious, interests, Iran clearly has good reasons to seek to be influential in Iraq, utilising both soft (religious and cultural) and hard (economic resources, military muscle) power. Yet, as Iraq seeks to develop as a sovereign and united state after the fall of Saddam and subsequent conflict, it is very likely to remain very wary of its eastern neighbour and, as a result, seek assiduously to limit Iran's influence within its borders. This necessarily will diminish the ability of Iran to achieve its goals. It is unlikely that Iran's religious and cultural soft power will take precedence in Iraq over a gradually emerging sense of Iraqi nationalism which, partly as a result of the 1980–88 conflict between the two countries, sees Iran as a significant threat despite deep religious ties.

In terms of the wider issue examined in this text – religion's variable role in international relations – the case of Iran's involvement in Iraq provides interesting food for thought. Iran's involvement in Iraq has clear policy relevance and important implications for the international relations literature on regional perceptions of threat and the balance of power, constructivist interpretations of what governments and other actors do, as well as wider issues of the links between religion and international security. As already noted, for many Iraqis, it appears that the – real or perceived – ideological, religious and political threat emanating from Iran is an important factor working to undermine any attempts to build a transnational Shia network involving the two countries.

We also examined a variety of transnational religious phenomena – including, the Roman Catholic Church, various Protestant evangelical entities (often conservative and American-based), as well as Islamist transnational entities, both 'militant' and 'moderate' (Voll, 2006; Casanova, 2005; Haynes, 2012b). The main purpose was to try to understand how such cross-border religious networks affect outcomes in international relations. But, as already noted, it took 9/11 to put transnational religious actors into the foreground of concern for international relations analysis. Before 9/11 international relations interest in transnational phenomena was often linked to questions of 'conventional' – that is, political and economic – security. Cross-border religious networks were often regarded as interesting but ultimately marginal phenomena, a niche area for those interested in exotica, remote from central, important questions affecting states and state power in international politics. This text has argued that such an approach is no longer sufficient, if ever it was. This is because, I have argued, various kinds of transnational religious actors directly and consistently affect international relations, for both 'good' and 'bad', which serves to qualify state power, as conventionally understood. Often, this activity is 'below the radar' of an international relations scholarship still focused mainly on conventional actors – states – and their efforts to affect outcomes in international relations.

We learned that *some* RTAs present significant challenges to international order and security, especially extremist Islamist organisations, such as al Qaeda, the key focus of the post-9/11 US-directed 'war on terror' (Shani, 2008; Marsden, 2008, 2011). The contemporary focus on al Qaeda has more generally helped to reignite debate on the 'Clash of Civilisations' controversy, while at the same time serving partly to obscure the emergence and development of a new transnational religious landscape, which is marked by *both* interreligious cooperation and conflict, focusing on democratisation and democracy, development, conflict, conflict resolution and peacebuilding (Rudolph and Piscatori, 1997; Thomas, 2005; Bouta et al., 2005; Haynes, 2007a, 2007b; Banchoff, 2008).

## Conclusion

The issue of religion and globalisation formed an often implicit backdrop to the text. We saw that, apparently irrespective of which religious tradition we are concerned with, religious ideas, experiences and practices are all significantly affected by globalisation. The impact of globalisation is encouraging many religions to adopt new or renewed agendas in relation to a variety of religious, social, political and economic concerns. It is also stimulating many religious individuals, organisations and movements to look beyond local or national contexts to regional or international environments.

The text also makes clear that religion has now reappeared as an important domestic and international political actor in part because of the impact of deepening globalisation, which has led to an expansion of channels, pressures and agents via which norms are diffused and interact through both transnational and international networks and interactions. As a result, religious actors now pursue a variety of goals in international relations that in many cases links their concerns to the economic, social and political consequences of globalisation.

We are now in a position to draw the following conclusions. First, the contemporary visibility of religious actors in international relations dramatically undermines a previously accepted 'law' of Western social sciences: modernisation goes hand in hand with secularisation and, as a result, religion is privatised, that is, socially and politically marginalised.

Second, certain events and developments – including, the 1979 Iranian revolution, the first Gulf War of 1990–91, the Vatican's encouragement of democratisation in various regions from the 1980s, including, Central and Eastern Europe (CEE) and Latin America, and al Qaeda attacks on the USA (11 September 2001) have had significant and still reverberating international effects. Collectively, these developments underline the propensity of religious actors of various kinds to affect international relations, especially issues of international development, order and security. Third, from the seventeenth to the twentieth century, both international order and security developed increasingly institutional procedures and mechanisms, while the public role of religion declined. Recently, however, religion and culture have returned to international relations, with major, yet not fully understood, ramifications for our understanding of international relations. Fourth, there are overlapping political, social and economic upheavals that have occurred following the end of the Cold War, including the collapse of the Soviet Union and associated communist systems and the contemporaneous onset of deepening, multifaceted globalisation. Fifth, as the forces of change have swept across the globe over the last quarter century, affecting alike both developed and underdeveloped regions and countries, large numbers of people seem to have become unconvinced by the secular values that had long underpinned international order and security. Many now seem to believe that they can most effectively pursue their goals through membership of religious groups or movements, a development with both domestic and international ramifications. According to Huntington (1993: 25), this has encouraged real or perceived differences between civilisational/cultural to become politically salient. He also claims that conflict between such groups will henceforward be both more prolonged and more violent than the secular conflicts of the Cold War, with serious impacts for both international order and international security. As a result, Thomas avers (1999: 32), 'in so far as it is a component of civilisational or ideational conflict, [religion] undermines the possibility of international society'.

Sixth, the material presented in the foregoing chapters is further affirmation – if any more is needed, which I doubt – that the relationship between religion and (international) politics is a complex one. A basic contrast can be drawn: between differences that divide secular democratic (Weberian/Schumpterian) politics – essentially rule-governed where there is consensus about the rules – and religious politics as 'ideological' politics. In this regard, we can note multiple examples not only from the contemporary era but also from the historical past, before and after the Reformation. It is not, however, clear – and this is one area where the complexity comes in – to what extent religion as a political actor is concerned with spiritual issues alone, or where – and how and in what ways – other, more material, concerns also impact on what religious actors do politically, both domestically and transnationally. Certainly, in the context of globalisation, there is evidence of both spiritual and material issues involving the attention of various religious transnational actors.

# Bibliography

'16 Members of Congress Urge Secretary Of State Clinton To Address Human Rights In China' (2009) Available at: http://www.chinaaid.org/2009/03/16-members-of-congress-urge-secretary.html.

'2008 Jewish Vote for Obama Exceeds All Expectations' (2008) National Jewish Democratic Council, 5 November. Available at: http://www.njdc.org/site/page/jewish_vote_for_obama_exceeds_all_expectations Accessed 1 April 2012.

'316 Confucious [sic] Institutes established worldwide' (2010) Xinhua news agency, 13 July. Available at: http://news.xinhuanet.com/english2010/culture/2010–07/13/c_13398209.htm. Accessed 20 April 2012.

'70,000 gather for violent Pakistan cartoons protest' (2006) *Times Online*, 15 February. Available at: http://www.timesonline.co.uk/article/0,,25689–2041723,00.html. Accessed 15 May 2006.

Abrams, F. (2011) 'Islamic schools flourish to meet demand', *The Guardian*, 28 November. Available at: http://www.guardian.co.uk/education/2011/nov/28/muslim-schools-growth. Accessed 1 April 2012.

Abramsky, S. (1996) 'Vote redneck', *The Observer, Life Magazine*, 27 October, pp. 16–19.

Abu-Nimer, M., and D. Augsburger (eds) (2009) *Peace-building by, Between, and Beyond Muslims and Evangelical Christians*, Lanham, MD: Rowman and Littlefield Publishers.

Abuza, Z. (2005) 'A conspiracy of silence: Who is behind the escalating insurgency in Southern Thailand?', *Terrorism Monitor*, 3, 9, pp. 4–6.

Acharya, A. and Stubbs, R. (1999) 'The Asia-Pacific region in the post-cold war era', in L. Fawcett and Y. Sayigh (eds), *The Third World Beyond the Cold War*, Oxford: Oxford University Press.

Achieng', J. (1998) 'Ruling on Muslim charities averts strike', International Press Syndicate, 18 September. Available at: http://www.hartford-hwp.com/archives/36/index-bfbc.html Accessed 5 January 2005.

Adler, J. (2011) 'Confucianism in China Today', 'Pearson Living Religions Forum', New York: April 14. Available at http://www2.kenyon.edu/Depts/Religion/Fac/Adler/Writings/Confucianism%20Today.pdf Accessed 20 April 2012.

Afrasiabi, K., and Maleki, A. (2003) 'Iran's foreign policy after September 11', *The Brown Journal of World Affairs*, 9, 2, pp. 255–265. Available at:

Bibliography

http://www.watsoninstitute.org/bjwa/archive/9.2/Iran/Afrasiabi.pdf Accessed 6 January 2006.

Ahmad, I. (2002) 'The needs of Muslim children can be met only through Muslim schools', *The Guardian*, 22 May.

Ahmed, A. (1992) *Postmodernism and Islam: Predicament and Promise*, London: Routledge.

Ahmed, K. (2003) 'And on the seventh day Tony Blair created . . .', *The Observer*, 3 August. Available at: http://observer.guardian.co.uk/politics/story/0,6903, 1011460,00.html. Accessed 26 May 2006.

Akbar, M. J. (2002) *The Shade of Swords. Jihad and the Conflict Between Islam & Christianity*, London: Routledge.

Alexiev, A. (2005) 'Tablighi Jamaat: Jihad's Stealthy Legions', *Middle East Quarterly*, 12, 1, pp. 3–11.

Ali, A. (2003) 'Islamic Revivalism: The case of the Tablighi Jamaat', *Journal of Muslim Minority Affairs*, 23, 1, pp. 176–187.

Ali, T. (1999) 'The panic button', *The Guardian*, 14 October.

Alkire, S. (2004) 'Religion and development', draft chapter for D. Clark (ed.), *The Elgar Companion to Development Studies*, October 2004.

Alkire, S. (2006) 'Religion and development', in D. Clark (ed.), *The Elgar Companion to Development Studies*, Cheltenham, UK: Edward Elgar.

Allen, D. (1992) *Religion and Political Conflict in South Asia: India, Pakistan and Sri Lanka*, London: Greenwood Press.

Almond, G., Scott Appleby, R. and Sivan, E. (2003) *Strong Religion: The Rise of Fundamentalisms Around the World*, Chicago and London: University of Chicago Press.

*American Heritage Dictionary of the English Language* (1985) New York: Houghton Mifflin Harcourt Publishing.

Amies, N. (2010) 'Alliance of Civilizations: Intercultural peace forum or talking shop?', *Deutsche Welle*, 28 May. Available at: http://www.dw.de/dw/article/ 0,,5610155,00.html. Accessed 15 March 2012.

Amin, H. (2011) 'Re-imagining the role of ulama', in G. ter Haar (ed.), *Religion and Development. Ways of Transforming the World*, London: Hurst and Co., pp. 273–292.

Amiraux, V. (2005) 'Discrimination and claims for equal rights amongst Muslims in Europe', in J. Cesari and S. McLoughlin (eds), *European Muslims and the Secular State*, Aldershot: Ashgate, pp. 25–38.

Amnesty International (2003) 'India: Best Bakery case – concerns for justice'. Amnesty International Press Release. AI Index: ASA 20/018/2003 (Public) News Service No: 165, 9 July. Available at: http://web.amnesty.org/library/ Index/ENGASA200182003?open&of=ENG-IND. Accessed 9 January 2006.

Anderson, B. (1983) *Imagined Communities*. London: Verso.

Anheier, H. and Themudo, N. (2002) 'Organisational forms of global civil society: Implications of going global', in M. Glasius, M. Kaldor and H. Anheier (eds), *Global Civil Society 2002*, Oxford: Oxford University Press, pp. 191–216.

Ansari, H. (2002) *Muslims in Britain*, London: Minority Rights Group International.

d'Antonio, M. (1990) *Fall From Grace. The Failed Crusade of the Christian Right*, London: Deutsch.

Appleby, R. Scott (2000) *The Ambivalence of the Sacred: Religion, Violence and Reconciliation*, Lanham, MD: Rowman and Littlefield.

Appleby, R. Scott (2006) 'Building sustainable peace: The roles of local and transnational religious actors'. Conference paper prepared for the Conference on New Religious Pluralism in World Politics, Georgetown University, 17 March.

Aquaviva, S. (1979) *The Decline of the Sacred in Industrial Society*, Oxford: Blackwell.

Arquilla, J. and Ronfeldt, D. (1999) *The Emergence of Noopolitik: Toward an American Information Strategy*, Santa Monica, CA: RAND.

Asad, T. (1993) *Genealogies of Religion: Discipline and Reasons of Power in Christianity and Islam*, Baltimore: The Johns Hopkins University Press.

Asad, T. (2006) 'Trying to understand French secularism', in H. de Vries and L. Sullivan (eds), *Political Theologies: Public Religions in a Post-Secular World*, New York: Fordham University Press.

Associated Press (2004) 'Election reinforces USA's religious schism', *USA Today*, 4 November. Available at: http://www.usatoday.com/news/politicselections/2004-11-04-religion_x.htm. Accessed 11 November 2005.

Astier, H. (2005) 'We want to be French!', 'Open Democracy', 22 November. Available at: http://www.opendemocracy.net/debates/article.jsp?id=6&debateId=28&articleId=3051. Accessed 5 June 2006.

'Attention Shifts to Moro Islamic Liberation Front' (2002) *Jane's Intelligence Review*, April, pp. 20–23.

Attina, A. (1989) 'The study of international relations in Italy', in H. Dyer and L. Mangasarian (eds), *The Study of International Relations. The State of the Art*, Basingstoke: Macmillan, pp. 344–357.

Ayoob, M. and Kosebaleban, H. (eds) (2008) *Religion and Politics in Saudi Arabia: Wahhabism and the State*, Boulder, CO: Lynne Rienner.

Ayubi, N. (1991) *Political Islam: Religion and Politics in the Arab World*, London: Routledge.

Bacevich, A. and Prodromou, E. (2004) 'God is not neutral: Religion and U.S. foreign policy after 9/11', *Orbis*, Winter, pp. 43–54.

Baer, R. (2005) 'The devil you think you know', *Newsweek*, 15 August. Available at: http://www.msnbc.msn.com/id/8853607/site/newsweek/. Accessed 13 June 2006.

Banchoff, T. (2005) 'Thematic Paper, August 5, 2005', prepared as background material for 'Conference on The New Religious Pluralism in World Politics', 16–17 March 2006, Berkley Center for Religion, Peace & World Affairs, Georgetown University. Available at: http://siteresources.worldbank.org/DEVDIALOGUE/Resources/GeorgeTown.doc. Accessed 7 April 2006.

Banchoff, T. (2008) 'Introduction: Religious pluralism in world affairs', in T. Banchoff (ed.), *Religious Pluralism, Globalization and World Politics*, New York and Oxford: Oxford University Press, pp. 3–38.

Bandhyodhyay, J. (1970) *The Making of India's Foreign Policy*, New Delhi: Sage.

Barbato, M. and Kratochwil, F. (2009) 'Towards a Postsecular Order?', *European Political Science Review*, 1, 3, pp. 320–336.

Bardi, L., Rhodes, M. and Nello, S. (2002) 'Enlarging the European Union: Challenges to and from Central and Eastern Europe – Introduction', *International Political Science Review*, 23, 3, pp. 227–233.

Barnes, H. and Bigham, A. (2006) *Understanding Iran: People, Politics and Power*, London: The Foreign Policy Centre.

Barr, M. (2002) *Cultural Politics and Asian Values. The Tepid War*, London: Routledge.

Barras, A. (2009) 'A rights-based discourse to contest the boundaries of state secularism? The case of the headscarf bans in France and Turkey', in J. Haynes (ed.), *Religion and Democratizations*, London: Routledge, pp. 197–220.

Barras, A. (2012) *A Rights-based Discourse to Contest the Boundaries of State Secularism? The Case of the Headscarf Bans in France and Turkey*, London: I. Tauris.

Barrett, D., Kurian, G. and Johnson, T. (eds) (2001) *World Christian Encyclopedia: A Comparative Survey of Churches and Religions in the Modern World*, Oxford: Oxford University Press.

Barringer, T. (2006) 'Taking faith seriously in International Relations and Development Studies'. Paper presented at the conference, 'Governance in the Commonwealth: Civic Engagement and Democratic Accountability', the Institute of Commonwealth Studies, London, 11–13 March. Available at: http://commonwealth.sas.ac.uk/events/csc_march11/barringer.pdf. Accessed 3 August 2006.

Bartoli, A. (2005) 'Conflict prevention: The role of religion is the role of its actors', *New Routes*, 10, 3, pp. 3–7.

Bates, S. (2006) 'Wing and a prayer: Religious right got Bush elected – now they are fighting each other', *The Guardian*, 31 May.

Bates, S. (2008) *God's Own Country: Religion and Politics in the USA*, London: Hodder.

Baumgart-Ochse, C. (2009) 'Democratization in Israel, Politicised Religion, and the Rise and Failure of the Oslo Peace Process', in J. Haynes (ed.), *Religion and Democratizations*, London: Routledge, pp. 75–102.

Baylis, J. (2005) 'International and global security in the post-cold war era', in J. Baylis and S. Smith (eds), *The Globalization of World Politics. An Introduction to International Relations*, 3rd edn, Oxford: Oxford University Press, pp. 297–324.

Bealey, F. (1999) *The Blackwell Dictionary of Political Science*, Oxford: Blackwell.

Beaumont, P. (2009) 'China's Falun Gong crackdown: The persecution is almost underground', *The Guardian*, 18 July.

Beck, U. (2005) *Power in the Global Age*, Cambridge: Polity Press.

Bellah, R. (1964) 'Religious evolution', *American Sociological Review*, 29, pp. 358–374.

Bellah, R. (1967) 'Civil religion in America', *Daedalus*, 96, 1, p. 1021.

Bellah, R. (1975; revised edn 1992) *The Broken Covenant*, Chicago: University of Chicago Press.

Ben Porat, G. (2010) 'Religion and secularism in Israel: Between politics and sub-politics', in J. Haynes (ed.), *Religion and Politics in Europe, the Middle East and North Africa*, London: Routledge, pp. 73–90.

Ben Porat, G. (2012) *Secularism and Religion in Israel*, Cambridge: Cambridge University Press.

Ben-Simon, D. (2005) 'French philosopher Alain Finkielkraut apologizes after death threats', *Ha'aretz*, 27 November. Available at: http://www.haaretz.com/hasen/pages/ShArt.jhtml?itemNo=650155. Accessed 23 June 2006.

Berger, J. (2003) 'Religious nongovernmental organisations: An exploratory analysis', *Voluntas*, 14, 1, pp. 15–39.

Berger, P. (1969) *The Sacred Canopy: Elements of a Sociological Theory of Religion*, New York: Anchor Books.

Berger, P. (1999) (ed.) *The Desecularization of the World: Resurgent Religion in World Politics*, Grand Rapids/Washington, DC: William B. Eerdmans/Ethics & Public Policy Center.

Berger, P. (2002) 'Introduction: The cultural dynamics of globalization', in P. Berger and S. Huntington (eds), *Many Globalizations: Cultural Diversity in the Contemporary World*, New York: Oxford University Press, pp. 1–15.

Berger, P. and Huntington, S. (eds) (2002) *Many Globalizations: Cultural Diversity in the Contemporary World*, New York: Oxford University Press.

Berman, R. (2005) 'The German perception of the United States since September 11', in V. Shlapentokh, J. Woods and E. Shiraev (eds), *America. Sovereign Defender or Cowboy Nation?*, Aldershot, UK, and Burlington, VT: Ashgate, pp. 15–28.

## Bibliography

Bernal, V. (1994) 'Gender, culture and capitalism', *Comparative Studies in Society and History*, 36, 1, pp. 36–67.

Besser, J. (2004) 'Bush gets 24 percent of Jewish vote – less than GOP hoped for', *The Jewish News* Weekly, 5 November. Available at: http://www.jewishsf.com/content/2–0-/module/displaystory/story_id/24038/format/html/displaystory.html. Accessed 11 November 2005.

Beyer, P. (1994) *Religion and Globalization*, London: Sage.

Beyer, P. (2003) 'Constitutional privilege and constituting pluralism: Religious freedom in national, global, and legal context', *Journal for the Scientific Study of Religion*, 42, 3, pp. 333–339.

Beyer, P. (2006) *Religions in Global Society*, London: Routledge.

Bhatia, S. (1996) 'A dark shadow descends on Israel', *The Observer*, 2 June.

Bhatt, C. (2001) *Hindu Nationalism: Origins, Ideologies and Modern Myths*, Oxford: Berg.

Bidwai, P. (2003) 'Critical moment for India', *Frontline*, 20, 13, 21 June. Available at: http://www.tni.org/archives/bidwai/critical.htm. Accessed 6 September 2005.

Bilefsky, D. (2006) 'Death toll mounts in rioting over cartoons', *International Herald Tribune*, February 8. Available at: http://www.iht.com/articles/2006/02/07/news/islam.php.

Bodansky, Y. (2001) *Bin Laden: The Man who Declared War on America*, New York: Crown Publishing Group.

Bose, S. (1994) *States, Nations, Sovereignty, Sri Lanka, India and the Tamil Eelam Movement*, New Delhi: Sage.

Bouta, T., Ayse Kadayifci-Orellana, S. and Abu-Nimer, M. (2005) *Faith-Based Peace-Building: Mapping and Analysis of Christian, Muslim and Multi-faith Actors*, The Hague: Netherlands Institute of International Relations.

Braam, E. (2006) 'Travelling with the Tablighi Jamaat in South Thailand', *ISIM Review*, 17, Spring, pp. 42–43.

Brass, P. (2005) *The Production of Hindu-Muslim Violence in Contemporary India*, Seattle: University of Washington Press.

Bright, A. (2006) 'Firestorm over Danish Mohammed cartoons continues', *Christian Science Monitor*, 1 February. Available at http://www.csmonitor.com/2006/0201/dailyUpdate.html. Accessed 27 April 2012.

Brody, D. (2012) *The Teavangelicals: The Inside Story of How the Evangelicals and the Tea Party are Taking Back America*, Grand Rapids, MI: Zondervan.

Brown, C. (2001) *Understanding International Relations*, 2nd edn, Basingstoke: Palgrave.

Brown, C. (2005) *Understanding International Relations*, 3rd edn, Basingstoke: Palgrave.

Brown, S. (1995) *New Forces, Old Forces and the Future of World Politics*, London: HarperCollins.

Bruce, S. (1992) 'Introduction', in S. Bruce (ed.), *Religion and Modernization*, Oxford: Clarendon Press, pp. 1–17.

Bruce, S. (2002) *God Is Dead: Secularization in the West*, Oxford: Blackwell.

Bruce, S. (2012) *Politics and Religion in the United Kingdom*, London: Routledge.

'Buddhism through Buddhist Eyes' (n.d.) Available at http://buddhism-eyes. blogspot.co.uk/2008/09/aung-san-suu-kyi-buddhist-hero.html. Accessed 20 April 2012.

Bull, H. (1977) *The Anarchical Society*, London: Macmillan.

Burchill, S. (2005) 'Liberalism', in Burchill, S., Linklater, A., Devetak, R., Dinnelly, J., Paterson, M., Reus-Smit, C. and True, J. (eds), *Theories of International Relations*, 3rd edn, Basingstoke and New York: Palgrave, pp. 55–82.

Burchill, S., Linklater, A., Devetak, R., Dinnelly, J., Paterson, M., Reus-Smit, C. and True, J. (2005) *Theories of International Relations*, 3rd edn, Basingstoke and New York: Palgrave.

Burke, J. (2004) *Al Qaeda: The True Story of Radical Islam*, Harmondsworth: Penguin.

Burke, J. (2010) 'Mumbai spy says he worked for terrorists – then briefed Pakistan', *The Guardian*, 18 October. Available at: http://www.guardian. co.uk/world/2010/oct/18/david-headley-mumbai-attacks-pakistan. Accessed 1 May 2012.

Butt, R. and Smith, D. (2011) 'Rowan Williams takes Mugabe to task in Zimbabwe sermon', *The Guardian*, 9 October 2011. Available at: http://www.guardian. co.uk/world/2011/oct/09/rowan-williams-zimbabwe-mugabe-sermon. Accessed 1 May 2012.

Buzan, B. (2004) *From International to World Society?: English School Theory and the Social Structure of Globalisation*, Cambridge: Cambridge University Press.

Byman, D. (2011) 'Regional consequences of internal turmoil in Iraq', in M. Kamrava (ed.), *International Politics of the Persian Gulf*, New York: Syracuse University Press, pp. 144–168.

Byrnes, T. (2011) *Reverse Mission. Transnational Religious Communities and the making of US Foreign Policy*, Washington, DC: Georgetown University Press.

Cady, L. and Simon, S. (eds) (2006) *Religion and Conflict in South and South-East Asia: Disrupting Violence*, London: Routledge.

Caeiro, A. (2005) 'Religious authorities or political actors? The Muslim leaders of the French Representative Body of Islam', in J. Cesari and S. McLoughlin (eds) *European Muslims and the Secular State*, Aldershot: Ashgate, pp. 71–84.

# Bibliography

Caeiro, A. (2006) 'An anti-riot fatwa', *ISIM Review*, 17, Spring, p. 32.

Carothers, T. (1997) 'Democracy without illusions', *Foreign Affairs*, 76, 1, pp. 85–99.

Carothers, T. (2002) 'The end of the transition paradigm', *Journal of Democracy*, 13, 1, pp. 5–21.

Carothers, T. (2004) *Critical Mission: Essays on Democracy Promotion*, Washington, DC: Carnegie Endowment for International Peace.

Casanova, J. (1994) *Public Religions in the Modern World*, Chicago and London: University of Chicago Press.

Casanova, J. (2005) 'Catholic and Muslim politics in comparative perspective', *Taiwan Journal of Democracy*, 1, 2, pp. 89–108.

Castelli, J. and McCarthy, J. (1997) 'Religion-sponsored social service providers: The not-so independent sector', New York: Aspen Institute Non-profit Sector Research Fund.

Ceccarini, Luigi (2009) 'The church in opposition. Religious actors, lobbying and Catholic voters in Italy', in Jeffrey Haynes (ed.), *Religion and Politics in Europe, the Middle East and North Africa,* London: Routledge, pp. 177–201.

Center Conversations (2003) An Occasional Publication of the Ethics and Public Policy Center, No. 17, February, 'Hindu Nationalism vs. Islamic Jihad: Religious Militancy in South Asia. A Conversation with Cedric Prakash, Teesta Setalvad, Kamal Chenoy, Sumit Ganguly, Sunil Khilnani, and Jonah Blank'. Available at: http://www.eppc.org/docLib/20030503_CenterConversation17.pdf. Accessed 1 September 2005.

Cesari, J. (ed.) (2010) *Muslims in the West after 9/11. Religion, Politics and Law*, London: Routledge.

Cesari, J. and McLoughlin, S. (eds) (2005) *European Muslims and the Secular State*, Aldershot: Ashgate.

'Challenge and Change for NATO. A US Perspective' (2002) Address by Stephen Hadley, US Deputy National Security Adviser, NATO/GMFUS Conference, Brussels, 3 October. Available at: http://www.nato.int/docu/speech/2002/s021003e.htm. Accessed 6 May 2005.

Chazan, N. (1991) 'The domestic foundations of Israeli foreign policy', in J. Kipper and H. H. Saunders (eds), *The Middle East in Global Perspective*, Boulder, CO: Westview Press, pp. 82–126.

Cherry, K. (2002) 'Defining terrorism down. What Muslim nations really think', *National Review Online*, 4 April. Available at: http://www.nationalreview.com/comment/comment-cherry040402.asp. Accessed 24 May 2006.

'China's human rights, in the red', 'A Christianity Today editorial', 13 March 2009. Available at: http://www.christianitytoday.com/ct/2009/marchweb-only/110–52.0.html.

Chiriyankandath, J. (1996) 'The 1996 Indian general election'. Briefing paper 31, London: Royal Institute of International Affairs.

Chiriyankandath, J. (2006) 'Hinduism and politics', in J. Haynes (ed.), *The Politics of Religion. A Survey*, London: Routledge, pp. 48–58.

Chomsky, N. (2000) 'Interview with Noam Chomsky', *Outlook* (India), 3 January.

Christiansen, T. (2001) 'European and regional integration', in J. Baylis and S. Smith (eds), *The Globalization of World Politics: An Introduction to International Relations*, Oxford: Oxford University Press, pp. 495–518.

Clark, I. (2005) 'Globalization and the post-Cold War order', in J. Baylis and S. Smith (eds), *The Globalization of World Politics. An Introduction to International Relations*, 3rd edn, Oxford: Oxford University Press, pp. 727–742.

Clark, V. (2003) 'The Christian Zionists', *Prospect*, July, issue no. 88. Available at: http://www.prospect-magazine.co.uk/article_details.php?id+5643. Accessed 12 December 2005.

Cohen, S. *The Idea of Pakistan*, Washington, DC: The Brookings Institution.

Coleman, S. (1996) 'Conservative Protetantism, politics and civil religion in the United States', in D. Weterlund (ed.) *Questioning the Secular State: The Worldwide Resurgence of Religion in Politics*, London: Hurst, pp. 24–47.

Conflict and Resolution Forum (2001) 'Faith-based peacemaking: The role of religious actors in preventing and resolving conflict worldwide', 10 April, Washington DC.

'Confucianism will never be religion' (2006) *China Daily*, 6 January. Available at: http://www.chinadaily.com.cn/english/doc/2006–01/06/content_509753.htm. Accessed 17 January 2006.

Corten, A. and Marshall-Fratani, R. (2001) *Between Babel and Pentecost: Transnational Pentecostalism in Africa and Latin America*, London: Hurst and Co.

Coulon, C. (1983) *Les Musulmans et le Pouvoir en Afrique Noire*, Paris. Karthala.

Council on Foreign Relations (2003) 'The role of Islamic groups in Pakistan's foreign policy'. Available at: http://www.cfr.org/publication.html?id=5773. Accessed 10 October 2005.

Council on Foreign Relations (2005) 'Abu Sayyaf Group (Philippines, Islamist separatists)', New York: Council on Foreign Relations.

Country Reports on Terrorism (2004) United States Department of State, April 2005. Available at: http://library.nps.navy.mil/home/tgp/asc.htm. Accessed 18 June 2006.

Cox, H. (1984) *Religion in the Secular City. Toward a Postmodern Theology*, New York: Simon and Schuster.

## Bibliography

Crawford, G. (2001) *Foreign Aid and Political Reform: A Comparative Analysis of Democracy Assistance and Political Conditionality*, Basingstoke: Palgrave.

Crispin, S. (2004) 'Thailand's war zone', *Far Eastern Economic Review*, 11 March.

Crumm, D. and Lords, E. (2002) 'Farrakhan says Bush, not Iraq, is world menace', *Detroit Free Press*, 10 October. Available at: http://www.freep.com/news/locway/farr9_20021009.htm. Accessed 17 August 2005.

Dagne, T. (2002) 'Africa and the war on terrorism', Congressional Research Service Report for US Congress, Library of Congress. Document catalogue number: m-u 41953–1 no. 02-RL31247.

Dalacoura, K. (2012) 'Turkey, Iran and the Arab uprisings: The failure of political Islam and the post-ideological politics', *Political Reflection Magazine*, 2, 4, pp. 68–73.

Dalferth, I. (2010) 'Post-secular society: Christianity and the dialectics of the secular', *Journal of the American Academy of Religion*, 78, 2, pp. 317–345.

Davie, G. (2000) *Religion in Modern Europe*, Oxford: Oxford University Press.

Davie, G. (2002) *Europe: The Exceptional Case. Parameters of Faith in the Modern World*, London: Darton, Longman and Todd.

Davie, G. (2007) *The Sociology of Religion*, New York: Sage.

Deegan, H. (2005) 'Culture and development', in S. Hunter and H. Malik (eds), *Modernization, Democracy, and Islam*, London: Praeger.

'Defense Report from AUSA's Institute of Land Warfare' (2002) 'A First Look at President Bush's June 2002 West Point Speech'. Available at: http://www.ausa.org/PDFdocs/dr02–2.pdf. Accessed 27 July 2005.

De Gruchy, J. (1995) *Christianity and Democracy. A Theology For a Just World Order*, Cambridge: Cambridge University Press.

De Waal, A. (ed.) (2004) *Islamism and Its Enemies in the Horn of Africa*, Bloomington, IN: Indiana University Press.

Diamond, L. (1993) 'The globalization of democracy', in R. Slater, B. Schutz, and S. Dorr (eds), *Global Transformation and the Third World*, Boulder, CO: Lynne Rienner, pp. 31–70.

Diamond, L. (1999) *Developing Democracy: Towards Consolidation*, Baltimore: Johns Hopkins University Press.

Dicklitch, S. and Rice, H. (2004) 'The Mennonite Central Committee (MCC) and faith-based NGO aid to Africa', *Development in Practice*, 14, 5, pp. 660–672.

Dinan, S. (2003) '9/11 spurred war, Rumsfeld says', *Washington Times*, 9 July. Available at: http://washingtontimes.com/national/20030709–114950–9370r.htm. Accessed 11 November 2005.

Dodd, V. (1996) 'Jews fear rise of the Muslim "underground"', *The Observer*, 18 February.

Dogan, N. (2005) 'The Organization of the Islamic Conference: An assessment of the role of the OIC in International Relations'. Paper prepared for the Third ECPR General Conference, Budapest, September 2005.

Dolan, C. (2005) *In War We Trust. The Bush Doctrine and the Pursuit of Just War*, Aldershot, UK: Ashgate.

Doran, M. Scott (2004) 'The Saudi paradox', *Foreign Affairs*, January/February. Available at: http://www.foreignaffairs.org/20040101faessay83105/michael-scott-doran/the-saudi-paradox.html. Accessed 11 November 2005.

Duffield, M. (2001) *Global Governance and the New Wars: The Merging of Development and Security*, London: Zed Books.

Duin, J. (2004) 'Bush makes significant gains in two polls of Catholic voters', *The Washington Times*, 4 October. Available at: http://www.washington-times.com/national/20041004–123844–3867r.htm. Accessed 11 November 2005.

Elazar, D. (n.d.) 'The future role of religion in Israel'. Available at: http://www.jcpa.org/dje/articles2/relinisr.htm. Accessed 5 June 2006.

Ehteshami, A. (2002) 'The Middle East: Iran and Israel', in M. Webber and M. Smith (eds), *Foreign Policy in a Transformed World*, Harlow: Prentice Hall, pp. 255–286.

Ehteshami, A. and Zweiri, M. (eds) (2012) *Iran's Foreign Policy: From Katami to Ahmadinejad*, New York: Ithaca Press.

Ellis, S. and ter Haar, G. (2004) *The Worlds of Power: Religious Thought and Political Practice in Africa*, London: Hurst.

Embassy of India (2003) 'Address by Shri Brajesh Mishra, National Security Advisor of India at the American Jewish Committee Annual Dinner', 8 May. Available at: http://www.indianembassy.org/indusrel/2003/nsa_ajc_may_8_03.htm. Accessed 6 September 2005.

Encarnacion, T. and Tadem, E. (1993) 'Ethnicity and separatist movements in South-East Asia', in P. Wignaraja (ed.), *New Social Movements in the South*, London: Zed Books, pp. 152–173.

Engels, D. and Marks, S. (eds) (1994) *Contesting Colonial Hegemony. State and Society in Africa and India*, London: German Historical Institute/British Academic Press.

Englund, H. (ed.) (2011) *Christianity and Public Culture in Africa*, Athens, OH: Ohio University Press.

Ervin, Kent C. (2006) 'Terrorism's soft targets', *The Washington Post*, 7 May. Available at http://www.washingtonpost.com/wp-dyn/content/article/2006/05/05/AR2006050501754.html. Accessed 10 May 2006.

Esposito, J. (1987) 'Islam in Asia: An introduction', in J. Esposito (ed.), *Islam in Asia: Religion, Politics, and Society*, New York: Oxford University Press, pp. 3–19.

Esposito, J. (2002) *Unholy War*, New York: Oxford University Press.

Esposito, J. (2007) 'It's the policy, stupid. Political Islam and US foreign policy', *Harvard International Review*, 2 May. Available at: http://hir.harvard.edu/articles/1453/. Accessed 21 July 2008.

Etienne, B. and Tozy, M. (1980) 'Le glissment des obligations islamiques vers le phenomene associatif à Casablanca', in Centre de Recherches et d'Etudes sur les Societés Mediterranéennes, *Le Maghreb Musulman en 1979*, Paris, CNRS, pp. 250–271.

Fandy, M. (1999) *Saudi Arabia and the Politics of Dissent*, Houndmills: Palgrave.

Federal Research Division of the Library of Congress (1995) 'India: the role of political and interest groups'. Country Studies Series. Available at: http://www.country-data.com/cgi-bin/query/r-6130.html. Accessed 9 January 2005.

Feng, Huiyun (2007) *Chinese Strategic Culture and Foreign Policy Decision-Making: Confucianism, Leadership and War*, London: Routledge.

Ferguson, N. (2003) 'What is power?', *Hoover Digest*, no. 2. Available at http://www.hooverdigest.org/032/ferguson.html. Accessed 14 April 2006.

Ferris, E. (2011) 'Faith and humanitarianism: It's complicated', *Journal of Refugee Studies*, 24, 3, pp. 606–625.

Finnemore, M. and Sikkink, K. (1998) 'Norms and international relations theory', *International Organization* 52, 4, pp. 887–917.

Fitzgerald, T. (2011) *Religion and Politics in International Relations. The Modern Myth*, London and New York: Continuum.

Flint, J. (1993) 'Sudan cracks down on Muslim rivals', *The Guardian*, 11 June.

Florini, A. (ed.) (2000) *The Third Force. The Rise of International Civil Society*, Tokyo and Washington, D.C: Japan Center for International Exchange/Carnegie Endowment for International Peace.

Fowler, Booth R., Hertzke, A., Olson, L. and Dulk, K. Den (2010) *Religion and Politics in America*, 4th rev. edn, Boulder, CO: Westview.

Fox, J. (2001a) 'Religion as an overlooked element of international relations', *International Studies Review*, 3, 2, pp. 53–73.

Fox, J. (2001b) 'Clash of civilizations or clash of religions. Which is a more important determinant of ethnic conflict?', *Ethnicities*, September, 1, 3, pp. 295–320.

Fox, J. (2008) *A World Survey of Religion and the State*, Cambridge: Cambridge University Press.

Fox, J. and Sandler, S. (2004) *Bringing Religion into International Relations*, Basingstoke, UK: Palgrave Macmillan.

Frankel, J. (1963) *The Making of Foreign Policy*, London: Oxford University Press.

Freedom House (2002) Available at: http://www.freedomhouse.org/template.cfm?page&year=2002&country=2309. Accessed 3 July 2009.

Freeman, C. (2002) 'Saudi Arabia's foreign and domestic dilemmas', Washington, DC: Middle East Policy Council.

Freston, P. (2001) *Evangelicals and Politics in Asia, Africa and Latin America*, Cambridge: Cambridge University Press.

Freston, P. (2004) *Protestant Political Parties. A Global Survey*, Aldershot: Ashgate.

Freston, P. (ed.) (2006) *Evangelical Christianity and Democracy in Latin America*, Oxford: Oxford University Press.

Friere, P. (1985) *The Politics of Education: Culture, Power and Liberation* (translated by Donaldo Macedo). Massachusetts: Bergin & Garvey Publishers, Inc.

Friere, P. (1999) *The Paulo Friere Reader*, London: Continuum Publishing Group.

Frost, F., Rann, A. and Chin, A. (2003) 'Terrorism in Southeast Asia', *Parliament of Australia – Parliamentary Library*. Available at: http://www.aph.gov.au/library/intguide/FAD/sea.htm. Accessed 16 January 2006.

Frum, D. (2003) *The Right Man: The Surprise Presidency of George W. Bush*, New York: Random House.

Fukuyama, F. (1992) *The End of History and the Last Man*, Harmondsworth: Penguin.

Fuller, G. (2003) *The Future of Political Islam*, New York and Basingstoke: Palgrave Macmillan.

Furedi, F. (1994) *Colonial Wars and the Politics of Third World Nationalism*, London: I. B. Tauris.

Gaborieau, M. (1999) 'Transnational Islamic movements: Tablighi Jamaat in politics', International Institute for the Study of Islam in the Modern World (ISIM) Newsletter, July, pp. 21–22.

Gaiya, M. (2002) 'The Pentecostal Revolution in Nigeria', Occasional Paper, Centre of African Studies.

Ganguly, S. (2003/4) 'India's foreign policy grows up', *World Policy Journal*, Winter, pp. 41–47

Ganiel, G. (2009) 'Spiritual capital and democratization in Zimbabwe: A case study of a progressive charismatic congregation', in J. Haynes (ed.), *Religion and Democratizations*, London: Routledge, pp. 132–153.

Gauchet, M. (1985) *Le déenchantement du monde*, Paris: Gallimard.

Gause III, F. Gregory (2011) 'Saudi Arabia's regional security strategy', in M. Kamrava (ed.), *International Politics of the Persian Gulf*, New York: Syracuse University Press, pp. 169–183.

Gellner, E. (1983) *Nations and Nationalism*. New York: Cornell University Press.

Geoghegan, V. (2000) 'Religious narrative, post-secularism and Utopia', *Critical Review of International Social and Political Philosophy*, 3, 2–3, pp. 205–224.

Ghandour, A.-R. (2002) Jihad humanitaire: enquête sur les OGN islamiques, Paris: Flammarion.

Gifford, P. (1994) 'Some recent developments in African Christianity', *African Affairs*, 93, 373, pp. 513–534.

Gifford, P. (2004) *Ghana's New Christianity: Pentecostalism In A Globalising African Economy*, Bloomington: Indiana University Press.

Gills, B., Rocamara, J. and Wilson, R. (eds) (1993) *Low-Intensity Democracy*, London: Pluto.

Glasius, M., Kaldor, M. and Anheier, H. (eds) (2006) *Global Civil Society 2005/6*, London: Thousand Oaks, New Delhi: Sage.

Goldstein, J. (2004) *International Relations*, 6th edn, London: Pearson.

Gopin, M. (2000) *Between Eden and Armageddon: The Future of World Religions, Violence and Peacemaking*, New York and London: Oxford University Press.

Gopin, M. (2005) 'World religions, violence, and myths of peace in international relations', in G. ter Haar and J. Busutill (eds), *Bridge or Barrier. Religion, Violence and Visions for Peace*, Leiden: Brill, pp. 35–56.

Goulborne, H. and Joly, D. (1989) 'Religion and the Asian and Caribbean minorities in Britain', *Contemporary European Affairs*, 2, 4, pp. 77–98.

Gozaydin, I. (2009) 'The Fethullah Gulen movement and politics in Turkey: A chance for democratization or a Trojan horse', in J. Haynes (ed.), *Religion and Democratizations*, London: Routledge, pp. 174–196.

Graham-Harrison, E. (2012) 'Nato apologise for Afghan Qur'an burning', *The Guardian*, 22 February. Available at: http://www.guardian.co.uk/world/2012/feb/21/us-nato-apologise-afghan-quran-burning. Accessed 1 May 2012.

Green, D. and Luehrmann, L. (2003) *Comparative Politics of the Third World. Linking Concepts and Cases*, Boulder, CO: Lynne Rienner.

Green, J. (2000) *The Diminishing Divide: Religion's Changing Role in American Politics*, Washington, DC: Brookings Institution Press.

Green, J. (2004) 'Karl Rove in a corner', *The Atlantic Monthly*, November.

Green, J., Rozell, M. and Wilcox, C. (eds) (2003) *The Christian Right in American Politics: Marching to the Millennium*, Washington, DC: Georgetown University Press.

Green, J., Smidt, C., Guth, J. and Kellstedt, L. (2005) 'The American religious landscape and the 2004 presidential vote: Increased polarization', Washington, DC: The Pew Forum on Religion & Public Life.

Griffiths, M. (1999) *Fifty Key Thinkers in International Relations*, London and New York: Routledge.

Grigoriadis, I. (2009) 'Islam and democratization in turkey: secularism and trust in a divided society', in J. Haynes (ed.), *Religion and Democratizations*, London: Routledge, pp. 154–173.

Gruber, T. R. (1993) 'A translation approach to portable ontologies', *Knowledge Acquisition*, 5, 2, pp. 199–220.

Gul, A. (2004) 'Turkey's Muslim identity did not prevent Turkey's intense relations with Europe', 16 December, 'Zaman Online. First Turkish paper on the Internet'. Available at: http://yaleglobal.yale.edu/display.article?id=5041. Accessed 15 November 2005.

Gunaratna, R. (2004) 'Defeating Al Qaeda – The pioneering vanguard of the Islamic movements', in R. Howard and R. Sawyer (eds), *Defeating Terrorism. Shaping the New Security Environment*, Guilford, CT: McGraw-Hill/Dushkin, pp. 1–28.

Gutierrez, G. (1973) *A Theology of Liberation. History, Politics and Salvation*, New York: Orbis.

ter Haar, G. (2005) 'Religion: Source of conflict or resource for peace?', in G. ter Haar and J. Busutill (eds), *Bridge or Barrier. Religion, Violence and Visions for Peace*, Leiden: Brill, pp. 3–34.

ter Haar, G. (ed.) (2011) *Religion and Development: Ways of Transforming the World*, London: Hurst.

ter Haar, G. and Busutill J. (eds) (2005) *Bridge or Barrier: Religion, Violence and Visions for Peace*, London: Brill.

Habermas, J. (2006) 'Religion in the public sphere', *European Journal of Philosophy*, 14, 1, pp. 1–25.

Hacker, J. and Pierson, P. (2005) *Off Center. The Republican Revolution & the Erosion of American Democracy*, New Haven and London: Yale University Press.

Haggerty, D. (2002) 'Ethnicity and Religion in International Politics: The Middle East, the Balkans, and India-Pakistan', Consortium of Social Science Associations Congressional Briefing, 19 September. Available at: http://www.cossa.org/ethnicity.htm. Accessed 10 January 2006.

Hague, R. and Harrop, M. (2001) *Comparative Government and Politics. An Introduction*, 5th ed., Basingstoke: Palgrave.

Hakki, M. (2003) 'Wolfowitz's America', *Al-Ahram Online* #627, 27 February– 5 March. Available at: http://middleeastinfo.org/article2120.html. Accessed 8 August 2005.

Halahoff, A. and D. Wright-Neville (2009) 'A missing peace? The role of religious actors in countering terrorism', *Studies in Conflict & Terrorism*, 32, pp. 921–932.

'Halal meat feeds French election debate' (2012), Al Arabiya News, 12 March. Available at http://www.alarabiya.net/articles/2012/03/10/199798.html. Accessed 1 April 2012.

Halliday, F. (2005) *The Middle East in International Relations: Power, Politics and Ideology*. Cambridge: Cambridge University Press.

Halper, S. and Clarke, J. (2004) *America Alone. The Neo-Conservatives and the Global Order*, Cambridge: Cambridge University Press.

Hammond, P. (2003) 'Review article: Making war and peace', *Contemporary Politics*, 9, 1, pp. 83–90.

Harris, F. (1999) *Something Within. Religion in African-American Political Activism*, Oxford: Oxford University Press.

Harris, H. (2000) 'Theological reflections on religious resurgence and international stability: a look at Protestant evangelicalism', in K. Dark (ed.), *Religion and International Relations*, Basingstoke, UK: Palgrave Macmillan, pp. 24–49.

Harris, I., Mews, S., Morris, P. and Shepherd, J. (1992) *Contemporary Religions: A World Guide*, Harlow, Essex: Longman.

Harrison, S. (2001) 'Pakistan: the destabilisation game', *Le Monde Diplomatique*, October, pp. 17–18.

Harsch, E. (2003) 'Africa builds its own peace forces', *Africa Recovery*, 17, 3, pp. 1, 14–16, 18–20.

Hasan, M. (2012) 'Netanyahu may want war on Iran, but his people don't', *The Guardian*, 30 April.

Hasenclever, A. and Ritberger, V. (2003) 'Does religion make a difference? Theoretical approaches to the impact of faith on political conflict', in F. Petito and P. Hatzopoulos (eds), *Religion in International Relations. The Return from* Exile, New York: Palgrave, pp. 107–146.

Hassner, P. (2002) 'The United States: the empire of force of the force of empire?', Chaillot Paper 54, September, Paris: European Union Institute for Security Studies.

Hastings, A. (1979) *A History of African Christianity, 1950–75*, Cambridge: Cambridge University Press.

Hauser, C. (2006) 'Bush says Iran leader's letter fails to address nuclear issue', *The New York Times*, 11 May. Available at: http://select.nytimes.com/gst/abstract.html?res=F00717FC3C5A0C728DDDAC0894DE404482&n=Top%2fNews%2fWorld%2fCountries%20and%20Territories%2fIran. Accessed 22 May 2006.

Haynes, J. (1993) *Religion in Third World Politics*, Buckingham: Open University Press.

Haynes, J. (1996) *Religion and Politics in Africa*, London: Zed.

Haynes, J. (1998) *Religion in Global Politics*, Harlow, UK: Longman.

Haynes, J. (2001a) *Democracy in the Developing World. Africa, Asia, Latin America and the Middle East*, Cambridge: Polity.

Haynes, J. (2001b) 'Transnational religious actors and international politics', *Third World Quarterly*, 22, 2, pp. 143–158.

Haynes, J. (2002) *Politics in the Developing World*, Oxford: Blackwell.

Haynes, J. (2003a) 'Religious fundamentalism and politics', in L. Ridgeon (ed.), *Major World Religions. From their Origins to the Present*, London: RoutledgeCurzon, pp. 324–375.

Haynes, J. (2003b) 'Democratic consolidation in Africa: the problematic case of Ghana', *The Journal of Commonwealth and Comparative Politics*, 41, 1, pp. 48–76.

Haynes, J. (2005a) *Comparative Politics in a Globalizing World*, Cambridge: Polity.

Haynes, J. (2005b) 'Review article: Religion and International Relations after "9/11"', *Democratization*, 12, 3, pp. 398–413.

Haynes, J. (2005c) 'Al Qaeda: ideology and action', *Critical Review of International Social and Political Philosophy*, 8, 2, pp. 177–191.

Haynes, J. (2005d) 'Islamic militancy in East Africa', *Third World Quarterly*, 26, 8, pp. 1321–1339.

Haynes, J. (ed.) (2005e) *Palgrave Advances in Development Studies*, Houndmills, Basingstoke: Palgrave Macmillan.

Haynes, J. (2006) 'Falun Gong – A-Z Glossary', in J. Haynes (ed.), *The Politics of Religion*, London: Taylor & Francis, pp. 47–48.

Haynes, J. (2007a). *Religion and Development. Conflict or Cooperation?* Basingstoke: Palgrave Macmillan.

Haynes, J. (2007b) *An Introduction to International Relations and Religion*, Harlow: Pearson.

Haynes, J. (2008a) 'Religion and foreign policy making in the USA, India and Iran: Towards a research agenda', *Third World Quarterly*, 29, 1, February, pp. 143–165.

Haynes, J. (2008b) 'Religion and a human rights culture in America', *The Review of Faith & International Affairs*, 6, 2, June, pp. 73–82.

Haynes, J. (2009) 'Transnational religious actors and international order', *Perspectives*, 17, 2, pp. 43–70.

Haynes, J. (2012a) Politics and democracy in Turkey: The case of the AKP', in J. Fox (ed.), *Religion and Politics*, Boulder, CO: Paradigm, pp. 73–87.

Haynes, J. (2012b) *Religious Transnational Actors and Soft Power*, Aldershot, UK: Ashgate.

Haynes, J. (2012c) 'Faith-based organisations, development and the World Bank', *International Development Policy*. Special issue on 'religion and development'.

Haynes, J. and A. Hennig (eds) (2011) *Religious Actors in the Public Sphere. Means, objectives and effects*, London: Routledge.

Haynes, J., Hough, P., Malik, S. and Pettiford, L. (2011) *World Politics*, London: Pearson.

## Bibliography

Hehir, B., Walzer, M., Richardson, L., Telhami, S., Krauthammer, C. and Lindsay, J. (2004) *Liberty and Power: A Dialogue on Religion and U.S. Foreign Policy in an Unjust World*, Washington, DC: Brookings Institution Press.

Held, D. (2003) 'Cosmopolitanism: Taming globalization', in D. Held and A. McGrew (eds), *The Global Transformations Reader*, 2nd edn, Cambridge: Polity Press, pp. 514–529.

Held, D. and McGrew, A. (2002) *Globalization/Anti-Globalization*, Cambridge: Polity.

Henley, J. (2004) 'French MPs vote for veil ban in state schools', *The Guardian*, 11 February.

Hennig, Anja (2009) 'Morality politics in a Catholic democracy. A hard road towards liberalisation of gay rights in Poland', in J. Haynes (ed.), *Religion and Politics in Europe, the Middle East and North Africa*, London: Routledge, pp. 202–226.

Hertzke, A. (1989) 'United States of America', in S. Mews (ed.), *Religion in Politics: A World Guide*, Harlow: Longman, pp. 298–317.

Hertzke, A. (2004) *Freeing God's Children: The Unlikely Alliance for Global Human Rights*, Lanham, MD: Rowman & Littlefield Publishers.

Hettne, B. (2001) 'Europe: paradigm and paradox', in M. Schulz, F. Söderbaum and J. Öjendal (eds), *Regionalization in a Globalizing World: A Comparative Perspective on Forms, Actors and Processes*, London: Zed Books, pp. 22–41.

Hinnebusch, R. (2005) 'The politics of identity in Middle East international relations', in L. Fawcett (ed.), *International Relations of the Middle East*, Oxford: Oxford University Press, pp. 151–171.

Hirohita, M. (2002) 'Muslims and Buddhists dialogue', Unitarian Universalist Fellowship of Frankfurt, 10 November. Available at http://www.uufrankfurt. de/MuslimsBuddhists021110.htm. Accessed 28 March 2006.

Hirst, P. and Thompson, G. (1999) *Globalization in Question*, Oxford: Blackwell.

Hirst, R. (2003) 'Social networks and personal beliefs', in G. Davie, P. Heelas and L. Woodhead (eds), *Predicting Religion*, Aldershot: Ashgate, pp. 86–94.

Hoare-Vance, S. (2009) 'The Confucius Institutes and China's evolving foreign policy'. Unpublished Master of Arts dissertation, University of Canterbury, New Zealand. Available at http://ir.canterbury.ac.nz/handle/10092/3619. Accessed 20 April 2012.

Hobsbawm, E. (1990) *Nations and Nationalism since 1780*, Cambridge: Cambridge University Press.

Hoekema, A. (1966) *What about Tongue-Speaking*, Exeter: Paternoster Press.

Hoffman, B. (1998–9) 'Old madness. New methods. Revival of religious terrorism begs for broader U.S. policy', *Rand Review*, 2, 22: 11–17.

Holenstein, A.-M. (2005) 'Role and significance of religion and spirituality in development co-operation. A reflection and working paper'. (Translated from German by Wendy Tyndale.) Bern: Swiss Agency for Development and Co-operation, March.

Holland, M. (2002) *The European Union and the Third World*, Basingstoke: Palgrave.

Hopkins, N. and Norton Taylor, R. (2012) 'Somalia: UK weighs up air strikes against rebels, *The Guardian*, 22 February. Available at: http://www.guardian.co.uk/world/2012/feb/21/uk-considers-air-strikes-somalia. Accessed 1 May 2012.

Hooker, M. (1997) *Islam in South-East Asia*, Leiden: Brill.

Horowitz, M. (2002) 'Research report on the use of identity concepts in international relations'. Available at: http://www.wcfia.harvard.edu/misc/initiative/identity/publications/horowitz1.pdf. Accessed 25 May 2006.

Howard, R. and Sawyer, R. (eds) *Defeating Terrorism. Shaping the New Security Environment*, Guilford, CT: McGraw-Hill/Dushkin.

Howenstein, N. (2006) 'Islamist networks: The case of Tablighi Jamaat', United States Institute of Peace, 'Peace Brief'. Available at: http://www.usip.org/publications/islamist-networks-case-tablighi-jamaat. Accessed 18 October 2011.

Hudson, M. (2005) 'The United States in the Middle East', in L. Fawcett (ed.), *International Relations of the Middle East*, Oxford: Oxford University Press, pp. 283–305.

Huiyun Feng (2007) *Chinese Strategic Culture and Foreign Policy Decision-Making: Confucianism, Leadership and War*, London: Routledge.

Human Rights Watch (2002) ' "We have no orders to save you". State Participation and Complicity in Communal Violence in Gujarat', New York: Human Rights watch.

*Human Security Report* (2005) Oxford: Oxford University Press.

*Human Security Report Project* (2010) Vancouver, Canada, Simon Fraser University Available at: http://www.hsrgroup.org/human-security-reports/20092010/overview.aspx. Accessed 1 May 2012.

Huntington, S. (1991) *The Third Wave. Democratization in the Late Twentieth Century*, Norman: University of Oklahoma Press.

Huntington, S. (1993) 'The clash of civilisations?', *Foreign Affairs*, 72, 3, pp. 22–49.

Huntington, S. (1996) *The Clash of Civilizations*, New York: Simon and Schuster.

Hurd, S. (2004) 'The political authority of secularism in international relations', *European Journal of International Relations*, 10, 2, June, pp. 235–262.

Hurd, Shakman, E. (2008) *The Politics of Secularism in International Relations*, Princeton: Princeton University Press.

Hurd, Shakman, E. (2011) 'Secularism and international relations theory', in J. Snyder (ed.), *Religion and International Relations Theory*, New York: Columbia University Press, pp. 60–90.

Hurrell, A. (2002) '"There are no rules" (George W. Bush): International order after September 11', *International Relations*, 16, 2, pp. 185–204.

Husain, M. Zohair (1995) *Global Islamic Politics*, New York: HarperCollins.

Hwang, K. (2005) 'Analysis: China resurrects Confucius', *Washington Times*, 12 August. Available at: http://www.washingtontimes.com/world/20050825–104920–5524r.htm. Accessed 26 August 2006.

Intermediate Technology Development Group–Eastern Africa (2002) News-letter, December. Available at: http://www.itdg.org/html/itdg_eastafrica/kit_dec_02.htm. Accessed 4 June 2005.

International Crisis Group (2005a) 'Bosnia's stalled police reform: No progress, no EU', Europe Report No. 164, 6 September. Available at: http://www.crisisgroup.org/home/index.cfm?id=3645&l=1. Accessed 21 November 2005

International Crisis Group (2005b) *Somalia's Islamists*, Africa Report No. 100, December.

International Islamic Relief Organisation (n.d.) Description of the IIRO's activities at http://www.gm-unccd.org/FIELD/NGO/IIRO/Res.htm. Accessed 3 June 2005.

Isaacs, D. (2003) 'Islam in Nigeria: Simmering tensions', BBC News online, 23 September. Available at: http://news.bbc.co.uk/1/hi/world/africa/3155279.stm. Accessed 1 December 2005.

Islam, I. and Chowdhury, A. (2001) *The Political Economy of East Asia: Post-Crisis Debates*, New York: Oxford University Press.

Jackson, D. (2004) 'Bush's Vatican strategy', *The Boston Globe*, 15 June. Available at: http://www.boston.com/news/globe/editorial_opinion/oped/articles/2004/06/15/bushs_vatican_strategy/. Accessed 11 November 2005.

Jackson, R. (1990) *Quasi-states: Sovereignty, International Relations and the Third World*, Cambridge: Cambridge University Press.

Jackson, R. and P. Owens, P. (2005) 'The evolution of international society', in J. Baylis and S. Smith (eds), *The Globalization of World Politics*, 3rd edn, Oxford: Oxford University Press, pp. 45–62.

Jacques, M. (2006) 'This is the relationship that will define global politics', *The Guardian*, 15 June.

Jain, P. and Groot, G. (2006) 'Beijing's "soft power" offensive', *Asia Times Online*, 17 May. Available at: http://www.atimes.com/atimes/China/HE17Ad01.html. Accessed 2 June 2006.

Jalalzai, M. K. (2004) *The Foreign Policy of Pakistan: Kashmir, Afghanistan and Internal Security Threats: 1947–2004*, Lahore: Ariana.

Jamal, A. (2009) 'Democratizing state-religion relations: a comparative study of Turkey, Egypt and Israel', in J. Haynes (ed.), *Religion and Democratizations*, London: Routledge, pp. 103–131.

Jamestown Foundation (2003a) 'Tanzania: Al Qaeda's East African beachhead?, Part 1', *Terrorism Monitor*, 1, 5, pp. 1–4.

Jamestown Foundation (2003b) 'Tanzania: Al Qaeda's East African beachhead?, Part 2', *Terrorism Monitor*, 1, 8, pp. 1–3.

James, P. (ed.) (2011) *Religion, Identity, and Global Governance. Ideas, Evidence, and Practice*, Toronto: University of Toronto Press.

Janson, M. (2006) 'The Prophet's path: Tablighi Jamaat in The Gambia', *ISIM Newsletter*, No. 17, Spring, pp. 44–45.

Jayawardena, L. (1992) *Buddhism Betrayed?: Religion, Politics and Violence in Sri Lanka*, Chicago: University of Chicago Press.

'JDW – Faith and development' (2011) Available at: http://go.worldbank.org/84GZJCRVU0. Accessed 18 August 2011.

Jefferis, J. (2011) *Religion and Political Violence. Sacred Protest in the Modern World*, London: Routledge.

Jervis, R. (2005) 'Why the Bush doctrine cannot be sustained, *Political Science Quarterly*, 120, 3, pp. 351–377.

Johnson, R. (n.d.; probably 2002) 'Reconstructing the Balkans: The effects of a global governance approach'. Unpublished manuscript. The Brookings Institution, Washington, DC. Available at: www.cpogg.org/paper%20amerang/Rebecca%20Johnson.pdf. Accessed 1 October 2003.

Johnson, T. (2011) 'Boko Haram'. Council for Foreign Relations Backgrounder. Available at: http://www.cfr.org/africa/boko-haram/p25739?cid=ppc-Google-boko_haram-122711&gclid=CJOpvtjKlq8CFUx76wodZFXP0Q. Accessed 2 April 2012.

Johnston, D. and Sampson, C. (eds) (1994) *Religion, the Missing Dimension of Statecraft*, Oxford: Oxford University Press.

Joyce, K. (2004) 'The Catholic Divide? Culture warriors try again with the "Catholic Divide"', *The Revealer*, 15 June. Available at: http://www.therevealer.org/archives/timely_000426.php. Accessed 11 November 2005.

Judis, J. (2005) 'The chosen nation: The influence of religion on US foreign policy', *Policy Brief*, no. 37, March. Available at: http://www.carnegieendowment.org/publications/index.cfm?fa=view&id=16668&prog=zgp&proj=zusr. Accessed 1 October 2005.

Juergensmeyer, M. (1993) *The New Cold War? Religious Nationalism Confronts the Secular State*, Berkeley: University of California Press.

Juergensmeyer, M. (2000) *Terror in the Mind of God: The Global Rise of Religious Violence*, Berkeley: University of California Press.

Juergensmeyer, M. (2005) 'Religion in the new global order'. Available at: http://www.maxwell.syr.edu/moynihan/programs/sac/paper%20pdfs/marks%20paper.pdf. Accessed 18 April 2006.

Kamrava, M. (1993) *Politics and Society in the Third World*, London: Routledge.

Kamrava, M. (ed.) (2011a) *International Politics of the Persian Gulf*, New York: Syracuse University Press.

Kamrava, M. (2011b) 'Iranian foreign policy and security policies in the Persian Gulf', in M. Kamrava (ed.), *International Politics of the Persian Gulf*, New York: Syracuse University Press, pp. 184–206.

Kapila, S. (2005) 'India's foreign policy challenges 2005: A perspective analysis', *South Asia Analysis Group*, 17 January. Available at: http://www.saag.org/papers13/paper1223.html. Accessed 10 January 2006.

Karl, T. Lynn (1995) 'The hybrid regimes of Central America', *Journal of Democracy*, 6, 3, pp. 72–86.

Katyala, K. (2004) 'Issues and trends in Indian elections', *South Asian Journal*, 5 (July–September). Available at: http://www.southasianmedia.net/Magazine/Journal/previousissues5.htm. Accessed 9 January 2006.

Katz, J. (2005) *Occultism: From the Renaissance to the Present Day*, London: Jonathan Cape.

Katzenstein, P. (2006) 'Multiple modernities as limits to secular Europeanization?', in T. Byrnes and P. Katzenstein (eds), *Religion in an Expanding Europe*, Cambridge: Cambridge University Press, pp. 1–31.

Katzman, K. (2002) 'Terrorism: Near Eastern groups and state sponsors, 2002', Congress Research Service Report for Congress, 13 February. Available at: http://www.fas.org/irp/crs/RL31119.pdf. Accessed 9 January 2006.

Kay, J. (2005) 'Pope Benedict XVI's political resume: theocracy and social reaction', 22 April. 'World Socialist Web Site'. Available at: http://www.wsws.org/articles/2005/apr2005/pope-a22.shtml. Accessed 15 November 2005.

Kelley, D. (1986) *Why Conservative Churches are Growing: A Study in Sociology of Religion*, New York: Harper and Row.

Kelley, K. (2001) 'Somalia "next US target" after Taliban', *The East African*, 19 November.

Kemp, G. (2005) 'Iran and Iraq. The Shia connection, soft power, and the nuclear connection', Washington, DC: United States Institute of Peace.

Kennedy, P. and Roudometof, V. (2002) *Communities Across Borders*, London: Routledge.

Keohane, R. (2002) 'The globalization of informal violence, theories of world politics, and the "liberalism of fear"', *Dialog-IO*, Spring, pp. 29–43.

Keohane, R. O., and Nye, J. S. (eds) (1972) *Transnational Relations and World Politics*, Cambridge, MA: Harvard University Press.

Keohane, R. and Nye, J. (1977) *International Relations Theory: A New Introduction*, London: Palgrave.

Keohane, R. and Nye, J. (2000) 'Introduction', in J. Nye and J. Donahue (eds), *Governance in a Globalizing World*, Washington DC: Brookings Press, pp. 1–15.

Kepel, G. (1994) *The Revenge of God*, Cambridge: Polity.

Kepel, G. (2004) *The War for Muslim Minds. Islam and the West*, London: Harvard University Press.

Khan, Muqtedar, M. A. (ed.) (2006) *Islamic Democratic Discourse. Theories, Debates and Philosophical Perspectives*, Lanham: Rowman and Littlefield.

Kim, S. (ed.) (1998) *China and the World: Chinese Foreign Policy Faces the New Millennium*, Boulder and London: Westview.

King, A. Y. C. (1993) 'A nonparadigmatic search for democracy in post-Confucian culture the case of Taiwan, R. O. C.', in L. Diamond (ed.), *Political Culture and Democracy in Developing Countries*, Boulder: Lynne Rienner, pp. 139–162.

King, M. (2000) 'Art and the postsecular', *Journal of Visual Art Practice*, 4, 1, pp. 3–17.

Kinzer, S. (2001) *The Crescent and the Star: Turkey Between Two Worlds*, New York: Farrar Straus Giroux.

Klicksberg, B. (2003a) *Social Justice: A Jewish Perspective*. New York: Gefen Publishing House.

Klicksberg, B. (2003b) 'Facing the inequalities of development: some lessons from Judaism and Christianity', *Development*, 46, 4, pp. 57–63.

Kohen, A. (1999) *From the Place of the Dead: The Epic Struggles of Bishop Belo of East Timor*, New York: St Martin's Press.

Kohli, A. (1994) 'Centralization and powerlessness: India's democracy in a comparative perspective', in J. Migdal, A. Kohli and V. Shue (eds), *State Power and Social Forces: Domination and Transformation in the Third World*, Cambridge: Cambridge University Press, pp. 93–136.

Kohut, A. and Rogers, M. (2002) 'Americans struggle with religion's role at home and abroad', 20 March, Washington, DC: Pew Research Council.

de Koning, M. (2006) 'Islamization of the French riots. Interview with Laurent Chambon', *ISIM Review*, 17, Spring, pp. 30–31.

Korany, B. (2005) 'The Middle East since the cold war: torn between geopolitics and geoeconomics', in L. Fawcett (ed.), *International Relations of the Middle East*, Oxford: Oxford University Press, pp. 59–76.

Krasner, S. (ed.) (1983) *International Regimes*, Ithaca, NY: Cornell University Press.

Krauthammer, C. (2004) 'When unilateralism is right and just', in J. B. Hehir, M. Walzer, L. Richardson, S. Telhami, C. Krauthammer and J. Lindsay, *Liberty and Power. A Dialogue on Religion and U.S. Foreign Policy in an Unjust World*, Washington DC: Brookings Institution Press, pp. 95–99.

Krishna, S. (2001) 'India's role in Sri Lanka's ethnic conflict', Colombo, Sri Lanka: Marga Institute.

Kristoff, N. (2002) 'Following God abroad', *New York Times*, 21 May, p. A21.

Kubálková, V. (2002) 'Toward an international political theology', *Fathom: The Source for Online Learning*. Available at: http://www.fathom.com/feature/35550/. Accessed 14 October 2005.

Kubálková, V. (2003) 'Toward an international political theology', in F. Petito and P. Hatzopoulos (eds) *Religion in International Relations. The Return from Exile*, New York: Palgrave, pp. 79–105.

Kumaraswamy, P. R. (1999) 'South Asia after the Cold War', in L. Fawcett and Y. Sayigh (eds), *The Third World Beyond the Cold War*, Oxford: Oxford University Press, pp. 170–199.

Künkler, M. and Leininger, J. (2009) 'The multi-faceted role of religious actors in democratization processes: empirical evidence from five young democracies', in J. Haynes (ed.), *Religion and Democratizations*, London: Routledge, pp. 18–52.

Kurop, M. Christoff (2001) 'Al Qaeda's Balkan Links', *The Wall Street Journal Europe*, 1 November. Available at: http://www.balkanpeace.org/hed/archive/nov01/hed4304.shtml. Accessed 10 March 2004.

Kurth, J. (1999) 'Religion and globalization'. The Templeton Lecture on Religion and World Affairs, *Foreign Policy Research Institute Wire*, 7, 7. Available at: http://www.fpri.org/fpriwire/0707.199905.kurth.religionglobalization.html. Accessed 18 March 2004.

Kurtz, L. (1995) *Gods in the Global Village*, Thousand Oaks, CA: Pine Forge Press.

LaFranchi, H. (2006) 'Evangelized foreign policy?', *The Christian Science Monitor*, 2 March. Available at: http://csmonitor.com/2006/0302/p01s01-usfp.htm. Accessed 2 June 2006.

Laing, A., and Flood, Z. (2012) 'Al-Shabaab: the growing menace of the al Qaeda affiliate', *The Telegraph*, 29 February. Available at: http://www.telegraph.co.uk/news/worldnews/al-qaeda/9113464/Al-Shabaab-the-growing-menace-of-the-al-Qaeda-affiliate.html. Accessed 2 April 2012.

Lall, M. (2005) 'Indian education policy under the NDA government', in K. Adeney and L. Saez (eds), *Coalition Politics and Hindu Nationalism*, London: Routledge, pp. 153–170.

Land, R. (2012) 'Romney and the evangelicals', *USA Today*, 2 April, p. 9A.

Lapid, Y. and Kratochwil, F. (eds) (1996) *The Return of Culture and Identity in International Relations Theory*, Boulder, CO: Lynne Reinner.

Lapidus, I. (1988) *A History of Islamic Societies*, Cambridge: Cambridge University Press.

Lasswell, H. D. (1936) *Politics: Who Gets What, When, How*, Cleveland, OH: Meridian Books.

Lawson, L. (1999) 'External democracy promotion in Africa: Another false start?', *The Journal of Commonwealth and Comparative Politics*, 37, 1, pp. 1–30.

Leftwich, A. (1993) 'Governance, democracy and development in the Third World', *Third World Quarterly*, 14, 3, pp. 517–536.

Leiken, R. (2012) *Europe's Angry Muslims*, New York: Oxford University Press.

Lerchner, F. and Boli, J. (eds) (2008) *The Globalization Reader,* 3rd edn. London: Blackwell.

LeVine, M. (2005) 'Assimilate or die. Do the French riots portend a coming cultural backlash against globalization?', Mother Jones. Available at: http://motherjones.com/commentary/columns/2005/11/assimilate_or_die.html. Accessed 5 June 2006.

Levinsohn, J. (2003) 'The World Bank's Poverty Reduction Strategy Paper approach: Good marketing or good policy', G-24 Discussion Paper Series, New York: United Nations Conference on Trade and Development.

Levitt, P. (2004) 'Redefining the boundaries of belonging: The institutional character of transnational religious life', *Sociology of Religion*, 65, 1, pp. 1–18.

Levitt, P. (2009) Roots and routes: Understanding the lives of the second generation transnationally', *Journal of Ethnic and Migration Studies*, 35, 7, pp. 1225–1242.

Lewis, B. (1990) 'The roots of Muslim rage', *The Atlantic Monthly*, September, pp. 52–60.

Lieven, A. (2001) 'Strategy for terror', *Prospect,* 67, pp. 19–23.

Lieven, A. (2004) *America, Right or Wrong: An Anatomy of American Nationalism,* Oxford and New York: Oxford University Press.

Lindquist, G. and Handelman, D. (2011), 'Religion, politics, and globalization: the long past foregrounding the short present – prologue and introdiction', in *idem.* (eds) *Religion, Politics & Globalization*, New York and Oxford: Bergahn Books, pp. 1–66.

Linz, Juan, and Alfred Stepan (1996) *Problems of Democratic Transition and Consolidation. Southern Europe, South America, and Post-Communist Europe.* Baltimore and London: John Hopkins University Press.

Lipschutz, R. (1992) 'Reconstructing world politics the emergence of global civil society', *Millennium*, 21, 3, p. 390.

Little, D. (1994) 'Religious nationalism and human rights', in G.F. Powers, D. Christiansen and R. Hennemeyer (eds) *Peacemaking: Moral and Policy Challenges for a New World*. Washington, DC: US Catholic Conference, pp. 84–95.

Louer, L. (2008) *Transnational Shia Politics: Religious and Political Networks in the Gulf*, London: C. J. Hurst and Co.

Luckmann, T. (1969) 'The decline of church-orientated religion', in R. Robertson (ed.), *The Sociology of Religion*, Baltimore, MD: Penguin, pp. 141–151.

Luhmann, N. (1989) *Ecological Communication*, London: Polity Press.

Lunn, J. (2009) 'The role of religion, spirituality and faith in development: a critical theory approach', *Third World Quarterly*, 30, 5, pp. 937–951.

Lyotard, J.-F. (1979) *The Post-Modern Condition a Report on Knowledge*, Manchester: Manchester University Press.

MacAskill, E. (2006) 'US blocking international deal on fighting Aids', *The Guardian*, 2 June.

MacAskill, E. and Tisdall, S. (2006) 'A year on, Ahmadinejad's popularity is soaring', *The Guardian*, 21 June.

MacFarquhar, L. (2003) 'Letter from. India. The Strongman', *The New Yorker*, 26 May, pp. 50–57.

Madeley, John T. S. (2009) '*E unum pluribus*. The role of religion in the project of European integration', in Jeffrey Haynes (ed.), *Religion and Politics in Europe, the Middle East and North Africa*, London: Routledge, pp. 114–135.

Maginnis, R. (2011) 'Muslim world more anti-American than ever', Human Events, 18 August. Available at: http://www.humanevents.com/article.php?id=45588. Accessed 1 April 2012.

Mahmud, E. (2005) 'The missing intra-Jammu & Kashmir dialogue'. Available at: http://www.stimson.org/southasia/?SN=SA20050301780. Accessed 12 January 2006.

Mian, Z. and Nayyar, A. H. (2008) 'Pakistan and the Islamist challenge', *Foreign Policy in Focus*. Available at: http://www.fpif.org/articles/pakistan_and_the_islamist_challenge. Accessed 2 August 2012.

Malek, C. (2004) 'Identity (inter-group) conflicts', The Conflict Resolution Information Source, University of Colorado. Available at: http://v4.crinfo.org/CK_Essays/ck_identity_issues.jsp. Accessed 25 October 2005.

Malik, I. (2002) *Religious Minorities in Pakistan*, London: Minority Rights Group International.

Marchesin, P. (2001) *Les nouvelles menaces: les relations Nord – Sud des anneés 1980 à nos jours*, Paris: Karthala.

Marchesin, P. (2003) 'The rise of Islamic fundamentalism in East Africa', *African Geopolitics*, no issue number. Available at: at http://www.african-geopolitics.org/show.aspx?ArticleId=3497. Accessed 4 April 2004.

'Married adolescents ignored in global agenda, says UNFPA' (2004) Press Release, 4 June.

Marshall, K. (2005a) 'Religious faith and development: Rethinking development debates', Religious NGOs and International Development Conference, Oslo, Norway, 7 April. Available at: http://www.global.ucsb.edu/orfaleacenter/luce/luce08/documents/Marshall_OsloNGObk-June1.pdf.

Marshall, K. (2005b) 'Faith and development: Rethinking development debates', World Bank paper, June, Washington, DC: World Bank.

Marshall, K. (2006) 'Religion and international development. Interview with *Katherine Marshall*, Director, Development Dialogue on Values and Ethics, The World Bank', The Pew Forum on Religion and Public Life, 6 March. Available at: http://pewforum.org/Government/Religion-and-International-Development.aspx. Accessed 19 August 2011.

Marshall, K. (2009) 'Faith and development leaders meeting. Faith-inspired networks and organizations: Their contributions to development programs and policies. A meeting organized by the Development Dialogue on Values and Ethics at the World Bank, the UK Department for International Development, and the World Faiths Development Dialogue, Accra, Ghana, July 1–3, 2009. Concluding remarks by Ms. Katherine Marshall, Executive Director, World faiths Development Dialogue.'

Marshall, K. (2011) 'Looking beyond growth', *Dharma World: For Living Buddhism and Interfaith Dialogue*, 38, pp. 4–6.

Marshall, K. and Keough, L. (2004) *Mind, Heart and Soul in the Fight against Poverty*, Washington, DC: World Bank.

Marshall, K. and Marsh, R. (eds) (2003) *Millennium Challenges for Development and Faith Institutions*, Washington, DC: World Bank.

Marsden, L. (2008) *For God's Sake: The Christian Right and US Foreign Policy*, London: Zed Books.

Marsden, L. (2011) 'Religion, identity and American power in the age of Obama', *International Politics*, 48, 2/3, pp. 326–343.

Marshall, P. (2003) 'Radical Islam's move on Africa', *The Washington Post*, 16 October.

Marshall, P. (2004) 'Hinduism and terror', *First Things: A Monthly Journal of Religion and Public Life*, 1 June. Available at: http://www.freedomhouse.org/religion/country/india/Hinduism%20and%20Terror.htm. Accessed 1 September 2005.

Martin, D. (1990) *Tongues of Fire. The Explosion of Protestantism in Latin America*, Oxford: Basil Blackwell.

Martin, W. (1999) 'The Christian right and American foreign policy', *Foreign Policy*, March.

Marty, M. and Appleby, R. Scott (eds) (1997) *Religion, Ethnicity and Self-Identity*, London: University Press of New England.

Marty, M., with J. Moore (2000) *Politics, Religion and the Common Good: Advancing a Distinctly American Conversation About Religion's Role in Our Shared Life*, San Francisco: Josey-Bass Publishers.

Mathews, G. (2000) *Global Culture/Individual Identity*, London: Routledge.

Maunder, J. (2005) 'Universally acknowledged, uniformly ignored?: Religion and international relations theory', *Polity@Carleton*, 1, 2, Summer. Available at: http://www.carleton.ca/polisci/Polity/Vol%201%20no2/Religion%20 and%20IR.htm. Accessed 10 June 2005.

Mazarr, M. (2003) 'George W. Bush, Idealist', *International Affairs*, 79, 3, pp. 503–522.

Mbembe, A. (1988) *Afriques indociles. Christianisme, Pouvoir et etat en societé postcoloniale*, Paris: Karthala.

McCargo, D. (2001) 'Democratic consolidation in Pacific Asia', in J. Haynes (ed.), *Towards Sustainable Democracy in the Third World*, Basingstoke and New York: Palgrave, pp. 141–162.

McCargo, D. (2009) 'Thai Buddhists and the South', *Journal of Southeast Asian Studies*, 40, 1, pp. 11–32.

McCarthy, R. (2002) 'Pearl trial told how Briton drove off with journalist', *The Guardian*, 23 April.

McGreal, C. (2005) 'Sharon breaks covenant with settlers', *The Guardian*, 18 August.

McGrew, A. (1992) 'Conceptualising global politics', in A. McGrew and D. Held (eds), *Global Politics*, Cambridge: Polity.

McGrory, D. (2005) 'Paying for ignoring the warnings', *Asian Affairs*, August, pp. 9–10.

McGrory, D., Ford, R. and Rice, X. (2005) 'Search for bombers centres on East Africa connection', *Times Online*. Available at: http://www.timesonline.co.uk/article/0,,22989-1708386,00.html. Accessed 6 August 2005.

McLoughlin, S. (2005) 'The state, new Muslim leaderships and Islam as a resource for public engagement in Britain', in J. Cesarai and S. McLoughlin (eds) *European Muslims and the Secular State*, Aldershot: Ashgate, pp. 55–70.

Mearsheimer, J. and S. Walt (2006) 'The Israel Lobby', *London Review of Books*, 28, 6, 23 March, pp. 3–12.

Mearsheimer, J. and Walt, S. (2008) *The Israel Lobby and U.S. Foreign Policy*, Harmondsworth, UK: Penguin.

Mendelsohn, B. (2005) 'Sovereignty under attack: the international society meets the Al Qaeda network', *Review of International Studies*, 31, pp. 45–68.

Menjivar, C. (1999) 'Religious institutions and transnationalism: A case study of Catholic and Evangelica; Salvadoran immigrants', *International Journal of Politics, Culture, and Society*, 12, 4, pp. 589–611.

Merlini, C. (2011) 'A Post-Secular World?', *Survival*, 53, 2, pp. 117–130.

Mesbahuddin, T. (2010) 'Religion in Development. An Islamic Model Emerging in Bangladesh', *Journal of South Asian Development*, 5, 2, pp. 221–241.

Metcalf, B. (2003) 'Travelers' tales in the Tablighi Jamaat', *The Annals of the American Academy of Political and Social Science*, 588, 1, pp. 136–148.

Micklethwait, J. and Wooldridge, A. (2009) *God is Back: How the Global Rise of Faith is Changing the World*, Harmondsworth, UK: Penguin.

Miles, J. (2004) 'Religion and American foreign policy', *Survival*, 46, 1, pp. 23–37.

Miller, M. (1997) 'Asia/Pacific', *Foreign Policy in Focus*, 2, 25, March, pp. 1–6.

Milton-Edwards, B. (2006) *Islam and Violence in the Modern Era*, Basingstoke and New York: Palgrave Macmillan.

Mitchell, M. (2003) 'A theology of engagement for the "newest internationalists" ', *The Brandywine Review of International Affairs*, Spring, pp. 11–19.

Moghadam, V. (2002) 'Violence and terrorism: Feminist observations on Islamist movements, states, and the international system', *Alternatives: Turkish Journal of International Relations*, 1, 2, pp. 8–27.

Mollov, B. (2006) 'Managing conflict: Can religion succeed where politics has failed? An Israeli addresses a Global Peace Forum in Malaysia', Jerusalem Center for Public Affairs, November 1. Available at: http://jcpa.org/JCPA/Templates/ShowPage.asp?DBID=1&TMID=111&LNGID=1&FID=375&PID=0&IID=1423. Accessed 5 December 2007

Moore, P. (1989) 'Greece', in S. Mews (ed.), *Religion in Politics. A World Guide*, Harlow: Longman, p. 88.

Moyser, G. (1991) 'Politics and religion in the modern world an overview', in G. Moyser (ed.), *Politics and Religion in the Modern World*, London: Routledge, pp. 1–27.

Mozjes, P. (2002) 'Report on the international conference on reconciliation in Bosnia, Dubrovnik, Croatia, September 12–14, 2002'. Available at: http://www.georgefox.edu/academics/undergrad/departments/soc-swk/ree/mojzes_rot.doc. Accessed 25 May 2006.

Mullally, S. (2004) 'Feminism and multicultural dilemmas in India: Revisiting the *Shah Bano* Case', *Oxford Journal of Legal Studies*, 24, 4, pp. 671–692.

'Muslim extremists seize Philippine health worker' (2012) Agence France-Presse, 20 March. Available at: http://news.ph.msn.com/regional/article.aspx?cp-documentid=6010312. Accessed 20 April 2012.

'Muslims voice anger over Mohammed cartoons' (2006) Worldpress.org, 'News and Views From Around the World'. Available at: http://www.worldpress.org/Europe/2261.cfm. Accessed 15 May 2006.

Naím, M. (2005) 'Three wise men', *Foreign Policy*, January–February. Available at: http://www.foreignpolicy.com/story/cms.php?story_id=2741. Accessed 2 September 2005.

Nasr, S. H. (1967; revised edn 1997) *Man and Nature: The Spiritual Crisis of Modern Man*, Chicago: Kazi Publications.

Nasr, S. H. (1975) *Islam and the Plight of Modern Man*, London: Longman.

Nasr, S. H. (1996) *Religion and the Order of Nature*, New York: Oxford University Press.

Nasr, S. Vali Reza (2001) *Islamic Leviathan. Islam and the Making of State Power*, Oxford: Oxford University Press.

National Commission on Terrorist Attacks (2004) *The 9/11 Commission Report*, Washington DC.

Nexon, D. (2011) 'Religion and international relations: No leap of faith required', in J. Snyder (ed.), *Religion and International Relations Theory*, New York: Columbia University Press, pp. 141–166.

Nicholson, M. (2002) *International Relations. A Concise Introduction*, 2nd edn, London: Palgrave.

Niebuhr, R. (1943) *The Nature and Destiny of Man, Vol. 1: Human Nature*, New York: Charles Scribners Sons.

Neilsen, J. (1992) 'Muslims, Christians and loyalties in the nation-states', in J. Nielsen (ed.), *Religion and Citizenship in Europe and the Arab World*, London: Grey Seal Books, pp. 1–18.

Nolan, A. and Broderick, R. (1987) *To Nourish our Faith. The Theology of Liberation in Southern Africa*, Hilton: Order of Preachers.

Nonneman, G. (1996) 'Muslim communities in post-Cold War Europe: themes and puzzles', in I. Hampsher-Monk and H. Stanyer (eds), *Contemporary Political Studies 1996, Volume One*, Proceedings of the Annual Conference of the Political Studies Association held at Glasgow, 10–12 April 1996, pp. 381–394.

Norris, P. and Inglehart, R. (2004) *Sacred and Secular. Religion and Politics Worldwide*, Cambridge: Cambridge University Press.

Novikov, E. (2005) 'The World Muslim League: agent of Wahhabi propagation in Europe', *Terrorism Monitor*, 3, 9, 6 May, pp. 8–10.

Nye, J. (1990) *Bound to Lead: The Changing Nature of American Power*, New York: Basic Books.

Nye, J. (2002) 'Globalism versus globalization', *The Globalist*, 15 April. Available at: http://www.theglobalist.com/StoryId.aspx?StoryId=2392. Accessed 13 April 2006.

Nye, J. (2004a) *Soft Power: The Means to Success in World Politics*, Washington, DC: Public Affairs.

Nye, J. (2004b) 'Soft power: The means to success in world politics', Carnegie Council. Available at: http://www.carnegiecouncil.org/resources/transcripts/4466.html. Accessed 1 May 2012.

Nye, J. (2004c) 'The benefits of soft power', *Harvard Business School Working Knowledge*, 2 August. Available at: http://hbswk.hbs.edu/item.jhtml?id=4290 &t=globalization. Accessed 10 April 2006.

Nye, J. (2004d) 'Sell it softly', *Los Angeles Times*, 25 April. Available at: http://www.ksg.harvard.edu/news/opeds/2004/nye-softly_lat_042504.htm. Accessed 1 June 2006.

Nye, J. (2005) 'Think again: soft power', *Foreign Policy*. Available at: http://yaleglobal.yale.edu/display.article?id=7059. Accessed 6 June 2007.

Oldfield, D. (2004) 'The evangelical roots of American unilateralism: The Christian Right's influence and how to counter it', *Foreign Policy in Focus*. Available at: http://www.fpif.org/papers/2004evangelical.html. Accessed 8 April 2005.

Ommerborn, W. (n.d., probably 2003) 'The importance of universal principles in Confucianism and the problems connected to Jiang Qing's concept of political Confucianism and his theory of particular principles'. Available at: http://www.eko-haus.de/menzius/universal.htm#_ftnref3]%20. Accessed 16 January 2006.

Orlik, T. (2011) 'Unrest grows as economy booms', *The Wall Street Journal*, 26 September.

Osborn, A. (2003) 'EU lifts Turkey's hopes', *The Guardian*, 27 March.

Overton, S. (2005) 'The Yemeni arms trade: Still a concern for terrorism and regional security', *Terrorism Monitor*, 3, 9, 6 May, pp. 6–7.

Page, S. (2005) 'Christian rights' alliances bend political spectrum', *USA Today*, 14 June. Available at: http://www.usatoday.com/news/washington/2005–06–14-christian-right-cover x.htm. Accessed 2 June 2006.

Pal, A. (2006) 'Sri Lanka on verge of civil war – again', *The Progressive*, May, p. 1.

Pan, P. (2004) 'Civil unrest challenges China's party leadership. Protests growing larger, more frequent, violent', *Washington Post*, 4 November.

Pararajasingham, A. (2004) 'India's Sri Lanka policy: Need for a review', South Asia Analysis Group, paper no. 1187, 13 December. Available at: http://www.saag.org/papers12/paper1187.html. Accessed 1 September 2005.

Pasic, S. C. (1996) 'Culturing International Relations theory: A call for extension', in Y. Lapid and F. Kratochwil (eds), *The Return of Culture and Identity in International Relations Theory*, London: Lynne Rienner, pp. 85–104.

## Bibliography

Patterson, E. (2011) *Politics in a Religious World. Building a religiously informed U.S. foreign policy*, New York and London: Continuum.

Pauly, Jr., R. J. (2004) *Islam in Europe. Integration or Marginalization?*, Aldershot: Ashgate.

Peter, F. (2006) 'Towards civil Islam? A comparison of Islam policies in Britain and France', *Recht van der Islam*, no. 23.

Petersen, A., Williams, P. and Vasquez, M. (eds), *Christianity, Social Change, and Globalization in the Americas*, New Brunswick, NJ: Rutgers, University Press.

Petito, F. (2007) 'The global political discourse of dialogue among civilizations: Mohammad Khatami and Vaclav Havel', *Global Change, Peace & Security*, 19, 2 pp. 103–125.

Petito, F. (2009) 'Dialogue of civilizations as an alternative model for world order', in M. Michalis and F. Petito (eds), *Civilizational Dialogue and World Order: The Other Politics of Cultures, Religions and Civilizations in International Relations*, New York: Palgrave, pp. 47–67.

Petito, F. and Hatzopoulos, P. (2003) *Religion in International Relations. The Return from Exile*, New York: Palgrave.

'Pew Forum on Religion and Public Life' (2003) Conference on 'Theology, Morality, and Public Life', The University of Chicago Divinity School, 26 February. Available at: http://pewforum.org/events/index.php?EventID=39. Accessed 5 October 2005.

Pew Global Attitudes Project (2005) 'Islamic extremism: Common concern for Muslims and Western publics', 14 July. Available at: http://pewglobal.org/reports/display.php?ReportID=248. Accessed 10 December 2005.

Pew Research Center (2011) 'Strengthen ties with China, but get tough on trade'. Available at: http://www.people-press.org/2011/01/12/strengthen-ties-with-china-but-get-tough-on-trade/

Philpott, D. (2002) 'The challenge of September 11 to secularism in international relations', *World Politics*, 55, October, pp. 66–95.

Philpott, D. (2004) 'The Catholic wave', *The Journal of Democracy*, 15, 2, pp. 32–46.

Phillips, K. (2006) *American Theocracy*, New York: Viking.

Pieterse, J. (1992) 'Christianity, politics and Gramscism of the right: Introduction', in J. Pieterse (ed.), *Christianity and Hegemony. Religion and Politics on the Frontiers of Social Change*, Oxford: Berg, pp. 1–31.

Pinkney, R. (1993) *Democracy in the Third World*, Buckingham: Open University Press.

Pinkney, R. (2005) *The Frontiers of Democracy: Challenges in the West, the East and the Third World*, Aldershot: Ashgate.

Piscatori, J. (1986) *Islam in a World of Nation-States*, Cambridge: Cambridge University Press.

Ploch, L. (2010) 'Countering terrorism in East Africa: The U.S. response', Congressional Research Service Report for Congress, 3 November. Available at: http://www.fas.org/sgp/crs/terror/R41473.pdf. Accessed 2 April 2012.

'President Bush discusses freedom in Iraq and Middle East' (2003) Remarks by the President at the 20th Anniversary of the National Endowment for Democracy, United States Chamber of Commerce, Washington, DC. Available at: http://www.whitehouse.gov/news/releases/2003/11/20031106–2.html. Accessed 5 October 2005.

'President Bush previews historic NATO summit in Prague' (2002) Remarks by the President to Prague Atlantic Student Summit Prague, Czech Republic 22 November. Available at: http://usa.usembassy.de/etexts/docs/bush201102. htm. Accessed 4 October 2005.

Pridham, G. (2000) *The Dynamics of Democratization. A Comparative Approach*, London and New York: Continuum.

Priesner, S. (2008) 'Gross national happiness – Bhutan's vision of development and its challenges'. Unpublished manuscript. Available at: http://www.bhutan 2008.bt/ndlb/typescripts/10/GNH_Ch3_Priesner.pdf. Accessed 20 April 2012.

Primor, A. (2011) 'The potential of Israel's relationship with India', *Haaretz*, 1 November. Available at: http://www.haaretz.com/print-edition/opinion/ the-potential-of-israel-s-relationship-with-india-1.393059. Accessed 2 August 2012.

Prusher, I. (2005a) 'Why is Israel pulling out settlers from Gaza, West Bank?', *The Christian Science Monitor*, 15 August. Available at: http://www. csmonitor.com/2005/0815/p10s01-wome.html?s=widep. Accessed 22 November 2005.

Prusher, I. (2005b) 'As Gaza empties, Israel looks ahead', *The Christian Science Monitor*, 22 August. Available at: http://www.csmonitor.com/2005/0822/ p06s01-wome.html. Accessed 22 November 2005.

Radhakrishnan, P. (2004) 'Religion under globalisation', *Economic and Political Weekly*, 27 March, pp. 1403–1411.

Raja Mohan, C. (2005) 'The Confucian Party of China', *The Indian Express* (Mumbai), 19 December. Available at: http://www.indianexpress.com/full_ story.php?content_id=84219. Accessed 17 January 2006.

Ram-Prasad, C. (2000) 'Hindu nationalism and the internaitonal relations of India', in K. Dark (ed.) *Religion and International Relations*, Basingstoke, Macmillan, pp. 140–198.

Ramadan, T. (2003) *Western Muslims and the Future of Islam*, Oxford and New York: Oxford University Press.

Ramadan, T. (2006) 'Before the trap springs shut on the Palestinian people, resign!'. Available at: http://www.tariqramadan.com/rubrique.php3?id_ rubrique=43&lang=en. Accessed 6 June 2006.

Ramazani, R. K. (2004) 'Ideology and pragmatism in Iran's foreign policy', *Middle East Journal*, 58, 4, pp. 549–559.

Ramet, S. (1995) 'Spheres of religio-political interaction: Social order, nationalism, and gender relations', in S. Ramet (ed.), *Render Unto Caesar. The Religious Sphere in World Politics*, Lanham, MD: The American University Press, pp. 51–70.

Rashid, T. (2009) 'Radical Islamic Movements: Gender construction in Jamaat-i-Islami and Tabligh-i-Jamaat in Pakistan', *Strategic Analysis*, 30, 2, pp. 354–376.

Ravitsky, A. (1993) *Messianism, Zionism and Jewish Religious Radicalism*, tel-Aviv: Am Oved.

Rees, J. (2009) 'The dynamics of religion in International Relations'. Unpublished PhD thesis, University of New South Wales, Australia.

Reichley, A. James (1986) 'Religion and the future of American politics', *Political Science Quarterly*, 101, 1, pp. 23–47.

Reichley, A. James (2002) *Faith in Politics*, Washington, DC: Brookings Institution Press.

Reiffer, B. (2003) 'Religion and nationalism: Understanding the consequences of a complex relationship', *Ethnicities* 3 (2), 215–242.

Religion and Ethics Newsweekly (2004) 'Interview: Leo Ribuffo', 23 April. Available at: http://www.pbs.org/wnet/religionandethics/week734/interview3.html. Accessed 17 March 2005.

'Remarks by the President in Address to Faculty and Students of Warsaw University' (2002) Warsaw University, Warsaw, Poland. Available at: http://www.whitehouse.gov/news/releases/2001/06/20010615–1.html. Accessed 4 October 2005.

Reoch, R. (2001) 'The "No Mercy War" in Sri Lanka', Asian Human Rights Commission. Available at: http://www.hrsolidarity.net/mainfile.php/1999vol 09no05/968/. Accessed 9 January 2006.

Reus-Smit, C. (2005) 'Constructivism', in S. Burchill, A. Linklater, R. Devetak, J. Donnelly, M. Paterson, C. Reus-Smit and J. True (eds), *Theories of International Relations*, 3rd edn, Basingstoke and New York: Palgrave Macmillan, pp. 161–187.

Reychler, L. (1997) 'Religion and conflict', *The International Journal of Peace Studies*, 2, 1. Available at: http://www.gmu.edu/academic/ijps/vol2_1/Reyschler.htm. Accessed 14 April 2006.

Rhodes, E. (2004) The good, the bad, and the righteous: Understanding the Bush vision of a new NATO partnership', *Millennium: Journal of International Studies*, 33, 1, pp. 123–143.

Rice, C. (2002) 'Remarks by National Security Advisor Condoleezza Rice on terrorism and foreign policy', Paul H. Nitze School of Advanced International

Studies, Johns Hopkins University, Kenney Auditorium Washington, DC. Available at: http://www.whitehouse.gov/news/releases/2002/04/20020429–9.html. Accessed 11 November 2005.

Rice, X., Burkeman, O. and Carroll, R. (2006) 'Fall of Mogadishu leaves US policy in ruins', *The Guardian*, 10 June.

Rizvi, G. (1995) 'South Asia and the New World Order', in H.-H. Holm and G. Sørensen (eds), *Whose World Order?*, Boulder: Westview, pp. 69–88.

Robbins, T. and Anthony, D. (1982) *In God We Trust: New Patterns of Religious Pluralism in America*, New Brunswick: Transaction.

Robinson, M. (ed.) (1998) *Corruption and Development*, London: Frank Cass.

Ronfeldt, D. and Arquilla, J. (eds) (2001) *Networks and Netwars*, Santa Monica, CA: Rand Corporation.

Rosen, D. (2005) 'Religion, identity and Mideast peace', 10th Annual Templeton Lecture on Religion and World Affairs. Available at: http://www.fpri.org/enotes/20050923.religion.rosen.religionidentitymideastpeace.html. Accessed 25 May 2006.

Rosenau, J. (1997) *Along the Domestic-Foreign Frontier*, Cambridge: Cambridge University Press.

Rosenberger, S. and Sauer, B. (eds) (2012) *Politics, Religion and Gender. Framing and Regulating the Veil*, London: Routledge.

Ross, R. and Johnston, A. (eds) (2006) *New Directions in the Study of China's Foreign Policy*, Stanford: Stanford University Press.

Roughneen, S. (2012) 'Muslim militants in south Thailand growing stronger', *Christian Science Monitor*, 1 April. Available at: http://www.csmonitor.com/World/Asia-Pacific/2012/0401/Muslim-militants-in-south-Thailand-growing-stronger. Accessed 20 April 2012.

Rousseau, J.-J. (2004 [1762]) *The Social Contract*, Harmondsworth: Penguin.

Roy, A. (2002) 'Fascism's firm footprint in India', *The Nation*, 30 September. Available at: http://www.ratical.org/co-globalize/AR093002.pdf. Accessed 26 May 2006.

Roy, O. (2004) *Globalised Islam. The Search for a New Ummah*, London: Hurst.

Roy, O. (2005) *La laicite face a l'islam*, Paris: Stock.

Roy, O. (2010) *Holy Ignorance*, London: Hurst.

Rudolph, Hoeber S. (1997a) 'Introduction', in S. Hoeber Rudolph and J. Piscatori (eds), *Transnational Religion and Fading States*, Boulder, CO, Westview Press, pp. 1–24.

Rudolph, Hoeber S. (1997b) 'Dehomogenizing religious formations', in S. Hoeber Rudolph and J. Piscatori (eds), *Transnational Religion and Fading States*, Boulder, CO, Westview Press, pp. 243–261.

Rudolph, Hoeber S. (2005) 'Religious Transnationalism', in M. Juergensmeyer (ed.), *Religion in Global Civil Society*, New York: Oxford University Press.

# Bibliography

Rudolph, S. Hoeber, and Piscatori, J. (eds) (1997) *Transnational Religion and Fading States*. Boulder, CO: Westview.

Rueschemeyer, D., Stephens, E. and Stephens, J. (1992) *Capitalist Development and Democracy*, Cambridge: Polity Press.

Russell, S. and Jones, E. (2004) 'Islam in Southeast Asia: A Summary', Center for Southeast Asian Studies, Northern Illinois University, December.

Ryall, D. (1994) 'The Roman Catholic Church and Socio-Political Change in South Africa, 1948–90'. Unpublished manuscript.

Sabirov, R. (2008) 'Buddhism in Mongolia: Tibetan or Mongolian?', paper presented at the CESS 9th Annual Conference 18–21 September 2008, Georgetown University, Washington, DC.

Sahliyeh, E. (1990) 'Introduction', in E. Sahliyeh (ed.), *Religious Resurgence and Politics in the Contemporary World*, Albany, NY: State University of New York Press, pp. 1–20.

Saikal, A. (2003) *Islam and the West. Conflict or Cooperation?*, New York and Basingstoke: Palgrave Macmillan.

Salamey, I. and Othman, Z. (2011) 'Shia revival and *welayat al-faqih* in the making of Iranian foreign policy', *Politics, Religion and Ideology*, 12, 2, pp. 197–212.

Salih, M. A. Mohamed (2002) 'Islamic NGOs in Africa: The Promise and Peril of Islamic Voluntarism', occasional paper, Centre of African Studies, University of Copenhagen, March.

Salih, M. A. (2004) 'Islamic NGOS in Africa. The promise and peril of Islamic voluntarism', in A. de Waal (ed.), *Islamism and its Enemies in the Horn of Africa*, London: Hurst and Company, pp. 146–181.

Sandal, N. and James, P. (2011) 'Religion and International Relations theory: Towards a mutual understanding', *European Journal of International Relations*, 17, 1, pp. 3–25.

Sandler, S. (2006) 'Judaism and politics', in J. Haynes (ed.), *The Politics of Religion. A Survey*, London: Routledge, pp. 37–47.

Sardar, Z. (1985) *Islamic Futures. The Shape of Ideas to Come*, London and New York: Mansell Publishing.

Sarioghalam, M. (2001) 'Iran's foreign policy and US-Iranian relations. A summary of remarks by Dr. Mahmood Sarioghalam, National University of Iran, at the Middle East Institute, February 5, 2001'. Available at: http://209.196.144.55/html/b-sarioghalam.html. Accessed 1 July 2006.

Schmitt, G. 'Confucius say – Caveat emptor. What China means by "peaceful rise"', *The Weekly Standard*, 11, 31, 1 May. Available at: http://www.weeklystandard.com/Content/Public/Articles/000/000/012/129bywdp.asp?pg=1. Accessed 2 May 2006.

Schoffeleers, M. (1988) 'Theological styles and revolutionary elan: An African discussion', in P. Q. van Ufford and Schoffeleers (eds), *Religion and Development. Towards an Integrated Approach*, Amsterdam: Free University Press, pp. 185–208.

Scott, J. (2003) *Exploring the Funding Relationships Between Community Foundations and Faith-Based Social Service Providers*, New York: The Roundtable on Religion and Social Welfare Policy/The Rockefeller Institute of Government/State University of New York.

Seabrook, J. (2004) 'Localizing cultures', *Korea Herald*, 13 January. Available at: http://www.globalpolicy.org/globaliz/cultural/2004/0113jeremyseabrook. htm. Accessed 18 April 2006.

Seiple, C. (2011) 'From ideology to identity: Building a foundation for communities of the willing', in P. James (ed.), *Religion, Identity, and Global Governance. Ideas, Evidence, and Practice*, Toronto: University of Toronto Press, pp. 292–310.

Seipel, R. and Hoover, D. (2004) *Religion and Security: The New Nexus in International Relations*, Lanham, MD: Rowman & Littlefield Publishers.

Sen, A. (2006) *Identity and Violence*, New York: Norton.

Shah, T. Samuel (2012) 'Introduction. Religion and world affairs: blurring the boundaries', in T. Samuel Shah, A. Stepan, and M. Duffy Toft (eds), *Rethinking Religion and World Affairs*, Oxford and New York: Oxford University Press, pp. 1–12.

Shah, T. Samuel and Philpott, D. (2011) 'The fall and rise of religion in International Relations: History and theory', in J. Snyder (ed.), *Religion and International Relations Theory*, New York: Columbia University Press, pp. 24–59.

Shankar, S. (2006) 'The tiger towards its territory', *South Asia Monitor*. Available at: http://www.southasiamonitor.org/2006/apr/news/10view1.shtml. Accessed 27 June 2006.

Shani, G. (2002) 'A revolt against the west': Politicized religion and the international order – A comparison of the Islamic *Umma* and the Sikh *Qaum*', *Ritsumeikan Annual Review of International Studies*, vol. 1, pp. 15–31.

Shani, G. (2008) 'Transnational Religious Actors and International Relations', in J. Haynes (ed.), *Handbook of Religion and Politics*, London: Routledge, pp. 308–322.

Shaw, T. (2005) 'The global political economy', in J. Haynes (ed.), *Palgrave Advances in Development Studies*, Basingstoke: Palgrave, pp. 249–267.

'Shi'ite supremacists emerge from Iran's shadows' (2005) *Asian Times Online*, 9 September. Available at: http://www.atimes.com/atimes/Middle_East/GI09Ak01.html. Accessed 13 June 2006.

# Bibliography

Shlapentokh, V., Woods, J. and Shirav, E. (eds) (2005) *America. Sovereign Defender or Cowboy Nation*, Aldershot: Ashgate.

Shupe, A. (1990) 'The stubborn persistence of religion in the global arena', in E. Sahliyeh (ed.), *Religious Resurgence and Politics in the Contemporary World*, Albany: State University of New York Press, pp. 17–26.

Siddiqi, F. (2012) 'Judicial democracy', *Dawn*, 12 July. Available at: http://dawn.com/2012/07/13/judicial-democracy/. Accessed 2 August 2012.

Silberstein, L. (1993) 'Religion, ideology, modernity: theoretical issues in the study of Jewish fundamentalism', in L. Silberstein (ed.), *Jewish Fundamentalism in Comparative Perspective: Religion, Ideology, and the Crisis of Modernity*, New York and London: New York University Press, pp. 3–26.

Simpson, J. (1992) 'Fundamentalism in America revisited the fading of modernity as a source of symbolic capital', in B. Misztal and A. Shupe (eds), *Religion and Politics in Comparative Perspective. Revival of Religious Fundamentalism in East and West*, Westport and London: Praeger, pp. 10–27.

Sivaraksa, Sulak (1992) *Seeds of Peace: A Buddhist Vision for Renewing Society*, ed. Tom Ginsburg. Berkeley, CA: Parallax Press.

Smith, A. (2003) *Chosen Peoples: Sacred Sources of National Identity*. Oxford: Oxford University Press.

Smith, C. (2005) 'The Arab-Israeli conflict', in L. Fawcett (ed.), *International Relations of the Middle East*, Oxford: Oxford University Press, pp. 217–235.

Smith, D. E. (1970) *Religion and Political Development*, Boston, MA: Little Brown.

Smith, S. (2002) 'The end of the unipolar moment? September 11 and the future of world order', *International Relations*, 16, 2, pp. 171–183.

Smock, D. (2001) 'Faith-Based NGOs and international peacebuilding', special report no. 76, United States Institute of Peace, October. Available at: http://www.usip.org/pubs/specialreports/sr76.html. Accessed 4 February 2006.

Smock, D. (2004) 'Divine intervention: Regional reconciliation through faith', *Religion*, 25, 4. Available at: http://hir.harvard.edu/articles/1190/3/. Accessed 1 September 2005.

Smock, D. (ed.) (2006) *Religious Contributions to Peacemaking. When Religion Brings Peace, Not War*, Washington, DC: United States Institute of Peace.

Snyder, J. (2011) 'Introduction', in J. Snyder (ed.), *Religion and International Relations Theory*, New York: Columbia University Press, pp. 1–23.

Soharabi, N. (2006) 'Conservatives, neoconservatives and reformists: Iran after the election of Mahmud Ahmadinejad', 'Middle East Brief', Crown Center for Middle East Studies, Brandeis University, April, No. 4.

Sommers, J. and Hoyer, D. (2005) 'The uses of France's riots'. Available at: http://www.zmag.org/content/showarticle.cfm?itemid=9154. Accessed June 5 2006.

'South Asia: Attacks on Indian Christians continue' (1998) BBC News, 30 December. Available at: http://news.bbc.co.uk/1/hi/world/south_asia/244653.stm. Accessed 23 May 2006.

Spickard, J. (2003) 'What is happening to religion? Six sociological narratives'. Unpublished manuscript. Available at: http://www.ku.dk/Satsning/Religion/indhold/publikationer/working_papers/what_is_happened.PDF. Accessed 14 April 2006.

Sprinzak, E. (1993) 'Fundamentalism, ultranationalism, and political culture: the case of the Israeli radical right, in L. Diamond (ed.), *Political Culture and Democracy in Developing Countries*, Boulder, CO and London: Lynne Rienner, pp. 247–278.

Stack, J. (2011) 'The religious challenge to International Relations theory', in P. James (ed.), *Religion, Identity, and Global Governance. Ideas, Evidence, and Practice*, Toronto: University of Toronto Press, pp. 19–36.

Stark, R. and Fink, R. (2000) *Acts of Faith: Explaining the Human Side of Religion*, Berkeley, CA: University of California Press.

Statement on the Organization of Islamic Conference (OIC) Summit Declaration (2005) Available at: http://www.whitehouse.gov/news/releases/2005/12/20051212.html. Accessed 22 May 2006.

Stepan, Alfred (1988) *Rethinking Military Politics. Brazil and the Southern Cone*. Princeton, NJ: Princeton University Press.

Stepan, Alfred (2000) 'Religion, democracy, and the "twin tolerations" ', *Journal of Democracy*, 11, 4, pp. 37–57.

Stiglitz, J. (2006) *Making Globalization Work: The Next Steps to Global Justice*, London: Allen Lane.

Støre, J. (2006) 'Managing conflict and building peace. Norwegian policy for peace and reconciliation', speech delivered by Norway's Minister of Foreign Affairs, Jonas Gahr Støre, at the Real Instituto Elcano, Madrid, 13 March.

Strindberg, A. and Wärn, M. (2011) *Islamism. Religion, Radicalism and Resistance*, Cambridge: Polity.

Stuart-Fox, M. (2006) 'Buddhism and politics in Laos, Cambodia, Myanmar and Thailand', paper presented at the Cambodia, Laos, Myanmar and Thailand Summer School, Asia Pacific Week, The Australian National University, Canberra, 30 January.

Sulak Sivaraksa (1993) *Seeds of Peace: A Buddhist Vision for Renewing Society*, Berkeley, CA: Parallax Press.

Sullivan, M. (2002) *Theories of International Relations. Transition vs. Persistence*, Basingstoke, UK, and New York: Palgrave.

Sunnideobandi (2011) 'Tablighi Jamaat'. Available at: http://sunnideobandi.wordpress.com/. Accessed 27 July 2012.

Sutcliffe, S. (2003) *Children of the New Age. A History of Spiritual Practices*, London: Routledge.

Swanson, A. (2004) 'Analysis: Iraq occupation endangers U.S.', *Washington Times*, 6 May. Available at: http://www.washingtontimes.com/upi-breaking/20040506–042407–9978r.htm. Accessed 17 August 2005.

Swanson, K. (2008) 'What happened to the Catholic vote? Interview with Fidelis President Brian Burch', Zenit: The Word Seen from Rome. Available at: http://www.zenit.org/article-24180?l=english.

Takeyh, R. (2009) *Guardians of the Revolution. Iran and the World in the Age of the Ayatollahs*, Oxford: Oxford University Press.

Tamney, J. and Hsueh-Ling Chiang, L. (2002) *Modernization, Globalization, and Confucianism in Chinese Societies*, Westport: Greenwood.

Tankel, S. (2009) 'Lashkar-e-Taiba: From 9/11 to Mumbai', report prepared for the International Centre for the Study of Radicalisation and Political Violence, Kings College, London, April/May. Available at: http://www.icsr. info/publications/papers/1240835356ICSRStephenTankelReport.pdf. Accessed 6 January 2010.

Tarrow, S. (1998) *Power in Movement. Social Movements and Contentious Politics*, 2nd edn, Cambridge: Cambridge University Press.

Taylor, C. (2007) *A Secular Age*, Cambridge, MA: Harvard University Press.

Taylor, I. (2005) 'Globalization and development', in J. Haynes (ed.), *Palgrave Advances in Development Studies*, Basingstoke: Palgrave, pp. 268–287.

Taylor, M. L. (2005) *Religion, Politics, and the Christian Right: Post-9/11 Powers in American Empire*, Minneapolis, MN: Augsburg Fortress Publishers.

Tehranian, M. (1997) 'Religious resurgence in global perspective', *Economic and Political Weekly* (New Delhi), 32, 50, December 13–19.

Telhami, S. (2004) 'Between faith and ethics', in J. B. Hehir, M. Walzer, L. Richardson, S. Telhami, C. Krauthammer and J. Lindsay, *Liberty and Power. A Dialogue on Religion and U.S. Foreign Policy in an Unjust World*, Washington DC: Brookings Institution Press, pp. 71–84.

Tenet, G. (2002) 'Worldwide Threat – Converging Dangers in a Post 9/11 World', testimony of Director of Central Intelligence George J. Tenet before the Senate Select Committee on Intelligence. Available at: http://www.cia. gov/cia/public_affairs/speeches/2002/dci_speech_02062002.html. Accessed 4 August 2005.

Tepe, S. (2005) 'Religious parties and democracy: A comparative assessment of Israel and Turkey', *Democratization*, 12, 3, pp. 283–307.

'The Common Goal of Universal Peace in Buddhism and the Baha'i Faith' (1990) A paper delivered to the Asian Buddhist Conference for Peace, Ulan Bator, Mongolia 16–25 September. Available at: http://statements.bahai.org/90–0916.htm. Accessed 22 September 2005.

The Royal Embassy of Saudi Arabia (2011) 'Specialized criminal court begins hearings against 85 people accused of terrorism'. Available at: http://www.saudiembassy.net/latest_news/news06261105.aspx. Accessed 25 April 2012.

*The Times of India* (2002) 'Venkaiah to Modi: No anti-minority remarks please', September 10. Available at: http://www1.timesofindia.indiatimes.com/cms.dll/articleshow?art_id=21793227. Accessed 9 January 2006.

'The WCC-IMF-WB high-level encounter' (2004) Synthesis of discussions and summary of agreements, 22 October 2004, Ecumenical Centre, Geneva, Switzerland. Available at: http://www.oikoumene.org/en/resources/documents/wcc-programmes/public-witness-addressing-power-affirming-peace/poverty-wealth-and-ecology/trade/wcc-imf-wb-high-level-encounter.html. Accessed 18 August 2011.

Thianh Duong (2003) *Hegemonic Globalisation. U.S. Centrality and Global Strategy in the Emerging World Order*, Aldershot: Ashgate.

Thirumalai, M. S. (2001) 'Language and culture in India's foreign policy – Part 1', *Language in India. Strength for Today and Bright Hope for Tomorrow*, 1, 3, May. Available at: http://www.languageinindia.com/may2001/foreign.html. Accessed 31 August 2005.

Thomas, C. and Reader, M. (2001) 'Development and inequality', in B. White, R. Little and M. Smith (eds), *Issues in World Politics*, Basingstoke: Palgrave, pp. 74–92.

Thomas, S. (1999) 'Religion and international society', in J. Haynes (ed.), *Religion, Globalization and Political Culture in the Third World*, Basingstoke: Macmillan, pp. 28–44.

Thomas, S. (2003) 'Taking religious and cultural pluralism seriously: The global resurgence of religion and the transformation of international society', in F. Petito and P. Hatzopoulos (eds), *Religion in International Relations. The Return from* Exile, New York: Palgrave, pp. 21–54.

Thomas, S. (2005) *The Global Transformation of Religion and the Transformation of International Relations. The Struggle for the Soul of the Twenty First Century*, New York and Basingstoke, UK: Palgrave Macmillan.

Tisdall, S. (2004) 'Islamists shift focus to Europe as jihad enters third phase', *The Guardian*, 18 November.

Tisdall, S. (2006) 'The land the world forgot', *The Guardian*, 23 May.

de Tocqueville, A. (2003 [1835]) *Democracy in America: And Two Essays on America*, Harmondsworth: Penguin.

Toft, M. Duffy (2011) 'Religion, rationalist, and violence', in J. Snyder (ed.), *Religion and International Relations Theory*, New York: Columbia University Press, pp. 115–140.

Toft, M. Duffy, Philpott, D. and Shah, T. Samuel (2011) *God's Century. Resurgent Religion and Global Politics*, New York and London: W. W. Norton.

## Bibliography

Travis, A. (2004) 'Desire to integrate on the wane as Muslims resent "war on Islam"', *The Guardian*, 16 March.

Traynor, I. (2005) 'A country with 14 governments where children refuse to cross ethnic divide', *The Guardian*, 18 November.

Troy, J. (2011) ' "Catholic waves" of democratization? Roman Catholicism and its potential for democratization', in J. Haynes (ed.), *Religion and Democratizations*, London: Routledge, pp. 53–74.

'Turkey, elections, and globalization' (2006) Available at: http://globalization. about.com/library/weekly/aa103102a.htm. Accessed 12 May 2006.

'Turkey–European Union' (2004) *AsiaNews.it*, 8 September. Available at: http://www.asianews.it/view.php?1=en&art+1442. Accessed 4 June 2006.

Turner, B. S. (1994) *Orientalism, Postmodernism and Globalism*, London: Routledge.

Turner, B. S. (2000) 'Liberal citizenship and cosmopolitan virtue', in A. Vandenberg (ed.), *Citzenship and Democracy in a Global Era*, Oxford: Polity Press, pp. 18–32.

Tyndale, W. (2004) 'Religions and the Millennium Development Goals: Whose agenda?', paper presented at the conference 'Religion and Development', 3 November, The Hague, The Netherlands.

United States Commission on International Religious Freedom (2004) 'Annual Report', May, Washington, DC: United States Commission on International Religious Freedom.

United States Institute of Peace (2003) 'Special Report: Can Faith-Based NGOs Advance Interfaith Reconciliation? The Case of Bosnia and Herzegovina' Available at: http://www.usip.org/pubs/specialreports/sr103.pdf. Accessed 1 February 2006.

Upreti, B. C. (n.d.) 'Gross national happyness (sic) and foreign policy of Bhutan: Interlinkages and imperatives', unpublished type script.

Upreti, B. C. (2005) 'Gross national happyness (sic) and foreign policy of Bhutan: Interlinkages and imperatives', paper presented at the conference 'Rethinking Development: Local Pathways to Global Wellbeing', St Francis Xavier University, Antigonish, Nova Scotia, Canada, June 20–24.

US Library of Congress (1986) 'Buddhism', *Area Handbook for Mongolia*, 2nd edn. Available at: http://countrystudies.us/mongolia/47.htm. Accessed 19 September 2005.

Vaillancourt, J.-G. (1980) *Papal Power. A Study of Vatican Control over Lay Catholic Elites*, Berkeley: University of California Press.

Voll, J. (2006) 'Trans-state Muslim movements in an era of soft power', paper prepared for the Conference on New Religious Pluralism in World Politics, Georgetown University, 17 March.

Vulliamy, E. (2003) 'Two men driving Bush into war', *The Observer* (London), 23 February.

Vyas, N. (2002) 'Hindutva opponents to get death: VHP', *Daily Times* (Pakistan), 19 December. Available at: http://www.dailytimes.com.pk/default.asp?page=story_19–12–2002_pg4_23. Accessed 9 January 2006.

de Waal, A. (2004) 'Counter-insurgency on the cheap', *London Review of Books*, 5 August 2004. Available at: http://www.lrb.co.uk/v26/n15/waal01_.html. Accessed 5 July 2005.

Wald, K. (1991) 'Social change and political response to the silent religious cleavage in North America', in G. Moyser (ed.), *Religion and Politics in the Modern World*, London: Routledge, pp. 239–284.

Wald, K. (2003) *Religion and Politics in the United States*, 4th edn, Lanham, MD: Rowman and Littlefield.

Waldron, A. (1999) 'Religious revivals in Communist China', *Foreign Policy Research Institute – FPRI Wire*, 7, 3, February. Available at: http://www.fpri.org/fpriwire/0703.199902.waldron.religiousrevivalscommunistchina.html. Accessed 18 January 2006.

Walker, M. (1996) 'Praying for a God-fearing president', *The Guardian*, 7 February.

Walker, M. (2004) 'Walker's world: Turkey's effect on Europe', *The Washington Times*, 6 October. Available at: http://www.washtimes.com/upi-breaking/20041006–014153–5595r.htm. Accessed 17 November 2005.

Walker, B. (2011) 'Vatican asks Hindus to end anti-Christian propaganda', *The New American*, 21 October. Available at: http://www.thenewamerican.com/world-news/asia/item/10430-vatican-asks-hindus-to-end-anti-christian-propaganda. Accessed 2 August 2012.

Walshe, P. (1992) 'South Africa Prophetic Christianity and the Liberation Movement', *Journal of Modern African Studies*, XXIX, 1, pp. 27–60.

Walt, S. (2005) *Taming American Power: The Global Response to U.S. Primacy*, New York and London: Norton.

Warburg, M. (2001) 'Religious organisations in a global world. A comparative perspective', University of Copenhagen, Denmark, paper presented at the 2001 international conference 'The Spiritual Supermarket: Religious Pluralism in the 21st Century', 19–22 April , London School of Economics.

Warner, C. and Walker, S. (2007) 'Thinking about the role of religion in foreign policy: A framework for analysis', *Foreign Policy Analysis*, 7, pp. 113–135.

Watson, M. (1994) 'Christianity and the green options in the new Europe', in J Fulton and P. Gee (eds), *Religion in Contemporary Europe*, Baltimore, MD: Penguin, pp. 19–41.

Watson, P. and Jones, A. (2005) 'The fruits of globalization: Rotten to the core. France erupts as rampant immigration reaps its vengeance'. Available at: http://www.prisonplanet.com/articles/november2005/081105rottentothe core.htm. Accessed 5 June 2006.

Watts, J. (2006) 'Land seizures threaten social stability, warns China's leader', *The Guardian*, 21 January.

Waylen, G. (2003) 'Gender and transitions: What do we know?', *Democratization*, 10, 1, pp. 157–78.

Webber, M. and Smith, M. (2002) *Foreign Policy in a Transformed World*, Harlow: Prentice Hall.

Weber, M. (1969) 'Major features of world religions', in R. Robertson (ed.), *Sociology of Religion*, Baltimore, MD: Penguin, pp. 19–41.

Weber, M. (1978) *Economy and Society*, Berkeley: University of California Press.

Weigel, G. (1992) *The Final Revolution: The Resistance Church and the Collapse of Communism*, Oxford: Oxford University Press.

Weigel, G. (2005) *Witness to Hope: The Biography of Pope John Paul II, 1920–2005*. New York: HarperCollins.

Weigel, G. (2007) *Faith, Reason, and the War against Jihadism: A Call to Action*. New York: Doubleday.

Weimann, G. (2006) *Terror on the Internet. The New Arena, the New Challenges*, Washington, DC: The United States Institute of Peace Press.

Weiss, G. (2011) *The Cage: The Fight for Sri Lanka & the Last Days of the Tamil Tigers*, London: Bodley Head.

'What World Leaders Say About RFE/RL' (2002) Available at: http://www.rferl.org/about/impact/bush.asp. Accessed 4 November 2005.

Whitehead, L. (1993) 'The alternatives to "liberal democracy". A Latin American Perspective', in D. Held (ed.), *Prospects for Democracy*, Cambridge: Polity, pp. 312–329.

Wilson, B. (1985) 'A typology of sects', in R. Bocock and K. Thompson (eds), *Religion and Ideology*, Manchester: Manchester University Press, pp. 301–316.

Wilson, B. (1992) 'Reflections on a many sided controversy', in S. Bruce (ed.), *Religion and Modernization*, Oxford: Clarendon Press, pp. 195–210.

Wilson, B. (2003) 'Prediction and prophecy in the future of religion', in G. Davie, P. Heelas, and L. Woodhead (eds), *Predicting Religion*, Aldershot: Ashgate, pp. 64–73.

Witte, J. Jr. (1993) 'Introduction' in *idem*. (ed.), *Christianity and Democracy in Global Context*, Boulder: Westview, p. 11.

'Wolf: China's record on human rights is "abysmal" Statement at Tom Lantos Human Rights Commission Hearing on China'. Available at: http://wolf.house.gov/index.cfm?sectionid=34&parentid=6&sectiontree=&itemid=1433

Woodward, B. (2004) *Plan of Attack*, London: Simon & Schuster.

Woollacott, M. (1995) 'Keeping our faith in belief', *The Guardian*, 23 December.

World Bank (2001) *World Development Report 2000/2001*, Oxford: Oxford University Press for the World Bank.

World Faiths Development Dialogue (1999) *Poverty and Development: An Inter-faith Perspective*. Available at: http://www.wfdd.org.uk/documents/publications/poverty_development_english.pdf. Accessed 2 March 2006.

World Faiths Development Dialogue (2003) 'Seminar proposal: Faith leaders and global economics'. Photocopy.

Wuthnow, R. (2000) *Linkages Between Religious Congregations and Nonprofit Service Organizations*. Working Paper Series. Washington, DC: Nonprofit Sector Research Fund. The Aspen Institute.

Yahuda, M. (2005) *The International Politics of the Asia Pacific*, 2nd edn, London: Routledge.

Yilmaz, H. (2002) 'External–internal linkages in democratization: developing an open model of democratic changes', *Democratization*, 9, 2, pp. 67–84.

Young, M. (2000) 'Sri Lanka's long war', *Foreign Policy in Focus*, 5, 35, October, pp. 1–3.

Yu Keping (2004) 'From the discourse of "Sino-West" to "globalization": Chinese perspectives on globalization', working paper GHC 04/1, Institute on Globalization and the Human Condition, Hamilton, Ontario, Canada, March.

Zhou, Qi (2005) 'Conflicts over human rights between China and the US', *Human Rights Quarterly*, 27, 1, February, pp. 105–124.

Ziyad, G. (2003) 'Saudi Arabia: lines in the sand'. Available at: http://www.worldpress.org/Mideast/1145.cfm. Accessed 27 June 2006.

Zunes, C. (2004) 'Christian Right's grip on US foreign policy'. Available at: http://www.couplescompany.com/Features/Politics/2004/ChristianRights.htm. Accessed 4 June 2006.

# Index